Applications of Differential Geometry to Econometrics

T0300463

Although geometry has always aided intuition in econometrics, it is only recently that differential geometry has become a standard tool in the analysis of statistical models, offering a deeper appreciation of existing methodologies and highlighting the essential issues which can be hidden in an algebraic development of a problem. This volume is the first collection of papers applying these techniques to econometrics.

An introductory chapter provides a brief tutorial for those unfamiliar with the tools of Differential Geometry. The topics covered in the following chapters demonstrate the power of the geometric method to provide practical solutions and insight into problems of econometric inference.

PAUL MARRIOTT is an Associate Professor in the Department of Statistics and Applied Probability at the National University of Singapore. He was previously based at the University of Surrey.

MARK SALMON is Deutsche Morgan Grenfell Professor of Financial Markets at City University Business School in London. He was previously Professor of Economics at the European University Institute in Florence.

Applications of differential geometry to econometrics

Edited by

PAUL MARRIOTT AND MARK SALMON

CAMBRIDGE
UNIVERSITY PRESS

CAMBRIDGE UNIVERSITY PRESS
Cambridge, New York, Melbourne, Madrid, Cape Town, Singapore,
São Paulo, Delhi, Dubai, Tokyo, Mexico City

Cambridge University Press
The Edinburgh Building, Cambridge CB2 8RU, UK

Published in the United States of America by Cambridge University Press, New York

www.cambridge.org
Information on this title: www.cambridge.org/9780521178297

First published 2000
First paperback edition 2010

A catalogue record for this publication is available from the British Library

ISBN 978-0-521-65116-5 Hardback
ISBN 978-0-521-17829-7 Paperback

Contents

vi   **Contents**

Figures and tables

Tables

Contributors

J. M. Corcuera   *Universitat de Barcelona*
Frank Critchley   *Open University*
Russell Davidson   *GREQEM, Marseille, and Queens University*
Kees Jan van Garderen   *CORE, Louvain-la-Neuve*
F. Giummolè   *Universita degli Studi di Padova*
Grant Hillier   *University of Southampton*
Uwe Jensen   *Institüt für Statistik und Ökonometrie, Kiel*
Maozu Lu   *University of Southampton*
Paul Marriott   *National University of Singapore*
Grayham Mizon   *European University Institute, Florence*
Ray O'Brien   *University of Southampton*
Thomas J. Rothenberg   *Berkeley University*
Mark Salmon   *City University Business School, London*
Richard J. Smith   *University of Bristol*

Editors' introduction

Geometry has always aided intuition in econometrics but has perhaps only very occasionally aided analytic development. However, advances in statistical theory have recently been greatly enhanced through a deeper understanding of differential geometry and the geometrical basis of statistical inference; see, for instance, Kass and Vos (1997), Barndorff-Nielsen and Cox (1994) and McCullagh (1987), as well as a rapidly expanding array of journal articles.

What value do these advances hold for econometrics? How can practical econometric methods be improved by a deeper understanding of the geometrical basis of the problems faced by econometricians?

This volume attempts to stimulate the appetite of econometricians to delve further into the sometimes complex but always enlightening world of differential geometry and its application to econometrics. The reward we have found is not only a deeper appreciation of existing methodologies but the recognition that further advance in a host of different directions can readily be made. It is this potential gained through studying what may be standard problems from an alternative perspective that makes the application of differential geometry to econometrics so exciting. Geometry is mathematically fundamental, and frequently a geometric understanding of a problem highlights the essential issues which can be hidden in an algebraic development of the same issue. Take for instance the basic notion of orthogonal projection that underlies much of econometric and statistical method and its extension to curved statistical spaces and the question of invariance to different parameterisations, the interpretation of higher-order asymptotic expansions and statistical curvature and the role of ancillarity and exogeneity. How can we formalise and hence understand more fundamentally the notions of encompassing in inference and the relationship between likelihood and method of moment based inference? These are some of the questions raised in the papers collected in this volume, which is in part based on the papers

1

presented at a conference held at the European University Institute on the Applications of Differential Geometry to Econometrics supported by a Human Capital and Mobility Grant (ERB CHRX-CT940514) from the European Union. We hope that you enjoy the experience of reading the papers gathered here and perhaps at the end appreciate the power of the geometric method.

We would like to thank the authors for their patience as this volume was put together – some more than others (!) and finally Tom and Tara for undertaking the burden of proofreading the first draft.

The first chapter in this volume, by Paul Marriott and Mark Salmon, surveys the mathematics needed to understand the methods of differential geometry and their application to econometric inference. A complete development of the tools required fully to understand differential geometry is clearly beyond the scope of this chapter, but we hope that this introduction provides the basis for understanding the issues and facilitates the reading of the later chapters in the volume. This is not to say that the papers collected here cannot be read without a deep understanding of differential geometry; indeed it is clearly the case that the intuition provided by the geometric framework can be grasped quite easily without the need for a full mastery of the techniques involved.

Maozu Lu and Grayham Mizon, in the second chapter, consider several aspects of the important issues of encompassing and nesting in model selection. Encompassing has a natural geometric intuition and feel but it is not necessarily straightforward to develop the associated geometry mathematically, partly because the concept of encompassing needs to be carefully defined. They investigate and develop the potentially surprising observation made by Gouriéroux and Monfort (1995) that it is not always the case that a more general model encompasses models that are simpler than itself. This has important implications for the inferential process of reduction from *general*-to-*simple* since in this case the sequence of parsimoniously encompassing models will not form a partial order and hence critical information might be lost if the intermediate models were discarded in the process. Lu and Mizon explore the conditions under which a general model encompasses simpler models independently of its relationship to the data-generation process (DGP). They explore the notion of nesting and demonstrate that nesting implies more than one model being an algebraic simplification of another. The importance of dimension-reducing nesting constraints is explained by showing that the nesting model will encompass models nested within it independently of the nature of the data-generation process when there is an orthogonal parameterisation. They define this property as *automatic encompassing* and show that it is not possible amongst non-nested models. They also discuss how the concept of parsimonious encompassing can be used to establish encompassing relationships between non-nested models given a competing model that nests each of the non-nested models. Encompassing hypotheses are considered as mappings in *Hilbert space* and it is shown that a sufficient condition for a model to encompass models nested within it is that these mappings are orthogonal projections in the relevant space.

Grant Hillier and Ray O'Brien apply a recently developed and geometrically motivated technique (Hillier and Armstrong (1996) for obtaining exact distribution results for implicitly defined estimators to study exact properties of the maximum likelihood estimator (MLE) in the exponential regression model. The method provides an integral formula for the exact density of the MLE, expressed as a surface integral over the manifold in the sample space upon which the MLE is defined. The method does not require that the MLE be a known function of data; all that is required is that the manifold or the level set of the MLE be known. This enables the formula to be used to get the exact density of the MLE even though the estimator may be only implicitly defined in terms of the data. Hillier and O'Brien provide a detailed discussion of the application of the approach to the exponential regression model. They show that the surface integral formula is tractable in general and that from particular numerical results for the exponential regression case the exact densities are well behaved and well approximated by the asymptotic density.

The generalised method of moments (GMM) approach to estimation and inference relaxes the need to have full knowledge of the likelihood function and is essentially a *semi-parametric* method. In consequence there is generally a trade-off between robustness and efficiency. Richard Smith considers instead empirical likelihood methods of inference, an approach that embeds the moment conditions used in GMM estimation within a non-parametric likelihood function through the use of additional parameters associated with these moment conditions. This enables equivalents of the test statistics based on classical likelihood to be developed and, in particular, tests of misspecification on the over-identifying moment conditions. He also considers the possibility of applying the empirical likelihood to testing non-nested hypotheses.

Russell Davidson develops a general geometric basis for the analysis of efficiency and robustness for estimators defined by estimating equations. The general class of such estimators was considered originally by Godambe (1960) and is essentially equivalent to the generalised method of moments. Davidson shows that, when a parameterised model is considered as a Hilbert manifold in an underlying space of DGPs, the tangent space at any particular DGP can be expressed as the direct sum of three mutually orthogonal subspaces. Robustness of an estimator is defined as its root-n consistency at all points in the model and efficiency by the asymptotic variance which is natural in the Hilbert spaces context. Consistent estimators of the model's parameters all have the same component in one of these subspaces which contains the asymptotically efficient estimator. Inefficient estimators have a non-vanishing component in the orthogonal complement of the tangent space to the model and they can then be seen to lose efficiency by including random variation in directions excluded by the model's specification. Information about parameters is represented geometrically by tangents that lie in the tangent space of the model. Efficient estimating equations for model parameters can be obtained by orthogonally projecting arbitrary root-n consistent estimators onto the efficient subspace. This projection can often be implemented by artificial regression.

Uwe Jensen provides a discussion of Rao distances and associated tests in certain two-parameter models. These tests are sometimes also called geodesic tests (see Critchley, Marriott and Salmon (1996)) and potentially offer an alternative approach to inference beyond the standard likelihood based trinity of the Likelihood Ratio, Lagrange multiplier and Wald tests. Jensen then develops an interesting earnings frontier model for German data and applies the Rao distance approach to examine various hypotheses on earnings differentials.

Jose Manuel Corcuera and Federica Giummolè consider the highly relevant issue of determining an optimal predictive density. They show how this predictive density may lie outside the class of the original parametric model describing the variable of interest and how geometrically a global solution can be constructed by considering formally all possible directions in which the original model may be extended. Their theory is based on minimising the leading term in the asymptotic expansion of risk based on general loss functions that reflect the discrepancy between distributions. Specifically they employ α divergences as loss functions to prove the existence of an optimal solution and to get explicit solutions for a number of examples in relevant econometric models, including the standard regression model and the AR(1) model.

Kees Jan van Garderen provides a detailed and powerful analysis of the effects of statistical curvature on the classical tests used in econometrics: the LR, LM, Wald and point optimal tests, as well as the geodesic test put forward by Critchley, Marriott and Salmon (1996). Most practical econometric models are statistically curved and yet the effects of statistical curvature are largely unrecognised. When a model is statistically curved, no uniformly powerful test will exist and any test will necessarily compromise power against different alternatives. Van

Garderen employs a geometric approach avoiding a complex mathematical development to graphically analyse the partitioning of the sample space into the critical and acceptance regions for the particular tests. The analysis is valid for all sample sizes and is global in that it considers the whole of the parameter and sample spaces. The standard asymptotic equivalence result often seems to suggest that the choice of which test to employ is simply a matter of computational convenience, but the approximate nature of this first-order asymptotic result can be highly misleading if the model is seriously curved, as van Garderen shows since the different tests employ very different critical regions. The point optimal and Lagrange multiplier tests give a straight boundary to the critical region and cannot guarantee global consistency. The Wald test gives a curved boundary but the numerical value of the statistic depends on the algebraic formulation of the restrictions, and the geodesic test begs the fundamental question of which geodesic to calculate. The likelihood ratio test uses the best critical region in the maximum likelihood direction and, since it implicitly and automatically takes into account the curvature of the model, it should be favoured over the other tests when the model is significantly curved. Van Garderen provides a detailed analysis of testing for serial correlation and unit roots.

Tom Rothenberg considers the question of testing for unit roots in autoregressive and moving-average models. These models are statistically curved and inference will often be critically affected. Moreover the effects of curvature get substantially larger the closer we get to the unit root (see van Garderen (1997)), indicating one aspect of the non-standard nature of inference in the unit root case. Although standard asymptotic theory does not apply, Rothenberg finds somewhat surprisingly that the large sample power curves and envelopes mimic those predicted by standard second-order asymptotic theory. This result requires further explanation.

Finally, Critchley, Marriott and Salmon consider the very general issue of the geometry of transformations and the role of parameterisation in econometric models. In particular, they provide an elementary and visual account of Amari's (1990) expected geometry, focusing on the full exponential family case. Formal definitions of affine connections are not exploited; instead they exploit the first two moments of the score function under the true distribution. Amari's fundamental non-metric affine connection appears as the natural measure of the non- constancy of the true covariance of the score across parameter space. This covariance is constant in the natural parameters. Non-linearity of the graph of the mean score in the natural parameter is then seen to reflect a curvature present in nearly all parametric families. They introduce the notion of ψ-duality, which is a natural duality between the score function in one parameterisation and the maximum likelihood estimator in another. It is seen to correspond to, and therefore provide a statistical interpretation of, the notion of duality in Amari's expected geometry. A number of generalised linear model examples are used throughout.

References

Amari, S. (1990), *Differential-Geometrical Methods in Statistics*, 2nd edn, Lecture Notes in Statistics No. 28, Berlin: Springer Verlag.

Barndorff-Nielsen, O.E. and D.R. Cox (1994), *Inference and Asymptotics*, Monographs on Statistics and Applied Probability No. 52, London: Chapman & Hall.

Critchley, F., P. Marriott and M. Salmon (1996), 'On the Differential Geometry of the Wald Test with Nonlinear Restrictions', *Econometrica*, 64: 1213–1222.

Garderen, K.J. van (1997), 'Exact Geometry of Explosive Autoregressive Models', University of Bristol Working Paper.

Godambe, V. P. (1960), 'An Optimum Property of Regular Maximum Likelihood Estimation', *Annals of Mathematical Statistics*, 31: 1208–1212.

Gouriéroux, C. and A. Monfort (1995), 'Testing, Encompassing and Simulating Dynamic Econometric Models', *Econometric Theory*, 11: 195–228.

Hillier, G.H. and M. Armstrong (1996), 'On the Density of the Maximum Likelihood Estimator', University of Southampton Discussion Papers in Economics and Econometrics No. 9645; also in *Econometrica*, 67(6),1999: 1459–1470.

Kass, R.E. and P.W. Vos (1997), *Geometrical Foundations of Statistical Inference*, Chichester: John Wiley.

McCullagh, P. (1987), *Tensor Methods in Statistics*, London: Chapman & Hall.

1 An introduction to differential geometry in econometrics

Paul Marriott and Mark Salmon

1 Introduction

In this introductory chapter we seek to cover sufficient differential geometry in order to understand its application to econometrics. It is not intended to be a comprehensive review either of differential geometric theory, or of all the applications that geometry has found in statistics. Rather it is aimed as a rapid tutorial covering the material needed in the rest of this volume and the general literature. The full abstract power of a modern geometric treatment is not always necessary and such a development can often hide in its abstract constructions as much as it illuminates.

In section 2 we show how econometric models can take the form of geometrical objects known as manifolds, in particular concentrating on classes of models that are full or curved exponential families.

This development of the underlying mathematical structure leads into section 3, where the tangent space is introduced. It is very helpful to be able to view the tangent space in a number of different but mathematically equivalent ways, and we exploit this throughout the chapter.

Section 4 introduces the idea of a metric and more general tensors illustrated with statistically based examples. Section 5 considers the most important tool that a differential geometric approach offers: the affine connection. We look at applications of this idea to asymptotic analysis, the relationship between geometry and information theory and the problem of the choice of parameterisation. Section 6 introduces key mathematical theorems involving statistical manifolds, duality, projection and finally the statistical application of the classic geometric theorem of Pythagoras. The last two sections look at direct applications of this geometric framework, in particular at the problem of inference in curved families and at the issue of information loss and recovery.

Note that, although this chapter aims to give a reasonably precise mathematical development of the required theory, an alternative and perhaps more intuitive approach can be found in the chapter by Critchley, Marriott and Salmon in this volume. For a more exhaustive and detailed review of current geometrical statistical theory see Kass and Vos (1997) or, from a more purely mathematical background, see Murray and Rice (1993).

2   Parametric families and geometry

In this section we look at the most basic relationship between parametric families of distribution functions and geometry. We begin by first introducing the statistical examples to which the geometric theory most naturally applies: the class of *full* and *curved exponential families*. Examples are given to show how these families include a broad range of econometric models. Families outside this class are considered in section 2.3.

Section 2.4 then provides the necessary geometrical theory that defines a *manifold* and shows how one manifold can be defined as a curved subfamily of another. It is shown how this construction gives a very natural framework in which we can describe clearly the geometrical relationship between full and curved exponential families. It further gives the foundations on which a fully geometrical theory of statistical inference can be built.

It is important at the outset to make clear one notational issue: we shall follow throughout the standard geometric practice of denoting components of a set of parameters by an upper index in contrast to standard econometric notation. In other words, if $\theta \in \mathbf{R}^r$ is an r-dimensional parameter vector, then we write it in component terms as

$$\theta = \left(\theta^1, \theta^2, \ldots, \theta^r\right)'.$$

This allows us to use the *Einstein summation convention* where a repeated index in both superscript and subscript is implicitly summed over. For example if $x = (x_1, \ldots, x_r)'$ then the convention states that

$$\theta^i x_i = \sum_{i=1}^{r} \theta^i x_i.$$

2.1   Exponential families

We start with the formal definition. Let $\theta \in \Theta \subseteq \mathbf{R}^r$ be a parameter vector, X a random variable, continuous or discrete, and $s(X) = (s_1(X), \ldots, s_r(X))'$ an r-dimensional statistic. Consider a family of continuous or discrete probability densities, for this random variable, of the form

$$p(x|\theta) = \exp\{\theta^i s_i - \psi(\theta)\}m(x). \tag{1}$$

Remember we are using the Einstein summation convention in this definition. The densities are defined with respect to some fixed dominating measure, ν. The function $m(x)$ is non-negative and independent of the parameter vector θ. We shall further assume that the components of s are not linearly dependent. We call Θ the *natural parameter space* and we shall assume it contains all θ such that

$$\int \exp\{\theta^i s_i\}m(x)\,d\nu < \infty.$$

A parametric set of densities of this form is called a *full exponential family*. If Θ is open in $\mathbf{R}^r$ then the family is said to be *regular*, and the statistics $(s_1, \ldots, s_r)'$ are called the *canonical statistics*.

The function $\psi(\theta)$ will play an important role in the development of the theory below. It is defined by the property that the integral of the density is one, hence

$$\psi(\theta) = \log\left(\int \exp\{\theta^i s_i\}m(x)d\nu\right).$$

It can also be interpreted in terms of the moment generating function of the canonical statistic S. This is given by $M(S; t, \theta)$ where

$$M(S; t, \theta) = \exp\{\psi(\theta + t) - \psi(\theta)\}; \tag{2}$$

see for example Barndorff-Nielsen and Cox (1994, p. 4).

The geometric properties of full exponential families will be explored later. However, it may be helpful to remark that in section 5 it is shown that they have a natural geometrical characterisation as the *affine subspaces* in the space of all density functions. They therefore play the role that lines and planes do in three-dimensional Euclidean geometry.

2.1.1   *Examples*

Consider what are perhaps the simplest examples of full exponential families in econometrics: the standard regression model and the linear simultaneous equation model. Most of the standard building blocks of univariate statistical theory are in fact full exponential families including the Poisson, normal, exponential, gamma, Bernoulli, binomial and multinomial families. These are studied in more detail in Critchley *et al.* in chapter 10 in this volume.

Example 1. The standard linear model Consider a linear model of the form

$$\mathbf{Y} = \mathbf{X}\boldsymbol{\beta} + \boldsymbol{\epsilon},$$

where $\mathbf{Y}$ is an $n \times 1$ vector of the single endogenous variable, $\mathbf{X}$ is an $n \times (k+1)$ matrix of the k weakly exogenous variables and the intercept term and $\boldsymbol{\epsilon}$ is the $n \times 1$ matrix of disturbance terms which we assume satisfies the Gauss–Markov conditions. In particular, for all i in $1, \ldots, n$

$$\epsilon_i \sim N(0, \sigma^2).$$

The density function of Y *conditionally* on the values of the exogenous variables can then be written as

$$\exp\left\{ \left(\frac{\beta}{\sigma^2}\right)' (\mathbf{X}'\mathbf{Y}) + \left(\frac{1}{-2\sigma^2}\right)(\mathbf{Y}'\mathbf{Y}) \right.$$
$$\left. - \left(\frac{\beta'\mathbf{X}'\mathbf{X}\beta}{2\sigma^2} + (n/2)\log(2\pi\sigma^2)\right) \right\}.$$

This is in precisely the form for a full exponential family with the parameter vector

$$\theta' = \left(\frac{\beta'}{\sigma^2}, \ \frac{1}{-2\sigma^2}\right)$$

and canonical statistics

$$(s(\mathbf{Y}))' = \left(\mathbf{Y}'\mathbf{X} \quad \mathbf{Y}'\mathbf{Y}\right).$$

Example 2. The simultaneous equation model Consider the set of simultaneous linear equations

$$\mathbf{B}\mathbf{Y}_t + \boldsymbol{\Gamma}\mathbf{X}_t = \mathbf{U}_t,$$

where $\mathbf{Y}$ are endogenous variables, $\mathbf{X}$ weakly exogenous, $\mathbf{U}$ the random component and $\mathbf{t}$ indexes the observations. Moving to the reduced form, we have

$$\mathbf{Y}_t = -\mathbf{B}^{-1}\boldsymbol{\Gamma}\mathbf{X}_t + \mathbf{B}^{-1}\mathbf{U}_t,$$

which gives a full exponential family in a similar way to Example 1. However, an important point to notice is that the natural parameters θ in the standard full exponential form are now highly non-linear functions of the parameters in the structural equations. We shall see how the geometric analysis allows us to understand the effect of such non-linear reparameterisations below.

Example 3. Poisson regression Moving away from linear models, consider the following Poisson regression model. Let μ_i denote the expected value for independent Poisson variables Y_i, $i = 1, \ldots, n$. We shall initially assume that the μ_i parameters are unrestricted. The density for $(y_1, \ldots, y_n)$ can be written as,

$$\exp\left\{\sum_{i=1}^{n} y_i \log(\mu_i) - \sum_{i=1}^{n} \mu_i\right\} \prod_{i=1}^{n} \frac{1}{y_i!}.$$

Again this is in full exponential family form, with the natural parameters and canonical statistics being

$$\theta^i = \log(\mu_i), \, s_i(y_1, \ldots, y_n) = y_i,$$

respectively. For a true Poisson regression model, the μ_i parameters will be predicted using covariates. This imposes a set of restrictions on the full exponential family which we consider in section 2.2.

2.1.2 Parameterisations

There is a very strong relationship between geometry and para-meterisation. In particular, it is important in a geometrically based theory to distinguish between those properties of the model that are dependent on a particular choice of parameterisation and those that are independent of this choice. Indeed, one can define the geometry of a space to be those properties that are invariant to changes in parameterisation (see Dodson and Poston (1991)).

In Example 2 we noted that the parameters in the structural equations need not be simply related to the natural parameters, θ. Structural para-meters will often have a direct econometric interpretation, which will be context dependent. However, there are also sets of parameters for full exponential families which always play an important role. The natural parameters, θ, are one such set. A second form are the *expected* para-meters η. These are defined by

$$\eta^i(\theta) = E_{p(x,\theta)}(s_i(x)).$$

From equation (2) it follows that these parameters can be expressed as

$$\eta^i(\theta) = \frac{\partial \psi}{\partial \theta^i}(\theta). \tag{3}$$

In a regular full exponential family the change of parameters from θ to η is a diffeomorphism. This follows since the Jacobian of this transformation is given from equation (3) as

$$\frac{\partial \eta^i}{\partial \theta^j} = \frac{\partial^2 \psi}{\partial \theta^i \partial \theta^j}(\theta).$$

This will be non-zero since for a regular family ψ is a strictly convex function (see Kass and Vos (1997), p. 16, Theorem 2.2.1).

2.1.3   *Repeated sampling and sufficient statistics*

One important aspect of full exponential families concerns the properties of their sufficient statistics. Let us assume that we have a random sample $(x_1, \ldots, x_n)$ where each observation is drawn from a density

$$p(x, \mid \theta) = \exp\{\theta^i s_i(x) - \psi(\theta)\}m(x).$$

The log-likelihood function for the full sample will be

$$\ell(\theta; (x_1, \ldots, x_n)) = \theta^i \sum_{j=1}^n s_i(x_j) - n\psi(\theta).$$

Thus if the parameter space is r-dimensional then there is always an r-dimensional sufficient statistic, namely

$$\left(\sum_{j=1}^n s_1(x_j), \ldots, \sum_{j=1}^n s_r(x_j)\right).$$

Note that the dimension of this sufficient statistic will be independent of the sample size n. This is an important property which we shall see in section 2.3 has important implications for the geometric theory.

2.2   Curved exponential families

In the previous section we mentioned that full exponential families will be shown to play the role of affine subspaces in the space of all density functions. Intuitively they can be thought of as lines, planes and higher-dimensional Euclidean spaces. We can then ask what would be the properties of *curved* subfamilies of full exponential families?

In general there are two distinct ways in which subfamilies can be defined: firstly by imposing restrictions on the parameters of the full family, and secondly as parametric families in their own right. We use this second approach as the basis of a formal definition.

Let Θ be the r-dimensional natural parameter space for the full exponential family given by

$$p(x \mid \theta) = \exp\{\theta^i s_i - \psi(\theta)\}m(x).$$

Assume that there is a mapping from Ξ, an open subset of $\mathbf{R}^p$ to Θ,

$$A : \Xi \to \Theta$$

$$\xi \mapsto \theta(\xi),$$

which obeys the following conditions:
1. the dimension of Ξ is less than that of Θ,
2. the mapping is one-to-one and smooth and its derivative has full rank everywhere,
3. if the sequence of points $\{\theta_i, i = 1, \ldots, r\} \subseteq A(\Xi)$ converges to $\theta_0 \in A(\Xi)$, then $A^{-1}(\theta_i)$ converges to $A^{-1}(\theta_0)$ in Ξ.

Under these conditions the parametric family defined by

$$p(x \mid \xi) = \exp\{\theta^i(\xi)s_i - \psi(\theta(\xi))\}m(x)$$

is called a *curved exponential* family. In particular noting the dimensions of the relevant spaces, it is an (r, p)-curved exponential family.

2.2.1   Examples

We now look at a set of examples to see how this class of curved exponential families is relevant to econometrics. For further examples see Kass and Vos (1997) or Barndorff-Nielsen and Cox (1994), where many forms of generalised linear models, including logistic, binomial and exponential regressions, non-linear regression models, time-series models and stochastic processes, are treated. Another important source of curved exponential families is the imposition and testing of parametric restrictions (see Example 5). Finally we mention some general approximation results which state that *any* parametric family can be approximated using a curved exponential family (see, for example, Barndorff-Nielsen and Jupp (1989)).

Example 3. Poisson regression (continued)   Let us now assume that the parameters in the Poisson regression model treated above are assumed to be determined by a set of covariates. As a simple example we could assume the means follow the equation

$$\log(\mu_i) = \alpha + \beta X_i,$$

where X is an exogenous variable. Hence, in terms of the natural parameters we have

$$\theta^i = \alpha + \beta X_i.$$

Thus the map defining the curved exponential family is

$$(\alpha, \beta) \rightarrow \left(\theta^1(\alpha, \beta), \dots, \theta^n(\alpha, \beta)\right),$$

and we have a $(n, 2)$-curved exponential family.

Example 4. $AR(1)$-model   Consider the simple $AR(1)$ model

$$x_t = \alpha x_{t-1} + \epsilon_t,$$

where the disturbance terms are independent $N(0, \sigma^2)$ variables, and we assume $x_0 = 0$. The density function will then be of the form

$$\exp\left\{ \left(\frac{-1}{2\sigma^2}\right) \sum_{i=1}^n x_i^2 + \left(\frac{\alpha}{\sigma^2}\right) \sum_{i=1}^n x_t x_{t-1} + \left(\frac{-\alpha^2}{2\sigma^2}\right) \sum_{i=1}^n x_{t-1}^2 \right.$$
$$\left. - \frac{n}{2} \log\left(2\pi\sigma^2\right) \right\}.$$

This is a curved exponential family since the parameters can be written in the form

$$\theta^1(\alpha, \sigma) = \frac{-1}{2\sigma^2}, \quad \theta^2(\alpha, \sigma) = \frac{\alpha}{\sigma^2}, \quad \theta^3(\alpha, \sigma) = \frac{-\alpha^2}{2\sigma^2}.$$

The geometry of this and more general $ARMA$-families has been studied in Ravishanker (1994).

Example 5. COMFAC model   Curved exponential families can also be defined by imposing restrictions on the parameters of a larger, full or curved, exponential family. As we will see, if these restrictions are non-linear in the natural parameters the restricted model will, in general, be a curved exponential family. As an example consider the COMFAC model,

$$y_t = \gamma x_t + u_t,$$

where x is weakly exogenous and the disturbance terms follow a normal $AR(1)$ process

$$u_t = \rho u_{t-1} + \epsilon_t.$$

Combining these gives a model

$$y_t = \rho y_{t-1} + \gamma x_t - \rho \gamma x_{t-1} + \epsilon_t$$

which we can think of as a restricted model in an unrestricted auto-regressive model

$$y_t = \alpha_0 y_{t-1} + \alpha_1 x_t + \alpha_2 x_{t-1} + w_t.$$

We have already seen that the autoregressive model gives rise to a curved exponential structure. The COMFAC restriction in this simple case is given by a polynomial in the parameters

$$\alpha_2 + \alpha_0\alpha_1 = 0.$$

The family defined by this non-linear restriction will also be a curved exponential family. Its curvature is defined by a non-linear restriction in a family that is itself curved. Thus the COMFAC model is curved exponential and testing the validity of the model is equivalent to testing the validity of one curved exponential family in another. We shall see later how the geometry of the embedding of a curved exponential family affects the properties of such tests, as discussed by van Garderen in this volume and by Critchley, Marriott and Salmon (1996), among many others.

2.3   Non-exponential families

Of course not all parametric families are full or curved exponential and we therefore need to consider families that lie outside this class and how this affects the geometric theory. We have space only to highlight the issues here but it is clear that families that have been excluded include the Weibull, generalised extreme value and Pareto distributions, and these are of practical relevance in a number of areas of econometric application. An important feature of these families is that the dimension of their sufficient statistics grows with the sample size. Although this does not make an exact geometrical theory impossible, it does considerably complicate matters.

Another property that the non-exponential families can exhibit is that the support of the densities can be parameter dependent. Thus members of the same family need not be mutually absolutely continuous. Again, although this need not exclude a geometrical theory, it does make the development more detailed and we will not consider this case.

In general the development below covers families that satisfy standard regularity conditions found, for instance, in Amari (1990, p. 16). In detail these conditions for a parametric family $p(x \mid \theta)$ are:
1. all members of the family have common support,
2. let $\ell(\theta ; x) = \log \text{Lik}(\theta ; x)$, then the set of functions

$$\left\{ \frac{\partial \ell}{\partial \theta^i}(\theta ; x) \mid i = 1, \ldots, n \right\}$$

are linearly independent,
3. moments of $\partial \ell / \partial \theta^i (\theta ; x)$ exist up to sufficiently high order,

4. for all relevant functions integration and taking partial derivatives with respect to θ are commutative.

These conditions exclude a number of interesting models but will not, in general, be relevant for many standard econometric applications. All full exponential families satisfy these conditions, as do a large number of other classes of families.

2.4   Geometry

We now look at the general relationship between parametric statistical families and geometric objects known as *manifolds*. These can be thought of intuitively as multi-dimensional generalisations of surfaces. The theory of manifolds is fundamental to the development of differential geometry, although we do not need the full abstract theory (which would be found in any modern treatment such as Spivak (1979) or Dodson and Poston (1991)). We develop a simplified theory suitable to explain the geometry of standard econometric models. Fundamental to this approach is the idea of an *embedded manifold*. Here the manifold is defined as a subset of a much simpler geometrical object called an *affine space*. This affine space construction avoids complications created by the need fully to specify and manipulate the infinite-dimensional space of all proper density functions. Nothing is lost by just considering this affine space approach when the affine space we consider is essentially defined as the space of all log-likelihood functions. An advantage is that with this construction we can trust our standard Euclidean intuition based on surfaces inside three-dimensional spaces regarding the geometry of the econometric models we want to consider.

The most familiar geometry is three-dimensional Euclidean space, consisting of points, lines and planes. This is closely related to the geometry of a real vector space except for the issue of the choice of origin. In Euclidean space, unlike a vector space, there is no natural choice of origin. It is an example of an affine geometry, for which we have the following abstract definition.

An affine space (X, V) consists of a set X, a vector space V, together with a translation operation $+$. This is defined for each $v \in V$, as a function

$$X \to X$$

$$x \mapsto x + v$$

which satisfies

$$(x + v_1) + v_2 = x + (v_1 + v_2)$$

and is such that, for any pair of points in X, there is a *unique* translation between them.

Most intuitive notions about Euclidean space will carry over to general affine spaces, although care has to be taken in infinite-dimensional examples. We shall therefore begin our definition of a manifold by first considering curved subspaces of Euclidean space.

2.4.1 Embedded manifolds

As with our curved exponential family examples, curved subspaces can be defined either using parametric functions or as solutions to a set of restrictions. The following simple but abstract example can most easily get the ideas across.

Example 6. The sphere model Consider in $\mathbf{R}^3$, with some fixed origin and axes, the set of points which are the solutions of

$$x^2 + y^2 + z^2 = 1.$$

This is of course the unit sphere, centred at the origin. It is an example of an embedded manifold in $\mathbf{R}^3$ and is a curved two-dimensional surface. At least part of the sphere can also be defined more directly, using parameters, as the set of points

$$\{(\cos(\theta^1)\sin(\theta^2), \sin(\theta^1)\sin(\theta^2), \cos(\theta^2)) \mid \theta^1 \in (-\pi, \pi), \theta^2 \in (0, \pi)\}.$$

Note that both the north and south poles have been excluded in this definition, as well as the curve

$$(-\sin(\theta^2), 0, \cos(\theta^2)).$$

The poles are omitted in order to ensure that the map from the parameter space to $\mathbf{R}^3$ is invertible. The line is omitted to give a geometric regularity known as an *immersion*. Essentially we want to keep the *topology* of the parameter space consistent with that of its image in $\mathbf{R}^3$.

The key idea here is we want the parameter space, which is an open set in Euclidean space, to represent the model as faithfully as possible. Thus it should have the same topology and the same smoothness structure.

We shall now give a formal definition of a manifold that will be sufficient for our purposes. Our manifolds will always be subsets of some fixed affine space, so more properly we are defining a submanifold.

Consider a smooth map from Φ, an open subset of $\mathbf{R}^r$, to the affine space (X, V) defined by

$$i : \Phi \to X.$$

The set $i(\Phi)$ will be an embedded manifold if the following conditions apply:

(A) the derivative of i has full rank r for all points in Φ,

(B) i is a *proper* map, that is the inverse image of any compact set is itself compact (see Bröcker and Jänich (1982), p. 71).

In the sphere example it is Condition (A) that makes us exclude the poles and Condition (B) that excludes the line. This is necessary for the map to be a diffeomorphism and this in turn is required to ensure the parameters represent unique points in the manifold and hence the econometric model is well defined and identified.

Another way of defining a (sub)manifold of an affine space it to use a set of restriction functions. Here the formal definition is: Consider a smooth map ρ from an n-dimensional affine space (X, V) to $\mathbf{R}^r$. Consider the set of solutions of the restriction

$$\left\{ x \mid \rho(x) = 0 \right\},$$

and suppose that for all points in this set the Jacobian of ρ has rank r, then the set will be an $(n - r)$-dimensional manifold.

There are two points to notice in this alternative definition. Firstly, we have applied it only to restrictions of finite-dimensional affine spaces. The generalisation to the infinite-dimensional case is somewhat more technical. Secondly, the two alternatives will be locally equivalent due to the inverse function theorem (see Rudin (1976)).

We note again that many standard differential geometric textbooks do not assume that a manifold need be a subset of an affine space, and therefore they require a good deal more machinery in their definitions. Loosely, the general definition states that a manifold is *locally* diffeomorphic to an open subset of Euclidean space. At each point of the manifold there will be a small local region in which the manifold looks like a curved piece of Euclidean space. The structure is arranged such that these local subsets can be combined in a smooth way. A number of technical issues are required to make such an approach rigorous in the current setting. Again we emphasise that we will always have an embedded structure for econometric applications, thus we can sidestep a lengthy theoretical development.

Also it is common, in standard geometric works, to regard parameters not as labels to distinguish points but rather as functions of these points. Thus if M is an r-dimensional manifold then a set of parameters $(\theta^1, \ldots, \theta^r)$ is a set of smooth functions

$$\theta^i : M \to \mathbf{R}.$$

In fact this is very much in line with an econometric view of parameters in which the structural parameters of the model are functions of the probability structure of the model. For example, we could parameterise a family of distributions using a finite set of moments. Moments are clearly most naturally thought of as functions of the points, when points of the manifolds are actually distribution functions.

2.4.2   Statistical manifolds

In this section we show how parametric families of densities can be seen as manifolds. First we need to define the affine space that embeds all our families, and we follow the approach of Murray and Rice (1993) in this development. Rather than working with densities directly we work with log-likelihoods, since this enables the natural affine structure to become more apparent. However, because of the nature of the likelihood function some care is needed with this definition.

Consider the set of all (smooth) positive densities with a fixed common support S, each of which is defined relative to some fixed measure ν. Let this family be denoted by $\mathcal{P}$. Further let us denote by $\mathcal{M}$ the set of all positive measures that are absolutely continuous with respect to ν. It will be convenient to consider this set up to scaling by a positive constant. That is, we will consider two such measures equivalent if and only if they differ by multiplication of a constant. We denote this space by $\mathcal{M}^*$. Define X by

$$X = \{\log(m) \mid m \in \mathcal{M}^*\}.$$

Because $m \in \mathcal{M}^*$ is defined only up to a scaling constant, we must have the identification in X that

$$\log(m) = \log(Cm) = \log(m) + \log(C), \quad \forall\, C \in \mathbf{R}^+.$$

Note that the space of log-likelihood functions is a natural subset of X. A log-likelihood is defined *only* up to the addition of a constant (Cox and Hinkley (1974)). Thus any log-likelihood $\log(p(x))$ will be equivalent to $\log(p(x)) + \log(C)$ for all $C \in \mathbf{R}^+$. Finally define the vector space V by $V = \{f(x) \mid f \in C^\infty(S, \mathbf{R})\}$.

The pair (X, V) is given an affine space structure by defining translations as

$$\log(m) \mapsto \log(m) + f(x) = \log(\exp(f(x)m)).$$

Since $\exp(f(x)m)$ is a positive measure, the image of this map does lie in X. It is then immediate that $(\log(m) + f_1) + f_2 = \log(m) + (f_1 + f_2)$ and the translation from $\log(m_1)$ to $\log(m_2)$ is uniquely defined by $\log(m_2) - \log(m_1) \in C^\infty(S, \mathbf{R})$, hence the conditions for an affine space apply.

Using this natural affine structure, consider a parametric family of densities that satisfies the regularity conditions from section 2.3. Condition 1 implies that the set of log-likelihoods defined by this family will lie in X. From Condition 2 it follows that Condition (A) holds immediately. Condition (B) will hold for almost all econometric models; in particular it will always hold if the parameter space is compact and in practice this will not be a serious restriction. Hence the family will be an (embedded) manifold.

We note further that the set $\mathcal{P}$ is defined by a simple restriction function as a subset of $\mathcal{M}$. This is because all elements of $\mathcal{P}$ must integrate to one. There is some intuitive value in therefore thinking of $\mathcal{P}$ as a submanifold of $\mathcal{M}$. However, as pointed out in section 2.4.1, the definition of a manifold by a restriction function works most simply when the embedding space is finite-dimensional. There are technical issues involved in formalising the above intuition, which we do not discuss here. However, this intuitive idea is useful for understanding the geometric nature of full exponential families. Their log-likelihood representation will be

$$\theta^i s_i(x) - \psi(\theta).$$

This can be viewed in two parts. Firstly, an affine function of the parameters θ fits naturally into the affine structure of X. Secondly, there is a normalising term $\psi(\theta)$ which ensures that the integral of the density is constrained to be one. Very loosely think of $\mathcal{M}$ as an affine space in which $\mathcal{P}$ is a curved subspace; the role of the function ψ is to project an affine function of the natural parameters back into $\mathcal{P}$.

      Example 4 $AR(1)$**-model (continued)**   We illustrate the previous theory with an explicit calculation for the $AR(1)$ model. We can consider this family as a subfamily of the n-dimensional multivariate normal model, where n is the sample size. This is the model that determines the innovation process. Thus it is a submodel of an n-dimensional full exponential family. In fact it lies in a three-dimensional subfamily of this full exponential family. This is the smallest full family that contains the $AR(1)$ family and its dimension is determined by the dimension of the minimum sufficient statistic. The dimension of the family itself is determined by its parameter space, given in our case by α and σ. It is a $(3, 2)$ curved exponential family.

Its log-likelihood representation is

$$\ell(\alpha, \sigma : x) = \left(\frac{-1}{2\sigma^2}\right) \sum_{i=1}^{n} x_i^2 + \left(\frac{\alpha}{\sigma^2}\right) \sum_{i=1}^{n} x_t x_{t-1}$$

$$+ \left(\frac{-\alpha^2}{2\sigma^2}\right) \sum_{i=1}^{n} x_{t-1}^2 - \frac{n}{2} \log(2\pi\sigma^2).$$

2.4.3 Repeated samples

The previous section has demonstrated that a parametric family $p(x|\theta)$ has the structure of a geometric manifold. However, in statistical application we need to deal with repeated samples – independent or dependent. So we need to consider a set of related manifolds that are indexed by the sample size n. The exponential family has a particularly simple structure to this sequence of manifolds.

One reason for the simple structure is the fact that the dimension of the sufficient statistic does not depend on the sample size. If X has density function given by (1), then an i.i.d. sample $(x_1, \ldots, x_n)$ has density

$$p((x_1, \ldots, x_n)|\theta) = \exp\left\{\theta^i \sum_{j=1}^{n} s_i(x_j) - n\psi(\theta)\right\} \prod_{j=1}^{n} m(x_j).$$

This is also therefore a full exponential family, hence an embedded manifold. Much of the application of geometric theory is concerned with asymptotic results. Hence we would be interested in the limiting form of this sequence of manifolds as $n \to \infty$. The simple relationship between the geometry and the sample size in full exponential families is then used to our advantage.

In the case of linear models or dependent data, the story will of course be more complex. There will still be a sequence of embedded manifolds but care needs to be taken with, for example, the limit distribution of exogenous variables. As long as the likelihood function for a given model can be defined, the geometric construction we have set up will apply. In general econometric models with dependent data and issues of exogeneity, the correct conditional distributions have to be used to define the appropriate likelihood for our geometric analysis, as was implicitly done in the $AR(1)$ example above with the prediction error decomposition.

2.4.4 Bibliographical remarks

The term *curved exponential family* is due to Efron (1975, 1978 and 1982) in a series of seminal papers that revived interest in the geometric aspects of statistical theory. This work was followed by a series of papers by Amari *et al.*, most of the material from which can be found in

Amari (1990). The particular geometry treatment in this section owes a lot to Murray and Rice's (1993) more mathematical based approach, as well as to the excellent reference work by Kass and Vos (1997). Since the exponential family class includes all the standard building blocks of statistical theory, the relevant references go back to the beginnings of probability and statistics. Good general references are, however, Brown (1986) and Barndorff-Nielsen (1978, 1988).

## 3	The tangent space

We have seen that parametric families of density functions can take the mathematical form of manifolds. However, this in itself has not defined the geometric structure of the family. It is only the foundation stone on which a geometric development stands. In this section we concentrate on the key idea of a differential geometric approach. This is the notion of a *tangent space*. We first look at this idea from a statistical point of view, defining familiar statistical objects such as the score vector. We then show that these are precisely what the differential geometric development requires. Again we shall depart from the form of the development that a standard abstract geometric text might follow, as we can exploit the embedding structure that was carefully set up in section 2.4.2. This structure provides the simplest accurate description of the geometric relationship between the score vectors, the maximum likelihood estimator and likelihood-based inference more generally.

### 3.1	Statistical representations

We have used the log-likelihood representation above as an important geometric tool. Closely related is the score vector, defined as

$$\left(\frac{\partial \ell}{\partial \theta^1}, \ldots, \frac{\partial \ell}{\partial \theta^r} \right)'.$$

One of the fundamental properties of the score comes from the following familiar argument. Since

$$\int p(x \mid \theta) dv = 1,$$

it follows that

$$\frac{\partial}{\partial \theta^i} \int p(x \mid \theta) dv = \int \frac{\partial}{\partial \theta^i} p(x \mid \theta) dv = 0$$

using regularity condition 4 in section 2.3, then

$$E_{p(x,\theta)}\left(\frac{\partial \ell}{\partial \theta^i}\right) = \int \frac{1}{p(x \mid \theta)} \frac{\partial}{\partial \theta^i} p(x \mid \theta) p(x \mid \theta) dv = 0. \tag{4}$$

We present this argument in detail because it has important implications for the development of the geometric theory.

Equation (4) is the basis of many standard asymptotic results when combined with a Taylor expansion around the maximum likelihood estimate (MLE), $\hat{\theta}$,

$$\hat{\theta}^i - \theta^i = \mathcal{I}^{ij} \frac{\partial \ell}{\partial \theta^j} + O\left(\frac{1}{n}\right) \tag{5}$$

where

$$\left(-\frac{\partial^2 \ell}{\partial \theta^i \partial \theta^j}(\hat{\theta})\right)^{-1} = \mathcal{I}^{ij}$$

(see Cox and Hinkley (1974)). This shows that, in an asymptotically shrinking neighbourhood of the data-generation process, the score statistic will be directly related to the MLE. The geometric significance of this local approximation will be shown in section 3.2.

The efficiency of the maximum likelihood estimates is usually measured by the covariance of the score vector or the expected Fisher information matrix:

$$I_{ij} = E_{p(x,\theta)}\left(-\frac{\partial^2 \ell}{\partial \theta^i \partial \theta^j}\right) = \text{Cov}_{p(x,\theta)}\left(\frac{\partial \ell}{\partial \theta^i}, \frac{\partial \ell}{\partial \theta^j}\right).$$

Efron and Hinkley (1978), however, argue that a more relevant and hence accurate measure of this precision is given by the observed Fisher information

$$\mathcal{I}_{ij} = -\frac{\partial^2 \ell}{\partial \theta^i \partial \theta^j}(\hat{\theta}),$$

since this is the appropriate measure to be used after conditioning on suitable ancillary statistics.

The final property of the score vector we need is its behaviour under conditioning by an ancillary statistic. Suppose that the statistic a is exactly ancillary for θ, and we wish to undertake inference conditionally on a. We then should look at the conditional log-likelihood function

$$\ell(\theta \mid a) = \log\left(p(x \mid \theta, a)\right).$$

However, when a is exactly ancillary,

$$\frac{\partial \ell}{\partial \theta^i}(\theta : |a) = \frac{\partial \ell}{\partial \theta^i}(\theta),$$

in other words, the conditional score will equal the unconditional. Thus the score is unaffected by conditioning on *any* exact ancillary. Because of this the statistical manifold we need to work with is the same whether we work conditionally or unconditionally because the affine space differs only by a translation that is invariant.

3.2   Geometrical theory

Having reviewed the properties of the score vector we now look at the abstract notion of a *tangent space* to a manifold. It turns out that the space of score vectors defined above will be a statistical representation of this general and important geometrical construction. We shall look at two different, but mathematically equivalent, characterisations of a tangent space.

Firstly, we note again that we study only manifolds that are embedded in affine spaces. These manifolds will in general be non-linear, or curved, objects. It is natural to try and understand a non-linear object by linear-ising. Therefore we could study a curved manifold by finding the best affine approximation at a point. The properties of the curved manifold, in a small neighbourhood of this point, will be approximated by those in the vector space.

The second approach to the tangent space at a point is to view it as the set of all *directions* in the manifold at that point. If the manifold were r-dimensional then we would expect this space to have the same dimension, in fact to be an r-dimensional affine space.

3.2.1   *Local affine approximation*
We first consider the local approximation approach. Let M be an r-dimensional manifold, embedded in an affine space N, and let p be a point in M. We first define a tangent vector to a curve in a manifold M. A curve is defined to be a smooth map

$$\gamma : (-\epsilon, \epsilon) \subset \mathbf{R} \to M$$

$$t \mapsto \gamma(t),$$

such that $\gamma(0) = p$. The tangent vector at p will be defined by

$$\gamma'(0) = \lim_{h \to 0} \frac{\gamma(h) - \gamma(0)}{h}.$$

We note that, since we are embedded in N, $\gamma'(0)$ will be an element of this affine space (see Dodson and Poston (1991)). It will be a vector whose origin is p. The tangent vector will be the best linear approximation to the curve γ, at p. It is the unique line that approximates the curve to first order (see Willmore (1959), p. 8).

We can then define TM_p, the tangent space at p, to be the set of all tangent vectors to curves through p. Let us put a parameterisation θ of an open neighbourhood which includes p on M. We define this as a map ρ

$$\rho : \Phi(\subseteq \mathbf{R}^r) \to N,$$

where $\rho(\Phi)$ is an open subset of M that contains p, and the derivative is assumed to have full rank for all points in Φ. Any curve can then be written as a composite function in terms of the parameterisation,

$$\rho \circ \gamma : (-\epsilon, \epsilon) \to \Phi \to N.$$

Thus any tangent vector will be of the form

$$\frac{\partial \rho}{\partial \theta^i} \frac{d\theta^i}{dt}.$$

Hence TM_p will be spanned by the vectors of N given by

$$\left\{ \frac{\partial \rho}{\partial \theta^i}, \ i = 1, \ldots, r \right\}.$$

Thus TM_p will be a p-dimensional affine subspace of N. For completeness we need to show that the construction of TM_p is in fact independent of the choice of the parameterisation. We shall see this later, but for details see Willmore (1959).

3.2.2 Space of directions

The second approach to defining the tangent space is to think of a tangent vector as defining a direction in the manifold M. We define a direction in terms of a directional derivative. Thus a tangent vector will be viewed as a differential operator that corresponds to the directional derivative in a given direction.

The following notation is used for a tangent vector, which makes clear its role as a directional derivative

$$\frac{\partial}{\partial \theta^i} = \partial_i.$$

It is convenient in this viewpoint to use an axiomatic approach. Suppose M is a smooth manifold. A tangent vector at $p \in M$ is a mapping

$$X_p : C^\infty(M) \to \mathbf{R}$$

such that for all $f, g \in C^\infty(M)$, and $a \in \mathbf{R}$:

1. $X_p(a.f + g) = aX_p(f) + X_p(g)$,
2. $X_p(f.g) = g.X_p(f) + f.X_p(g)$.

It can be shown that the set of such tangent vectors will form an r-dimensional vector space, spanned by the set

$$\{\partial_i, \ i = 1, \ldots, r\};$$

further that this vector space will be isomorphic to that defined in section 3.2.1. For details see Dodson and Poston (1991).

It is useful to have both viewpoints of the nature of a tangent vector. The clearest intuition follows from the development in section 3.2.1, whereas for mathematical tractability the axiomatic view, in this section, is superior.

3.2.3   The dual space

We have seen that the tangent space TM_p is a vector space whose origin is at p. We can think of it as a subspace of the affine embedding space. Since it is a vector space it is natural to consider its dual space TM_p^*. This is defined as the space of all linear maps

$$TM_p \rightarrow \mathbf{R}.$$

Given a parameterisation, we have seen we have a basis for TM_p given by

$$\{\partial_1, \ldots, \partial_r\}.$$

The standard theory for dual spaces (see Dodson and Poston (1991)) shows that we can define a basis for TM_p^* to be

$$\{d\theta^1, \ldots, d\theta^r\},$$

where each $d\theta^i$ is defined by the relationship

$$\partial_i(d\theta^j) = \begin{cases} 1 & \text{if } i = j \\ 0 & \text{if } i \neq j. \end{cases}$$

We can interpret $d\theta^i$, called a 1-*form* or *differential*, as a real valued function defined on the manifold M which is constant in all tangent directions apart from the ∂_i direction. The level set of the 1-forms defines the coordinate grid on the manifold given by the parameterisation θ.

3.2.4   The change of parameterisation formulae

So far we have defined the tangent space explicitly by using a set of basis vectors in the embedding space. This set was chosen through the choice of parameterisation. Since this parameterisation is not intrinsic to the geometry of the manifold we must be able to convert from the basis defined in terms of one parameterisation to that defined in terms of another. Indeed we must show that the tangent space and its dual exist independently of the choice of parameters used.

The change of parameterisation formulae in fact turn out to be repeated applications of the standard chain rule from multivariate calculus. Suppose we have two parameterisations θ and η, for an open subset of the manifold M. Owing to the full rank of the derivative of parameterisations there is a diffeomorphism connecting the parameters, i.e. $\eta = \eta(\theta)$ is a smooth invertible map, whose inverse is smooth. This follows from the inverse function theorem and the fact that we are only working locally in an open neighbourhood of some point in the manifold (see for example Kass and Vos (1997), p. 300). We write $\partial_a \eta^i$ to denote the i'th partial derivative of η with respect to the a'th component of θ. So we have

$$\partial_a \eta^i = \frac{\partial \eta^i}{\partial \theta^a}(\theta).$$

Application of the chain rule then allows us to connect the basis in the θ-parameters, which we denote by $\{\partial_a \mid a = 1, \ldots, r\}$, indexed by a, with the basis relative to the η-parameterisation, which is denoted by $\{\partial_i \mid i = 1, \ldots, r\}$. Thus, recalling from section 3.2.2 that the basis elements are defined as differential operators, we can apply the chain rule. This gives the formula connecting the two bases as being

$$\partial_a = (\partial_a \eta^i)\partial_i.$$

Note here, as throughout, the use of the Einstein summation notation. Since this is just an invertible linear transformation, this result immediately implies that the tangent space spanned by the two basis sets will be the same. Hence we have shown that the previous definitions are indeed well defined.

Further, to complete the change of basis formulae, suppose we have a tangent vector X. We could write it in component terms relative to the θ-parameterisation as

$$X = X^a \partial_a.$$

Thus, changing basis gives

$$X = X^a (\partial_a \eta^i)\partial_i$$
$$= (X^a \partial_a \eta^i)\partial_i.$$

Hence the *components* will have the following change of basis formula

$$(X^1, \ldots, X^r) \mapsto (X^a \partial_a \eta^1, \ldots, X^a \partial_a \eta^1). \tag{6}$$

The change of basis formulae for the dual space can be derived in a similar way. The relationship connecting the basis relative to the θ-parameterisation, $\{d\theta^a \mid : a = 1, \ldots, r\}$, with that of the η-parameterisation, $\{d\eta^i \mid : i = 1, \ldots, r\}$, is given by

$$d\theta^a = \partial_i \theta^a \, d\eta^i,$$

where $\partial_i \theta^a = \partial \eta^i / \partial \theta^a$. Note that there is also the important relationship between the two changes of basis matrices, which states

$$\partial_i \theta^a \partial_a \eta^j = \begin{cases} 1 & \text{if } i = j \\ 0 & \text{if } i \neq j. \end{cases} \tag{7}$$

That is, viewed as matrices, $\partial_i \theta^a$ and $\partial_a \eta^j$ are mutual inverses.

3.2.5   *Statistical interpretation*

We can now relate this previous theory to our statistical manifolds. Recall that we are representing the manifolds by their log-likelihood representations. Let us now consider the representation of the tangent space in terms of the local affine approximation to the manifold.

Let the parametric family be given by $p(x \mid \theta)$, then its log-likelihood representation is given by $\log p(\theta \mid x) = \ell(\theta)$. A path in this manifold, through the point represented by θ_0, is given by

$$\gamma : (-\epsilon, \epsilon) \to \Phi \to X$$

$$t \mapsto \ell(\theta(t)).$$

Thus the tangent space will be spanned by the set of random variables

$$\left\{ \frac{\partial \ell}{\partial \theta^1}, \ldots, \frac{\partial \ell}{\partial \theta^r} \right\}.$$

Hence the set of score vectors spans the tangent space.

It will be convenient to swop freely between the two interpretations of tangent vectors – firstly random variables, which are elements of the above vector space, and secondly directional derivatives. We shall use the following notation throughout,

$$\partial_i \ell(\theta) = \frac{\partial \ell}{\partial \theta^i}$$

when we wish to emphasise the random variable nature of the tangent vector.

3.2.6   Taylor's theorem

Suppose we have a real valued function h defined on our statistical manifold M. Most asymptotic theory is defined using a form of
expansion of such functions. Using the machinery we have already developed, we can look at a first-order Taylor expansion that is relevant for
curved manifolds. Suppose we have a parameterisation θ on the manifold, then Taylor's expansion will be

$$h(\theta) = h(\theta_0) + \partial_i h(\theta_0) d\theta^i + \text{higher-order terms.}$$

We note however, owing to the change of basis formulae in section 3.2.4,
in particular equation (7), that this expansion will be invariant. That is to
say, the expansion will be the same for all parameterisations. The question of invariance to reparameterisation is an important one in statistics,
and has motivated much of our geometric development. We shall see that
the extension of this formula, which is needed for higher-order asymptotics, requires more knowledge of the underlying geometry of the manifold, and is considered in detail in Blæsild (1987).

3.2.7   Further structures

Having defined a single tangent space for a manifold M at the
point $p \in M$, we can define the *tangent bundle*, denoted by TM. This is
the collection of all tangent spaces, i.e.

$$TM = \{TM_p \mid p \in M\}.$$

The tangent bundle itself will have the structure of a manifold; in fact, if
M is r-dimensional then TM will be a $2r$-dimensional manifold (see
Dodson and Poston (1991)).

We will also use the notion of a tangent field on the manifold.
Intuitively we can think of this associating a tangent vector at each
point p that lies in the tangent space TM_p. Formally, a tangent field X
is a (smooth) map between manifolds

$$X : M \to TM$$

$$p \mapsto X(p) \in TM_p.$$

We denote the set of all tangent fields by $\chi(M)$. In a similar way we can
define the cotangent bundle T^*M by

$$T^*M = \{T^*M_p \mid p \in M\},$$

and a cotangent field X^* by

$$X^* : M \to T^*M$$

$$p \mapsto X^*(p) \in T^*M_p.$$

We denote the set of all cotangent fields by $\chi^*(M)$.

4   Metric tensors

Having carefully defined the tangent and cotangent spaces we are now able to define part of the underlying geometrical structure of a statistical manifold. Given that the tangent space can be viewed as a vector space, it is natural to ask if we have some way of measuring lengths of tangent vectors and angles between tangent vectors. We will see how this will enable us to define, amongst other things, lengths of paths. The tool that we use is called a *metric tensor*.

Since each tangent space is a vector space, the simplest way to measure lengths and angles is to prescribe a quadratic form for each tangent space. However, we would require that this quadratic form varies smoothly across the manifold. This gives the definition: a metric tensor, denoted by $\langle , \rangle$, is a smooth function

$$\langle , \rangle : \chi(M) \times \chi(M) \to C^\infty(M)$$

$$(X, Y) \mapsto \langle X, Y \rangle.$$

It satisfies the properties that for all $X, Y, Z \in \chi(M)$, and for all $f \in C^\infty(M)$:

1. $\langle X, Y \rangle = \langle Y, X \rangle$ (symmetry),
2. $\langle fX, Y \rangle = f \langle X, Y \rangle$ and $\langle X + Y, Z \rangle = \langle X, Z \rangle + \langle Y, Z \rangle$ (bilinearity),
3. $\langle X, X \rangle > 0$ (positive definiteness).

This definition is best understood when you consider what happens at the tangent space at a particular point p. On this vector space, T_pM, the metric $\langle , \rangle_p$ is simply a quadratic form. The key to the above definition lies in ensuring that this quadratic form varies smoothly across the manifold with p.

Suppose now that we introduce a parameterisation, θ. Since the metric is a bilinear form it can be written as an element of the tensor product of 1-forms, $T^*M \otimes T^*M$. We can express it in terms of the basis for T^*M given by the parameterisation, i.e. relative to $\{d\theta^1, \ldots, d\theta^r\}$. Thus we have the expression

$$\langle , \rangle = g_{ab} d\theta^a d\theta^b, \quad \text{where } g_{ab} = \langle \partial_a, \partial_b \rangle.$$

Just as we write any tangent vector in terms of its components with respect to the basis $\{\partial_1, \ldots, \partial_r\}$, the metric is often simply denoted by its components $g_{ab} = g_{ab}(\theta)$ relative to the basis $\{d\theta^1, \ldots, d\theta^r\}$. It is important then to understand how this 'component form' representation of the metric changes with a change of parameters. Suppose that η is another parameterisation, then we have

$$\langle , \rangle = g_{ab}\partial_i\theta^a\partial_j\theta^b\,d\eta^i d\eta^j = \tilde{g}_{ij}d\eta^i d\eta^j,$$

where $\tilde{g}_{ij}$ is the coordinate form for the η-parameterisation. Hence the change of basis formula for the coordinate version of the metric is

$$\tilde{g}_{ij} = \partial_i\theta^a\partial_j\theta^b g_{ab}. \tag{8}$$

Remember that we are using the Einstein convention. From the above definition we can see that, as long as the components of the metric obey the transformation rule in equation (8), then lengths and angles defined by the metric will be invariant to changes in parameterisation.

The following example shows how the metric can be induced by the geometry on the embedding space.

Example 6. The sphere example (continued)   Consider the sphere embedded in $\mathbf{R}^3$, which is given parametrically by

$$\{(\cos(\theta^1)\sin(\theta^2), \sin(\theta^1)\sin(\theta^2), \cos(\theta^2)) \mid \theta^1 \in (-\pi, \pi), \theta^2 \in (0, \pi)\}.$$

The tangent space at the point (θ^1, θ^2) is spanned by the vectors in $\mathbf{R}^3$

$$\partial_1 = \left(-\sin(\theta^1)\sin(\theta^2), \cos(\theta^1)\sin(\theta^2), 0\right)$$
$$\partial_2 = \left(\cos(\theta^1)\cos(\theta^2), \sin(\theta^1)\cos(\theta^2), -\sin(\theta^2)\right).$$

This surface is embedded in $\mathbf{R}^3$. Let us suppose we impose on $\mathbf{R}^3$ the standard Euclidean inner product, $\langle , \rangle_{\mathbf{R}^3}$. Since $\partial_1, \partial_2 \in \mathbf{R}^3$ we can measure their lengths and angles with this inner product. Thus we can define

$$g_{ij} = \langle \partial_i, \partial_j \rangle_{\mathbf{R}^3},$$

and we have the metric

$$\begin{pmatrix} \sin^2(\theta^2) & 0 \\ 0 & 1 \end{pmatrix}.$$

In general, if the embedding space N is not just an affine space, but also has a fixed inner product $\langle , \rangle_N$, then this will induce the *embedding metric*. In component form, relative to a parameterisation θ, this will be

$$g_{ij} = \langle \partial_i, \partial_j \rangle_N.$$

We shall return to this notion in section 4.2.

Having a metric tensor on the manifold not only defines the length of tangent vectors; it also can be used to define the length of curves. Suppose that the curve

$$\gamma : (0, 1)(\subset \mathbf{R}) \to M$$

$$t \mapsto \gamma(t)$$

is a smooth map such that $\gamma(0) = p_1$ and $\gamma(1) = p_2$. For any $t \in (0, 1)$ the corresponding tangent vector is $\frac{d\gamma}{dt}(t)$, with length

$$\sqrt{\left\langle \frac{d\gamma}{dt}(t), \frac{d\gamma}{dt}(t) \right\rangle_{\gamma(t)}}$$

and the length of the curve from p_1 to p_2 is defined as

$$\int_0^1 \sqrt{\left\langle \frac{d\gamma}{dt}(t), \frac{d\gamma}{dt}(t) \right\rangle_{\gamma(t)}} \, dt.$$

Owing to the invariance properties of the metric, this will be an invariant measure of arc-length.

Given two such points on a manifold we can ask the natural geometric question: what is the shortest path connecting them? Although this is a natural question, in general the complete answer is rather complex. There are examples where there will not be a shortest path in a manifold, or there may be many. There is a simpler answer, however, to the question: is it a path of *locally* minimum length, in a variational sense? That is, its length is a local minimum in the class of all paths joining p_1 and p_2. A path that satisfies this condition is called a *geodesic*.

Given a metric on a manifold, its geodesics can be characterised by a set of differential equations. We will see this representation in section 5.

4.1   Tensors

Tangent vectors, cotangent vectors and metrics are all examples of the general geometric notion of a *tensor*. All of these examples show how the careful definition of transformation rules allows definitions of invariant quantities to be made. This invariance to the choice of parameterisation is very important not only geometrically but also for statistical purposes. In general we would not want the tools of inference to depend on arbitrary choices in the model specification. Using a geometric approach will, almost by definition, avoid these problems; for an example of this see Critchley, Marriott and Salmon (1996). For a good reference to where tensors have had a direct application to statistical theory, see McCullagh (1987).

A general tensor is made up of multivariate linear functions and functionals of the tangent fields. They come in two types. The first are *covariant* tensors, which on each tangent space are high-dimensional generalisations of matrices. For example, the metric is simply a bilinear form that varies smoothly with the point of evaluation. The second type are called *contravariant* tensors, which are simply products of tangent vectors when evaluated at each point. We have the following formal definitions:

A *covariant tensor* of degree r on T_pM is an r-linear real valued function on the r-fold product $T_pM \times \ldots \times T_pM$. A *contravariant tensor field* of degree r is an r-linear real valued function on the r-fold product $T_p^*M \times \ldots \times T_p^*M$. A tensor field is a set of tensors on T_pM that varies smoothly with $p \in M$.

4.1.1 *Components of tensors*

To work with these tensors in computations it is necessary to write them out in component form with respect to the bases which span TM_p and TM_p^*. Given a parameter system θ, these bases will be

$$\{\partial_1, \ldots, \partial_r\}$$

and

$$\{d\theta^1, \ldots, d\theta^r\}.$$

Thus a k-covariant tensor can be written as

$$A_{i_1 i_2 \ldots i_k} d\theta^{i_1} d\theta^{i_2} \ldots d\theta^{i_k}.$$

This is, by definition, a k-linear real valued function on the k-fold product $T_pM \times \ldots \times T_pM$, which acts on tangent vectors in the following way. If we have a set of k tangent vectors $v_1, \ldots, v_k$, which we write with respect to the basis as

$$v_i = v_i^j \partial_j,$$

then the tensor acts on the set of vectors as

$$A_{i_1 i_2 \ldots i_k} d\theta^{i_1} d\theta^{i_2} \ldots d\theta^{i_k}(v_1, \ldots, v_k) = A_{i_1 i_2 \ldots i_k} v_1^{i_1} \ldots v_k^{i_k},$$

recalling again the Einstein convention.

To see how the components of this tensor will transform under a change of parameters, we apply the same methodology as we did for the metric. Let θ be the original parameterisation and let the components of the tensor with respect to this parameterisation be $A_{a_1 a_2 \ldots a_k}$. Let η be

the new parameterisation, with components $\tilde{A}_{i_1 i_2 \ldots i_k}$. This will give a transformation rule

$$\tilde{A}_{i_1 i_2 \ldots i_k} = \partial_{i_1}\theta^{a_1}\partial_{i_2}\theta^{a_2}\ldots\partial_{i_k}\theta^{a_k}A_{a_1 a_2 \ldots a_k}. \tag{9}$$

For a contravariant tensor the component form will be

$$A^{i_1 i_2 \ldots i_k}\partial_{i_1}\ldots\partial_{i_k},$$

which acts on k cotangent vectors $v^1, \ldots, v^k$, which we write as

$$v^i = v^i_j d\theta^j.$$

The action is then

$$A^{i_1 i_2 \ldots i_k \partial_{i_1}\ldots\partial_{i_k}}(v^1, \ldots, v^k) = A^{i_1 i_2 \ldots i_k}v^1_{i_1}\ldots v^k_{i_k},$$

and the transformation rule will then be

$$\tilde{A}^{i_1 i_2 \ldots i_k} = \partial_{a_1}\eta^{i_1}\partial_{a_2}\eta^{i_2}\ldots\partial_{a_k}\eta^{i_k}A^{a_1 a_2 \ldots a_k}. \tag{10}$$

4.1.2   *Raising and lowering indices*
The general theory of dual spaces tells us that if V is a vector
space and V^* its dual space, there will be a natural isomorphism between
V and V^{**}, the dual of the dual space, defined by

$$V \to V^{**}$$

$$v \mapsto \alpha_v,$$

where $\alpha_v : V^* \to \mathbf{R}$ is defined by $\alpha_v(A) = A(v)$ for all $A \in V^*$. However,
in general there will not be a *natural* isomorphism between V and V^*
unless there is an inner product $\langle , \rangle$ on V. In that case the isomorphism is
defined by

$$V \to V^*$$

$$v \mapsto \langle v, . \rangle,$$

where we interpret $\langle v, . \rangle$ as an element of V^* since

$$\langle v, . \rangle : V \to \mathbf{R}$$

$$w \mapsto \langle v, w \rangle.$$

For a manifold with a metric, of course, we do have an inner product
on each of the vector spaces defined by the tangent space. This will, by
the above theory, allow us to define a *natural* isomorphism between
tangent space TM and dual space T^*M. More generally it will enable

us to convert between covariant and contravariant tensors. Thus, if in component terms we have a 1-covariant tensor, given by A_i, then it can be converted to a contravariant tensor by using the metric. In detail we get $A^j = g^{ij} A_i$, where g^{ij} is the inverse to the metric g_{ij}.

4.2   Statistical metrics

Having seen the concept of a metric and a tensor in generality, we turn now to statistical applications. In this section we shall see that these tools are not new to statistical theory and that they are essential to understanding the nature of invariance. We look first at three examples of metrics in statistics and their application.

4.2.1   *Expected Fisher information*
We have already seen the expected Fisher information matrix in section 3.1:

$$I_{ij} = E_{p(x,\theta)} \left(-\frac{\partial^2 \ell}{\partial \theta^i \partial \theta^j} \right) = \text{Cov}_{p(x,\theta)} \left(\frac{\partial \ell}{\partial \theta^i}, \frac{\partial \ell}{\partial \theta^j} \right).$$

These are the components of a covariant 2-tensor which can be easily checked by seeing how it transforms under a change of parameters using equation (9). This is a simple exercise in the chain rule. Further, it will, under regularity, be positive definite and a smooth function of the parameter. Hence it has the properties of the components of a metric tensor. In general we will abuse notation and refer to I_{ij} as being a metric, dropping reference to components and explicit parameter dependence.

For a full exponential family, in the natural parameterisation, the expected Fisher information matrix will be given by

$$I_{ij}(\theta) = \frac{\partial^2 \psi}{\partial \theta^i \partial \theta^j}(\theta).$$

Applying equations (3) and (8) shows immediately that the components in the expected η-parameters will be

$$\left(\frac{\partial^2 \psi}{\partial \theta^i \partial^j}(\theta(\eta)) \right)^{-1}.$$

Using the convexity of ψ we see that the positive definiteness is assured, hence in the full exponential family case the expected Fisher information matrix is a metric tensor.

Although this has the formal properties of being a metric, we have to ask in what way does this act on the tangent space? In particular, what statistical interpretation can be given? This will become clear if we use the interpretation of the tangent vectors as being random variables, elements of the space spanned by

$$\left\{ \frac{\partial \ell}{\partial \theta^1}, \ldots, \frac{\partial \ell}{\partial \theta^r} \right\}.$$

The expected Fisher information is the covariance for this space of random variables. Due to the additive properties of the log-likelihood, the central limit theorem tells us that asymptotically linear combinations of score vectors will be normally distributed. Equation (4) tells us that the mean will be zero, thus the metric completely determines the stochastic behaviour of the space, at least to first order. This interpretation, although being completely standard, does need careful refinement in our geometric viewpoint. We will return to this issue below.

Having seen the expected Fisher information metric in the case of full exponential families, it is natural to ask what form it takes in a curved exponential family. Given an (r, t)-curved exponential family

$$p(x \mid \xi) = \exp\{\theta^i(\xi)s_i - \psi(\theta(\xi))\}m(x),$$

the tangent space to this family will be spanned by the set

$$\left\{ \frac{\partial \ell}{\partial \xi^1}, \ldots, \frac{\partial \ell}{\partial \xi^t} \right\},$$

where

$$\frac{\partial \ell}{\partial \xi^i} = \frac{\partial \theta^j}{\partial \xi^i}\left(s_j - \frac{\partial \psi}{\partial \theta^j} \right) = \frac{\partial \theta^j}{\partial \xi^i} \partial \ell_j.$$

The construction of an embedding metric, as seen in Example 6, can be used here. The metric on the curved family is completely determined by that on the embedding full exponential family. In component form this is given by g_{ij}, where

$$g_{ij} = \frac{\partial \theta^k}{\partial \xi^i} \frac{\partial \theta^l}{\partial \xi^j} I_{kl}. \tag{11}$$

4.2.2 Applications

We now give two examples where the metric properties of the expected Fisher information have found application in statistics. The first concerns the question of an invariant definition of length, and the second an invariant definition of angle.

The first example concerns the score test. Suppose we have an $(r, 1)$-curved exponential family

$$p(x \mid \xi) = \exp\{\theta^i(\xi)s_i(x) - \psi(\theta(\xi))\},$$

and we wish to test the null hypothesis $\xi = \xi_0$ using the score test. The components of the score vector will be

$$S(\theta(\xi_0)) = \left(s_i - \frac{\partial \psi}{\partial \theta^i}(\theta(\xi_0))\right) \frac{d\theta^i}{d\xi}(\theta(\xi_0)).$$

The variance of the score is the expected Fisher information matrix, which can be calculated using equation (11) as

$$V = \frac{d\theta^k}{d\xi} \frac{d\theta^l}{d\xi} I_{kl}.$$

Hence the score statistic is $S'V^{-1}S$. This is an invariant quantity for any reparameterisation of ξ. It has the geometric interpretation of the length of a cotangent vector which is a tensor. For an example of how this invariance is important in econometrics, see Critchley, Marriott and Salmon (1996).

The second example is where an angle is measured invariantly. Parameter orthogonality is a useful property when estimation is being made in the presence of nuisance parameters. For an example of this, see Barndorff-Nielsen and Cox (1994, p. 49).

4.2.3 Preferred point metrics

The expected Fisher information metric is not the only possible statistically based metric. The concept of a *preferred point geometry* and the related *preferred point metric* was introduced in Marriott (1989). This is a very natural geometric and statistical construction for the embedding given in section 2.4.2. The embedding space can be viewed as a space of random variables. These random variables are simply functions of the data. It seems natural then that the data-generation process (DGP) plays some role in defining the geometry. Let us suppose that we have a parametric family $p(x \mid \theta)$ and the data-generation process is given by a member of this family, namely $p(x \mid \phi)$. The point ϕ, although unknown, plays a distinctive role in the family $p(x \mid \theta)$. It is called the *preferred point*. The tangent space at a general point θ is spanned by the random variables

$$\left\{ \frac{\partial \ell}{\partial \theta^1}(\theta), \ldots, \frac{\partial \ell}{\partial \theta^r}(\theta) \right\}.$$

We can define the covariance matrix of this space relative to the DGP, i.e.

$$I_{ij}^{\phi}(\theta) = \text{Cov}_{p(x \mid \phi)} \left(\frac{\partial \ell}{\partial \theta^i}(\theta), \frac{\partial \ell}{\partial \theta^j}(\theta) \right). \tag{12}$$

The important difference between this and the expected Fisher information matrix is that the covariance here is evaluated with respect to some
fixed distribution for *all* tangent spaces. In the Fisher information case
the evaluating distribution varies with tangent space.

By the same argument as for the Fisher information, equation (12)
defines the components of a metric tensor, at least for all θ in a neighbourhood of ϕ. The properties of such preferred point metrics are
explored in Critchley, Marriott and Salmon (1993, 1994, and in this
volume).

We note further that we must reconsider equation (4) in the preferred
point context. The mean value of the score vector will be zero only in the
tangent space of the preferred point. In general we define

$$\mu_i^{\phi}(\theta) = E_{p(x \mid \phi)} \left(\frac{\partial \ell}{\partial \theta^i}(\theta) \right). \tag{13}$$

This defines a covariant 1-tensor on the manifold.

For a full exponential family it is easy to check that the preferred point
metric, in the natural parameters, is given by

$$I_{ij}^{\phi}(\theta) = \frac{\partial^2 \psi}{\partial \theta^i \partial \theta^j}(\phi).$$

Note that this is independent of θ and thus is constant across all tangent
spaces. We return to this property later.

4.2.4   Observed information metrics

As mentioned in section 3.1, Efron and Hinkley (1978) argue
that in general the observed Fisher information

$$\mathcal{I}_{ij} = -\frac{\partial^2 \ell}{\partial \theta^i \partial \theta^j}(\hat{\theta}),$$

is a better measure of the covariance of the score vector at $\hat{\theta}$, since it
reflects the conditional distribution of the score. This will also give a
statistically based metric. Here, though, the change of parameterisation
rule requires some care. By applying the chain rule to

$$\frac{\partial^2 \ell}{\partial \theta^i \partial \theta^j}(\theta)$$

twice, we have the following formula:

$$\frac{\partial^2 \ell}{\partial \eta^i \partial \eta^j}(\eta(\theta)) = \frac{\partial \theta^a}{\partial \eta^i} \frac{\partial \theta^b}{\partial \eta^j} \frac{\partial^2 \ell}{\partial \theta^a \partial \theta^b}(\theta) + \frac{\partial^2 \theta^a}{\partial \eta^i \partial \eta^j} \frac{\partial \ell}{\partial \theta^a}(\theta).$$

The second term on the right-hand side of this expression disappears when evaluated at $\hat\theta$, giving the correct covariant 2-tensor transformation rule. At all other values of θ, however, this will not transform as a tensor.

For a full exponential family the metric has components

$$\mathcal{I}_{ij}(\hat\theta) = \frac{\partial^2 \psi}{\partial \theta^i \partial \theta^j}(\hat\theta), \tag{14}$$

the same as the expected Fisher metric. However, for a curved exponential family the metrics will differ. The observed information metric will be a stochastic function, whereas the expected form will be deterministic.

The use of the observed information metric is best explained in the context of conditional inference. Let us suppose that we can write the minimum sufficient statistic, $(s_1(x), \ldots, s_r(x))$, for the curved exponential family $p(x \mid \xi)$ in the form $(\hat\xi(x), a(x))$, where a is any ancillary statistic for ξ and $\hat\xi$ is the maximum likelihood estimate. We have seen in section 3.1 that the tangent space is invariant under conditioning on an exact ancillary statistic. Thus, as an asymptotic approximation the observed metric will be the *conditional* covariance of the tangent vector and this will be the observed information matrix.

4.2.5 Bibliographical notes

The fact that the expected Fisher information has the properties of a metric tensor was first observed by Rao (1945, 1987). The full theory of so-called *expected* geometry was developed in a series of papers by Amari (see Amari (1987, 1990)). Preferred point metrics were introduced by Marriott (1989). The relationship between these two forms of geometry is explored in the companion chapter in this volume by Critchley, Marriott and Salmon. The *observed* geometry was developed by Barndorff-Nielsen (1987) and developed to a more general theory of *yokes*, by Blæsild (1987, 1991).

5 Affine connections

In section 2 it was stated that full exponential families can be thought of as affine subspaces, and that curved exponential families are curved subfamilies of these affine subspaces. In this section we shall see the formalisation of these statements. We have already studied the construction of the manifold, tangent bundle and metric structure of a parametric family. One final structure is needed before a satisfactory geometric theory for statistics can be developed. This is the idea of *curvature* and the absence of curvature, *straightness* and *flatness*. The tool used in differential geometry to describe these features is called an *affine connection*.

Consider for motivation a one-dimensional subfamily of a parametric family $p(x \mid \theta)$. We have already seen two ways in which we might consider this to be 'straight'. Firstly, we have the affine structure of the embedding space. Affine subspaces are often considered to be straight. Secondly, we have the concept of a geodesic with respect to a metric tensor. Loosely, a geodesic is a curve of minimum length, and this is often intuitively thought of as being equivalent to straightness. However, detailed investigation shows that for parametric families these two notions are quite different. A curve that is 'straight' according to this first criterion will not be 'straight' according to the second. Amari (1990) realised that the way out of this seeming paradox lay in the careful definition of the correct connection structure for statistics.

In this section we shall first examine the general geometric theory of connections and then define the relevant statistical examples.

5.1   Geometric affine connections

We take as our fundamental notion of straightness for a curve that its tangent vectors are always parallel to some fixed direction. However, to formalise this we must have a way of measuring the rate of change of a tangent field. An affine connection gives us that tool. It can be thought of as a way to calculate the rate of change of one tangent field with respect to another. We would want the result of the differentiation itself to be a tangent field.

Formally we define a symmetric affine connection ∇ to be a function

$$\nabla : \chi(M) \times \chi(M) \to \chi(M)$$

$$(X, Y) \mapsto \nabla_X Y,$$

which satisfies the following properties: for all $X, X_1, X_2, Y, Y_1, Y_2 \in \chi(M)$ and $f \in C^\infty(M)$, we have
1. $\nabla_{X_1 + X_2} Y = \nabla_{X_1} Y + \nabla_{X_2} Y$,
2. $\nabla_X(Y_1 + Y_2) = \nabla_X Y_1 + \nabla_X Y_2$,
3. $\nabla_{fX} Y = f \nabla_X Y$,
4. $\nabla_X(fY) = f \nabla_X Y + X(f)Y$,
5. $\nabla_X Y - \nabla_Y X = XY - YX$.

Note that here we are explicitly using the derivative version of the tangent vector given in section 3.2.2. Thus $X(f)$ is the directional derivative of the function f in the direction stipulated by the tangent vector X. Conditions

1, 2 and 3 define the linearity properties of the connection. Condition 4 states that the connection is a derivative and hence satisfies the product rule. Condition 5 is the condition that makes the connection symmetric. We shall consider only symmetric connections.

Just as in the case of a metric, we can write a connection in component form. Let us suppose that the vector fields X and Y are given with respect to the basis defined by the parameterisation θ, i.e.

$$X = X^i \partial \theta_i$$

$$Y = Y^i \partial \theta_i.$$

By definition $\nabla_X Y$ is also a tangent field. If we define

$$\nabla_{\partial_i} \partial_j = \Gamma_{ij}^k \partial_k,$$

then by the above Conditions 1–5 it must follow that

$$\nabla_X Y = (X^i \partial_i Y^k + X^i Y^j \Gamma_{ij}^k) \partial_k. \tag{15}$$

Thus the connection is completely determined by the three-way array Γ_{ij}^k. These are called the *Christoffel symbols* for the connection. Note that Condition 5 implies that, for all i, j and k,

$$\Gamma_{ij}^k = \Gamma_{ji}^k,$$

hence the connection is called symmetric.

It is important to note that the Christoffel symbols do not transform as tensors. If Γ_{ab}^c are the Christoffel symbols relative to the θ-parameters and $\tilde{\Gamma}_{ij}^k$ relative to the η-parameters, then the two sets of components are connected according to the rule

$$\Gamma_{ab}^c = \partial_k \theta^c \left(\partial_{ab}^2 \eta^k + \partial_a \eta^i \partial_b \eta^j \tilde{\Gamma}_{ij}^k \right). \tag{16}$$

One consequence of this not being a tensor rule is that Christoffel symbols can be identically zero with respect to one parameterisation, but non-zero in another.

Having defined a connection, we can see how the symbols are able to define a straight line, or, as it is called, a *geodesic*. Let us define a path in terms of a parameterisation,

$$\gamma : [0, 1](\subset \mathbf{R}) \to M$$

$$t \mapsto \theta(t).$$

Note that this is a slight abuse of notation, identifying $(\theta^1(t), \ldots, \theta^r(t))$ with the point in M with those parameters. The path will be a geodesic if it satisfies the equation

$$\frac{d^2\theta^k}{dt^2} + \frac{d\theta^i}{dt}\frac{d\theta^j}{dt}\Gamma^k_{ij} = 0. \tag{17}$$

If the tangent vector to this path is $X(t)$, this equation is the component form of the equation

$$\nabla_X X = 0. \tag{18}$$

5.1.1   Connections and projections

In order to understand the nature of a connection operator it is helpful to return to the sphere example and see how the most natural connection there operates on tangent fields.

Example 6. Sphere example (continued) For the sphere embedded in $\mathbf{R}^3$ with parameterisation

$$\{(\cos(\theta^1)\sin(\theta^2), \sin(\theta^1)\sin(\theta^2), \cos(\theta^2)) \mid \theta^1 \in (-\pi, \pi), \theta^2 \in (0, \pi)\},$$

consider a path

$$(\theta^1, \theta^2) = (t, \pi/2).$$

In $\mathbf{R}^3$ it is the path

$$(\cos(t), \sin(t), 1),$$

the equator of the sphere. Suppose we differentiate with respect to t, giving a vector in $\mathbf{R}^3$

$$X(t) = (-\sin(t), \cos(t), 0).$$

This is the tangent vector to the curve. A connection allows us to differentiate tangent fields. The result of this differentiation should itself be a tangent vector, since the tangent space gives the set of all directions in the manifold. However, differentiating $X(t)$ directly gives

$$\dot{X} = (-\cos(t), -\sin(t), 0).$$

This does not lie in the tangent space, which is spanned by

$$\partial_1 = (-\sin(t), \cos(t), 0) \quad \text{and} \quad \partial_2 = (0, 0, -1).$$

If we want the derivative of the tangent field, to be a tangent field we must project $\dot{X}(t)$ back into TM_p. Using the standard inner product on $\mathbf{R}^3$, $\langle\, ,\, \rangle_{\mathbf{R}^3}$, we find that $\dot{X}(t)$ is in fact orthogonal to the tangent space. Hence the rate of change of X, relative to the sphere, will be zero. In other words, in the sphere the curve is straight. This is completely consistent with intuition. The equator is a *great circle* that is well known to provide the shortest distance between two points on a sphere.

The intuition from the above example gives an interpretation of equation (15). It can be viewed as a standard derivative operation combined with a projection onto the tangent space. The exact form of the projection will depend on the form of the Christoffel symbols. For details of this construction, see Dodson and Poston (1991). We return to this view of the connection in section 5.2.1.

5.1.2   Metric connections

Having seen how a connection defines a geodesic, we return to the second definition of straightness. In section 4 a geodesic was defined as a path of (locally) minimum length. It can be shown, that given a metric, there is a unique affine connection ∇^0, called the Levi–Civita connection, for which the two definitions of geodesic agree. That is to say, defining a metric automatically defines a particular connection, such that if a path satisfies equation (18) it will be a path of minimum length. We quote here two important ways of characterising the Levi–Civita connection.

Theorem

(i)   *For a manifold M with a metric $\langle \, , \, \rangle_p$, the Levi–Civita connection ∇^0 is characterised as the only symmetric connection that satisfies*

$$X\langle Y, Z\rangle_p = \langle \nabla^0_X Y, Z\rangle_p + \langle Y, \nabla^0_X Z\rangle_p, \tag{19}$$

for all tangent fields X, Y, Z.

(ii)   *If we introduce a parameter system θ, the Christoffel symbols of the Levi–Civita connection are given by*

$$\Gamma^{0k}_{\ \ ij} = g^{kl}\left(\frac{\partial g_{il}}{\partial \theta^j} + \frac{\partial g_{jl}}{\partial \theta^i} - \frac{\partial g_{ij}}{\partial \theta^l}\right), \tag{20}$$

where g_{ij} are the components of the metric. The proof of this theorem can be found in Dodson and Poston (1991).

5.1.3   Non-metric connections

Connections do not, however, have to be constructed in this way. Any connection that is not the Levi–Civita connection of some underlying metric will be called a non-metric connection. Formally, all that is required is the definition of a set of Christoffel symbols that transform under a change of parameters according to equation (16). We shall see in the following section that for statistical purposes non-metric connections play a more important role than metric ones.

5.2   Statistical connections

As we have previously noted, we have two distinct notions of straightness or flatness for our statistical manifolds: firstly from the affine structure of the embedding space, and secondly from the Levi–Civita connection of a statistically based metric. Initially we consider the case with the expected Fisher information as the metric tensor on the manifold which represents the parametric family.

5.2.1   *The +1-connection*

We wish to define a connection that is consistent with the affine structure of the embedding space. Relative to this embedding we have the tangent vector

$$\partial_i = \frac{\partial \ell}{\partial \theta^i},$$

and hence

$$\partial_i \partial_j = \frac{\partial^2 \ell}{\partial \theta^i \partial \theta^j}(\theta; x),$$

a random variable. This, as we have seen in section 5.1.1, will not necessarily lie in the tangent space. The embedding structure gives a possible way of projecting into TM_θ. It is natural to use

$$\langle f, g \rangle = \mathrm{Cov}_{p(x \mid \theta)}(f, g)$$

for all elements f, g of X. Using this we project $\partial_i \partial_j$ onto the tangent space, which is spanned by the set

$$\left\{ \frac{\partial \ell}{\partial \theta^1}(\theta), \ldots, \frac{\partial \ell}{\partial \theta^r}(\theta) \right\}.$$

This will then define a connection whose Christoffel symbols are

$$\Gamma^{+1}{}_{ij}^{k}(\theta) = I^{kl}(\theta) E_{p(x \mid \theta)} \left(\frac{\partial^2 \ell}{\partial \theta^i \partial \theta^j}(\theta) \frac{\partial \ell}{\partial \theta^l}(\theta) \right). \tag{21}$$

This connection will be denoted by ∇^{+1}.

Calculating the Christoffel symbols for a full exponential family in its natural parameterisation and exploiting equation (4), gives that, for all $i, j, k \in \{1, \ldots, r\}$,

$$\Gamma^{+1}{}^{k}_{ij}(\theta) = 0.$$

We will return to this result later.

5.2.2 The 0-connection

In section 5.1.2 it was shown that the metric tensor gives rise to the Levi–Civita connection. The Christoffel symbols are defined by equation (20). If we take I, the expected Fisher information matrix, as our metric, then the associated Levi–Civita connection will be given by

$$\Gamma^{+1}{}^{k}_{ij} = I^{kl}(\theta)E_{p(x\,|\,\theta)}\left(\frac{\partial^2 \ell}{\partial\theta^i\partial\theta^j}(\theta)\frac{\partial \ell}{\partial\theta^l}(\theta)\right)$$

$$+\frac{1}{2}I^{kl}(\theta)E_{p(x\,|\,\theta)}\left(\frac{\partial \ell}{\partial\theta^i}(\theta)\frac{\partial \ell}{\partial\theta^j}(\theta)\frac{\partial \ell}{\partial\theta^l}(\theta)\right).$$

For the full exponential family in the natural parameterisation, the Christoffel symbols are given by

$$\Gamma^{0}{}^{k}_{ij} = \frac{1}{2}I^{kl}\frac{\partial^3 \psi}{\partial\theta^i\partial\theta^j\partial\theta^l}.$$

This connection will be denoted by ∇^0.

5.2.3 The −1-connection

Again considering connections as the combination of a derivative operation followed by a projection to the tangent space gives us yet another plausible connection.

As in section 5.2.1, we wish to project the random variable

$$\frac{\partial^2 \ell}{\partial\theta^i\partial\theta^j}(\theta)$$

into the tangent space. From equation (4) it is clear that any member of the tangent space *must* have zero expectation. Hence this motivates the projection

$$\frac{\partial^2 \ell}{\partial\theta^i\partial\theta^j}(\theta)\mapsto\frac{\partial^2 \ell}{\partial\theta^i\partial\theta^j}(\theta)-E_{p(x\,|\,\theta)}\left(\frac{\partial^2 \ell}{\partial\theta^i\partial\theta^j}(\theta)\right).$$

This operation is enough to define a connection, ∇^{-1}, and its Christoffel symbols will be

$$\Gamma^{-1}{}^{k}_{ij} = I^{kl}E_{p(x,\,|\,\theta)}\left(\left\{\frac{\partial^2 \ell}{\partial\theta^i\partial\theta^j}(\theta)+\frac{\partial \ell}{\partial\theta^i}(\theta)\frac{\partial \ell}{\partial\theta^j}(\theta)\right\}\frac{\partial \ell}{\partial\theta^l}(\theta)\right).$$

In the full exponential family, again in the natural coordinates, this has the form

$$\Gamma^{-1}{}^k_{ij}(\theta) = I^{kl}(\theta)\frac{\partial^3\psi}{\partial\theta^i\partial\theta^j\partial\theta^l}(\theta).$$

Notice the similarity to the ∇^0 case.

5.2.4   The α-connection

Amari (1987) pointed out that these different connections are all special cases of a large family of connections that have many statistical uses. They are called the α-connections, and denoted by ∇^α. They can be thought of as a linear combination of any two of the above types. The general definition is that the Christoffel symbols are given by

$$\Gamma^{\alpha}{}^k_{ij} = I^{kl}E_{p(x,\,|\,\theta)}\left(\left\{\frac{\partial^2\ell}{\partial\theta^i\partial\theta^j}(\theta) + \frac{1-\alpha}{2}\frac{\partial\ell}{\partial\theta^i}(\theta)\frac{\partial\ell}{\partial\theta^j}(\theta)\right\}\frac{\partial\ell}{\partial\theta^l}(\theta)\right).$$

In the full exponential family this simplifies to be

$$\Gamma^{\alpha}{}^k_{ij}(\theta) = \frac{1-\alpha}{2}I^{kl}\frac{\partial^3\psi}{\partial\theta^i\partial\theta^j\partial\theta^l}(\theta).$$

in the natural parameterisation.

5.2.5   Statistical manifolds

The development in the previous section concentrated on expected geometry. As we have seen, this is not the only sensible or important geometrical structure for a parametric family of distributions. However, the structure that was developed does seem to have a general applicability across most of the possible geometric structures. This was recognised by Lauritzen (1987). He defined a general structure that encompassed most forms of statistical geometry. A *statistical manifold* is defined as (M, g, T), where M is a manifold of distribution functions, g is a metric tensor and T is a covariant 3-tensor that is symmetric in its components and called the skewness tensor. For this structure there will always be a set of affine connections that parallels the structure in the previous section.

Theorem   *For any statistical manifold (M, g, T) there is a one-dimensional family of affine connections defined by*

$$\Gamma^{\alpha}{}_{ijk} = \Gamma^0{}_{ijk} - \frac{\alpha}{2}T_{ijk},$$

where ∇^0 is the Levi–Civita connection for the metric g.

In the case of expected geometry we have that

$$T_{ijk} = E_{p(x \mid \theta)} \left(\frac{\partial \ell}{\partial \theta^i} \frac{\partial \ell}{\partial \theta^j} \frac{\partial \ell}{\partial \theta^k} \right).$$

For the observed geometry we assume that the data can be written in the conditional resolution form $x = (\hat{\theta}, a)$, where a is ancillary. The likelihood can then be written as

$$\ell(\theta \, ; \, x) = \ell(\theta \, ; \, \hat{\theta}, a).$$

We use the following notation

$$\ell_i = \frac{\partial}{\partial \theta^i} \ell(\theta \, ; \, \hat{\theta}, a), \quad \text{and} \quad \ell_{,i} = \frac{\partial}{\partial \hat{\theta}^i} \ell(\theta \, ; \, \hat{\theta}, a). \tag{22}$$

In this notation it can be shown that $g_{ij} = -\ell_{ij} = \ell_{i,j}$ is the observed Fisher information metric, and $T_{ijk} = \ell_{ijk}$ is the skewness tensor.

6   Three key results

In this section we look at the key mathematical theorems of statistical manifolds; the applications to statistics are shown in sections 7 and 8. Throughout we shall assume that we have the structure of a statistical manifold (M, g, T) as defined in section 5.2.5.

6.1   Duality

The concept of duality for a statistical manifold is tied up with that of *flatness*. A connection defines the geometry of a manifold; in particular, it defines the curvature. There are many ways in which we can measure the curvature of a manifold. One issue of great interest is when there is no curvature, which is measured using the Riemann curvature tensor. This is a covariant 2-tensor defined in component terms using a connection as

$$R_{ijkl} = g_{lm}(\partial_i \Gamma^m_{jk} - \partial_j \Gamma^m_{ik}) + (\Gamma_{iml} \Gamma^m_{jk} - \Gamma_{jml} \Gamma^m_{ik}). \tag{23}$$

If this tensor is identically zero for all θ and all $i, j, k, l \in \{1, \ldots, r\}$, then the manifold is said to be *flat*. It is an important theorem of differential geometry that if a manifold is flat then there exists a parameterisation θ that has the property that the components of the Christoffel symbol in this parameterisation will be identically zero (see section 7). If the connection that defines the Riemann curvature is the Levi–Civita connection of the metric g, then this theorem extends. In this case there exists a parameterisation that has the property that the components $g_{ij}(\theta)$ will be independent of θ, so that the metric will be a constant. In either of these cases the parameterisation is called an *affine parameterisation*.

The duality theorem for statistical manifolds then states

> **Theorem**   *If (M, g, T) is a statistical manifold such that M is flat with respect to the connection ∇^α, then it will be flat with respect to $\nabla^{-\alpha}$.*

We say that the $-\alpha$-connection is *dual* to the α-connection. The 0-connection, which is the Levi–Civita connection derived from the metric, will be self dual.

One important application of this theorem is to the full exponential family. In section 5.2.1 it is shown that in the natural parameterisation the Christoffel symbols of the ∇^{+1}-connection are identically zero. Thus for this connection a full exponential family is flat and the natural parameters are affine. The theorem states that a full exponential family will also be flat with respect to the -1-connection. There is also therefore a set of parameters that is affine for this connection. These parameters are the expectation parameters defined in section 2.1.2.

The relationship between a dual pair of connections is illuminated by the following result, which should be compared with the defining equation for the Levi–Civita connection, equation (19).

> **Theorem**   *If the metric is denoted by $\langle\,,\rangle$, then for a statistical manifold (M, g, T)*

$$X\langle Y, Z\rangle = \langle \nabla_X^\alpha Y, Z\rangle + \langle Y, \nabla_X^{-\alpha} Z\rangle. \tag{24}$$

6.2   Projection theorem

In the following two sections we concentrate on the statistical manifold structure defined by Amari (1990).

The geodesic distance in a manifold is one way to measure distances between points of the manifold. However, for probability distributions there are other more statistically natural ways of defining a form of distance. Consider the following definition:

An α-divergence between $p(x)$ and $q(x)$, two density functions, is defined as

$$D_\alpha(p, q) = \begin{cases} E_q(\log(q) - \log(p)) & \alpha = 1 \\ E_p(\log(p) - \log(q)) & \alpha = -1. \end{cases} \tag{25}$$

Note that these divergences are the Kullback–Leibler information from q to p when $\alpha = 1$ and from q to p when $\alpha = -1$. These are not formally distance functions as they do not obey the standard axioms for a distance, such as symmetry or the triangle inequality. For a clarification of their geometric role, see Critchley, Marriott and Salmon (1994).

Amari's projection theorem connects these divergence functions with the geodesic structure. We give a simplified version of his theorem here, for exponential families. For more details see Amari (1990, p. 89).

Theorem *Let $p(x \mid \theta)$ be a full exponential family, and $p(x \mid \xi)$ a curved subfamily. Let θ_1 represent a distribution in the embedding family. Let ξ_α be an extremal point for the α-divergence, that is, in Ξ, ξ_α is an extremal point of the function*

$$D_\alpha(p(x \mid \theta_1), p(x \mid \xi)).$$

If ξ_α is an α extremal point, then the α geodesic connecting $p(x \mid \theta_1)$ and $p(x \mid \xi_\alpha)$ cuts the family $p(x \mid \xi)$ orthogonally.

One natural application here is in the case of a misspecified model. Suppose that the model is incorrectly specified as being the curved exponential family $p(x \mid \xi)$, while the data-generation process lies in the embedding family, and is denoted by $p(x \mid \theta_0)$. It is well known that the MLE on the misspecified model will converge to the value that is closest to $p(x \mid \theta_0)$ in terms of the Kullback–Leibler divergence. Hence it will be a -1-extremal point and the DGP and the pseudo-true estimate are connected by a -1-projection.

6.3   Pythagoras theorem

The final result presented in this section brings to the geometry of statistical families the classical geometric theorem of Pythagoras. We state the theorem for completeness.

Theorem *Let θ_1, θ_2 and θ_3 be three points in the parameter space of a full exponential family. Suppose that the α-geodesic joining θ_1 and θ_2 is orthogonal to the $-\alpha$-geodesic joining θ_2 and θ_3. For this triangle we have the Pythagorean relationship*

$$D_\alpha(\theta_1, \theta_2) + D_\alpha(\theta_2, \theta_3) = D_\alpha(\theta_1, \theta_3). \tag{26}$$

A more complete version of this theorem can be found in Amari (1990, p. 86).

7   Inference in curved families

In the final two sections of this chapter we look at how the machinery previously set up enables us to understand both the problem of inference in curved families and how to assess the information content of a general statistic. This issue is taken up in several chapters in this volume, in particular by Kees Jan van Garderen and Tom Rothenberg.

7.1   Curvature due to parameterisations

We have seen how the connection structure of a manifold enables us to define curvature, both of a curve and of a set of parameters. We look first at the issue of parameter-dependent curvature.

Example 7. Non-linear regression models   Bates and Watts (1988, p. 241) distinguish between two types of parameterisation that are important in the analysis of non-linear regression models. These curvatures are called the *parameter effects* and *intrinsic* curvatures. The first of these will be dependent on the exact form of the parameterisation and can be removed in principle by reparameterisation. The second will be independent of the parameterisation chosen. This distinction carries over from the non-linear regression case to a general statistical manifold.

One example where parameter effects are important is the bias of the maximum likelihood estimate. In the case of a full exponential family, the first-order bias of the maximum likelihood estimate is given by

$$b^i(\xi) = \frac{-1}{2n} g^{ij} g^{kl} \Gamma_{jkl}^{-1}. \tag{27}$$

Consider this formula in the context of linear models.

Example 1. The linear model (continued)   There is a natural geometric interpretation for ordinary least squares (OLS) estimation, which connects Euclidean geometry and regression (see, for example, Bates and Watts (1988)). For presentational simplicity we consider the case where the variance parameter is fixed and known. We have the model

$$\mathbf{Y} = \mathbf{X}\boldsymbol{\beta} + \boldsymbol{\epsilon}.$$

There is an n-dimensional space of possible response vectors Y and a $(k+1)$-dimensional submanifold of this affine space is defined by the expectation surface

$$\boldsymbol{\beta} \rightarrow X\boldsymbol{\beta} \subset \mathbf{R}^n.$$

This is a $(k+1)$-dimensional affine subspace. When σ is known, the geometry of the model is simply that of Euclidean geometry.

In this model the natural parameters are given by β and the expectation parameters by

$$\frac{\mathbf{X}'\mathbf{X}\beta}{\sigma^2}.$$

Thus there is a fixed linear relationship between the $+1$-affine and -1-affine parameters. Equation (16) implies that the Christoffel symbols for the ∇^{+1} and ∇^{-1} connections will be simultaneously zero in both the natural and expectation parameterisations. Equation (27) then implies that estimating β using maximum likelihood estimation will have zero bias in both those parameterisations. However, in any non-linear reparameterisation of the model the Christoffel symbols Γ^{-1} need not be zero. A simple example of this is given by a simultaneous equation model, when we parameterise by the parameters in the structural equations.

In general, choosing a parameterisation can improve statistical properties. This was recognised by Hougaard (1982), and similar results are found in Amari (1990). In section 6.1 we have seen that the Riemann curvature tensor can characterise the existence of a set of affine parameters. The following theorem formalises this idea.

Theorem *For a manifold M with metric g and connection ∇ we have the following:*
(a) Assume that the Riemann curvature tensor vanishes identically for all points in a sufficiently small open neighbourhood U. Then there exists an affine parameterisation θ covering U such that the Christoffel symbols for ∇ vanish identically. Further all ∇-geodesics in U are characterised by being affine functions of the θ-parameters.
(b) In the general case, the Riemann curvature tensor will be non-zero. For any point $p_0 \in M$ there will be a parameterisation θ around p_0 such that the Christoffel symbols for ∇ vanish at p. Further, the set of geodesics through p_0, in U, are all affine functions of the θ-parameters.

The parameterisation in case (b) is often called the *geodesic normal* parameterisation. For details of this and the related *exponential* map, see Dodson and Poston (1991). When a manifold has an affine parameterisation, the geometry becomes that of an affine space. All geodesics are the one-dimensional affine subspaces. This is the simplest possible geometry. When the Riemann curvature is non-zero, the fundamental geometry of the manifold creates an obstruction to the existence of such an affine parameterisation. In this case the geodesic normal parameterisation is, in a sense, closest to being truly affine.

In the case where the connections come from the expected geometric statistical manifold, then affine parameterisations, when they exist, and geodesic normal parameters, when they do not exist, have useful statistical properties. The following list summarises the properties of some of the more important of these. Each of these is global property if the parameterisation is affine, otherwise they hold locally in the neighbourhood of a fixed point.

- +1-connection: The affine parameters for these are the natural parameters for the full exponential family.
- 1/3-connection: This is the quadratic log-likelihood parameterisation. In this parameterisation, the expectation of the third derivative of the log-likelihood

$$E_{p(x \mid \theta)}(\partial_i \partial_j \partial_k \ell)$$

vanishes. Thus the likelihood closely approximates that from a normal family. This is the expected form of the *directed likelihood* parameterisation, which has been shown to be a very effective tool in classical and Bayesian analysis (see Sweeting (1996) and references therein).
- 0-connection: This is the covariance stabilising parameterisation in which the Fisher information will be (locally) constant.
- −1/3-connection: This is called the *zero asymptotic skewness* parameterisation, because any first-order efficient estimator will have zero asymptotic skewness in this parameterisation.
- −1-connection: We have already seen that in this parameterisation we have asymptotically minimum bias.

7.2   Intrinsic curvature

The distinction raised by Bates and Watts between parameter effects and intrinsic curvature is an important one in geometry. In this section we look at how intrinsic curvature is particularly important when undertaking inference on curved exponential families.

Suppose that N is the manifold representing the (r, t)-curved exponential family $p(x \mid \xi)$. N is embedded in the r-dimensional full exponential family, $p(x \mid \theta)$, which is denoted by M. In terms of manifolds, N is an embedded submanifold of M (see section 2.4.1). In the natural parameters, M has many of the properties of an affine space, and intuitively it is useful to think of N as a curved subspace of an affine space. It is this curvature that will define the intrinsic curvature of the model.

We first define a set of parameters that is suited to describe the embedding of N in M.

Theorem   *For each $\xi_0 \in N$ there exists an open neighbourhood U of M, such that $p(x \mid \xi_0) \in U$ and U can be parameterised by*

$$\Xi \times X (\subset \mathbf{R}^t \times \mathbf{R}^{r-t}) \to U \subset M$$

$$(\xi, \chi) \mapsto p(x \mid \theta(\xi, \chi))$$

where

$$U \cap N = \{ p(x \mid \theta(\xi, 0)) \mid \xi \in \Xi \}.$$

The parameters for the full family are split such that the first t components refer to the submanifold, while the remaining $(r - t)$ components fill out the rest of the space, in such a way that they are zero on the submanifold. For notational convenience we will denote the first t components of such a system by indices $i, j, k, \ldots$, while the remaining $(r - t)$ indices will be denoted by $a, b, c, \ldots$.

Hence, if we consider the tangent space to M at a point in N, denoted by p_0, in this space there will be directions that also lie in tangent space to N. In the above parameterisation these are spanned by the set $\{ \partial_i = \frac{\partial}{\partial \xi^i} \mid i = 1, \ldots, t \}$. There will remain those directions that are not tangent to N. The set of tangent vectors $\{ \partial_a = \frac{\partial}{\partial \chi^a} \mid a = 1, \ldots, (r - t) \}$ all have this property. We think of TN_{p_0} as being a subspace of TM_{p_0}.

In fact a parameterisation (ξ, χ) can be refined to have the property that

$$\langle \partial_i, \partial_a \rangle_M = \left\langle \frac{\partial}{\partial \xi^i}, \frac{\partial}{\partial \chi^a} \right\rangle_M = 0$$

for all $i = 1, \ldots, t$ and for all $a \in 1, \ldots, (r - t)$. Hence the splitting of the tangent space TM_{p_0} can be made into TN_{p_0} and its orthogonal component. It will be convenient to use such a parameterisation throughout this section.

Suppose now that there is a metric and a connection on M. These will induce a metric and a connection on the submanifold N in the following way. Let g_{ij} be the components of the metric on M relative to the (ξ, χ)-parameterisation. By definition, the parameterisation has the property that

$$g_{ia} = 0$$

for all $i = 1, \ldots, t$ and for all $a \in 1, \ldots, (r - t)$. Relative to the ξ-parameterisation, define the metric on N, $\tilde{g}$ to have components

$$\tilde{g}_{ij} = \langle \partial_i, \partial_j \rangle_M. \tag{28}$$

Let X, Y be tangent fields on N. They can then also be thought of, slightly loosely, as tangent fields on M. Hence we can define the rate of change of Y relative to X using the connection on M. This gives $\nabla_X Y$ a tangent field in M. However, a connection on N gives this rate of change as a tangent field on the submanifold. Hence we need to project $\nabla_X Y$ from TM to TN. We do this using the metric on M and an orthogonal projection. The connection $\tilde{\nabla}$ on N is defined by

$$\tilde{\nabla}_X Y = \Pi_N (\nabla_X Y) \tag{29}$$

where Π_N is the orthogonal projection of TM to TN.

The embedding curvature of N in M is defined as the difference between the result of using the connection relative to M and relative to N. Formally it is a 2-tensor H defined by

$$H(X, Y) = \nabla_X Y - \tilde{\nabla}_X Y. \tag{30}$$

$H(X, Y)$ will lie in the orthogonal complement to TN. It can be written with respect to the parameterisation defined above as

$$H(\partial_i, \partial_j) = \tilde{\Gamma}_{ij}^a \partial_a = H_{ij}^a \partial_a. \tag{31}$$

7.2.1   Auxiliary spaces

Suppose that we now wish to conduct inference in a curved exponential family N. An estimator is a function that maps the data x to a point in N. It is convenient to use the fact that in the full exponential family M, which embeds N, there is a bijection between x and $\hat{\theta}(x)$, the maximum likelihood estimate in M. We can therefore think of an estimator, geometrically, as a function

$$T : M \to N$$

$$\hat{\theta}(x) \mapsto T(\hat{\theta}(x)).$$

We then study the properties of the estimator in terms of the geometry of this function. T is said to be *regular* if it is a smooth map with derivative of full rank and the restriction of T to the subspace, $T|_N$, is the identity.

Define the *auxiliary space* of the estimator to be the points in M given by the set of parameters

$$A(\xi) = \{ \theta \mid T(\theta) = \xi \}. \tag{32}$$

We shall assume that for each point $\xi_0 \in N$ there exists an open subset U of M such that $A(\xi_0) \cap M$ is an $(r - t)$-dimensional submanifold of M. This assumption will be satisfied by all of the commonest estimators used in econometrics and in practice it will not be restrictive. We shall use the geometry of these submanifolds together with that of N to explore the behaviour of estimators.

A simple way of measuring the efficiency of an estimator is in terms of mean square error. We define an estimator to be k'th-order efficient if the asymptotic expansion of its mean square error is minimal among all $(k - 1)$'th efficient estimators. The following theorems, due to Amari, characterise this asymptotic efficiency.

Theorem *A consistent estimator is* first-order efficient *if the associated auxiliary space $A(\xi)$ cuts N orthogonally with respect to the expected Fisher information metric.*

Theorem *The first-order bias of a consistent estimator is defined* to be

$$b^a(\xi) = \frac{-1}{2n} g^{ij} \left\{ g^{kl} \Gamma_{ijk}^{-1} + g^{ab} h_{abj}^{-1} \right\}, \tag{33}$$

where h is the embedding curvature of the submanifold $A(\xi)$ with respect to the -1-connection and is defined as

$$h_{abj}^{-1} = \langle H^{-1}(\partial_a, \partial_b), \partial_j \rangle.$$

Thus for a curved exponential family the bias term comes in two parts. The first, as we have seen before, is parameterisation dependent; the second, however, depends only on the intrinsic geometry of the auxiliary space. This depends on the exact form of the estimator but *not* on the parameterisation use. Thus we have a decomposition into parameter effects and intrinsic curvature.

Using this geometric characterisation, the third-order most efficient estimator for a curved exponential family can be found.

Theorem *The biased correct maximum likelihood estimator is third-order efficient for a curved exponential family.*

All the results shown in this section are proved in Amari (1990); for a good treatment, see Kass and Vos (1997, p. 227).

8   Curvature and information loss

Once we move from the full exponential family case we lose the property that the maximum likelihood estimate (MLE) will be a sufficient statistic. Fisher (1925) was the first to suggest using the observed information as the best means of recovering information lost by reducing the data to just the maximum likelihood estimate. There is an elegant geometric extension to higher-order recovery which provides a complete decomposition of the information in a minimal sufficient statistic. The geometry provides a natural framework for expressing the higher-order calculations but also an explanation of why these terms successfully recover additional information. Having analysed the decomposition of the information in a statistic in geometric terms, there remains the question of how to use this information for inference.

8.1   Information loss

Since the MLE is a sufficient statistic for a full exponential family, standard inferential procedures will automatically make use of all available information in the data. We look at geometrical properties that make a family exponential, and hence ensure that the full information content in the data is exploited.

8.1.1   One-dimensional case

First consider a one-dimensional family as in Efron (1975). If we have an r-dimensional full exponential family defined by

$$p(x \mid \theta) = \exp\{\theta^i s_i(x) - \psi(\theta)\}m(x),$$

then any one-dimensional affine map

$$\xi \mapsto \theta^i(\xi) = \alpha^i \xi + \beta^i$$

will define a one-dimensional full exponential family. In general we have the following result.

Theorem   *A one-dimensional curved exponential family*

$$p(x \mid \xi) = \exp\{\theta(\xi)s_i(x) - \psi(\theta(\xi))\}m(x) \tag{34}$$

is a full exponential family if and only if there exist constants $(\alpha^1, \ldots, \alpha^r)$ *and* $(\beta^1, \ldots, \beta^r)$ *such that*

$$\theta(\xi) = \alpha^i f(\xi) + \beta^i$$

for some smooth monotone function f.

Hence we see that being a full exponential family depends on the family being defined as an affine subspace of the natural parameters of the embedding family. In section 5.2.1 we saw that the ∇^{+1} connection is the appropriate tool for measuring curvature relative to the natural parameters. Efron (1975) approached this question more directly. He defined the *statistical curvature* of equation (34) to be

$$\gamma = \gamma(\theta) = \frac{\langle \theta''(\xi)_N, \theta''(\xi)_N \rangle^{1/2}}{\langle \theta'(\xi), \theta'(\xi) \rangle} \tag{35}$$

where $\theta'(\xi) = d\theta/d\xi$ and $\theta''(\xi)_N$ denotes the component of the second derivative which is normal to the tangent direction $\theta'(\xi)$. The inner product is the expected Fisher information metric. The motivation for this comes directly from the definition of the curvature of a one-dimensional path in $\mathbf{R}^n$. The important result concerning statistical curvature is given by the following theorem.

Theorem *The curved exponential family given by equation (34) is a one-parameter full exponential family if and only if its statistical curvature is zero.*

One important property of the full exponential family is that the observed information equals the expected Fisher information. They both equal $[(\partial^2 \psi)/(\partial \theta^i \partial \theta^j)](\hat{\theta})$ in the natural parameterisation. The randomness of the observed information is purely a function of the MLE. In fact Murray and Rice (1993) characterise a full exponential family by the property that the second derivative of the log-likelihood lies in the span of the first derivatives. In a curved family, the expected and observed information matrices will differ. The statistical curvature, defined above, gives a useful measure of the amount of variability in the observed information, given the MLE. This comes from the following result (see Efron and Hinkley (1978)).

Theorem *In a regular curved exponential family, if $\mathcal{I}(\hat{\xi})$ is the observed Fisher information and $I(\hat{\xi})$ the expected information for one observation, then*

$$\frac{(\mathcal{I}(\hat{\xi}) - nI(\hat{\xi}))}{\sqrt{n}I(\hat{\xi})\gamma(\hat{\theta})} \rightarrow N(0, 1) \tag{36}$$

where the convergence is in law as $n \rightarrow \infty$.

8.1.2   The general case

Suppose now that we are working in an (r, t)-curved exponential family. Again we wish to understand the amount of information lost if we use only the statistic $\hat{\xi}$. To do this we need to define the information contained in a general statistic $T(x)$. Using an asymptotic measure of information, the information in a statistic T is defined as being the expected Fisher information for the likelihood for ξ based on the statistic $T(x)$. That is

$$I^T(\xi) = E_{p(t \mid \xi)}\left(-\frac{\partial^2 \ell}{\partial \xi^i \partial \xi^j}(t \; ; \; \xi)\right).\tag{37}$$

This measures, by the Cramer–Rao theorem, the variance of the best possible estimator based only on the statistic $T(x)$. Of course, with this notation we would have $I^X(\xi) = I(\xi)$, the standard Fisher information. We can generalise the previous results on information loss to multi-dimensional families.

Theorem   *In a curved exponential family $p(x \mid \xi)$ then*

$$nI_{ij} - I_{ij}^{\hat{\xi}} = g^{kl}\langle H^{+1}(\partial_i, \partial_k), H^{+1}(\partial_j, \partial_l)\rangle,\tag{38}$$

where H^{+1} is the embedding curvature of the family relative to the $+1$-connection, and the inner product is relative to the expected Fisher metric.

For a proof of this result, see Kass and Vos (1997, p. 222). Thus the $+1$-embedding curvature plays the role of Efron's statistical curvature in higher dimensions.

8.2   Information recovery

Having seen that the geometric structure of a family allows the measurement of loss in information, we now ask in what way this information can be recovered and used in inference. Since the MLE, $\hat{\xi}$, will not in general be sufficient, we need to add a further statistic that will recover (approximate) sufficiency. It is convenient to construct the *conditional resolution*. This is a decomposition of the sufficient statistic into $(\hat{\xi}, a)$, where a is (approximately) ancillary, combined with an (approximate) expression for $p(\hat{\xi} \mid \theta, a)$. For more details of this construction, see Barndorff-Nielsen and Cox (1994).

8.2.1 Choosing ancillaries

One difficulty with using a conditional resolution structure is the problem of the non-uniqueness of the ancillary statistic, raised by Basu (1964). Solutions to this problem were considered by Barnard and Sprott (1971) and Cox (1971). We look at a geometrical construction defined in Kass and Vos (1997, p. 222), which gives a way of ensuring that the ancillary constructed captures information to progressively higher asymptotic order.

First we use geometry to construct approximately sufficient statistics for a curved exponential family. These are then transformed into approximately ancillary statistics. Consider the (r, t)-curved exponential family N given by $\exp\{\theta^i(\xi)s_i(x) - \psi(\theta(\xi))\}m(x)$. Clearly the statistic $(s_1(x), \ldots, s_r(x))$ is sufficient, but this can be very high dimensional. In fact, as Examples 3, 4 and 5 show, in econometric examples this sufficient statistic can be of order n. It is therefore natural to see if we can reduce the dimension of the sufficient statistic. Using the definition of tangent vector and the affine embedding given in section 3.2.1, the best local affine approximation to N at ξ_0 will be given by the t-dimensional full exponential family, $M_{[1]}$,

$$p(x \mid (\alpha^1, \ldots, \alpha^t)) = \exp\{(\theta^i(\xi_0) + \alpha^j \partial_j \theta^i(\xi_0))s_i(x)$$

$$- \psi(\theta(\xi_0) + \alpha^j \partial_j \theta^i(\xi_0))\}m(x)$$

$$= \exp\{\alpha^j (\partial_j \theta^i(\xi_0)s_i(x)) - \psi(\alpha)\}m_1(x)$$

$$= \exp\{\alpha^j \tilde{s}_j - \psi(\alpha)\}m_1(x),$$

say, for a measure $m_1(x)$. The natural parameters are given by $(\alpha^1, \ldots, \alpha^t)'$. It follows from the theorems in section 8.1.1 that this will be a full exponential family. Its sufficient statistic will be equivalent to $\hat{\xi}$, the MLE for the curved family. This is defined by the equations

$$\frac{\partial \theta^i}{\partial \xi^j}(\hat{\xi})\left(s_i - \frac{\partial \psi}{\partial \theta^i}\right) = \tilde{s}_i - \frac{\partial \theta^i}{\partial \xi^j}(\hat{\xi})\frac{\partial \psi}{\partial \theta^i}(\hat{\xi})$$

$$= 0.$$

Owing to the regularity conditions of section 2.3, this equation will be invertible. Hence the information in $\hat{\xi}$ is precisely equivalent to $(\tilde{s}_1, \ldots, \tilde{s}_t)'$.

In general we can define a sequence of full exponential families $M_{[1]}, M_{[2]}, \ldots, M_{[k]}$ where $M_{[k]}$ is the family

$$p(x \mid \alpha_i, \alpha_{ij}, \ldots, \alpha_{i_1 \ldots i_k}) = \exp\{(\theta^i(\xi_0) + \alpha^j \partial_j \theta^i(\xi_0) + \alpha^{j_1 j_2} \partial^2_{j_1 j_2} \theta^i(\xi_0)$$

$$+ \cdots + \alpha^{j_1 \cdots j_k} \partial^k_{j_1 \cdots j_k} \theta^i(\xi_0))s_i(x)$$

$$- \psi(\theta(\alpha))\}m(x).$$

The sufficient statistic for this full exponential family is given by

$$(\hat{\xi}, \partial_{i_1 i_2} \ell(\hat{\xi}), \ldots, \partial^k_{i_1 \ldots i_k} \ell(\hat{\xi})).$$

We therefore have constructed a sequence of full exponential families, which give progressively better approximations to the curved family N. These in turn give a sequence of statistics, which become progressively better approximations to the sufficient statistic for N.

It is necessary to check that this construction is geometrically well defined, so that the sufficient statistics generated will be independent of any choice of parameterisation. This follows since the linear spaces given by

$$T_{[k]} = span\{\partial_i \theta, \partial^2_{i_1 i_2} \theta, \ldots, \partial^k_{i_1 \cdots i_k} \theta\}$$

will be parameterisation independent (see Murray and Rice (1993)).

The sequence of sufficient statistics $(\hat{\xi}, \partial_{i_1 i_2} \ell(\hat{\xi}), \ldots, \partial^k_{i_1 \ldots i_k} \ell(\hat{\xi}))$ can then be transformed to be approximately in the conditional resolution form $(\hat{\xi}, a)$. Define

$$h_{i_1 \cdots i_{k+1}} = P^{\perp}_{[k]} \partial^{k+1}_{i_1 \cdots i_{k+1}},$$

where $P^{\perp}_{[k]}$ is the orthogonal projection into $T_{[k]}$. This orthogonalisation ensures that the terms are uncorrelated and asymptotically independent; further, the expected Fisher information based on $h_{i_1 \cdots, i_{k+1}}$ will be of asymptotic order n^{-k+1}. To achieve approximate ancillarity these statistics are adjusted to give zero mean and unit variance to the correct asymptotic order. For further details, see Kass and Vos (1997). Note that the terms $h_{i_1 \cdots i_k}$ are simply generalisations of the embedding curvature in section 7.2.

8.2.2   *The p*-formula*

Having used geometry in the construction of an approximately sufficient statistic of the form $(\hat{\xi}, a)$, the second part of a conditional resolution is to approximate the distribution $p(\hat{\xi} \mid a)$. Barndorff-Nielsen, in a series of papers, proposes a very good higher-order approximation, based on the saddlepoint method given by the so-called p^*-formula. For a derivation of results in this section, see Barndorff-Nielsen and Cox (1994, p. 238). The p^*-approximation is given by

$$p^*(\hat{\xi} \mid \xi, a) = c|\hat{j}|^{1/2} e^{\bar{\ell}}, \tag{39}$$

where

$$\hat{j} = \frac{\partial^2 \ell}{\partial \xi^i \partial \xi^j}(\hat{\xi})$$

and

$$\bar{\ell}(\xi \mid \hat{\xi}, a) = \ell(\xi \mid \hat{\xi}, a) - \ell(\hat{\xi} \mid \hat{\xi}, a).$$

The constant c is defined to make the above density integrate to one. When this is not known, the approximation

$$p^\dagger(\hat{\xi} \mid \theta, a) = (2\pi)^{-t/2} |\hat{j}|^{1/2} e^{\bar{\ell}} \tag{40}$$

can be used. This version is accurate to order $O(n^{-1})$, whereas the p^*-formula is accurate to order $O(n^{-3/2})$. For a further discussion of this issue of the distribution of the maximum likelihood estimator, see chapter 3 by Grant Hillier and Ray O'Brien in this volume.

References

Amari, S.I. (1987), 'Differential Geometric Theory of Statistics', in S.I. Amari, O.E. Barndorff-Nielsen, R.E. Kass, S.L. Lauritzen and C.R. Rao (eds.), *Differential Geometry in Statistical Inference*, Hayward, Calif.: Institute of Mathematical Statistics.

(1990), *Differential-Geometrical Methods in Statistics*, 2nd edn, Lecture Notes in Statistics No. 28, Berlin: Springer.

Barnard, G.A. and D.A. Sprott (1971), 'A Note on Basu's Examples of Anomalous Ancillary Statistics (with Discussion)', in V.P. Godambe and D.A. Sprott (eds.), *Foundations of Statistical Inference*, Toronto: Holt, Rinehart & Winston, pp. 163–176.

Barndorff-Nielsen, O.E. (1978), *Information and Exponential Families in Statistical Theory*, London: Wiley.

(1987), 'Differential Geometry and Statistics: Some Mathematical Aspects', *Indian Journal of Mathematics*, 29, Ramanujan Centenary Volume.

(1988), *Parametric Statistical Families and Likelihood*, New York: Springer.

Barndorff-Nielsen O.E. and D.R. Cox (1994), *Inference and Asymptotics*, Monographs on Statistics and Applied Probability 52, London: Chapman & Hall.

Barndorff-Nielsen, O.E. and P. Jupp (1989), 'Approximating Exponential Models', *Annals of Statistical Mathematics*, 41: 247–267.

Basu, D. (1964), 'Recovery of Ancillary Information', *Sankya A*, 26: 3–16.

Bates, M. and D.G. Watts (1988), *Nonlinear Regression Analysis and Its Applications*, London: Wiley.

Blæsild, P. (1987), 'Yokes: Elemental Properties with Statistical Applications', in C.T.J. Dodson (ed.), *Geometrization of Statistical Theory, Proceedings for the GST Workshop, University of Lancaster*, ULDM Publications, University of Lancaster, pp. 193–198.

(1991), 'Yokes and Tensors Derived from Yokes', *Annals of the Institute of Statistical Mathematics*, 43: 95–113.

Bröcker, T.H. and Jänich, K. (1982), *Introduction to Differential Geometry*, Cambridge: Cambridge University Press.

Brown, L.D. (1986), *Fundamentals of Statistical Exponential Families with Applications in Statistical Decision Theory*, Haywood, Calif.: Institute of Mathematical Statistics.

Cox, D.R. (1971), 'The Choice between Alternative Ancillary Statistics', *Journal of the Royal Statistical Society C*, 33: 251–255.

Cox, D.R., and D.V. Hinkley (1974), *Theoretical Statistics*, London: Chapman & Hall.

Critchley, F., P.K. Marriott and M. Salmon (1993), 'Preferred Point Geometry and Statistical Manifolds', *Annals of Statistics*, 21: 1197–1224.

(1994), 'On the Local Differential Geometry of the Kullback–Leibler Divergence', *Annals of Statistics*, 22: 1587–1602.

(1996), 'On the Differential Geometry of the Wald Test with Nonlinear Restrictions', *Econometrica*, 64: 1213–1222.

Dodson, C.T. and T. Poston (1991), *Tensor Geometry: The Geometric Viewpoint and Its Uses*, 2nd edn, New York: Springer Verlag.

Efron, B. (1975), 'Defining the Curvature of a Statistical Problem (with Applications to Second Order Efficiency)', *Annals of Statistics*, 3: 1189–1217.

(1978), 'The Geometry of Exponential Familes', *Annals of Statistics*, 6: 362–376.

(1982), 'Maximum Likelihood and Decision Theory', *Annals of Statistics*, 10: 340–356.

Efron, B. and D.V. Hinkley (1978), 'Assessing the Accuracy of the Maximum Likelihood Estimator: Observed versus Expected Fisher Information', *Biometrika*, 65: 457–481.

Fisher, R.A. (1925), 'Theory of Statistical Estimation', *Proceedings of Cambridge Philosophical Society*, 22: 700–725.

Hougaard, P. (1982), 'Parametrisations of Nonlinear Models', *Journal of the Royal Statistical Society, Series B Methodological*, 44: 244–252.

Kass, R.E. and P.W. Vos (1997), *Geometrical Foundations of Asymptotic Inference*, Probability and Statistics series, New York: Wiley.

Lauritzen, S.L. (1987), 'Statistical Manifolds', in S.I. Amari, O.E. Barndorff-Nielsen, R.E. Kass, S.L. Lauritzen and C.R. Rao (eds.), *Differential Geometry in Statistical Inference*, Hayward, Calif.: Institute of Mathematical Statistics, pp. 163–216.

McCullagh, P. (1987), *Tensor Methods in Statistics*, Monographs on Statistics and Applied Probability No. 29, London: Chapman & Hall

Marriott, P.K. (1989), 'Applications of Differential Geometry to Statistics', Ph.D. dissertation, University of Warwick.

Murray, M.K. and J.W. Rice (1993), *Differential Geometry and Statistics*, Monographs on Statistics and Applied Probability No. 48, London: Chapman & Hall.

Rao, C.R. (1945), 'Asymptotic Efficiency and Limiting Information', *Proceedings of the Fourth Berkeley Symp. Math. Statist. Probab.*, 1: 531–545.

(1987), 'Differential Metrics in Probability Spaces', in S.I. Amari, O.E. Barndorff-Nielsen, R.E. Kass, S.L. Lauritzen and C.R. Rao (eds.), *Differential Geometry in Statistical Inference*, Hayward, Calif.: Institute of Mathematical Statistics, pp. 217–240.

Ravishanker, N. (1994), 'Relative Curvature Measure of Nonlinearity for Time-Series Models', *Communications in Statistics–Simulation and Computation*, 23(2): 415–430.

Rudin, W. (1976), *Principles of Mathematical Analysis*, 3rd edn, New York: McGraw-Hill.

Spivak, M. (1979), *A Comprehensive Introduction to Differential Geometry*, 2nd edn, Boston: Publish and Perish.

Sweeting, T. (1996), 'Approximate Bayesian Computation Based on Signed Roots of Log-density Ratios (with Discussion)', in *Bayesian Statistics 5* (ed. J.M. Bernardo, J.O. Berger, A.P. Dawid and A.F.M. Smith), Oxford: Oxford University Press, pp. 427–444.

Willmore, T.J. (1959), *An Introduction to Differential Geometry*, Oxford: Clarendon.

2 Nested models, orthogonal projection and encompassing

Maozu Lu and Grayham E. Mizon

1 Introduction

An important objective in econometric modelling is to obtain congruent and encompassing models, which are thus consistent with data evidence and economic theory, and are capable of explaining the behaviour of rival models for the same economic phenomena. Hendry (1995) and Mizon (1995b) *inter alia* present this view of modelling, as well as recording that a *general-to-simple* modelling strategy is an efficient way to isolate congruent models. Indeed such a modelling strategy requires the models under consideration to be thoroughly tested and progressively evaluated within a sequence of nested hypotheses, so that each model not rejected in the process is a valid simplification of (i.e. *parsimoniously encompasses*) all models more general than it in the sequence. Models arrived at as the limit of the reduction process therefore contain all relevant information available in the initial models, thus rendering the latter inferentially redundant. Testing the ability of models to parsimoniously encompass more general ones, thus ensuring that no information is lost in the reduction process, creates a partially ordered sequence of models. Further, Lu and Mizon (1997) point out that the intermediate models considered while testing the parsimonious encompassing ability of models in a nested sequence are mutually encompassing models and hence observationally equivalent to each other. Note, though, that there is an important distinction between observational equivalence in the population and in a sample, which may contain weak evidence.

In the theory of reduction, attention is focused on parsimonious encompassing, and not on the ability of nesting models to encompass

Financial support from the UK Economic and Social Research Council, under grant R000233447, and from the EUI Research Council grant *Econometric Modelling of Economic Time Series*, is gratefully acknowledged. We also thank Søren Johansen for helpful discussions on the topic.

simplifications of themselves. Though the latter might be thought to be automatic, Gouriéroux and Monfort (1995) give a counter-example, thus showing that it is not always the case that a general model encompasses models simpler than itself. Clearly, if this happens in a process of reduction, the sequence of parsimonious encompassing models will not form a partial order, and some vital information might be lost if the intermediate models were discarded. It is therefore important to investigate the conditions under which a general model encompasses simpler models independently of its relationship to the *data-generation process* (DGP). This is the topic of the present chapter. Bontemps and Mizon (1997), on the other hand, establish that congruence of a general model is a sufficient condition for it to encompass models that it nests.

The chapter is organised as follows. In section 2 nesting is defined, it being emphasised that nesting is more than one model being an algebraic simplification of another model. A distinction is drawn between exact and inequality constraints on parameters, the former being dimension reducing and the latter not. The importance of dimension-reducing nesting constraints is illustrated by showing that the nesting model in cases where there is an orthogonal parameterisation will encompass models nested within it independently of the nature of the process generating the data. This property is defined as automatic encompassing. Section 2.3 records that automatic encompassing is not possible amongst non-nested models. Section 3 indicates how the concept of parsimonious encompassing can be used to establish encompassing relationships between non-nested models within the framework of a completing model that nests each of the non-nested models. In section 4 encompassing hypotheses are considered as mappings in *Hilbert* space, and it is shown that a sufficient condition for a model to encompass models nested within it is that these mappings are orthogonal projections. Section 5 presents concluding remarks.

2   Nested and restricted models

A parametric probability model for the n random variables $(x_{1,t}, x_{2,t}, \ldots, x_{n,t}) = \mathbf{x}_t'$ defined on the probability space $(S, \Im, P(.))$ consists of a family of sequential densities indexed by a parameter vector $\boldsymbol{\theta}$:

$$M_1 = \{f(\mathbf{x}_t \mid \mathbf{X}_{t-1}, \boldsymbol{\theta}), \quad \boldsymbol{\theta} \in \boldsymbol{\Theta} \subseteq \mathbb{R}^p\} \tag{1}$$

when $\mathbf{X}_{t-1} = (\mathbf{X}_0, \mathbf{x}_1, \ldots, \mathbf{x}_{t-1}) = (\mathbf{X}_0, \mathbf{X}_{t-1}^1)$, with $\mathbf{X}_0$ being initial conditions. Denoting this probability model by M_1 and considering the alternative probability model M_2:

$$M_2 = \{g(\mathbf{x}_t \mid \mathbf{X}_{t-1}, \boldsymbol{\psi}), \quad \boldsymbol{\psi} \in \boldsymbol{\Psi} \subseteq \mathbb{R}^q\} \tag{2}$$

enables nesting to be defined.

Definition 1 M_2 *is nested within* M_1 *if and only if* $M_2 \subseteq M_1$.

Hence nesting is a property of the joint density of all the variables involved in M_1 and M_2, and heuristically requires M_2 to be a restricted version of M_1. However, there are important differences between nested and restricted models. In particular, note that if $\boldsymbol{\Theta}$ were restricted (e.g. the model was restricted to have only seasonal dynamics) but $\boldsymbol{\Psi}$ were not so restricted, then M_2 cannot be nested in M_1 since M_2 could not be a subset of M_1. Further, the nature of restrictions applied to models can affect the nesting and encompassing relationships between models. This is illustrated in section 2.1 for the important cases of equality and inequality restrictions.

There exist alternative definitions of nested models in the literature, one of which, based on an information criterion, was proposed by Pesaran (1987):

Definition 2   *For the models* M_1 *and* M_2 *defined in (1) and (2)* M_2 *is nested within* M_1 *if and only if for* $\forall \boldsymbol{\psi}^* \in \boldsymbol{\Psi}$, $\exists \boldsymbol{\theta}^* \in \boldsymbol{\Theta}$, *such that*

$$\int \log\left(\frac{g(\boldsymbol{\psi}^*)}{f(\boldsymbol{\theta}^*)}\right) g(\boldsymbol{\psi}^*) \, dy = 0 \tag{3}$$

where $f(\boldsymbol{\theta}^*) = f(\mathbf{x}_t \mid \mathbf{X}_{t-1}; \boldsymbol{\theta}^*)$ *and* $g(\boldsymbol{\psi}^*) = g(\mathbf{x}_t \mid \mathbf{X}_{t-1}; \boldsymbol{\psi}^*)$.

Despite their apparent differences, these definitions are essentially the same. In particular, it is shown in A.1 of the Appendix that, for any given $\boldsymbol{\psi}^* \in \boldsymbol{\Psi}$, $\boldsymbol{\theta}^*$ is the pseudo true value $\theta(\boldsymbol{\psi}^*)$ that solves the minimisation problem:

$$\min_{\theta \in \boldsymbol{\Theta}} \int \log\left(\frac{g(\boldsymbol{\psi}^*)}{f(\theta)}\right) g(\boldsymbol{\psi}^*) \, dy = \int \log\left(\frac{g(\boldsymbol{\psi}^*)}{f(\theta(\boldsymbol{\psi}^*))}\right) g(\boldsymbol{\psi}^*) \, dy.$$

It is further shown in A.2 that, if M_2 is nested in M_1 in the sense of (3), the parameter space $\boldsymbol{\Psi}$ is a subset of $\boldsymbol{\Theta}$ with probability one. It then follows that, although the concept of nesting defined by (3) employs a measure of distance between densities, it is closely concerned with parameter restrictions leading to $\boldsymbol{\Psi} \subseteq \boldsymbol{\Theta}$.

2.1   Nested models with exact restrictions

A special case of Definition 1, which is commonly used in the discussion of nesting, arises when $f(\mathbf{x}_t | \mathbf{X}_{t-1}, \theta)$ and $g(\mathbf{x}_t | \mathbf{X}_{t-1}, \psi)$ belong to the same family of densities but $\Psi \subseteq \Theta$ with $q < p$, so that $M_2 \subseteq M_1$ solely as a result of restrictions on Θ defining the restricted parameter space Ψ. In this latter case, when Θ is an unrestricted parameter space and the constraints on Θ that lead to Ψ are exact or equalities, a reparameterisation of M_1 is possible that makes explicit the relationship between M_1 and M_2.

Proposition 1   *In the context of (1) and (2) let $\phi(\theta) = 0$ be the $r = p - q > 0$ exact, continuous, and differentiable constraint equations on θ which define ψ, with rank $\left(\partial\phi/\partial\theta'\right)_{N_{\theta_0}} = r$ when N_{θ_0} is a neighbourhood of the pseudo-true value θ_0 of the maximum likelihood (ML) estimator $\hat{\theta}_T$ of θ. Then there exists an isomorphic reparameterisation λ of $\theta : \lambda = \lambda(\theta) = \left(\lambda_1(\theta)', \lambda_2(\theta)'\right)' = \left(\lambda_1(\theta)', \phi(\theta)'\right)' \forall \theta \in N_{\theta_0}$ such that rank $\left(\partial\lambda/\partial\theta'\right)_{N_{\theta_0}} = p$ and $(\lambda_1, \lambda_2) \in \Lambda_1 \times \Lambda_2$.*
(See Sargan (1988, p. 143) for discussion of such a reparameterisation.)

Note that the r constraint equations $\phi(\theta) = 0$ are dimension reducing, in that when applied they reduce the dimension of parameter space from dim $\Theta = p$ to dim $\Psi = q = p - r$. Further note that $\lambda_2(\theta)$ is equal to the parameters of the constraint equations, and although $\lambda_1(\theta) \neq \psi$ in general, when the constraints are satisfied $\lambda_1(\theta) = \psi \quad \forall \theta \in \Theta_0 = \{\theta \mid \theta \in \Theta$ such that $\phi(\theta) = 0\}$. Hence $\Psi = \{\psi \mid \psi = \lambda_1(\theta)$ such that $\phi(\theta) = 0 \quad \forall \theta \in \Theta_0\}$. Another important property of the reparameterisation is the fact that $\lambda_1(\theta)$ and $\lambda_2(\theta)$ are variation free. These properties of the reparameterisation do not ensure that $M_1 \mathcal{E} M_2$. A special class of model that does ensure that $M_1 \mathcal{E} M_2$ is that in which the parameters λ_1 and λ_2 are orthogonal. An important feature of this special case is that the expected information matrix for the parameters $\lambda_1(\theta)$ and $\lambda_2(\theta)$ (and hence $\phi(\theta)$) is block diagonal, so that the score vectors with respect to λ_1 and λ_2 are asymptotically uncorrelated. Thus, if $\phi(\theta)$ were set to zero, the ML estimator of λ_1 will be unaffected asymptotically. In particular, when there are T observations on $\mathbf{x}_t$ available, the log-likelihood function for M_1 is:

$$L_1(\theta) = \sum_{t=1}^{T} \log f(\mathbf{x}_t \mid \mathbf{X}_{t-1}; \theta)$$

$$= \sum_{t=1}^{T} \log f(\mathbf{x}_t \mid \mathbf{X}_{t-1}; \lambda_1, \phi) = L_1(\lambda_1, \phi), \tag{4}$$

and when $M_2 \subseteq M_1$ as a result of the exact restrictions $\phi(\theta) = \mathbf{0}$ the log-likelihood function for M_2 is:

$$L_2(\psi) = \sum_{t=1}^{T} \log f(\mathbf{x}_t \mid \mathbf{X}_{t-1}; \psi, \mathbf{0}).$$ (5)

The parameters $\lambda_1(\theta)$ and $\phi(\theta)$ are globally orthogonal when:

$$\mathrm{E}_{\mathrm{DGP}}\left[\frac{\partial^2 L_1(\lambda_1, \phi)}{\partial \lambda_1 \partial \phi'}\right] = \mathbf{0} \quad \forall \, \theta \in \Theta$$ (6)

and locally orthogonal at θ_0 when (6) holds for $\theta = \theta_0$ – see *inter alia* Cox and Reid (1987) and Barndorff-Nielsen and Cox (1994), who also point out that parameter orthogonality is achievable in the regular exponential family of densities.

In this special case Proposition 1 has the following corollary.

Corollary 2   *Under the conditions of Proposition 1 the condition that $\lambda_1(\theta)$ and $\lambda_2(\theta)$ are locally orthogonal at θ_0 is sufficient for $M_1 \, \mathcal{E} \, M_2(\psi)$ independently of the data-generation process (DGP), i.e. $\psi_0 = \lambda_1(\theta_0) = \psi(\theta_0)$ $\forall$ DGPs when ψ_0 is the pseudo-true value of the maximum likelihood (ML) estimator $\hat{\psi}_T$ of ψ.*

As an example, consider the following two nested regression models $(M_2 \subseteq M_1)$ when $\mathbf{x}_t' = (y_t, \mathbf{z}_t')$ with $n = 3$, and the validity of conditioning on $\mathbf{z}_t$ is assumed:

$$
\begin{aligned}
M_1: \quad & y_t = z_{1,t}\beta_1 + z_{2,t}\beta_2 + \epsilon_t & \epsilon_t \mid \mathbf{z}_t \sim N(0, \sigma^2) \\
M_2: \quad & y_t = z_{1,t}\delta + v_t & v_t \mid \mathbf{z}_t \sim N(0, \tau^2).
\end{aligned}
$$ (7)

Note that model M_2 may be obtained by setting $\beta_2 = 0$ in model M_1, so that $\delta = \beta_1$ and $\sigma^2 = \tau^2$ *when the restriction $\beta_2 = 0$ is valid.* However, it is also possible to reparameterise M_1 as:

$$M_1: \quad y_t = z_{1,t}\delta + z_{2,t}^*\beta_2 + \epsilon_t \qquad \epsilon_t \mid \mathbf{z}_t \sim N(0, \sigma^2)$$ (8)

when $z_{2,t}^* = (z_{2,t} - z_{1,t}\sum_{s=1}^{T} z_{1,s}z_{2,s} / \sum_{s=1}^{T} z_{1,s}^2)$ is the projection of $z_{2,t}$ onto the space orthogonal to $z_{1,t}$ so that the relationship between M_1 and M_2 is explicit, in that they both involve δ, independently of the restriction $\beta_2 = 0$. This reparameterisation leaves δ and β_2 variation free, and it is valid independently of the DGP. Hence M_1 encompasses M_2 with respect to δ $(M_1 \, \mathcal{E} \, M_2(\delta))$ independently of the DGP (see Mizon and Richard (1986)). Heuristically this means that anything that can be learned about δ from M_2, can be obtained equally from M_1. In particular, note that the ML estimator of δ in M_2 is $\hat{\delta}_T = \sum_{t=1}^{T} z_{1,t} y_t / \sum_{t=1}^{T} z_{1,t}^2$, which has a pseudo-true value of δ_0 under the DGP. Further, using (8) yields:

$$\hat{\delta}_T = \left[\sum_{t=1}^{T} z_{1,t}(z_{1,t}\delta + z_{2,t}^* \beta_2 + \epsilon_t) \right] \Bigg/ \left[\sum_{t=1}^{T} z_{1,t}^2 \right]$$

$$= \delta + \left[\sum_{t=1}^{T} z_{1,t} z_{2,t}^* \beta_2 + \sum_{t=1}^{T} z_{1,t} \epsilon_t \right] \Bigg/ \left[\sum_{t=1}^{T} z_{1,t}^2 \right]$$

$$= \delta + \sum_{t=1}^{T} z_{1,t} \epsilon_t \Bigg/ \sum_{t=1}^{T} z_{1,t}^2$$

so that $\hat{\delta}_T$ has a probability limit under M_1 given by:

$$\plim_{T \to \infty} \hat{\delta}_T M_1 = \delta = \delta_0.$$

The latter equality holds since the ML estimator of δ in M_1 is identical to that for δ in M_2 as a result of $z_{1,t}$ and $z_{2,t}^*$ being orthogonal. This example and Corollary 2 serve to indicate the value in econometric and statistical modelling of adopting orthogonal parameterisations, a point made by Barndorff-Nielsen and Cox (1994, section 3.6) and Hendry (1995, p. 552). Section 4 further illustrates the importance of orthogonality by interpreting encompassing as involving mappings in *Hilbert* space and proving that a sufficient condition for automatic encompassing ($M_1 \mathcal{E} M_2(\psi)$) is that the mappings be orthogonal projections.

Although the nesting of M_2 in M_1 in the above example (7) was determined by parameter restrictions, the form of the densities $f(\mathbf{x}_t \mid \mathbf{X}_{t-1}, \boldsymbol{\theta})$ and $g(\mathbf{x}_t \mid \mathbf{X}_{t-1}, \boldsymbol{\psi})$ can also affect the nestedness of models. For example, the models in (7) are still nested when the normality of ϵ_t and v_t is replaced by the assumption that they are i.i.d. with zero means and finite variances. However, they are non-nested when $\epsilon_t \mid \mathbf{z}_t \sim N(0, \sigma^2)$ and $v_t \mid \mathbf{z}_t \sim U(-\boldsymbol{\theta}, +\boldsymbol{\theta})$ since then $\boldsymbol{\Phi}_2$ is no longer a subset of $\boldsymbol{\Phi}_1$. On the other hand, the following conditional models:

$$M_3: \quad y_t = \beta z_t + \eta_t \qquad \eta_t \mid \mathbf{z}_t, \mathbf{X}_{t-1} \sim \text{i.i.d.}(0, \sigma^2)$$

$$M_4: \quad y_t = \gamma y_{t-1} + \xi_t \qquad \xi_t \mid \mathbf{z}_t, \mathbf{X}_{t-1} \sim \text{i.i.d.}(0, \tau^2)$$

are non-nested when η_t and ξ_t are i.i.d., but if η_t is serially dependent the models might be nested. For example, if η_t were specified as being generated by the stationary $AR(1)$ process $\eta_t = \rho \eta_{t-1} + \zeta_t$ ($|\rho| < 1$), then M_3 can be rearranged as:

$$M_3^*: \quad y_t = \beta z_t + \rho y_{t-1} - \beta \rho z_{t-1} + \zeta_t,$$

so that the restriction $\beta = 0$ applied to M_3^* yields M_4 with $\rho = \gamma$ and $\sigma^2 = \tau^2$ *when the common factor restriction involved in the $AR(1)$ error process is valid*, in which case these models are nested (see Hendry and Mizon (1978), Mizon (1995a) and Sargan (1980)). However, M_3^* has a restricted parameter space in that though it has 3 regression coefficients they involve only 2 parameters β and ρ, and as a result M_3^* does not nest M_4 in general. Indeed, only if the DGP belonged to M_3^* would the latter nest M_4. Note that in this example, and that developed in Mizon (1995a), a model that appears to be an algebraic simplification of another (e.g., the restriction $\beta = 0$ renders M_3^* algebraically the same as M_4) is neither nested nor encompassed by the more general model as a result of an auxiliary restriction on the parameter space of the general model (the common factor restriction) not being a feature of the parameter space of the simple model. Thus the requirement that Θ be unrestricted, or if restricted the same restrictions apply to Ψ, is critical for M_1 to nest M_2, and hence for an apparently more general model to encompass its algebraic simplification.

2.2   Nested models with inequality restrictions

In addition to the requirement that Θ be unrestricted in order for the reparameterisation presented in Proposition 1 to hold, it is also necessary that the constraint equations be exact (and hence dimension reducing), and not inequality restrictions as the following example illustrates. Let M_1^* be an inequality restricted version of M_1 from (7):

$$M_1^* : y_t = z_{1,t}\beta_1 + z_{2,t}\beta_2 + u_t \tag{9}$$

$$s.t. \quad 0 \le \beta_2 \le \beta_1, \qquad if \ \beta_1 \ge 0$$

$$0 \le \beta_2 \le |\beta_1| \qquad if \ \beta_1 \le 0$$

then $M_1^* \subseteq M_1$, but since the constraints are inequalities they are not dimension reducing and Proposition 1 does not apply. Indeed, for the generic nested models M_1 and M_2, whenever $M_2 \subseteq M_1$ as a result of restrictions on the parameter space, but the constraints defining the nested model are inequalities (e.g. $\phi(\theta) > 0 \ \forall \ \theta \in \Theta$), neither Proposition 1 nor its Corollary 2 apply. As a result, the nesting model M_1 will not in general encompass the nested model M_2, though if the DGP lies in M_1 it will. Hence the nature of the restrictions relating the nested model M_2 to the nesting model M_1 can determine whether $M_1 \ \mathcal{E} \ M_2$ independently of the DGP.

2.3   Non-nested models

Now consider the relationship of M_1^* in (9) to M_2 in (7). Even though M_2 appears as an algebraic simplification of M_1^* it is not nested in M_1^* since it is not subject to the inequality restrictions in (9). Further, although M_1^* and M_2 are each nested in M_1 of (7), and model M_1 in (7) encompasses M_2 independently of the DGP, M_1^* does not encompass M_2 unless the DGP lies in M_1^* of (9) or the inequality restrictions are not binding. Indeed, if y_t were generated by a process not contained in M_1^*, it can be shown that, as long as the projection of y_t on the space spanned by z_{1t} and z_{2t} is in the *interior* of the area of $0 \le \beta_2 \le |\beta_1|$, M_1^* will encompass M_2 irrespective of the actual form of the DGP.

A more revealing case arises when the minimum distance from y_t to M_1, generated by a DGP $h(\mathbf{x}_t \mid \mathbf{X}_{t-1}, \alpha_0)$ other than M_1^* or M_2, lies in the parameter subspace in which $\beta_1 = \beta_2$. Given this relationship between M_1 and the unknown data-generation process, the apparently more general model M_1^* may not encompass the simple model M_2. Within the parameter subspace the restriction $\beta_1 = \beta_2$ holds, so model M_1 in (7) becomes:

$$M_1^\dagger : y_t = \beta_1(z_{1t} + z_{2t}) + w_t \tag{10}$$

$$= \beta_1 z_t^\dagger + w_t$$

where $z_t^\dagger = z_{1t} + z_{2t}$. Model $M_1^\dagger$ encompasses M_2 in (7) if and only if:

$$\delta(\alpha_0) - \delta(\boldsymbol{\beta}(\alpha_0)) = 0,$$

that is:

$$\operatorname*{plim}_{T\to\infty}\left(\sum_{t=1}^{T} z_{1t}^2\right)^{-1} \operatorname*{plim}_{T\to\infty} \sum_{t=1}^{T} z_{1t}\left\{ y_t - z_t^\dagger \frac{\displaystyle\sum_{t=1}^{T} z_t^\dagger y_t}{\displaystyle\sum_{t=1}^{T} z_t^{\dagger 2}} \right\} = 0 \tag{11}$$

(see Mizon and Richard (1986)). The condition in (11) requires that the residuals

$$y_t - z_t^\dagger \frac{\displaystyle\sum_{s=1}^{T} z_s^\dagger y_s}{\displaystyle\sum_{s=1}^{T} z_s^{\dagger 2}}, \qquad t = 1, 2, \ldots, T \tag{12}$$

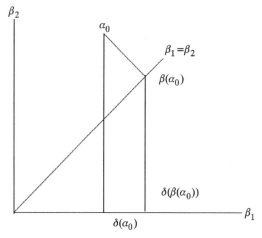

Figure 2.1 $\delta(\alpha_0) \neq \delta(\beta(\alpha_0))$

be orthogonal to z_{1t}, and it is shown in A.3 of the Appendix that this is equivalent to:

$$\text{plim}_{T \to \infty} \sum_{t=1}^{T} z_{2t} \left\{ y_t - z_t^\dagger \sum_{s=1}^{T} z_s^\dagger y_s \sum_{s=1}^{T} z_s^{\dagger 2} \right\} = 0. \tag{13}$$

Hence, the condition (11) requires that the residuals (12) be orthogonal to the space $\mathcal{S}(\beta)$ spanned by z_{1t} and z_{2t}. However, M_1^* will encompass only M_2 when the orthogonal projection of y_t onto $\mathcal{S}(\beta)$ lies in the subspace satisfying the triangular restriction in (9). This is illustrated by the graph in figure 2.1 (see also figure 1 in Gouriéroux and Monfort (1995)).

The analysis of section 2 can be summarised in the following proposition.

Proposition 3   *In the context of the generic models M_1 and M_2 of (1) and (2) respectively and Definition 2:*
(i)   if $M_2 \subseteq M_1$ with $\phi(\theta) = 0$ being the constraints on θ defining the lower dimensional parameters ψ then $M_1 \, \mathcal{E} \, M_2(\psi)$ for all DGPs whenever ψ and ϕ are orthogonal;
(ii) if $M_2 \subseteq M_1$ with $\phi(\theta) < 0$ being the constraints on θ defining the nested model M_2 then $M_1 \, \mathcal{E} \, M_2(\psi)$ if the DGP belongs to M_1;
(iii) if M_1 and M_2 are non-nested then $M_1 \, \mathcal{E} \, M_2(\psi)$ if the DGP belongs to M_1 and conversely $M_2 \, \mathcal{E} \, M_1(\psi)$ if the DGP belongs to M_2.

Hence nesting and the nature of the restrictions defining the nested relationship, as well as the class of density used, are critical in determining whether a general model will automatically encompass a simple model. An implication of this proposition is that it is important to establish carefully that models thought to be nested are indeed nested. The fact that a restriction placed on the parameters of an apparently more general model yields a simple model does not imply that the general model nests the simple model. Further, since the presence of auxiliary restrictions on the parameter space of a general model will generally result in that model not nesting an algebraic simplification of it, it is important to test the validity of such auxiliary restrictions, and to proceed to a comparison of the general and simple models only if they are not rejected. Thus the congruence of general models is important whenever a *general-to-simple* modelling strategy is adopted.

3   Encompassing and parsimonious encompassing

In this section the role of nested models in encompassing is discussed further, and it is shown that when a completing model exists for non-nested models it is possible to use the concept of parsimonious encompassing to establish encompassing relationships amongst the non-nested models.

Although general conditions for encompassing amongst non-nested models are difficult to establish, and will usually involve the unknown DGP, the concept of parsimonious encompassing can be used to yield encompassing relationships amongst non-nested models that are nested within the completing model. For example, M_1^* in (9), $M_1^\dagger$ in (10) and M_2 in (7) are all non-nested, but they are each nested within M_1 in (7). Hence if any of the three non-nested models is a valid reduction of M_1 (i.e. parsimoniously encompasses M_1) it contains as much relevant information as M_1, and hence at least as much as each of the other non-nested models. In other words, when any of M_1^*, $M_1^\dagger$ and M_2 parsimoniously encompasses M_1 it will also encompass the other two non-nested models. This result can now be stated more generally for generic non-nested models M_1 and M_2 as follows.

Definition 3 *M_2 parsimoniously encompasses M_c (denoted $M_2 \mathcal{E}_p M_c$) when $M_2 \mathcal{E} M_c$ and $M_2 \subseteq M_c$ with $M_c = M_2 \cup M_1^\perp$ being the completing model which contains M_2 and all aspects of M_1 that are not already in M_2.*
(See Hendry and Richard (1989) and Hendry (1995).)

This definition and the following theorem provide a framework for establishing encompassing relationships between non-nested models.

Theorem 4 *If $M_1 \subseteq M_c$ and $M_2 \subseteq M_c$ then $M_2 \, \mathcal{E} \, M_1$ if and only if $M_2 \, \mathcal{E}_p M_c$.*
(See Hendry and Richard (1989) and Hendry (1995, pp. 511–512).)

Hence it is possible to compare alternative non-nested models via their encompassing properties within the framework of an appropriate choice of completing model. For example, since each of M_1^* in (9), $M_1^\dagger$ in (10) and M_2 in (7) is nested within M_1, if any of them parsimoniously encompasses M_1 in the population, that model will encompass the other two models. If more than one of these models parsimoniously encompasses M_1 then they are mutually encompassing and hence observationally equivalent – see Lu and Mizon (1997) for more details.

4   Encompassing and orthogonal projection

In this section a generalisation of the results in section 2 is presented which interprets encompassing as orthogonal projections in *Hilbert* space. In particular, a more general sufficient condition for a model to encompass models nested within it, when the DGP need not be parametric, is given.

4.1   Mapping and orthogonal projection

Let a *Hilbert* space $\mathcal{R}^T$, of which the random vectors $\mathbf{y}_1$ and $\mathbf{y}_2$ are elements, be defined as a T-dimensional complete linear space equipped with the scalar product:

$$\langle \mathbf{y}_1, \mathbf{y}_2 \rangle = E\left(\sum_{j=1}^{T} y_{1,j} \, y_{2,j} \right) \qquad \forall \, \mathbf{y}_1, \mathbf{y}_2 \in \mathcal{R}^T$$

and the norm of any element $\mathbf{y} \in \mathcal{R}^T$ is given by:

$$\| \mathbf{y} \| = (\langle \mathbf{y}, \mathbf{y} \rangle)^{1/2} = \left(E \sum_{j=1}^{T} y_j^2 \right)^{1/2},$$

where 'E' is expectation taken under the specification of $\mathbf{y}$. Two $T \times 1$ random vectors $\mathbf{y}_1$ and $\mathbf{y}_2 \in \mathcal{R}^T$ are equal if and only if:

$$\| \mathbf{y}_1 - \mathbf{y}_2 \| = 0,$$

which requires $\mathbf{y}_1$ and $\mathbf{y}_2$ be equivalent with probability one.
With these definitions and notation it is possible to discuss encompassing in a *Hilbert* space generated by $T \times 1$ random vectors $\mathbf{y} =$

$(y_1, \ldots, y_T)$. In order to do so, it is convenient to translate the encompassing relationship, which is often defined in parameter space, to the mapping relationship between the elements $\mathbf{y}$ in $\mathcal{R}^T$. This not only facilitates the discussion in $\mathcal{R}^T$, but also has the advantage of accommodating those random vectors $\mathbf{y}$ that are generated by a non-parametric DGP (cf. Gouriéroux and Monfort (1995)).

Let $\mathbf{x}_t$ be partitioned as $\mathbf{x}'_t = (y_t, \mathbf{z}'_t)$ and consider the conditional models M_1 and M_2:

$$M_1 : \quad \{f(y_t | \mathbf{z}_t, \mathbf{X}_{t-1}, \theta), \quad \theta \in \Theta \subseteq \mathbb{R}^p\}$$
$$M_2 : \quad \{g(y_t | \mathbf{z}_t, \mathbf{X}_{t-1}, \psi), \quad \psi \in \Psi \subseteq \mathbb{R}^q\}$$
(14)

which are such that the conditional densities $f(y_t | \mathbf{z}_t, \mathbf{X}_{t-1}, \theta)$ and $g(y_t | \mathbf{z}_t, \mathbf{X}_{t-1}, \psi)$ are sufficiently well-behaved functions to ensure the global uniqueness of the pseudo-true values θ_0 and ψ_0. It is assumed that conditioning on $\mathbf{z}_t$ is valid (see Engle, Hendry and Richard (1983)), and that y_t does not Granger cause $\mathbf{z}_t$ (see Granger (1969)). It is also assumed that the random variable of interest, y_t, can be uniquely expressed as:

$$y_t = y_t(\theta) = \mathrm{r}_t(\mathbf{z}_t, \mathbf{X}_{t-1}, \epsilon_{1,t}; \theta)$$

and

$$y_t = y_t(\psi) = \mathrm{k}_t(\mathbf{z}_t, \mathbf{X}_{t-1}, \epsilon_{2,t}; \psi)$$

from models M_1 and M_2, respectively. Further, the functions

$$\mathrm{r}_t(\mathbf{z}_t, \mathbf{X}_{t-1}, \epsilon_{1,t}; \theta) \qquad \text{and} \qquad \mathrm{k}_t(\mathbf{z}_t, \mathbf{X}_{t-1}, \epsilon_{2,t}; \psi)$$

are assumed to have derivatives for all arguments, and to be contraction mappings (with probability one) with respect to $\mathbf{X}_{t-1}$ when it includes lagged values of y_t. Let

$$y_t(\hat{\psi}_T) = \mathrm{k}_t(\mathbf{z}_t, \mathbf{X}_{t-1}, \mathbf{0}; \hat{\psi}_T)$$

and

$$y_t(\psi_1(\hat{\theta}_T)) = \mathrm{k}_t(\mathbf{z}_t, \mathbf{X}_{t-1}, \mathbf{0}; \psi_1(\hat{\theta}_T))$$

when $\psi_1(\theta)$ is the M_1 pseudo-true value of $\hat{\psi}_T$, or binding function from Θ to Ψ (see Gouriéroux and Monfort (1995)). Under these conditions, the encompassing contrast $\psi_0 - \psi_1(\theta_0)$ for the hypothesis $M_1 \mathcal{E} M_2(\psi)$ takes the form:

$$\psi_0 - \psi_1(\theta_0) = \plim_{T \to \infty}\{\hat{\psi}_T - \psi_1(\hat{\theta}_T)\} = 0.$$
(15)

The contrast in (15) can be translated to the following relationship in $\mathcal{R}^T$:

$$\{\mathbf{y}(\hat{\boldsymbol{\psi}}_T) - \mathbf{y}(\boldsymbol{\psi}_1(\hat{\boldsymbol{\theta}}_T))\} = \mathbf{0}$$

where $\mathbf{y}' = (y_1, \ldots, y_T)$. $\mathbf{y}(\hat{\boldsymbol{\psi}}_T)$ and $\mathbf{y}(\boldsymbol{\psi}_1(\hat{\boldsymbol{\theta}}_T)) \in \mathcal{R}^T$ are two $T \times 1$ random vectors constrained by parameter sets $\boldsymbol{\Theta}$ and $\boldsymbol{\Psi}$. Therefore, since $\hat{\boldsymbol{\psi}}_T$ and $\hat{\boldsymbol{\theta}}_T$ are functions of $\mathbf{y}' = (y_1, y_2, \ldots, y_T)$, $\mathbf{y} \to \mathbf{y}(\hat{\boldsymbol{\psi}}_T)$ and $y \to y(\boldsymbol{\psi}_1(\hat{\boldsymbol{\theta}}_T))$ define two mappings on $\mathcal{R}^T \to \mathcal{R}^T$. These mappings will form the basis of the following discussion of encompassing.

In addition, define the following mapping for $\hat{\boldsymbol{\psi}}_T \in \boldsymbol{\Psi}$:

$$\mathcal{M}_\psi^T : \mathcal{R}^T \mapsto \mathcal{S}^T(\boldsymbol{\Psi}) \subset \mathcal{R}^T$$

such that for $\forall \mathbf{y} \in \mathcal{R}^T$,

$$\mathcal{M}_\psi^T(\mathbf{y}) = \mathbf{y}(\hat{\boldsymbol{\psi}}_T) \in \mathcal{S}^T(\boldsymbol{\Psi}) \subset \mathcal{R}^T, \quad \hat{\boldsymbol{\psi}}_T \in \boldsymbol{\Psi}; \tag{16}$$

and the corresponding mapping for $\hat{\boldsymbol{\theta}}_T \in \boldsymbol{\Theta}$:

$$\mathcal{M}_\theta^T : \mathcal{R}^T \mapsto \mathcal{S}^T(\boldsymbol{\Theta}) \subset \mathcal{R}^T$$

such that for $\forall \mathbf{y} \in \mathcal{R}^T$,

$$\mathcal{M}_\theta^T(\mathbf{y}) = \mathbf{y}(\hat{\boldsymbol{\theta}}_T) \in \mathcal{S}^T(\boldsymbol{\Theta}) \subset \mathcal{R}^T, \quad \hat{\boldsymbol{\theta}}_T \in \boldsymbol{\Theta}. \tag{17}$$

When the only restrictions on the parameter spaces $\boldsymbol{\Psi}$ and $\boldsymbol{\Theta}$ are of the form $\varphi(\psi) = \mathbf{0}$ and $\phi(\theta) = \mathbf{0}$ so that they are dimension reducing, $\mathcal{S}^T(\boldsymbol{\Psi})$ and $\mathcal{S}^T(\boldsymbol{\Theta})$ are subspaces of $\mathcal{R}^T$. By the construction of $\mathcal{M}_\psi^T$ and $\mathcal{M}_\theta^T$, $\mathbf{y}(\boldsymbol{\psi}_1(\hat{\boldsymbol{\theta}}_T))$ can be expressed as:

$$\mathbf{y}(\boldsymbol{\psi}_1(\hat{\boldsymbol{\theta}}_T)) = \mathcal{M}_\psi^T \cdot \mathcal{M}_\theta^T(\mathbf{y}),$$

where $(\mathcal{M}_\psi^T \cdot \mathcal{M}_\theta^T)$ denotes the product mapping. Hence the condition for $M_1 \,\mathcal{E}\, M_2$ at $\mathbf{y} \in \mathcal{R}^T$ is equivalent to:

$$\| \mathcal{M}_\psi^T(\mathbf{y}) - \mathcal{M}_\psi^T \cdot \mathcal{M}_\theta^T(\mathbf{y}) \| = 0. \tag{18}$$

The nature of the mappings $\mathcal{M}_\psi^T$, $\mathcal{M}_\theta^T$ and $\mathcal{M}_\psi^T \cdot \mathcal{M}_\theta^T$ not only depends on the functional form of $f(\theta)$ and $g(\psi)$ and the relation between $\mathcal{S}^T(\boldsymbol{\Psi})$ and $\mathcal{S}^T(\boldsymbol{\Theta})$, but also depends on the nature of the DGP. This makes the derivation of general conditions for (18) to hold impossible – in general the encompassing relation between $f(\theta)$ and $g(\psi)$ requires separate investigation for each particular case. However, there is a degenerate case of (18), in which

$$\mathcal{M}_\psi^T(\mathbf{y}) = \mathcal{M}_\psi^T \cdot \mathcal{M}_\theta^T(\mathbf{y}) \tag{19}$$

holds independently of the nature of the DGP, and this is referred to as *automatic* encompassing as it does not provide any relevant information about the DGP.

Corollary 2 in section 2.1 gives sufficient conditions for a nesting model M_1 automatically to encompass a nested model M_2. An important component of those sufficient conditions is the requirement that nesting model M_1 has orthogonal parameters. A similar, but more general, condition can be derived for (19) when the mappings $\mathcal{M}_\psi^T$ and $\mathcal{M}_\theta^T$ are orthogonal projections defined on $\mathcal{S}^T(\mathbf{\Psi})$ and $\mathcal{S}^T(\mathbf{\Theta})$, respectively. A continuous linear mapping $\mathcal{M}_\psi^T$ defined on subspace $\mathcal{S}^T(\mathbf{\Psi}) \subset \mathcal{R}^T$ is orthogonal, if it is self-adjoint – $\mathcal{M}_\psi^T = \mathcal{M}_\psi^{T*}$, where $\mathcal{M}_\psi^{T*}$ is the adjoint projection – and idem-potent so that $\mathcal{M}_\psi^T \cdot \mathcal{M}_\psi^T = \mathcal{M}_\psi^T$. This condition is often satisfied, especially when both densities $f(\theta)$ and $g(\psi)$ belong to the linear exponential family. In the sequel it is assumed that the mappings $\mathcal{M}_\psi^T$ and $\mathcal{M}_\theta^T$ are orthogonal projections defined on $\mathcal{S}^T(\mathbf{\Psi})$ and $\mathcal{S}^T(\mathbf{\Theta})$, respectively.

Since $\mathcal{M}_\psi^T$ is an orthogonal projection, for (19) to hold it is necessary that the product projection $\mathcal{M}_\psi^T \cdot \mathcal{M}_\theta^T(\cdot)$ also be orthogonal. However, the fact that $\mathcal{M}_\psi^T$ and $\mathcal{M}_\theta^T$ are orthogonal projections is not sufficient for the orthogonality of the product projection $\mathcal{M}_\psi^T \cdot \mathcal{M}_\theta^T$. A necessary and sufficient condition for $\mathcal{M}_\psi^T \cdot \mathcal{M}_\theta^T$ to be an orthogonal projection is provided by the following proposition.

Proposition 4   *Let $\mathcal{M}_\psi^T$ and $\mathcal{M}_\theta^T$ be orthogonal projections defined on $\mathcal{S}^T(\mathbf{\Psi})$ and $\mathcal{S}^T(\mathbf{\Theta})$, respectively. A necessary and sufficient condition for the product projection $\mathcal{M}_\psi^T \cdot \mathcal{M}_\theta^T$ to be an orthogonal projection is that $\mathcal{M}_\psi^T$ and $\mathcal{M}_\theta^T$ commute, i.e.*

$$\mathcal{M}_\psi^T \cdot \mathcal{M}_\theta^T = \mathcal{M}_\theta^T \cdot \mathcal{M}_\psi^T. \tag{20}$$

In this case $\mathcal{M}_\psi^T \cdot \mathcal{M}_\theta^T$ is the orthogonal projection on $\mathcal{S}^T(\mathbf{\Psi}) \cap \mathcal{S}^T(\mathbf{\Theta})$. (For a proof see e.g. Bachman and Narici (1966).)

An implication of Proposition 4 is that the product projection $\mathcal{M}_\psi^T \cdot \mathcal{M}_\theta^T$ cannot define the same orthogonal projection as $\mathcal{M}_\psi^T$ if the two subspaces are disjoint, i.e. $\mathcal{S}^T(\mathbf{\Psi}) \cap \mathcal{S}^T(\mathbf{\Theta}) = \{\}$. Since having disjoint parameter sets is a defining characteristic of non-nested models, it follows that *automatic* encompassing can never occur between non-nested models.

As an illustration of the result in (20) consider the following two conditional regression models:

$$M_1: \quad \mathbf{y} = \mathbf{Z}_1 \gamma_1 + \mathbf{u}_1$$
$$M_2: \quad \mathbf{y} = \mathbf{Z}_2 \gamma_2 + \mathbf{u}_2$$

(21)

when $\mathbf{y}$ is $T \times 1$, $\mathbf{Z}_i$ is $T \times k_i$, γ_i is $k_i \times 1$, and $\mathbf{u}_i \sim N(0,1)$ for $i = 1, 2$. Let $\mathbf{Z} = (\mathbf{Z}_1, \mathbf{Z}_2)$ have rank $k = k_1 + k_2$ so that the two parameter subspaces Ψ and Θ are disjoint, when $\theta = \gamma_1$ and $\psi = \gamma_2$. The two subspaces $\mathcal{S}^T(\Psi)$ and $\mathcal{S}^T(\Theta)$ are given by:

$$\mathcal{S}^T(\Psi) = \{\mathbf{y}(\hat{\gamma}_2) = \mathcal{M}_\psi^T(\mathbf{y}) = \mathbf{Z}_2(\mathbf{Z}_2'\mathbf{Z}_2)^{-1}\mathbf{Z}_2'y = P_2\mathbf{y}, \quad \hat{\gamma}_2 \in \Psi\}$$

$$\mathcal{S}^T(\Theta) = \{\mathbf{y}(\hat{\gamma}_1) = \mathcal{M}_\theta^T(\mathbf{y}) = \mathbf{Z}_1(\mathbf{Z}_1'\mathbf{Z}_1)^{-1}\mathbf{Z}_1'y = P_1\mathbf{y}, \quad \hat{\gamma}_1 \in \Theta\}$$

when $\hat{\gamma}_i = (\mathbf{Z}_i'\mathbf{Z}_i)^{-1}\mathbf{Z}_i'y$ for $i = 1, 2$. It is easy to see that the product projection $\mathcal{M}_\psi^T \cdot \mathcal{M}_\theta^T$ is not orthogonal because in general $\mathcal{M}_\psi^T$ and $\mathcal{M}_\theta^T$ do not commute:

$$P_1 P_2 \neq P_2 P_1.$$

(22)

The next result shows that, when the two models are nested, the orthogonality of $\mathcal{M}_\psi^T$ and $\mathcal{M}_\theta^T$ is sufficient for the product projection to be orthogonal.

Proposition 5 *Let $\mathcal{M}_\psi^T$ and $\mathcal{M}_\theta^T$ be orthogonal projections defined on $\mathcal{S}^T(\Psi)$ and $\mathcal{S}^T(\Theta)$, respectively. If M_2 is nested in M_1 with $\Psi \subseteq \Theta$ so that $\mathcal{S}^T(\Psi) \subset \mathcal{S}^T(\Theta)$, then the product projection $\mathcal{M}_\psi^T \cdot \mathcal{M}_\theta^T(\cdot)$ is an orthogonal projection defined on $\mathcal{S}^T(\Psi)$.*
(Proof see A.4 in the Appendix.)

Note that the nesting of M_2 in M_1 alone is not sufficient for this result. The requirement that $\mathcal{M}_\psi^T$ and $\mathcal{M}_\theta^T$ are orthogonal projections is critical. Also note that when $\mathcal{M}_\psi^T$ and $\mathcal{M}_\psi^T \cdot \mathcal{M}_\theta^T$ are orthogonal projections defined on $\mathcal{S}^T(\Psi)$ it follows that $\mathcal{M}_\psi^T = \mathcal{M}_\psi^T \cdot \mathcal{M}_\theta^T$ on $\mathcal{S}^T(\Psi)$, which implies the following proposition.

Proposition 6 *If $\mathcal{M}_\psi^T$ and $\mathcal{M}_\theta^T$ are orthogonal projections on $\mathcal{S}^T(\Psi)$ and $\mathcal{S}^T(\Theta)$, respectively, and $\mathcal{S}^T(\Psi)$ is a subspace of $\mathcal{S}^T(\Theta)$, then*

$$\mathcal{M}_\psi^T = \mathcal{M}_\psi^T \cdot \mathcal{M}_\theta^T$$

and hence $M_1 \mathcal{E} M_2(\psi)$ automatically.

Note that Proposition 3(i) is the special case of 6 that arises when both Ψ and Θ are *Euclidean* subspaces with $\phi(\theta) = 0$ being the dimension-reducing constraints that define Ψ as a subspace of Θ.

As an illustration, consider the previous example but further assume that $\mathbf{Z}_2 \subset \mathbf{Z}_1$ so that $M_2 \subseteq M_1$, and $\mathbf{Z}_2 = \mathbf{Z}_1\mathbf{\Pi}$. Hence substituting for $\mathbf{Z}_2$ into (22) yields:

$$\mathbf{P}_2\mathbf{P}_1 = \mathbf{P}_1\mathbf{P}_2 = \mathbf{P}_2$$

and thus, from Proposition 6, $M_1 \, \mathcal{E} \, M_2(\psi)$ automatically irrespective of the nature of the DGP.

4.2   Limit of orthogonal projection $\mathcal{M}_\psi^T$

Finally, it is shown that the above analysis remains valid when the dimension T of the *Hilbert* space $\mathcal{R}^T$ tends to infinity. This is important since much statistical inference using econometric models, including encompassing analyses, relies on limiting distribution theory.

Noting that $\mathcal{S}^T(\mathbf{\Psi})$ is the subspace on which the orthogonal projection $\mathcal{M}_\psi^T$ is defined, it is necessary to show that as $T \to \infty$ the limit of $\mathcal{M}_\psi^T$ exists and defines an orthogonal projection in the infinite-dimensional *Hilbert* space $\mathcal{H} = \lim_{T \to \infty} \mathcal{R}^T$. Let $\{\mathcal{S}^T(\mathbf{\Psi}), T = l, l+1, \ldots\}$ be a series of T-dimensional subspaces of the *Hilbert* space $\mathcal{R}^T$, $\{\mathcal{M}_\psi^T, T = l, l+1, \ldots\}$ be a series of orthogonal projections defined on $\mathcal{R}^T \mapsto \mathcal{S}^T(\mathbf{\Psi})$, and $\mathcal{S}(\mathbf{\Psi}) = \lim_{T \to \infty} \cup_l^T \mathcal{S}^T(\mathbf{\Psi})$. It is shown in A.5 of the Appendix that $\mathcal{M}_\psi$ is the orthogonal projection defined on $\mathcal{H} \mapsto \mathcal{S}(\mathbf{\Psi})$, where

$$\mathcal{M}_\psi^T \to \mathcal{M}_\psi.$$

The limits of $\mathcal{M}_\theta^T$ and $\mathcal{M}_\psi^T \cdot \mathcal{M}_\theta^T$ also exist for the same reasons, thus yielding:

Proposition 7 *If $\mathcal{M}_\psi^T$ and $\mathcal{M}_\theta^T$ are orthogonal projections on $\mathcal{S}^T(\mathbf{\Psi})$ and $\mathcal{S}^T(\mathbf{\Theta})$, respectively, and $\mathcal{S}^T(\mathbf{\Psi})$ is a subspace of $\mathcal{S}^T(\mathbf{\Theta})$, then*

$$\mathcal{M}_\psi^T = \mathcal{M}_\psi^T \cdot \mathcal{M}_\theta^T$$

so that $M_1 \, \mathcal{E} \, M_2(\psi)$. This encompassing relation remains valid when $T \to \infty$, since

$$\mathcal{M}_\psi = \lim \mathcal{M}_\psi^T = \lim \mathcal{M}_\psi^T \cdot \mathcal{M}_\theta^T = \mathcal{M}_\psi \cdot \mathcal{M}_\theta$$

defines an orthogonal projection on $\mathcal{H}$.

5   Conclusion

The ability of a general model to encompass a simplification of itself has been questioned rarely. However, Gouriéroux and Monfort (1995) presented an example in which a general model was unable to encompass a simple model. This paper has presented conditions under which a model encompasses models nested within it independently of the nature of the DGP, and thus *automatically* encompasses the nested models. Equally importantly it was pointed out that nesting is more than one model being an algebraic simplification of another. By interpreting encompassing as the existence of orthogonal projections in *Hilbert* space, it was shown that, when the model M_2 is nested within M_1, a sufficient condition for M_1 to encompass M_2 is that the individual mappings associated with the models are orthogonal projections. As a by-product, it was also pointed out that *automatic* encompassing cannot occur between non-nested models. One of the important methodological implications of these findings is that care should be taken to establish the presence and nature of nesting amongst models prior to implementing hypothesis tests for model reduction, as for example is done in *general-to-simple* modelling.

Appendix

A.1

If ψ^* and θ^* satisfy (3), then:

$$
\begin{aligned}
0 &= \int \log\left(\frac{g(\psi^*)}{f(\theta^*)}\right) g(\psi^*)\, dy \\
&\geq \min_{\theta \in \Theta} \int \log\left(\frac{g(\psi^*)}{f(\theta)}\right) g(\psi^*)\, dy \\
&= \int \log\left(\frac{g(\psi^*)}{f(\theta(\psi^*))}\right) g(\psi^*)\, dy \\
&\geq 0.
\end{aligned}
$$

Therefore, $\theta^* = \theta(\psi^*)$ is the M_2 pseudo-true value of $\theta \in \Theta \ \forall \ \psi^* \in \Psi$. Gouriéroux and Monfort (1995) define $\theta^* = \theta(\psi^*)$ as the binding function from Ψ to Θ.

A.2

Here it is shown that if $g(\psi)$ is nested in $f(\theta)$ in the sense of (3) then $\Psi \subseteq \Theta$, or $\Psi \cap \Theta = \Psi$ with probability one. $g(\psi)$ is nested in $f(\theta)$ in the sense of (3) if $\forall \ \psi \in \Psi$, there exists $\theta^* \in \Theta^* \subseteq \Theta$, such that

$$
\int \log\left(\frac{g(\psi)}{f(\theta^*)}\right) g(\psi)\, dy = 0. \tag{23}
$$

First, if for each $\psi \in \Psi$, there exists $\theta^* \in \Theta^* \subseteq \Theta$, then it is necessary and sufficient that $g(\psi)$ and $f(\theta^*)$ are equivalent with probability one. Therefore, there is a *one-to-one* mapping between $\{g(\psi) \mid \psi \in \Psi\}$ and $\{f(\theta^*) \mid \theta^* \in \Theta^*\}$. Otherwise, if both $g(\psi_1)$ and $g(\psi_2)$ are mappings to $f(\theta^*)$, then $g(\psi_1)$ and $g(\psi_2)$ are identical with probability one, and hence $\psi_1 = \psi_2$. Further, the equivalence between $g(\psi)$ and $f(\theta^*)$ holds under any absolutely continuous measure, so $\{g(\psi) \mid \psi \in \Psi\}$ and $\{f(\theta^*) \mid \theta^* \in \Theta^*\}$ are *isomorphic*. Let Ω_0 define the set of zero measure on which $g(\psi) \neq f(\theta^*)$, $g(\psi)$ can then be equally written as

$$g(\psi) = \begin{cases} f(\theta^*) & \text{on } \Theta^* - \Omega_0 \\ g(\psi) & \text{on } \Omega_0 \end{cases}$$

$g(\psi)$ is a density function defined on Θ^*, and $\Psi \subseteq \Theta$ with probability one.

On the other hand, if for each $\psi \in \Psi$, $g(\psi)$ can be obtained as a special case of $f(\theta)$, then there exists $\theta^* \in \Theta$ so that (23) holds.

A.3

Here, it is shown that:

$$\operatorname*{plim}_{T \to \infty} \sum_{t=1}^{T} z_{1t} \left\{ y_t - z_t^\dagger \frac{\sum_{s=1}^{T} z_s^\dagger y_s}{\sum_{s=1}^{T} z_s^{\dagger 2}} \right\} = 0 \tag{24}$$

implies:

$$\operatorname*{plim}_{T \to \infty} \sum_{t=1}^{T} z_{2t} \left\{ y_t - z_t^\dagger \frac{\sum_{s=1}^{T} z_s^\dagger y_s}{\sum_{s=1}^{T} z_s^{\dagger 2}} \right\} = 0 \tag{25}$$

and *vice versa*. The following are equivalent to the orthogonal condition in (24):

$$\operatorname*{plim}_{T \to \infty} \left\{ \sum_{t=1}^{T} z_t^{\dagger 2} \sum_{t=1}^{T} z_{1t} y_t - \sum_{t=1}^{T} z_{1t} z_t^\dagger \sum_{t=1}^{T} (z_{1t} + z_{2t}) y_t \right\}$$

$$= \operatorname*{plim}_{T \to \infty} \left\{ \sum_{t=1}^{T} z_{1t} y_t \sum_{t=1}^{T} \left(z_t^\dagger - z_{1t} \right) z_t^\dagger - \sum_{t=1}^{T} z_{1t} z_t^\dagger \sum_{t=1}^{T} z_{2t} y_t \right\}$$

$$= \operatorname*{plim}_{T \to \infty} \left\{ \sum_{t=1}^{T} z_{1t} y_t \sum_{t=1}^{T} z_{2t} z_t^\dagger - \sum_{t=1}^{T} z_{1t} z_t^\dagger \sum_{t=1}^{T} z_{2t} y_t \right\} = 0. \tag{26}$$

On the other hand, condition (25) can be rewritten as:

$$\text{plim}_{T\to\infty}\left\{\sum_{t=1}^{T}z_t^\dagger\sum_{t=1}^{T}z_{2t}y_t - \sum_{t=1}^{T}z_{2t}z_t^\dagger\sum_{t=1}^{T}(z_{1t}+z_{2t})y_t\right\}$$

$$=\text{plim}_{T\to\infty}\left\{\sum_{t=1}^{T}z_{2t}y_t\sum_{t=1}^{T}\left(z_t^\dagger-z_{2t}\right)z_t^\dagger - \sum_{t=1}^{T}z_{2t}z_t^\dagger\sum_{t=1}^{T}z_{1t}y_t\right\}$$

$$=\text{plim}_{T\to\infty}\left\{\sum_{t=1}^{T}z_{2t}y_t\sum_{t=1}^{T}z_{1t}z_t^\dagger - \sum_{t=1}^{T}z_{2t}z_t^\dagger\sum_{t=1}^{T}z_{1t}y_t\right\}=0. \qquad (27)$$

Therefore, the conditions in (26) and (27) are equivalent.

A.4

Proof. Consider any $\mathbf{y}\in\mathcal{R}^T$ that can be decomposed in the following form:

$$y = z + z^\perp, \qquad \mathbf{z}\in\mathcal{S}^T(\mathbf{\Psi}), \qquad \mathbf{z}^\perp\in\mathcal{S}^T(\mathbf{\Psi})^\perp.$$

Therefore,

$$\mathcal{M}_\psi^T(\mathbf{y}) = \mathbf{z}\in\mathcal{S}^T(\mathbf{\Psi})\subset\mathcal{S}^T(\mathbf{\Theta}),$$

which implies,

$$\mathcal{M}_\theta^T\cdot\mathcal{M}_\psi^T(\mathbf{y}) = \mathbf{z}$$

and it follows that

$$\mathcal{M}_\theta^T\cdot\mathcal{M}_\psi^T(\cdot) = \mathcal{M}_\psi^T(\cdot). \qquad (28)$$

Taking adjoints in (28), we have,

$$\mathcal{M}_\psi^{T*} = \left(\mathcal{M}_\theta^T\cdot\mathcal{M}_\psi^T\right)^{T*} = \mathcal{M}_\psi^{T*}\cdot\mathcal{M}_\theta^{T*}$$

$$= \mathcal{M}_\psi^T\cdot\mathcal{M}_\theta^T = \mathcal{M}_\psi^T. \qquad (29)$$

The last equality sign holds because of the orthogonality $\mathcal{M}_\theta^T$ and $\mathcal{M}_\psi^T$. Combining (28) and (29) yields

$$\mathcal{M}_\psi^T\cdot\mathcal{M}_\theta^T(\cdot) = \mathcal{M}_\theta^T\cdot\mathcal{M}_\psi^T(\cdot),$$

i.e. $\mathcal{M}_\psi^T(\cdot)$ and $\mathcal{M}_\theta^T(\cdot)$ commute. Therefore, $\mathcal{M}_\psi^T\cdot\mathcal{M}_\theta^T(\cdot)$ is an orthogonal projection defined on $\mathcal{S}^T(\mathbf{\Psi})\cap\mathcal{S}^T(\mathbf{\Theta}) = \mathcal{S}^T(\mathbf{\Psi})$. ∎

A.5

Proof. First, the orthogonal projection $\mathcal{M}_\psi^T$ on $\mathcal{S}^T(\Psi)$ is continuous and bounded, and for $\forall \mathbf{y} \in \mathcal{R}^T$

$$\| \mathcal{M}_\psi^T(\mathbf{y}) \| \le \| \mathbf{y} \| < \infty.$$

On the other hand, the subspaces $\{\mathcal{S}^T(\Psi), T = l, l+1, \ldots,\}$ form an increasing sequence:

$$\mathcal{S}^l(\Psi) \subset \mathcal{S}^{l+1}(\Psi) \subset \cdots$$

therefore:

$$\mathcal{M}_\psi^T \cdot \mathcal{M}_\psi^{T+1} = \mathcal{M}_\psi^T$$

and

$$\| \mathcal{M}_\psi^T(\mathbf{y}) \|^2 = \| \mathcal{M}_\psi^T \cdot \mathcal{M}_\psi^{T+1}(\mathbf{y}) \|^2$$
$$\le \| \mathcal{M}_\psi^T \|^2 \cdot \| \mathcal{M}_\psi^{T+1}(\mathbf{y}) \|^2$$
$$\le \| \mathcal{M}_\psi^{T+1}(\mathbf{y}) \|^2 \le \| \mathbf{y} \|^2 .$$

Hence,

$$\| \mathcal{M}_\psi^T(\mathbf{y}) \|^2 \le \| \mathcal{M}_\psi^{T+1}(\mathbf{y}) \|^2 \le \cdots \le \| \mathbf{y} \|^2$$

implies $\mathcal{M}_\psi^T(\cdot)$ strongly converges in the norm $\|\cdot\|$ to the projection $\mathcal{M}_\psi(\cdot)$ which is defined on $\mathcal{S}(\Psi) \subset \mathcal{H}$. ∎

References

Bachman, G. and L. Narici (1966), *Functional Analysis*, New York: Academic Press.

Barndorff-Nielsen, O.E. and D.R. Cox (1994), *Inference and Asymptotics*, Monographs on Statistics and Applied Probability No. 52, London: Chapman & Hall.

Bontemps, C. and G.E. Mizon (1997), 'Congruence and Encompassing', European University Institute, mimeograph.

Cox, D.R. and N. Reid (1987), 'Parameter Orthogonality and Approximate Conditional Inference', *Journal of the Royal Statistical Society, Series B*, 49: 1–49.

Engle, R.F., D.F. Hendry and J.-F. Richard (1983), 'Exogeneity', *Econometrica*, 51: 277–304.

Gouriéroux, C. and A. Monfort (1995), 'Testing, Encompassing and Simulating Dynamic Econometric Models', *Econometric Theory*, 11: 195–228.

Granger, C.W.J. (1969), 'Investigating Causal Relations by Econometric Models and Cross-Spectral Methods', *Econometrica*, 37: 424–438.

Hendry, D.F. (1995), *Dynamic Econometrics*, Oxford: Oxford University Press.

Hendry, D.F. and G.E. Mizon (1978), 'Serial Correlation as a Convenient Simplification, Not a Nuisance: A Comment on a Study of the Demand for Money by the Bank of England', *Economic Journal*, 88: 549–563.

Hendry, D.F. and J.-F. Richard (1989), 'Recent Developments in the Theory of Encompassing', in B. Cornet and H. Tulkens (eds.), *Contributions to Operations Research and Economics. The XXth Anniversary of CORE*, Cambridge, Mass.: MIT Press, pp. 393–440.

Lu, M. and G.E. Mizon (1997), 'Mutual Encompassing and Model Equivalence', EUI Economics Department Working Paper No. 97/17.

Mizon, G.E. (1995a), 'A Simple Message for Autocorrelation Correctors: Don't', *Journal of Econometrics*, 69: 267–288.

(1995b), 'Progressive Modelling of Macroeconomic Time Series – The LSE Methodology', in K.D. Hoover (ed.), *Macroeconometrics: Developments, Tensions, and Prospects*, Dordrecht: Kluwer Academ Press, pp. 107–170.

Mizon, G. E. and J.-F. Richard (1986), 'The Encompassing Principle and Its Application to Non-nested Hypothesis Tests', *Econometrica*, 54: 657–678.

Pesaran, M.H. (1987), 'Global and Partial Non-nested Hypotheses and Asymptotic Local Power', *Econometric Theory*, 3: 69–97.

Sargan, J.D. (1980), 'Some Tests of Dynamic Specification for a Single Equation', *Econometrica*, 48: 879–897.

(1988), *Lectures on Advanced Econometric Theory*, Oxford: Basil Blackwell.

3 Exact properties of the maximum likelihood estimator in exponential regression models: a differential geometric approach

Grant Hillier and Ray O'Brien

1 Introduction

In a recent paper Hillier and Armstrong (1996) have given an integral formula for the (exact) density of the maximum likelihood estimator (MLE). The formula,[1] which expresses the density at a point t, does not require that the estimator be a known function of the data, but does require that the manifold on which the MLE is fixed (i.e. the level set of the MLE) be known. One situation, but by no means the only case, in which this occurs is when the MLE is uniquely defined by the vanishing of the score vector. The importance of this result lies in the fact that the formula can be used to obtain the exact density even when the estimator is only implicitly defined in terms of the data. The exponential regression model is well known to be of this type, and in this chapter we apply the Hillier and Armstrong result to the MLE for this model.

The observations $x_1, \ldots, x_n$ are assumed to be independent realisations of exponential random variables with means

$$\lambda_i = \exp\{\theta'w_i\}, \quad i = 1, \ldots, n, \tag{1}$$

where θ is a $k \times 1$ vector of parameters, and w_i is a $k \times 1$ vector of covariates, assumed non-random. The joint density of the data is thus:

$$pdf(x_1, \ldots, x_n; \theta) = \exp\{-n\theta'\bar{w}\} \exp\left\{-\sum_{i=1}^{n} x_i \exp[-\theta'w_i]\right\}, \tag{2}$$

---

[1] A surface integral over the manifold in the sample space upon which the MLE has the value t.

for $x_i > 0, i = 1, \ldots, n$, where $\bar{w}$ is the vector of sample means of the w_i. Let $x = (x_1, \ldots, x_n)'$, and abbreviate the condition $x_i > 0$ for $i = 1, \ldots, n$ to simply $x > 0$. The log-likelihood, score vector and observed information matrix are:

$$\ell(x; \theta) = -n\theta'\bar{w} - \sum_{i=1}^{n} x_i \exp\{-\theta'w_i\}, \tag{3}$$

$$u(x; \theta) = u(x; \theta, W) = \partial\ell(x; \theta)/\partial\theta$$

$$= -n\bar{w} + \sum_{i=1}^{n} x_i w_i \exp\{-\theta'w_i\}, \tag{4}$$

$$j(x; \theta) = j(x; \theta, W) = -\partial^2\ell(x; \theta)/\partial\theta\partial\theta'$$

$$= \sum_{i=1}^{n} x_i w_i w_i' \exp\{-\theta'w_i\}, \tag{5}$$

respectively. Provided the matrix $W(n \times k)$ with rows w_i', $i = 1, \ldots, n$, has rank k, it is well known that the MLE for θ is the unique solution to the equations $u(x; \theta) = 0$, but the MLE cannot be expressed directly in terms of $x_1, \ldots, x_n$. This has hitherto prevented an analysis of the small-sample properties of the MLE in this model, but the Hillier/Armstrong formula makes such results accessible, at least for small values of k, as we shall see.

To the best of our knowledge the only other analytic study of the exact properties of the MLE in this model is Knight and Satchell (1996). This used an approach suggested by Huber (1964; see also Shephard (1993)) and characteristic function inversion techniques to deduce some properties of the density for the cases $k = 1$ and $k = 2$, but this approach does not generalise easily. In fact, our differential geometric formula can be regarded as a generalisation of the Huber approach to the multi-parameter case, avoiding the need for characteristic function inversion.

We denote the MLE for θ by $T = T(x) = T(x; W)$, and a particular value of T by t. The density of T (with respect to Lebesgue measure, dt) at $T = t$ will be denoted by $pdf_T(t; \theta)$, or, if the dependence on W is important, by $pdf_T(t; \theta, W)$. From Hillier and Armstrong (1996, equation (26)), we have the following expression for the density of T:

$$pdf_T(t; \theta) = \exp\{-n\theta'\bar{w}\} \left| \sum_{i=1}^{n} w_i w_i' \exp\{-2t'w_i\} \right|^{-1/2}$$

$$\times \int_{S(t)} \left| \sum_{i=1}^{n} x_i w_i w_i' \exp\{-t'w_i\} \right|$$

$$\times \exp\left[-\sum_{i=1}^{n} x_i \exp\{-\theta'w_i\} \right] (dS(t)), \tag{6}$$

where $S(t) = \{x; x > 0, \sum_{i=1}^{n} x_i w_i \exp\{-t'w_i\} = n\bar{w}\}$, and $(dS(t))$ denotes the (canonical) volume element on the manifold $S(t)$ (see Hillier and Armstrong (1996), Appendix A, for definitions and technical details). That is, $S(t)$ is the intersection of an $(n-k)$-dimensional hyperplane with the non-negative orthant.

The key problem, therefore, is the evaluation of the surface integral in (6). Because the surface $S(t)$ is, in this case, flat, $S(t)$ admits a global coordinate chart, so that this surface integral can be reduced to an ordinary integral over a region in R^{n-k}. Nevertheless, the evaluation of this integral presents considerable difficulties: the region of interest consists of a polyhedron in R^{n-k} bounded by the coordinate axes and k intersecting hyperplanes. In the present chapter we give details of the evaluation of this integral for the cases $k = 1$ and $k = 2$. The completely general case can no doubt be dealt with similarly; see Schechter (1998) for one possible algorithm.

2   Some properties of the density in the general case

Before considering the evaluation of (6) in detail we make some general observations on the density of T that follow almost trivially from equations (4)–(6). Consider first a transformation of the w_i; $w_i \to A'w_i$, $i = 1, \ldots, n$, where A is a $k \times k$ non-singular matrix, so that $W \to WA$. From (4) we see that $u(x; \theta, WA) = A'u(x; A\theta, W)$. Hence, $T(x; W) = AT(x; WA)$, so that the transformation $W \to WA$ induces the transformation $T \to A^{-1}T$ on the MLE. It follows from this observation that $pdf_T(t; \theta, W) = \|A\|^{-1} pdf_{T^*}(t^*; \theta, WA)$, where $T^* = T(x; WA) = A^{-1}T(x; W)$, and $t = At^*$. That is, the density of $T = T(x; W)$ is trivially obtainable from the density of $T^* = T(x; WA)$, the MLE when W is replaced by WA, so that there is no loss of generality in standardising the w_i's so that, for instance, $W'W = I_k$. Note that $W'W$ is the Fisher information matrix for θ.

Next, for a fixed value of t one can transform variables in equation (6) from x_i to $\tilde{x}_i = \exp\{-t'w_i\}x_i$, $i = 1, \ldots, n$. This maps the manifold $\mathcal{S}(t)$ into a new manifold $\tilde{\mathcal{S}}(t)$, say, and using Hillier and Armstrong (1996, equation (A4)), the volume elements on $\mathcal{S}(t)$ and $\tilde{\mathcal{S}}(t)$ are related by:

$$(d\tilde{\mathcal{S}}(t)) = \exp\{-nt'\bar{w}\}\left|\sum_{i=1}^{n} x_i w_i w_i' \exp\{-2t'w_i\}\right|^{-1/2}$$

$$\times \mid W'W \mid^{1/2} (d\mathcal{S}(t)).$$

Rewriting (6) in terms of the transformed x_i we obtain:

$$pdf_T(t; \theta) = \exp\{n(t - \theta)'\bar{w}\} \mid W'W \mid^{-1/2}$$

$$\times \int_{\mathcal{S}} \left|\sum_{i=1}^{n} x_i w_i w_i'\right| \exp\left[-\sum_{i=1}^{n} x_i \exp\{(t - \theta)'w_i\}\right](d\mathcal{S}),$$

$$(7)$$

where $\mathcal{S} = \{x; x > 0, \sum_{i=1}^{n} x_i w_i = n\bar{w}\}$ does not depend on t. It follows at once from (7) that the density of T depends on (t, θ) only through their difference $(t - \theta)$. When regarded as a function of $d = (t - \theta)$, it is easy to see that, *at each point on the surface* $\mathcal{S}$, the integrand (with the term $\exp\{nd'\bar{w}\}$ attached) is maximised at $d = 0$. Hence, the mode of the (joint) density is at the point $t = \theta$.

Write the density of $T = T(x, W)$ in (7) as $f(d, W)$. It is clear from (7) that $f(d, W)$ is invariant under permutations of the rows of W, and also that the density of $T^* = T(x, WA) = A^{-1}T(x, W)$ is $f(d, WA) = \|A\|f(Ad, W)$ for any non-singular $k \times k$ matrix A. In particular, $f(d, -W) = f(-d, W)$ (on choosing $A = -I_k$), and thus, if $-W = PW$ for some permutation matrix P, the density of $(t - \theta)$ is symmetric about the origin. If the model contains an intercept, and the remaining variables are symmetric about their means, the density of the estimates of the coefficients of those variables will be symmetric about the corresponding true values, and hence will be unbiased if their means exist.

3   The one-parameter case

We consider first the case $k = 1$, and work from expression (7) for the density, which becomes (on replacing w_i by z_i):

$$pdf_T(t; \theta) = \exp\{n(t - \theta)\bar{z}\}\left[\sum_{i=1}^{n} z_i^2\right]^{-1/2} \int_S \left[\sum_{i=1}^{n} x_i z_i^2\right]$$

$$\times \exp\left[-\sum_{i=1}^{n} x_i \exp\{(t - \theta)z_i\}\right](d\mathcal{S}), \qquad (8)$$

where $\mathcal{S}$ is the intersection of the hyperplane $\sum_{i=1}^{n} x_i z_i = n\bar{z}$ with the non-negative orthant. To simplify matters we assume that the z_i are all of the same sign, and there is no loss of generality in taking this to be positive. Results for the case where the z_i''s are of mixed signs require only minor modifications in what follows. We also assume for convenience that the z_i''s are distinct.

The manifold $\mathcal{S}$ admits a global coordinate chart, and we can use $x_2, \ldots, x_n$ as coordinates, setting

$$x_1 = z_1^{-1}\left(n\bar{z} - \sum_{i=2}^{n} x_i z_i\right). \qquad (9)$$

We then have (from Hillier and Armstrong (1996), equation (A3)):

$$(d\mathcal{S}) = z_1^{-1}\left[\sum_{i=1}^{n} z_i^2\right]^{1/2} dx_2 dx_3 \ldots dx_n,$$

and, in view of (9), the region of integration becomes:

$$\mathcal{R} = \left\{x_i > 0, i = 2, \ldots, n; \sum_{i=2}^{n} x_i z_i < n\bar{z}\right\}.$$

To further simplify the integration it will be helpful to 'lift' the term $[\sum_{i=1}^{n} x_i z_i^2]$ in the integrand in (8) into the exponential. This can be done by writing

$$\left[\sum_{i=1}^{n} x_i z_i^2\right]\exp\left\{-\sum_{i=1}^{n} x_i r_i\right\} = (\partial/\partial w)\left[\exp\left\{-\sum_{i=1}^{n} x_i(r_i - w z_i^2)\right\}\right]_{w=0},$$

where we have put $r_i = \exp\{(t - \theta)z_i\}, i = 1, \ldots, n$. Substituting for x_1 from (9), and noting that the differentiation (with respect to w) commutes with the integration, the density becomes:

$$pdf_T(t; \theta) = z_1^{-1} \exp\{n(t - \theta)\bar{z}\}(\partial/\partial w)[\exp\{-(n\bar{z}a_1/z_1)\}$$

$$\times \int_R \exp\left\{-\sum_{i=2}^{n} x_i[a_i z_1 - a_1 z_i]/z_1 dx_2 \ldots dx_n\right]_{w=0}$$

$$\tag{10}$$

where we have now set $a_i = r_i - wz_i^2$, $i = 1, \ldots, n$. The essential problem, therefore, is the evaluation of the integral in (10).

Define

$$d_{si} = (z_s a_i - z_i a_s)/z_s, \quad i = 2, \ldots, n; \quad s < i. \cdot \tag{11}$$

The x_2-integral in (10) is (with the term $\exp\{-n\bar{z}a_1/z_1\}$ attached):

$$\exp\left\{-n\bar{z}a_1/z_1 - \sum_{i=3}^{n} x_i d_{1i}\right\}\left\{\int_0^{u_2} \exp\{-x_2 d_{12}\}dx_2\right\}, \tag{12}$$

where $u_2 = z_2^{-1}[n\bar{z} - \sum_{i=3}^{n} x_i z_i]$, giving, on integrating out x_2,

$$\exp\left\{-n\bar{z}a_1/z_1 - \sum_{i=3}^{n} x_i d_{1i}\right\}d_{12}^{-1}\{1 - \exp(-d_{12}u_2)\}$$

$$= d_{12}^{-1}\left\{\exp\left\{-n\bar{z}a_1/z_1 - \sum_{i=3}^{n} x_i d_{1i}\right\}\right.$$

$$\left. - \exp\left\{-n\bar{z}a_2/z_2 - \sum_{i=3}^{n} x_i d_{2i}\right\}\right\}, \tag{13}$$

since $a_1/z_1 + d_{12}/z_2 = a_2/z_2$ and $d_{1i} - z_i d_{12}/z_2 = d_{2i}$. The integral is interpreted as zero if $u_2 \leq 0$.

Integrating now with respect to x_3 we have:

$$d_{12}^{-1}\left\{\exp\left\{-n\bar{z}a_1/z_1 - \sum_{i=4}^{n} x_i d_{1i}\right\}d_{13}^{-1}[1 - \exp\{-d_{13}u_3\}]\right.$$

$$\left. - \exp\left\{-n\bar{z}a_2/z_2 - \sum_{i=4}^{n} x_i d_{2i}\right\}d_{23}^{-1}[1 - \exp\{-d_{23}u_3\}]\right\}, \tag{14}$$

where $u_3 = z_3^{-1}[n\bar{z} - \sum_{i=4}^{n} x_i z_i]$. There appear to be four distinct terms here, but identities similar to those below (13) yield:

$$(d_{12}d_{13})^{-1} \exp\left\{-n\bar{z}a_1/z_1 - \sum_{i=4}^{n} x_i d_{1i}\right\} - (d_{12}d_{23})^{-1}$$

$$\times \exp\left\{-n\bar{z}a_2/z_2 - \sum_{i=4}^{n} x_i d_{2i}\right\}[(d_{12}d_{13})^{-1} - (d_{12}d_{23})^{-1}]$$

$$\times \exp\left\{-n\bar{z}a_3/z_3 - \sum_{i=4}^{n} x_i d_{3i}\right\}. \tag{15}$$

The iterative relation is now clear: the p'th step in the integration yields a linear combination of terms

$$\exp\left\{-n\bar{z}a_s/z_s - \sum_{i=p+1}^{n} x_i d_{si}\right\}, \quad s = 1, \ldots, p,$$

in which the coefficients are simply the coefficients at the previous step multiplied by $d_{1p}^{-1}, d_{2p}^{-1}, \ldots, d_{p-1,p}^{-1}$, respectively, except for the last term ($s = p$), whose coefficient is minus the sum of the coefficients of all lower terms. Thus, if we denote by c_p the $p \times 1$ vector of coefficients of the terms $\exp\{-n\bar{z}a_s/z_s - \sum_{i=p+1}^{n} x_i d_{si}\}$ after integrating out x_p, we may write:

$$c_p = L_p c_{p-1},$$

where L_p is the $p \times (p-1)$ matrix:

$$L_p = \begin{bmatrix} d_{1p}^{-1} & 0 & .. & 0 \\ 0 & d_{2p}^{-1} & .. & . \\ . & . & .. & . \\ 0 & 0 & .. & d_{p-1,p}^{-1} \\ -d_{1p}^{-1} & -d_{2p}^{-1} & .. & -d_{p-1,p}^{-1} \end{bmatrix}. \tag{16}$$

After integrating out $x_2, \ldots, x_n$, therefore, we are left with a linear combination of the terms

$$g_n(j) = \exp\{-n\bar{z}a_j/z_j\}, \quad j = 1, \ldots, n, \tag{17}$$

with vector of coefficients, c_n, given by the recursive relation:

$$c_n = L_n L_{n-1} \ldots L_2 = \prod_{i=1}^{n-1} L_{n-i+1}, \tag{18}$$

starting with

$$L_2 = \begin{pmatrix} d_{12}^{-1} \\ -d_{12}^{-1} \end{pmatrix}.$$

We therefore have a very simple expression for the density:

$$pdf_T(t;\theta) = z_1^{-1} \exp\{n\bar{z}(t-\theta)\}(\partial/\partial w)[c_n' g_n]_{w=0}$$

$$= z_1^{-1} \exp\{n\bar{z}(t-\theta)\}[(\partial c_n/\partial w)' g_n + c_n'(\partial g_n/\partial w)]_{w=0}, \tag{19}$$

where g_n is the $n \times 1$ vector with elements $g_n(j)$ given in (17).

It remains to evaluate the derivatives in (19), and then set $w = 0$. It is easy to see that

$$\partial g_n(j)/\partial w \mid_{w=0} = n\bar{z}z_j \exp\{-n\bar{z}r_j/z_j\} = n\bar{z}z_j\tilde{g}_n(j), \text{ say.} \tag{20}$$

Defining $\tilde{L}_p$ as L_p has been defined above, but with the d_{sp} replaced by $\tilde{d}_{sp} = [z_s r_p - z_p r_s]/z_s$ (since $a_i = r_i$ when $w = 0$), we define

$$\tilde{c}_n \equiv c_n \mid_{w=0} = \prod_{i=1}^{n-1} \tilde{L}_{n-i+1}. \tag{21}$$

This deals with the second term in the [·] in (19).

Now, from the definition of c_n in terms of the L_p in (18), we have that:

$$\partial c_n/\partial w = \sum_{i=1}^{n-1}[L_n L_{n-1} \ldots L_{n-i+2}(\partial L_{n-i+1}/\partial w)L_{n-i}L_{n-i-1} \ldots L_2].$$

The matrices

$$\partial L_p/\partial w \mid_{w=0}$$

that occur here have the same structure as the $\tilde{L}_p$ except that the elements $\tilde{d}_{sp}^{-1}$ are replaced by $z_p(z_p - z_s)\tilde{d}_{sp}^{-2}$. Denote these matrices by $\tilde{L}_p^*$, $p = 2, \ldots, n$. Then clearly

$$\partial c_n/\partial w \mid_{w=0} = \sum_{i=1}^{n-1}[\tilde{L}_n \ldots \tilde{L}_{n-i+2}\tilde{L}_{n-i+1}^*\tilde{L}_{n-i} \ldots \tilde{L}_2] = \tilde{c}_n^*, \text{ say.}$$

Hence we finally have an expression for the density in the form:

$$pdf_T(t;\theta) = z_1^{-1} \exp\{n\bar{z}(t-\theta)\} \sum_{j=1}^{n} \tilde{g}_n(j)\{\tilde{c}_n^*(j) + n\bar{z}z_j\tilde{c}_n(j)\}. \tag{22}$$

Unfortunately, because the vectors $\tilde{c}_n^*$ and $\tilde{c}_n$ are both defined only by recursive formulae, it is difficult to study the properties of the density (22) analytically. In section 5 below we briefly summarise some results obtained by direct numerical evaluation of (22).

4   Inclusion of a constant term

Suppose now that $E(x_i) = \exp\{\alpha + \theta z_i\}$, so that $w_i = (1, z_i)'$ in the notation used in the Introduction. We denote the (fixed values of) the MLEs for (α, θ) by (a, t). From equation (7) we have:

$$pdf_{A,T}(a, t; \alpha, \theta) = \lambda_0^n \exp\{n(t - \theta)\bar{z}\} \left| \sum_{i=1}^{n} \begin{pmatrix} 1 \\ z_i \end{pmatrix} \begin{pmatrix} 1 \\ z_i \end{pmatrix}' \right|^{-1/2}$$

$$\times \int_{\mathcal{S}} \left| \sum_{i=1}^{n} x_i \begin{pmatrix} 1 \\ z_i \end{pmatrix} \begin{pmatrix} 1 \\ z_i \end{pmatrix}' \right|$$

$$\times \exp\left\{ -\lambda_0 \sum_{i=1}^{n} x_i r_i \right\} (d\mathcal{S}) \qquad (23)$$

where $\lambda_0 = \exp(a - \alpha)$, and we have again put $r_i = \exp\{(t - \theta)z_i\}$, $i = 1, \ldots, n$. The integral is now over the surface $\mathcal{S}$ defined by:

$$\sum_{i=1}^{n} x_i = n, \quad \text{and} \quad \sum_{i=1}^{n} x_i z_i = n\bar{z},$$

and $x_i > 0, i = 1, \ldots, n$. In what follows we assume that the z_i''s are distinct, and are ordered so that $z_1 < z_2 < \cdots < z_n$. It is clear from (23) that the density is invariant to the order of the z_i''s, so the assumption that the z_i''s are ordered is not restrictive. The assumption that the z_i''s are distinct is restrictive, but unlikely to be important in practice.

We first choose $n - 2$ coordinates for the surface $\mathcal{S}$, and for this purpose it will be convenient to use $x_2, \ldots, x_{n-1}$. Writing x_1 and x_n in terms of $x_2, \ldots, x_{n-1}$ we have:

$$x_1 = n(z_n - \bar{z})/(z_n - z_1) - \sum_{i=2}^{n-1} x_i[(z_n - z_i)/(z_n - z_1)] \qquad (24)$$

$$x_n = n(\bar{z} - z_1)/(z_n - z_1) - \sum_{i=2}^{n-1} x_i[(z_i - z_1)/(z_n - z_1)]. \qquad (25)$$

Note that the constants, and the coefficients of the x_i, in both of these expressions are all positive, because of our ordering of the z_i''s.

With these coordinates the integral (23) becomes an ordinary integral over $x_2, \ldots, x_{n-1}$, and the volume element becomes:

$$(dS) = [(z_n - z_1)]^{-1} \left| \sum_{i=1}^{n} \binom{1}{z_i} \binom{1}{z_i}' \right|^{1/2} (dx_2 dx_3 \ldots dx_{n-1}). \quad (26)$$

Because x_1 and x_n in (24) and (25) must be positive, the region of integration becomes that part of the non-negative orthant (for $x_2, \ldots, x_{n-1}$) within which:

$$\sum_{i=2}^{n-1} x_i(z_n - z_i) < n(z_n - \bar{z}) \quad \text{and} \quad \sum_{i=2}^{n-1} x_i(z_i - z_1) < n(\bar{z} - z_1).$$

$$(27)$$

That is, the region of integration becomes the subset, $\mathcal{R}$ say, of the $(n-2)$-dimensional non-negative orthant below both of the hyperplanes defined by replacing the inequalities in (27) by equalities. It is straightforward to check that the two hyperplanes involved must intersect, so neither lies entirely below the other. This obviously complicates the integration problem to be dealt with.

We first set out a notation that will be helpful in the evaluation of the integral in (23). First, we define $b_i = z_i - \bar{z}, i = 1, \ldots, n$, and $b_{jk} = z_j - z_k, j, k = 1, \ldots, n, j \neq k$. Note that b_{jk} will be positive for $j > k$ because of the ordering of the z_i, and that the b_i will necessarily be negative for i less than some integer p, say, $(1 \leq p < n)$, and positive thereafter. This property of the b_i's will be important in what follows. The following identities, easily derived from the definitions of the b_i and b_{jk}, will be used repeatedly in what follows to combine products of terms:

$$b_r b_{is} + b_s b_{ri} - b_i b_{rs} = 0 \qquad (28)$$

$$b_{ir} b_{js} - b_{ij} b_{rs} - b_{is} b_{jr} = 0. \qquad (29)$$

Next we define

$$\ell_{rs} = nb_s + \sum_{i=r}^{n-1} x_i b_{is} \quad (r = 2, \ldots, n-2, s < r), \qquad (30)$$

and

$$\bar{\ell}_r = nb_n - \sum_{i=r}^{n-1} x_i b_{ni}. \qquad (31)$$

Substituting for x_1 and x_n from (24) and (25) into the determinantal factor in the integrand of (23) we find that:

$$\left| \sum_{i=1}^{n} x_i \begin{pmatrix} 1 \\ z_i \end{pmatrix} \begin{pmatrix} 1 \\ z_i \end{pmatrix}' \right| = n^2 \{ (b_n z_1^2 - b_1 z_n^2)/b_{n1} - \bar{z}^2 \}$$

$$+ n \sum_{i=2}^{n-1} x_i \{ b_{n1} z_i^2 - b_{ni} z_1^2 - b_{i1} z_n^2 \}/b_{n1}. \qquad (32)$$

Note that this is linear in $x_2, \ldots, x_{n-1}$, *not* quadratic.

As before, it will be helpful to 'lift' the determinantal factor (32) into the exponential term in the integrand. We thus write the integrand in the form:

$$n\lambda_0^{-1}[\partial/\partial w] \left[\exp\{-n\lambda_0 w \bar{z}^2\} \right.$$

$$\left. \times \exp\left\{ -n\lambda_0([b_n a_1 - b_1 a_n]/b_{n1}) - \lambda_0 \sum_{i=2}^{n-1} x_i d_{n1i} \right\} \right]_{w=0},$$

where we have defined

$$d_{ijk} = [a_k b_{ij} - a_i b_{kj} - a_j b_{ik}]/b_{ij}, \qquad (33)$$

and

$$g_{ij} = [b_i a_j - b_j a_i]/b_{ij}, \qquad (34)$$

with

$$a_i = (r_i - w z_i^2), \quad i = 1, \ldots, n. \qquad (35)$$

Assuming that differentiation with respect to w commutes with the integration, we therefore have:

$$pdf_{A,T}(a, t; \alpha, \theta) = n\lambda_0^{n-1} \exp\{n(t - \theta)\bar{z}\}[b_{n1}]^{-1}(\partial/\partial w)$$

$$\times \left[\exp\{-n\lambda_0 w \bar{z}^2\} \exp\{-n\lambda_0 g_{n1}\} \right.$$

$$\left. \times \int_{\mathcal{R}} \exp\left\{ -n\lambda_0 \sum_{i=2}^{n-1} x_i d_{n1i} \right\} dx_2 \ldots dx_{n-1} \right]_{w=0}. \qquad (36)$$

Our first task is therefore to evaluate the integral in the last line of (36), though in what follows we shall include the term $\exp\{-n\lambda_0 g_{n1}\}$ in the derivation of the results, because this will facilitate their simplification as we proceed.

Consider now the integral with respect to x_2. From (27), the range of x_2 is restricted by

$$x_2 < \left[nb_n - \sum_{i=3}^{n-1} x_i b_{ni} \right]/b_{n2} = \bar{\ell}_3/b_{n2},$$

and

$$x_2 < \left[-nb_1 - \sum_{i=3}^{n-1} x_i b_{i1} \right]/b_{21} = -\ell_{31}/b_{21}.$$

Now, the difference between these two upper bounds is

$$\bar{\ell}_3/b_{n2} + \ell_{31}/b_{21} = (b_{n1}/(b_{n2}b_{21})) \left[nb_2 + \sum_{i=3}^{n-1} x_i b_{i2} \right]$$

$$= (b_{n1}/(b_{n2}b_{21}))\ell_{32}. \tag{37}$$

For $x_3, \ldots, x_{n-1}$ such that $\ell_{32} > 0$ and $\ell_{31} < 0$, the x_2-integral is over the interval $(0, -\ell_{31}/b_{21})$, while for $x_3, \ldots, x_{n-1}$ such that $\ell_{32} < 0$ and $\bar{\ell}_3 > 0$, it is over the interval $(0, \bar{\ell}_3/b_{n2})$. Notice that, because all coefficients other than b_2 in ℓ_{32} are positive, if $b_2 = z_2 - \bar{z} > 0$ the only possibility is $\ell_{32} > 0$. However, assume for the moment that $b_2 < 0$, so that ℓ_{32} can be either positive or negative. Since the regions of subsequent integration with respect to $x_3, \ldots, x_{n-1}$ are disjoint, the integral with respect to x_2 may be expressed as a sum of two terms, each to be subsequently integrated over *different* regions for $x_3, \ldots, x_{n-1}$. The result of integrating out x_2 is thus the sum of two terms:

$$[\lambda_0 d_{n12}]^{-1} \exp\left\{ -\lambda_0 \left[ng_{n1} + \sum_{i=3}^{n-1} x_i d_{n1i} \right] \right\} [1 - \exp(\lambda_0 d_{n12}\ell_{31}/b_{31})],$$

to be integrated over the region $\{\ell_{32} > 0, \bar{\ell}_3 < 0\}$, and

$$[\lambda_0 d_{n12}]^{-1} \exp\left\{ -\lambda_0 \left[ng_{n1} + \sum_{i=3}^{n-1} x_i d_{n1i} \right] \right\} [1 - \exp(-\lambda_0 d_{n12}\bar{\ell}_3/b_{n2})],$$

to be integrated over the region $\{\ell_{32} < 0, \bar{\ell}_3 > 0\}$.

After some tedious algebra the two results above for the x_2-integral become (apart from the factor $[\lambda_0 d_{n12}]^{-1}$):

$$\left[\exp\left\{ -\lambda_0 \left[ng_{n1} + \sum_{i=3}^{n-1} x_i d_{n1i} \right] \right\} - \exp\left\{ -\lambda_0 \left[ng_{21} + \sum_{i=3}^{n-1} x_i d_{21i} \right] \right\} \right],$$

$$\tag{38}$$

to be integrated over $\{\ell_{32} > 0,\ \ell_{31} < 0\}$, plus

$$\left[\exp\left\{-\lambda_0\left[ng_{n1} + \sum_{i=3}^{n-1}x_id_{n1i}\right]\right\} - \exp\left\{-\lambda_0\left[ng_{n2} + \sum_{i=3}^{n-1}x_id_{n2i}\right]\right\}\right], \tag{39}$$

to be integrated over $\{\ell_{32} < 0,\ \bar{\ell}_3 > 0\}$.

Now, the first terms in (38) and (39) are the same, but are to be integrated over two disjoint regions. When added, therefore, the integral of this term will be over the union of the regions $\{\ell_{32} > 0,\ \ell_{31} > 0\}$ and $\{\ell_{32} < 0,\ \bar{\ell}_3 > 0\}$, i.e. over the region $\{\ell_{31} > 0,\ \bar{\ell}_3 > 0\}$. The result of the x_2-integration is therefore a sum of three terms, each to be integrated over a different region of $(x_3, \ldots, x_{n-1})$-space. These are (again apart from the term $[\lambda_0 d_{n12}]^{-1}$), together with their respective regions of subsequent integration:

$$+\exp\left\{-\lambda_0\left[ng_{n1} + \sum_{i=3}^{n-1}x_id_{n1i}\right]\right\}, \qquad (\ell_{31} < 0,\ \bar{\ell}_3 > 0); \tag{40}$$

$$-\exp\left\{-\lambda_0\left[ng_{n2} + \sum_{i=3}^{n-1}x_id_{n2i}\right]\right\}, \qquad (\ell_{32} < 0,\ \bar{\ell}_3 > 0); \tag{41}$$

$$-\exp\left\{-\lambda_0\left[ng_{21} + \sum_{i=3}^{n-1}x_id_{21i}\right]\right\}, \qquad (\ell_{32} > 0,\ \ell_{31} < 0). \tag{42}$$

Note that if ℓ_{32} cannot be negative (i.e. if $z_2 > \bar{z}$), the second term here is missing.

The final form of the result we seek is certainly not yet apparent, so we need to proceed to integrate out x_3 in the same way. To do so we need to deal with the three terms in (40) to (42) separately, since each has a different region of integration for $(x_3, \ldots, x_{n-1})$. Proceeding as above for the x_2-integration, after isolating x_3 each region gives rise to a sum of two x_3-integrals, and each of these yields two distinct terms. At this stage we have:

from (40)

$$+[\lambda_0 d_{n13}]^{-1} \text{ multiplied by}$$

$$\exp\left\{-\lambda_0\left[ng_{n1} + \sum_{i=4}^{n-1}x_id_{n1i}\right]\right\}[1 - \exp(\lambda_0 d_{n13}\ell_{41}/b_{31})]$$

$$(\ell_{43} > 0,\ \ell_{41} < 0)$$

plus

$$\exp\left\{-\lambda_0\left[ng_{n1} + \sum_{i=4}^{n-1} x_i d_{n1i}\right]\right\}[1 - \exp(-\lambda_0 d_{n13}\bar{\ell}_4/b_{n3})]$$

$$(\ell_{43} < 0, \quad \bar{\ell}_4 > 0)$$

from (41)

$-[\lambda_0 d_{n23}]^{-1}$ multiplied by

$$\exp\left\{-\lambda_0\left[ng_{n2} + \sum_{i=4}^{n-1} x_i d_{n2i}\right]\right\}[1 - \exp(\lambda_0 d_{n23}\ell_{42}/b_{32})]$$

$$(\ell_{43} > 0, \quad \ell_{42} < 0)$$

plus

$$\exp\left\{-\lambda_0\left[ng_{n2} + \sum_{i=4}^{n-1} x_i d_{n2i}\right]\right\}[1 - \exp(-\lambda_0 d_{n23}\bar{\ell}_4/b_{n3})]$$

$$(\ell_{43} < 0, \quad \bar{\ell}_4 > 0)$$

from (42)

$-[\lambda_0 d_{213}]^{-1}$ multiplied by

$$\exp\left\{-\lambda_0\left[ng_{21} + \sum_{i=4}^{n-1} x_i d_{21i}\right]\right\}[\exp(\lambda_0 d_{213}\ell_{42}/b_{32})$$

$$- \exp(\lambda_0 d_{213}\ell_{41}/b_{31})] \quad (\ell_{43} > 0, \quad \ell_{42} < 0)$$

plus

$$\exp\left\{-\lambda_0\left[ng_{21} + \sum_{i=4}^{n-1} x_i d_{21i}\right]\right\}[1 - \exp(\lambda_0 d_{213}\ell_{41}/b_{31})]$$

$$(\ell_{41} < 0, \quad \ell_{42} > 0)$$

From the first of these sets of results we get three terms (ignoring the factor $[\lambda_0]^{-1}$ which occurs in all terms):

d_{n13}^{-1} multiplied by:

$$+ \exp\left\{-\lambda_0\left[ng_{n1} + \sum_{i=4}^{n-1} x_i d_{n1i}\right]\right\} \qquad (\ell_{41} < 0, \quad \bar{\ell}_4 > 0) \qquad (43)$$

$$- \exp\left\{-\lambda_0\left[ng_{31} + \sum_{i=4}^{n-1} x_i d_{31i}\right]\right\} \qquad (\ell_{43} > 0, \quad \ell_{41} < 0) \qquad (44)$$

$$- \exp\left\{-\lambda_0\left[ng_{n3} + \sum_{i=4}^{n-1} x_i d_{n3i}\right]\right\} \qquad (\ell_{43} < 0, \quad \bar{\ell}_4 > 0). \qquad (45)$$

From the second group we get:

$-d_{n23}^{-1}$ multiplied by:

$$+ \exp\left\{-\lambda_0\left[ng_{n2} + \sum_{i=4}^{n-1} x_i d_{n2i}\right]\right\} \qquad (\ell_{42} < 0, \quad \bar{\ell}_4 > 0) \qquad (46)$$

$$- \exp\left\{-\lambda_0\left[ng_{32} + \sum_{i=4}^{n-1} x_i d_{32i}\right]\right\} \qquad (\ell_{43} > 0, \quad \ell_{42} < 0) \qquad (47)$$

$$- \exp\left\{-\lambda_0\left[ng_{n3} + \sum_{i=4}^{n-1} x_i d_{n3i}\right]\right\} \qquad (\ell_{43} < 0, \quad \bar{\ell}_4 > 0). \qquad (48)$$

Finally, from the third group we get:

$-d_{213}^{-1}$ multiplied by:

$$+ \exp\left\{-\lambda_0\left[ng_{21} + \sum_{i=4}^{n-1} x_i d_{21i}\right]\right\} \qquad (\ell_{41} < 0, \quad \ell_{42} > 0) \qquad (49)$$

$$+ \exp\left\{-\lambda_0\left[ng_{32} + \sum_{i=4}^{n-1} x_i d_{32i}\right]\right\} \qquad (\ell_{43} > 0, \quad \ell_{42} < 0) \qquad (50)$$

$$- \exp\left\{-\lambda_0\left[ng_{31} + \sum_{i=4}^{n-1} x_i d_{31i}\right]\right\} \qquad (\ell_{43} > 0, \quad \ell_{41} < 0). \qquad (51)$$

To simplify the summary of these results, write

$$f_{ns}^{(k)} = \exp\left\{-\lambda_0\left[ng_{ns} + \sum_{i=k}^{n-1} x_i d_{nsi}\right]\right\}, \qquad k = 3, \dots, n-1, s < k;$$

$$(52)$$

and, for $j > s$,

$$f_{js}^{(k)} = \exp\left\{-\lambda_0\left[ng_{js} + \sum_{i=k}^{n-1} x_i d_{jsi}\right]\right\}, \quad k = 3, \ldots, n-1, s < k.$$

(53)

From (40)–(42), the result after integrating out x_2 may, with this notation, be expressed as:

$$[\lambda_0 d_{n12}]^{-1}\{-f_{21}^{(3)} + f_{n1}^{(3)} - f_{n2}^{(3)}\},$$

(54)

with respective regions of integration: for $f_{n1}^{(3)}$, $\{\ell_{31} < 0, \bar{\ell}_3 > 0\}$, for $f_{n2}^{(3)}$, $\{\ell_{32} < 0, \bar{\ell}_3 > 0\}$, and for $f_{21}^{(3)}$, $\{\ell_{32} > 0, \ell_{31} < 0\}$. Likewise, from (43)–(51), the result after integrating out x_3 may be expressed in the form:

$$[\lambda_0^2 d_{n12}]^{-1}\{d_{n13}^{-1}f_{n1}^{(4)} - d_{n23}^{-1}f_{n2}^{(4)} - [d_{n13}^{-1} - d_{n23}^{-1}]f_{n3}^{(4)} - d_{213}^{-1}f_{21}^{(4)}$$

$$-[d_{n13}^{-1} - d_{213}^{-1}]f_{31}^{(4)} - [d_{213}^{-1} - d_{n23}^{-1}]f_{32}^{(4)}\},$$

(55)

with subsequent regions of integration:

for $f_{ns}^{(4)}$, $\{\ell_{4s} < 0, \bar{\ell}_4 > 0\}$, $s = 1, 2, 3$;

for $f_{js}^{(4)}$, $\{\ell_{4j} > 0, \ell_{4s} < 0\}$, $j = 2, 3$, $s < j$.

Evidently, so long as $(k-1) < p$ (recall that p is the first value of i for which $b_i = z_i - \bar{z} > 0$), the result of integrating out $x_2, \ldots, x_{k-1}$ will be a linear combination of $k(k-1)/2$ terms, the $(k-1)$ terms $f_{ns}^{(k)}$, $s = 1, \ldots, k-1$, together with the $(k-1)(k-2)/2$ terms $f_{js}^{(k)}$, $j = 2, \ldots, (k-1)$, $s = 1, \ldots, (j-1)$, each term to be subsequently integrated over a different region for $(x_k, \ldots, x_{n-1})$. As in the one-parameter case, the coefficients in this linear combination can be generated recursively. To deduce the transition rules for the recursion, write the result of integrating out $x_2, \ldots, x_{k-1}$ (assuming $k-1 < p$) in the form:

$$\sum_{s=1}^{k-1} a_{ns}^{(k)} f_{ns}^{(k)} + \sum_{r=2}^{k-1}\sum_{s=1}^{r-1} a_{rs}^{(k)} f_{rs}^{(k)},$$

(56)

with regions of subsequent integration:

for $f_{ns}^{(k)}$: $(\ell_{ks} < 0, \quad \bar{\ell}_k > 0)$

for $f_{rs}^{(k)}$: $(\ell_{kr} > 0, \quad \ell_{ks} < 0)$.

We proceed now to integrate out x_k. There are two cases to consider: (i) the case $k < p$, and (ii) the case $k = p$.

Case (i): $k < p$

We begin with the first sum in (56). Isolating x_k in the inequalities ($\ell_{ks} < 0$, $\bar{\ell}_k > 0$), we find that x_k must satisfy both of the inequalities:

$$x_k < -\ell_{k+1,s}/b_{ks} \quad \text{and} \quad x_k < \bar{\ell}_{k+1}/b_{nk}.$$

Using the identities (28) and (29), the difference between these upper bounds is

$$\bar{\ell}_{k+1}/b_{nk} + \ell_{k+1,s}/b_{ks} = (b_{ns}/(b_{nk}b_{ks}))\ell_{k+1,k}.$$

The x_k-integral of an $f_{ns}^{(k)}$ term in (56) therefore splits into a sum of two terms (each multiplied by $f_{ns}^{(k+1)}$):

$$\int_0^{-\ell_{k+1,s}/b_{ks}} \exp(-\lambda_0 x_k d_{nsk})dx_k = [\lambda_0 d_{nsk}]^{-1}\left[1 - \exp(\lambda_0 d_{nsk}\ell_{k+1,s}/b_{ks})\right]$$

$$(\text{if } \ell_{k+1,k} > 0, \quad \ell_{k+1,s} < 0), \quad (57)$$

plus

$$\int_0^{\bar{\ell}_{k+1}/b_{nk}} \exp(-\lambda_0 x_k d_{nsk})dx_k = [\lambda_0 d_{nsk}]^{-1}\left[1 - \exp(\lambda_0 d_{nsk}\bar{\ell}_{k+1}/b_{nk})\right]$$

$$(\text{if } \ell_{k+1,k} < 0, \quad \bar{\ell}_{k+1} > 0). \quad (58)$$

As before, the sum of the two equal terms $f_{ns}^{(k+1)}$ to be integrated over the disjoint regions ($\ell_{k+1,k} > 0$, $\ell_{k+1,s} < 0$) and ($\ell_{k+1,k} < 0$, $\bar{\ell}_{k+1} > 0$) is simply the integral over the union of those regions, i.e. over the region ($\ell_{k+1,s} < 0$, $\bar{\ell}_{k+1} > 0$). Using the identities (28) and (29) again, we see that

$$f_{ns}^{(k+1)} \exp(\lambda_0 \ell_{k+1,s} d_{nsk}/b_{ks}) = f_{ks}^{(k+1)},$$

and

$$f_{ns}^{(k+1)} \exp(-\lambda_0 \bar{\ell}_{k+1} d_{nsk}/b_{nk}) = f_{nk}^{(k+1)}.$$

Hence, integration of the first sum in (56) yields the sum:

$$\lambda_0^{-1}\sum_{s=1}^{k-1}[a_{nsk}/d_{nsk}]\{f_{ns}^{(k+1)} - f_{ks}^{(k+1)} - f_{nk}^{(k+1)}\}, \quad (59)$$

with regions of subsequent integration:

$$\text{for } f_{ns}^{(k+1)} : \{\ell_{k+1,s} < 0, \quad \bar{\ell}_{k+1} > 0\},$$

$$\text{for } f_{ks}^{(k+1)} : \{\ell_{k+1,k} > 0, \quad \ell_{k+1,s} < 0\},$$

$$\text{for } f_{nk}^{(k+1)} : \{\ell_{k+1,k} < 0, \quad \bar{\ell}_{k+1} > 0\}.$$

Consider now the second sum in (56). Isolating x_k in the inequalities $(\ell_{kr} > 0, \ell_{ks} < 0)$ gives:

$$x_k > -\ell_{k+1,r}/b_{kr} \quad \text{and} \quad x_k < -\ell_{k+1,s}/b_{ks}.$$

The difference between the upper and lower limits is

$$\ell_{k+1,r}/b_{kr} - \ell_{k+1,s}/b_{ks} = (b_{rs}/(b_{kr}b_{ks}))\ell_{k+1,k}.$$

The integral vanishes, of course, if this is non-positive, i.e. if $\ell_{k+1,k} \leq 0$. We again get a sum of two terms (each to be multiplied by $f_{rs}^{(k+1)}$):

$$\int_{-\ell_{k+1,r}/b_{kr}}^{-\ell_{k+1,s}/b_{ks}} \exp(-\lambda_0 x_k d_{rsk}) dx_k$$

$$= [\lambda_0 d_{rsk}]^{-1}[\exp(\lambda_0 \ell_{k+1,r} d_{rsk}/b_{kr}) - \exp(\lambda_0 \ell_{k+1,s} d_{rsk}/b_{ks})]$$

$$(\text{if } \ell_{k+1,r} < 0, \quad \ell_{k+1,k} > 0) \quad (60)$$

plus

$$\int_{0}^{-\ell_{k+1,s}/b_{ks}} \exp(-\lambda_0 x_k d_{rsk}) dx_k$$

$$= [\lambda_0 d_{rsk}]^{-1}[1 - \exp(\lambda_0 \ell_{k+1,s} d_{rsk}/b_{ks})]$$

$$(\text{if } \ell_{k+1,r} < 0, \quad \ell_{k+1,s} < 0). \quad (61)$$

Again using the identities (28) and (29) we find that:

$$f_{rs}^{(k+1)} \exp(\lambda_0 \ell_{k+1,r} d_{rsk}/b_{kr}) = f_{kr}^{(k+1)},$$

and

$$f_{rs}^{(k+1)} \exp(\lambda_0 \ell_{k+1,s} d_{rsk}/b_{ks}) = f_{ks}^{(k+1)}.$$

The two equal terms in (60) and (61) combine as usual to give the term $f_{ks}^{(k+1)}$, to be integrated over $\{\ell_{k+1,k} > 0, \ell_{k+1,s} < 0\}$. Hence the second sum in (56) becomes, after integrating out x_k,

$$\lambda_0^{-1} \sum_{r=2}^{k-1} \sum_{s=1}^{r-1} [a_{rs}^{(k)}/d_{rsk}]\{f_{rs}^{(k+1)} + f_{kr}^{(k+1)} - f_{ks}^{(k+1)}\} \quad (62)$$

with regions of subsequent integration:

for $f_{rs}^{(k+1)}$: $\{\ell_{k+1,r} > 0, \quad \ell_{k+1,s} < 0\}$,

for $f_{kr}^{(k+1)}$: $\{\ell_{k+1,r} < 0, \quad \ell_{k+1,k} > 0\}$,

for $f_{ks}^{(k+1)}$: $\{\ell_{k+1,s} < 0, \quad \ell_{k+1,k} > 0\}$.

Case (ii): $k = p$

In the case $k = p$, $\ell_{p+1,p}$ cannot be negative, so only (57) occurs when x_p is integrated out in the first term of (56). We therefore get, in place of (59),

$$\lambda_0^{-1} \sum_{s=1}^{p-1} [a_{ns}^{(p)}/d_{nsp}] \{f_{ns}^{(p+1)} - f_{ps}^{(p+1)}\}, \tag{63}$$

with both terms to be integrated over the region (for $x_{p+1}, \ldots, x_{n-1}$) determined by the single condition $\ell_{p+1,s} < 0$. Notice that the term $f_{np}^{(p+1)}$ does not appear in (63).

Turning to the second term in (56), equations (60) and (61) apply with $k = p$, but the condition $\ell_{p+1,p} > 0$ in (60) is automatically satisfied. Hence the only change needed for this case is that the regions of subsequent integration of the terms $f_{pr}^{(p+1)}$ and $f_{ps}^{(p+1)}$ in (62) are determined by the single inequalities $\ell_{p+1,r} < 0$ and $\ell_{p+1,s} < 0$, respectively.

Combining these results, the result of integrating out x_k in (56) is, apart from the factor $[\lambda_0]^{-1}$,

for case (i): $k < p$

$$\sum_{s=1}^{k-1} [a_{ns}^{(k)}/d_{nsk}] \{f_{ns}^{(k+1)} - f_{ks}^{(k+1)} - f_{nk}^{(k+1)}\}$$

$$+ \sum_{r=2}^{k-1} \sum_{s=1}^{r-1} [a_{rs}^{(k)}/d_{rsk}] \{f_{rs}^{(k+1)} + f_{kr}^{(k+1)} - f_{ks}^{(k+1)}\} \tag{64}$$

for case (ii): $k = p$

$$\sum_{s=1}^{p-1} [a_{ns}^{(p)}/d_{nsp}] \{f_{ns}^{(p+1)} - f_{ps}^{(p+1)}\}$$

$$+ \sum_{r=2}^{p-1} \sum_{s=1}^{r-1} [a_{rs}^{(p)}/d_{rsp}] \{f_{rs}^{(p+1)} + f_{pr}^{(p+1)} - f_{ps}^{(p+1)}\}. \tag{65}$$

Identifying (64) with the analogue of (56):

$$\sum_{s=1}^{k} a_{ns}^{(k+1)} f_{ns}^{(k+1)} + \sum_{r=2}^{k} \sum_{s=1}^{r-1} a_{rs}^{(k+1)} f_{rs}^{(k+1)} \tag{66}$$

the 'new' terms are $f_{nk}^{(k+1)}$(in the first sum) and $f_{k1}^{(k+1)}, \ldots, f_{k,k-1}^{(k+1)}$ (in the second), a total of k new terms. Now, for $s = 1, \ldots, k-1$, $f_{ns}^{(k+1)}$ occurs only in the first line of (64). Hence, if $k < p$,

$$a_{ns}^{(k+1)} = a_{ns}^{(k)}/d_{nsk}, \quad s = 1, \ldots, (k-1). \tag{67}$$

Also, the term $f_{nk}^{(k+1)}$ occurs only in the first line of (64), so that

$$a_{nk}^{(k+1)} = -\sum_{s=1}^{k-1}[a_{ns}^{(k)}/d_{nsk}]. \tag{68}$$

In the second line of (64), the terms $f_{rs}^{(k+1)}$ with $r < k$ occur with coefficients $a_{rs}^{(k)}/d_{rsk}$, so that

$$a_{rs}^{(k+1)} = a_{rs}^{(k)}/d_{rsk}, \quad r = 2,\ldots,(k-1); \quad s = 1,\ldots,(r-1). \tag{69}$$

The new terms $f_{kj}^{(k+1)}$, $j = 1,\ldots,k-1$, occur in the first line of (64) with coefficients $-a_{ns}^{(k)}/d_{nsk}$, and twice in the second line of (64), in the second term with coefficients

$$+\sum_{s=1}^{j-1}\left[a_{js}^{(k)}/d_{jsk}\right], \quad (j > 1)$$

and in the third term with coefficients

$$-\sum_{r=j+1}^{k-1}\left[a_{rj}^{(k)}/d_{rjk}\right], \quad (j < k-1).$$

Hence the coefficients of the terms $f_{kj}^{(k+1)}$ in (64) are:

$$a_{k1}^{(k+1)} = -a_{n1}^{(k)}/d_{n1k} - \sum_{r=2}^{k-1}[a_{r1}^{(k)}/d_{r1k}];$$

$$a_{kj}^{(k+1)} = -a_{nj}^{(k)}/d_{njk} + \sum_{s=1}^{j-1}[a_{js}^{(k)}/d_{jsk}] - \sum_{r=j+1}^{k-1}[a_{rj}^{(k)}/d_{rjk}],$$

$$j = 2,\ldots,k-2;$$

$$a_{k,k-1}^{(k+1)} = -a_{n,k-1}^{(k)}/d_{n,k-1,k} + \sum_{s=1}^{k-2}[a_{k-1,s}^{(k)}/d_{k-1,s,k}]. \tag{70}$$

Equations (67)–(70) specify the recursive relations between the coefficients in equation (56) up to the integration with respect to x_{p-1}. For the next step, integration with respect to x_p, we need to identify (65) with (66) (with k replaced by p). This gives:

$$a_{ns}^{(p+1)} = a_{ns}^{(p)}/d_{nsp}, \quad s = 1,\ldots,p-1; \tag{71}$$

$$a_{np}^{(p+1)} = 0; \tag{72}$$

$$a_{rs}^{(p+1)} = a_{rs}^{(p)}/d_{rsp}, \quad r = 2,\ldots,p-1, \quad s = 1,\ldots,r-1; \tag{73}$$

$$a_{p1}^{(p+1)} = -a_{n1}^{(p)}/d_{n1p} - \sum_{r=2}^{p-1} [a_{r1}^{(p)}/d_{r1p}]$$

$$a_{pj}^{(p+1)} = -a_{nj}^{(p)}/d_{njp} + \sum_{s=1}^{j-1} [a_{js}^{(p)}/d_{jsp}] - \sum_{r=j+1}^{p-1} [a_{rj}^{(p)}/d_{rjp}],$$

$$j = 2, \ldots, p-2$$

$$a_{p,p-1}^{(p+1)} = -a_{n,p-1}^{(p)}/d_{n,p-1,p} + \sum_{s=1}^{p-2} [a_{p-1,s}^{(p)}/d_{p-1,s,p}]. \tag{74}$$

Thus, after integrating out x_p, we shall have an expression:

$$\sum_{s=1}^{p-1} a_{ns}^{(p+1)} f_{ns}^{(p+1)} + \sum_{r=2}^{p-1} \sum_{s=1}^{r-1} a_{rs}^{(p+1)} f_{rs}^{(p+1)} + \sum_{s=1}^{p-1} a_{ps}^{(p+1)} f_{ps}^{(p+1)} \tag{75}$$

with regions of subsequent integration:

for $f_{ns}^{(p+1)} : \ell_{p+1,s} < 0;$

for $f_{rs}^{(p+1)} : \{\ell_{p+1,r} > 0, \quad \ell_{p+1,s} < 0\} \quad (r \le p-1);$

for $f_{ps}^{(p+1)} : \ell_{p+1,s} < 0, \quad s = 1, \ldots, p-1.$

In general, after integrating out x_{k-1}, with $p < k-1 < n-1$, we shall have an expression of the form:

$$\sum_{s=1}^{p-1} a_{ns}^{(k)} f_{ns}^{(k)} + \sum_{r=2}^{p-1} \sum_{s=1}^{r-1} a_{rs}^{(k)} f_{rs}^{(k)} + \sum_{r=p}^{k-1} \sum_{s=1}^{p-1} a_{rs}^{(k)} f_{rs}^{(k)} \tag{76}$$

with regions of subsequent integration:

for $f_{ns}^{(k)} : \ell_{ks} < 0, \quad s = 1, \ldots, p-1;$

for $f_{rs}^{(k)} : \ell_{kr} > 0, \quad \ell_{ks} < 0, \quad r = 2, \ldots, p-1, \quad s = 1, \ldots, r-1;$

for $f_{rs}^{(k)} : \ell_{ks} < 0, \quad r = p, \ldots, n-2, \quad s = 1, \ldots, p-1.$

Integration of (76) with respect to x_k then yields (apart from the factor λ_0^{-1}):

$$\sum_{s=1}^{p-1}[a_{ns}^{(k)}/d_{nsk}]\{f_{ns}^{(k+1)} - f_{ks}^{(k+1)}\}$$

$$+\sum_{r=2}^{p-1}\sum_{s=1}^{r-1}[a_{rs}^{(k)}/d_{rsk}]\{f_{rs}^{(k+1)} + f_{kr}^{(k+1)} - f_{ks}^{(k+1)}\}$$

$$+\sum_{r=p}^{k-1}\sum_{s=1}^{p-1}[a_{rs}^{(k)}/d_{rsk}]\{f_{rs}^{(k+1)} - f_{ks}^{(k+1)}\}. \tag{77}$$

Identifying this with the analogue of (76) with $k-1$ replaced by k:

$$\sum_{s=1}^{p-1} a_{ns}^{(k+1)}f_{ns}^{(k+1)} + \sum_{r=2}^{p-1}\sum_{s=1}^{r-1} a_{rs}^{(k+1)}f_{rs}^{(k+1)} + \sum_{r=p}^{k}\sum_{s=1}^{p-1} a_{rs}^{(k+1)}f_{rs}^{(k+1)}, \tag{78}$$

the only additional terms are the $p-1$ terms $f_{ks}^{(k+1)}$, $s = 1,\ldots,p-1$.

Comparison of (77) with (78) yields the recursive relations for the coefficients for terms beyond the p'th, but with $k < n-1$:

$$a_{ns}^{(k+1)} = a_{ns}^{(k)}/d_{nsk}, \quad s = 1,\ldots,p-1; \tag{79}$$

$$a_{rs}^{(k+1)} = a_{rs}^{(k)}/d_{rsk}, \quad r = 2,\ldots,p-1, \quad s = 1,\ldots,r-1; \tag{80}$$

$$a_{rs}^{(k+1)} = a_{rs}^{(k)}/d_{rsk}, \quad r = p,\ldots,k-1, \quad s = 1,\ldots,p-1; \tag{81}$$

$$a_{k1}^{(k+1)} = -a_{k1}^{(k)}/d_{n1k} - \sum_{r=2}^{p-1}[a_{r1}^{(k)}/d_{r1k}],$$

$$a_{kj}^{(k+1)} = -a_{kj}^{(k)}/d_{njk} - \sum_{r=j+1}^{p-1}[a_{rj}^{(k)}/d_{rjk}]$$

$$+\sum_{s=1}^{j-1}[a_{js}^{(k)}/d_{jsk}], \quad j = 2,\ldots,p-2$$

$$a_{k,p-1}^{(k+1)} = -a_{k,p-1}^{(k)}/d_{n,p-1,k} + \sum_{s=1}^{p-2}[a_{p-1,s}^{(k)}/d_{p-1,s,k}],$$

$$a_{ks}^{(k+1)} = 0, \quad s > p-1. \tag{82}$$

Note that each integration with respect to an x_k, with $k > p-1$, adds only $p-1$ terms to the sum, not k.

Consider now the integral with respect to the last variable, x_{n-1}. We assume that $p < n-2$; slight modifications of what follows are needed in the cases $p = n - 1$ or $p = n$, but since these cases are unlikely in practice we omit those details. We need to integrate (78) (with k replaced by $n - 2$) with respect to x_{n-1}. For the terms $f_{ns}^{(n-1)}$ the range of integration is $\ell_{n-1,s} < 0$, or $nb_s + x_{n-1}b_{n-1,s} < 0$, so that

$$x_{n-1} < -nb_s/b_{n-1,s}, \quad s = 1, \ldots, p - 1.$$

Hence, integration of these terms with respect to x_{n-1} yields the sum:

$$\lambda_0^{-1} \sum_{s=1}^{p-1} [a_{ns}^{(n-1)}/d_{ns,n-1}]\{f_{ns} - f_{n-1,s}\}, \tag{83}$$

where here and below we set $f_{rs} = \exp\{-n\lambda_0 g_{rs}\}$.

For the second sum in (78), the inequalities $\ell_{n-1,r} > 0$ and $\ell_{n-1,s} > 0$ give $x_{n-1} < -nb_r/b_{n-1,r}$ and $x_{n-1} > -nb_s/b_{n-1,s}$. The difference between the upper and lower limits here is a positive multiple of b_{n-1}, and is thus positive unless $p = n$, which we rule out. Since the lower limit is certainly positive (because $b_s < 0$ when $s < p - 1$), integration with respect to x_{n-1} yields:

$$\lambda_0^{-1} \sum_{r=2}^{p-1} \sum_{s=1}^{r-1} [a_{rs}^{(n-1)}/d_{rs,n-1}]\{f_{n-1,r} - f_{n-1,s}\}. \tag{84}$$

Note particularly that (84) yields no terms f_{rs} with $r < p$.

Finally, the third sum in (78) yields

$$\lambda_0^{-1} \sum_{r=p}^{n-2} \sum_{s=1}^{p-1} [a_{rs}^{(n-1)}/d_{rs,n-1}]\{f_{rs} - f_{n-1,s}\}. \tag{85}$$

Hence, after integrating out the final variable x_{n-1}, we shall have a linear combination of $(n - p + 1)(p - 1)$ terms:

$$f_{rs} = \exp\{-n\lambda_0 g_{rs}\}, \quad r = p, \ldots, n, \quad s = 1, \ldots, p - 1. \tag{86}$$

If we write this linear combination in the form:

$$\sum_{r=p}^{n} \sum_{s=1}^{p-1} a_{rs} f_{rs}, \tag{87}$$

equations (79)–(85) yield the relations between the a_{rs} and the $a_{rs}^{(n-1)}$:

$$a_{rs} = a_{rs}^{(n-1)}/d_{rs,n-1}, \quad r = p, \ldots, n - 2, \quad s = 1, \ldots, p - 1; \tag{88}$$

$$a_{n-1,1} = -a_{n1}^{(n-1)}/d_{n1,n-1} - \sum_{r=2}^{n-2} [a_{r1}^{(n-1)}/d_{r1,n-1}]; \tag{89}$$

$$a_{n-1,s} = -a_{ns}^{(n-1)}/d_{ns,n-1} + \sum_{j=1}^{s-1}[a_{sj}^{(n-1)}/d_{sj,n-1}]$$

$$- \sum_{r=s+1}^{n-2}[a_{rs}^{(n-1)}/d_{rs,n-1}], \quad s = 2, \ldots, p-1; \tag{90}$$

$$a_{ns} = a_{ns}^{(n-1)}/d_{ns,n-1}, \quad s = 1, \ldots, p-1. \tag{91}$$

As in the single-parameter case, these recursive relations can be expressed in terms of a product of matrices of increasing dimension. To do so, first assume that $k < p$, and let c_k be the $[k(k+1)/2] \times 1$ vector of coefficients of the $f_{rs}^{(k+1)}$ after integrating out x_k, with an analogous definition of c_{k-1} (which, of course, is $[k(k-1)/2] \times 1$). Assume that the elements of c_k are arranged in lexicographic order, i.e. in the order (for $k < p$):

$$((21), (31), (32), \ldots, (k1), (k2), \ldots, (k, k-1), (n1), \ldots, (nk)).$$

In the case $k \geq p$, only pairs (rs) with $s \leq p - 1$ occur. In the transition from c_{k-1} to c_k ($k < p$) the terms $((k1), \ldots, (k, k-1))$ and (nk) are added. Let L_k denote the $[k(k+1)/2] \times [k(k-1)/2]$ matrix that takes c_{k-1} to $c_k : c_k = L_k c_{k-1}$. From the results in (67)–(70), the structure of the matrix L_k, for $k < p$, is as follows:

$$L_k = \begin{bmatrix} L_{k11} & 0 \\ L_{k21} & L_{k22} \\ 0 & L_{k32} \\ 0 & L_{k42} \end{bmatrix}, \tag{92}$$

where

$$L_{k11} = \text{diag}\{d_{21k}^{-1}, d_{31k}^{-1}, d_{32k}^{-1}, \ldots, d_{k-1,1k}^{-1}, \ldots, d_{k-1,k-2,k}^{-1}\} \tag{93}$$

is a $[(k-1)(k-2)/2] \times [(k-1)(k-2)/2]$ diagonal matrix,

$$L_{k32} = \text{diag}\{d_{n1k}^{-1}, \ldots, d_{n,k-1,k}^{-1}\} \tag{94}$$

is a $(k-1) \times (k-1)$ diagonal matrix, $L_{k22} = -L_{k32}$,

$$L_{k42} = (-d_{n1k}^{-1}, \ldots, -d_{n,k-1,k}^{-1}) \tag{95}$$

is a $1 \times (k-1)$ vector, and L_{k21} is a $(k-1) \times [(k-1)(k-2)/2]$ matrix with the following structure:

for $j = 1, \ldots, (k - 1)$, the non-zero elements in row j are, in their lexicographic positions, the terms $-d_{rjk}^{-1}$ for $r > j$, and the terms d_{jsk}^{-1} for $s = 1, \ldots, j - 1$.

Row 3, for instance, is:

$$\{0, d_{31k}^{-1}, d_{32k}^{-1}, 0, 0, -d_{43k}^{-1}, 0, 0, -d_{53k}^{-1}, \ldots, -d_{k-1,3,k}^{-1}, 0, \ldots, 0\}.$$

For $p \leq k < n - 1$ the following modifications to L_k must be made: (1) the last row is absent; (2) $L_{k32} = \text{diag}\{d_{n1k}^{-1}, \ldots, d_{n,p-1,k}^{-1}\}$ is $(p - 1) \times (p - 1)$, and hence so is $L_{k22} = -L_{k32}$; (3) in L_{k11}, the diagonal terms d_{rsk}^{-1} for $r > p$ appear only for $s = 1, \ldots, (p - 1)$, so that L_{k11} is square of dimension $[p(p - 1)/2 + (k - p)(p - 1)]$, and, correspondingly, (4) L_{k21} is now $(p - 1) \times [p(p - 1)/2 + (k - p)(p - 1)]$, with the same structure as above except that the d_{rsk}^{-1} that occur are for $r = 1, \ldots, (p - 1)$ only. Hence, for $p \leq k < n - 1$, L_k is

$$[p(p - 1)/2 + (k - p + 1)(p - 1)] \times [p(p - 1)/2 + (k - p + 2)(p - 1)].$$

Finally, the matrix L_{n-1} is $[(n - p + 1)(p - 1)] \times [(n - p)(p - 1) + p(p - 1)/2]$ with the following structure:

$$L_n = \begin{bmatrix} L_{n-1,11} & 0 \\ L_{n-1,21} & L_{n-1,22} \\ 0 & L_{n-1,32} \end{bmatrix}$$

where $L_{n-1,32} = \text{diag}\{d_{ns,n-1}^{-1}; \ s = 1, \ldots, p - 1\}$ is $(p - 1) \times (p - 1)$, $L_{n-1,22} = -L_{n-1,32}$, $L_{n-1,21}$ is $(p - 1) \times [(n - p - 1)(p - 1) + p(p - 1)/2]$ with the same structure as in the case $p \leq k < n - 1$ above, and $L_{n-1,11}$ is $(n - p - 1)(p - 1) \times [(n - p - 1)(p - 1) + p(p - 1)/2]$ with the form:

$$L_{n-1,11} = [0, \text{diag}\{d_{rs,n-1}^{-1}; \quad r = p, \ldots, n - 2, \ s = 1, \ldots, p - 1\}],$$

where the initial block of zeros is $(n - p - 1)(p - 1) \times [(p - 1)(p - 2)/2]$.

The final vector c_{n-1}, of dimension $[(n - p + 1)(p - 1)] \times 1$, is then given by the recursive formula:

$$c_{n-1} = L_{n-1}L_{n-2} \ldots L_2, \tag{96}$$

starting with

$$L_2 = d_{n12}^{-1} \begin{pmatrix} -1 \\ +1 \\ -1 \end{pmatrix} \tag{97}$$

(see (54) above). Letting f_{n-1} denote the vector of functions

$$f_{rs} = \exp\{-n\lambda_0[b_r a_s - b_s a_r]/b_{rs}\},$$

ordered lexicographically as above, we have:

$$pdf_{A,T}(a, t; \alpha, \theta) = (n\lambda_0 b_{n1}^{-1}) \exp\{n\bar{z}(t - \theta)\}(\partial/\partial w)$$

$$\times [\exp\{-n\lambda_0 w\bar{z}^2\}c'_{n-1} f_{n-1}]_{w=0}.$$

It remains now to evaluate the differential operator, and set $w = 0$. The results are exactly analogous to those for the single-parameter case given earlier. First we define

$$\tilde{c}_{n-1} = c_{n-1}|_{w=0} = \tilde{L}_{n-1}\tilde{L}_{n-2}\ldots\tilde{L}_2, \tag{98}$$

where the $\tilde{L}_p$ are defined exactly as the L_p are defined above, but with d_{ijk} replaced by

$$\tilde{d}_{ijk} = [b_{ij}r_k - b_{kj}r_i - b_{ik}r_j]/b_{ij}. \tag{99}$$

Before proceeding we note that, at the point $t = \theta, r_i = 1$ for all i, and $\tilde{d}_{ijk} = 0$, so that the $\tilde{L}_r$ are not defined at $t = \theta$. The results that follow therefore hold everywhere except at $t = \theta$. At the point $t = \theta$ we have, directly from (23),

$$pdf_{A,T}(a, t = \theta; \alpha, \theta) = \lambda_0^n \exp\{-n\lambda_0\} \times c_n(z), \tag{100}$$

where $c_n(z)$ is a constant. (100) follows from (23) when $t = \theta$ because, in the integrand of (23), the exponential term becomes

$$\exp\left\{-\lambda_0 \sum_{i=1}^{n} x_i\right\} = \exp\{-n\lambda_0\}$$

on S (since, on S, $\sum_{i=1}^{n} x_i = n$). The integral is then a function only of $z = (z_1, \ldots, z_n)'$ and n. Since (100) is proportional to the conditional density of A given that $T = \theta$, which must integrate to one, we also obtain an expression for the density of T at $t = \theta$:

$$pdf_T(t = \theta; \theta) = n^{-n}\Gamma(n)c_n(z). \tag{101}$$

The constant $c_n(z)$ in (100) and (101) can be evaluated by methods like those above, but we omit these details.

Next, let $\tilde{f}_{n-1}$ be defined as f_{n-1}, which has been defined above, but with the f_{rs} replaced by

$$\tilde{f}_{rs} = \exp\{-n\lambda_0[b_r r_s - b_s r_r]/b_{rs}\}, \tag{102}$$

and define $\tilde{f}^*_{n-1}$ to be the vector with elements

$$(\partial/\partial w)[\exp\{-n\lambda_0 w\bar{z}^2\}f_{rs}]\,|_{w=0} = -n\lambda_0 b_r b_s \tilde{f}_{rs}. \tag{103}$$

As before,

$$\partial c_{n-1}/\partial w \mid_{w=0} = \sum_{i=1}^{n-2} [\tilde{L}_{n-1} \ldots \tilde{L}^*_{n-i+1} \ldots \tilde{L}_2] = \tilde{c}^*_{n-1}, \text{say}, \qquad (104)$$

where $\tilde{L}^*_p$ is again defined as L_p is defined above but with d_{ijk}^{-1} replaced by

$$[b_{ij}z_k^2 - b_{kj}z_i^2 - b_{ik}z_j^2]/[b_{ij}\tilde{d}_{ijk}^2] = b_{ki}b_{kj}/\tilde{d}_{ijk}^2. \qquad (105)$$

Combining these results, we have a relatively simple expression for the density of (A, T):

$$pdf_{A,T}(a, t; \alpha, \theta) = \exp\{n\bar{z}(t - \theta)\}(n\lambda_0 b_{n1}^{-1})[\tilde{c}^{*\prime}_{n-1}\tilde{f}_{n-1} + \tilde{c}^{\prime}_{n-1}\tilde{f}^*_{n-1}]. \qquad (106)$$

4.1   The marginal density of T

Remarkably, it is straightforward to integrate out a in (106) to obtain the marginal density of T, because the two terms in the [·] in (106) are linear combinations of terms $\exp\{-n\lambda_0 g_{rs}\}$ and $(-nb_r b_s \lambda_0)\exp\{-n\lambda_0 g_{rs}\}$, respectively, with coefficients that do not depend on a. Transforming from $(a - \alpha)$ to $\lambda_0 = \exp\{(a - \alpha)\} > 0$, and integrating out λ_0 we obtain:

$$pdf_T(t; \theta) = \exp\{n\bar{z}(t - \theta)\}b_{n1}^{-1}[\tilde{c}^{*\prime}_{n-1}h_{n-1} + \tilde{c}^{\prime}_{n-1}h^*_{n-1}], \qquad (107)$$

where h_{n-1} has elements g_{rs}^{-1}, and h^*_{n-1} has elements $-b_r b_s g_{rs}^{-2}$. Again, the density is defined by (107) at all points other than $t = \theta$. At $t = \theta$ expression (101) must be used.

5   Properties of the exact densities

Because the coefficients in the exact expressions (22), (106) and (107) are generated recursively it is difficult to study the properties of the densities analytically. However, given a choice for the vector z, it is straightforward to analyse the densities numerically, although in the two-parameter case we did have some difficulty with the numerical stability of the calculations near $t = \theta$ (see below).

5.1   Properties in the case $k = 1$

From the remarks in section 2, the density depends only on $d = (t - \theta)$, has its mode at $t = \theta$, and the density at d when $z > 0$ is the density at $-d$ with $z < 0$, so that the density with negative z's is simply the density with positive z's reflected about the origin.

Table 3.1. *Means, variances and skewness for figure 3.1*

n	Mean	Variance	Skewness
2	−0.429	1.386	−0.841
4	−0.315	1.216	−0.628
8	−0.227	1.114	−0.454
16	−0.161	1.058	−0.323

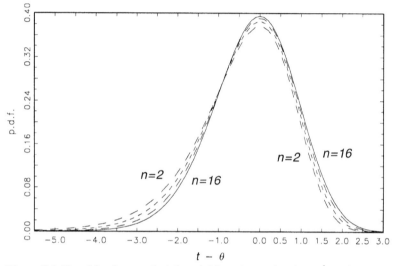

Figure 3.1 Densities for $n = 2, 4, 8$ and 16 equispaced points $z'z = 1$

It also follows from the remarks in section 2 that there is no loss of generality in scaling the z_i's so that $z'z$, the (expected) Fisher information for θ, is unity, corresponding to an asymptotic variance of one. Figure 3.1 shows the density, calculated from equation (22), for the case of equi-spaced positive z's, scaled so that $z'z = 1$, for the cases $n = 2, 4, 8$ and 16. Different patterns of z's produce little change in the graphs. In table 3.1 we give the means, variances and skewness for the cases that appear in figure 3.1 (calculated by numerical integration).

Both figure 3.1 and table 3.1 suggest that the approach to the asymptotic distribution of the MLE is quite rapid, that (with positive z's) the estimator is slightly negatively biased, and that the asymptotic variance (= 1 in this example) slightly understates the true variance.

5.2   Properties for the model with a constant term

In view of the remarks in section 2, the joint density has its mode at the point $(a, t) = (\alpha, \theta)$. Further properties must be derived from the formulae above.

Consider first the case $n = 3$. In this case no recursion is needed, and we have directly from (54):

$$pdf_{A,T}(a, t; \alpha, \theta) = \exp\{3(t - \theta)\bar{z} - 3\lambda_0\tilde{g}_{31}\}[3\lambda_0 b_{31}^{-1}]$$

$$\times [-b_{21}b_{32}\phi_2(\tilde{d}_{312}) - \lambda_0 b_1 b_3 \phi_1(\tilde{d}_{312})] \qquad (108)$$

where

$$\phi_1(y) = [1 - e^{-yy}]/y, \qquad (109)$$

and

$$\phi_2(y) = [1 - (1 + \gamma y)e^{-yy}]/y^2, \qquad (110)$$

with $\gamma = n\lambda_0 b_3/b_{32}$ if $p = 3$ and $\gamma = -n\lambda_0 b_1/b_{21}$ if $p = 2$. Note that (108) is well defined for all (a, t), including $t = \theta$, since both ϕ_1 and ϕ_2 in fact do not involve negative powers of $\tilde{d}_{312}$.

The marginal density of T is readily obtained from (108) by direct integration, giving:

$$pdf_T(t; \theta) = \exp\{3(t - \theta)\bar{z}\}b_{31}^{-1}$$

$$\times [-\beta^2 b_{21}b_{32}\tilde{g}_{31} - b_1 b_3 \beta(6\tilde{g}_{31}$$

$$+ \beta\tilde{d}_{312})]/[\tilde{g}_{31}^2(3\tilde{g}_{31} + \beta\tilde{d}_{312})], \qquad (111)$$

where now $\beta = \gamma/\lambda_0$. The marginal density of A does not seem to be obtainable analytically from (108), but is easily obtained from the joint density by numerical integration.

Figure 3.2 presents three cases of the marginal density of t in (111) corresponding to vectors $z' = [-1, -0.9, 1]$, $[-1, 0, 1]$, and $[-1, 0.9, 1]$ that were subsequently standardised to have $\bar{z} = 0$ and $\sum z_i^2 = 1$ (so that the asymptotic covariance matrix of $[\sqrt{n}(a - \alpha), (t - \theta)]$ is an identity matrix). The first and third cases, of course, are identical except for reflection about the origin. Even for such a small sample size, figure 3.2 reveals that the density is quite concentrated around zero, showing slight skewness (depending on the pattern of the z's). Table 3.2 presents some properties of the marginal densities for the case $n = 3$, and the two (unstandardised) z-vectors (a) $[-1, -0.9, 1]$, (b) $[1, 0, 1]$.

Figure 3.3 shows the joint density $pdf_{A,T}(a, t; \alpha, \theta; z)$ for case (b). The marginal density of A, $pdf_A(a; \alpha; z)$, can be obtained by numerical

Table 3.2. *Properties of the marginal densities: n = 3*

	$pdf_T(t; \theta)$		$pdf_A(a; \alpha)$	
Case	(a)	(b)	(a)	(b)
Mean	−0.25	0.0	−0.64	−0.62
Variance	1.53	1.65	1.39	1.38
Skewness	−0.56	0.0	−0.61	−0.62
Kurtosis	4.22	4.15	3.64	3.68
Correlation	−0.03	0.03	−0.03	0.03

(a) $z' = [-1, -0.9, 1]$; (b) $z' = [1, 0, 1]$.

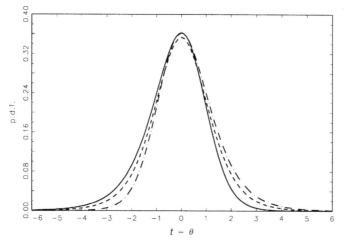

Figure 3.2 Marginal densities for $t - \theta, n = 3$

integration, and is shown for all three cases in figure 3.4 (although cases (a) and (c) are exactly superimposed). It does not exhibit the mirror symmetry of $pdf_T(t; \theta; z)$, being always negatively skewed. The density for (b) lies slightly to the right. The density of A has variance and kurtosis closer to the asymptotic values than those for T, but the mean and skewness are further from their asymptotic values. The correlation between A and T is negative for case (a), and positive for cases (b) and (c), which is the mirror image of (a). Given the small sample size, the results look well behaved.

For $n = 4$, the marginal density of T is symmetric if the data are symmetric about its mean (e.g. $z' = [0.1, 0.2, 0.3, 0.4]$), and positively skewed z's (e.g. $z' = [0.1, 0.26, 0.33, 0.4]$) give the mirror image of the

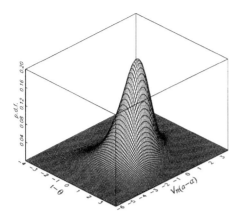

Figure 3.3 Joint density for $t - \theta$, $a - \alpha$, $n = 3$

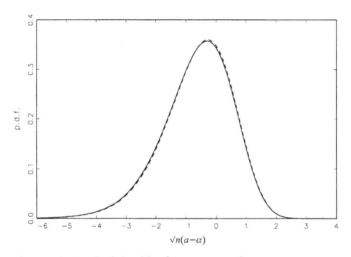

Figure 3.4 Marginal densities for $a - \alpha$, $n = 3$

density with negatively skewed z's (e.g. $z' = [0.1, 0.17, 0.24, 0.4]$).
Accordingly we can illustrate almost the full range of behaviour by
using the symmetric z above, and the negatively skewed case
$z' = [0.1, 0.11, 0.12, 0.4]$. Table 3.3 shows the resulting moments in its
first two columns. For $n = 5$, the cases $z' = [0.1, 0.2, 0.29, 0.4, 0.5]$,
which gives the mirror image of the results with z_3 changed to 0.31,
and $z' = [0.1, 0.11, 0.12, 0.13, 0.5]$, are illustrated in columns 3 and 4 of
table 3.3. The z-vectors given for table 3.3 (and elsewhere) are in their
unstandardised form. Progress towards limiting normality is masked by
the possibility of greater skewness for $n = 5$ observations than for $n = 4$.

Table 3.3. *Moments of the marginal density of* T

	$n = 4$		$n = 5$	
	(a)	(b)	(a)	(b)
Mean	0.00	−0.329	−0.016	−0.393
Variance	1.43	1.45	1.40	1.55
Skewness	0.00	−0.56	−0.05	−0.77
Kurtosis	3.48	3.58	3.71	4.22

For $n = 4$: (a) $z' = [0.1, 0.2, 0.3, 0.4]$, (b) $z' = [0.1, 0.11, 0.12, 0.4]$
For $n = 5$: (a) $z' = [0.1, 0.2, 0.29, 0.4, 0.5]$, (b) $z' = [0.1, 0.11, 0.12, 0.13, 0.5]$

Table 3.4. *Marginal density of* T. *Tail areas:* n = 5 *and* n = 10

Nominal tail area	lower%	upper%	sum%	$n = 10$, sum%
10	14.4	2.3	16.7	17.2
5	10.4	0.9	11.3	12.0
1	7.0	0.3	7.3	8.7

$n = 5$: $z' = [0.1, 0.11, 0.12, 0.13, 0.5]$
$n = 10$: $z' = [0.1, 0.11, 0.12, 0.13, 0.14, 0.15, 0.16, 0.17, 0.18, 1.0]$

Because of the numerical instability of the calculations near $t = \theta$, and because the cases above for small n suggest reasonably rapid convergence to the asymptotic distribution, we now concentrate on the tail area of the densities. Table 3.4 gives the exact tail area in the marginal density of T (obtained by numerical integration) for $n = 5$ and $n = 10$, and for three nominal (i.e. asymptotic) levels.

If one chooses z in this way, so that, for example, when $n = 10$, all the observations except the largest are crowded together at the lower end of the range, the skewness increases, and this acts against the effect of increasing n, to leave the tail areas more or less unchanged over the range $n = 5, \ldots, 10$, as the last column of table 3.4 illustrates. However, for uniformly distributed z's, for example

$$z' = [0.1, 0.2, 0.3, 0.4, 0.5, 0.6, 0.7, 0.8, 0.9, 1.0],$$

the distribution is symmetric, the tail probabilities are equal, and are given in table 3.5. There is evidently steady progress towards the nominal values as n increases, slightly slower the further one is into the tails. For larger values of n the computational difficulties mentioned above have so

Table 3.5. *Marginal density of* T. *Tail area (uniformly distributed z's); combined tails*

Nominal %	1	5	10
$n = 6$	4.7	8.7	14.3
$n = 8$	4.0	7.8	13.3
$n = 10$	3.6	7.3	12.7
$n = 12$	3.3	6.9	12.3

far prevented us from carrying out a more detailed analysis of the densities.

6   Conclusion

We have shown that the surface integral formula for the exact density of the MLE given by Hillier and Armstrong (1996) provides a tractable expression for the exact density in the case of an exponential regression model with a k-covariate exponential mean function, at least for small values of k. It seems clear that an algorithm could, in principle, be written to provide similar results for arbitrary k.

The discussion in section 2 also shows that, even for arbitrary k, the general formula can, by itself, provide considerable information about the properties of the exact density. It is also worth noting that the general approach used here extends easily to more general specifications for the mean function (i.e. non-exponential functions of the w_i), provided only that the level set of the MLE is known. It will remain true for more general models that the surface integral that needs to be evaluated is over an $(n - k)$-dimensional hyperplane.

Finally, as far as the results for the specific model under consideration are concerned, our main conclusion is that the exact densities are well behaved and well approximated by the asymptotic densities, even for quite small sample sizes. The sample behaviour of the covariates certainly has an impact on the properties of the estimator, as one would expect, but this effect is not dramatic.

References

Hillier, G.H. and M. Armstrong (1996), 'On the Density of the Maximum Likelihood Estimator', University of Southampton Discussion Papers in Economics and Econometrics No. 9645; also in *Econometrica*, 67 (6), 1999: 1459–1470.

Huber, P.J. (1964), 'Robust Estimation of a Location Parameter', *Annals of Mathematical Statistics*, 35: 73–101.

Knight, J.L. and S.E. Satchell (1996), 'The Exact Distribution of the Maximum Likelihood Estimator for the Linear-regression Negative-exponential Model', *Journal of Statistical Planning and Inference*, 1: 91–102.

Schechter, M. (1998), 'Integration over a Polyhedron: An Application of the Fourier–Motzkin Elimination Method', *American Mathematical Monthly*, 105: 246–251.

Shephard, N. (1993), 'Distribution of the ML Estimator of the MA(1) and a Local Level Model', *Econometric Theory*, 9: 377–401.

4   Empirical likelihood estimation and inference

Richard J. Smith

1   Introduction

Since Hansen's (1982) seminal paper, the *generalised method of moments* (GMM) has become an increasingly important method of estimation in econometrics. Given assumed population moment conditions, the GMM estimation method minimises a quadratic form in the sample counterparts of these moment conditions. The quadratic form is constructed using a positive definite metric. If this metric is chosen as the inverse of a positive semi-definite consistent estimator for the asymptotic variance matrix of the sample moments, then the resultant GMM estimator is asymptotically efficient. Estimation using GMM is *semi-parametric* and, therefore, a particular advantage of GMM is that it imposes less stringent assumptions than, for example, the method of *maximum likelihood* (ML). Although consequently more robust, GMM is of course generally less efficient than ML. There is some Monte Carlo evidence indicating that GMM estimation may be biased in small samples where the bias seems to arise mainly from the metric used. For example, Altonji and Segal (1996) suggest that GMM estimators using an identity matrix metric may perform better in finite samples than an efficient GMM estimator obtained using the inverse of the estimated asymptotic variance matrix of the sample moments.[1]

When the variables of interest in the data-generation process (DGP) are independent and identically distributed, an important recent paper (Qin and Lawless (1994)) shows that it is possible to embed the components of the sample moments used in GMM estimation in a *non-parametric* likelihood function; namely, an *empirical likelihood* (EL)

---

[1] See also the special issue of *Journal of Business and Economic Statistics* (1996), vol. 14, no. 3, for further evidence on the finite sample performance of GMM estimators and test statistics.

framework. The resultant *maximum* EL estimator (MELE) shares the same first-order properties as Hansen's (1982) efficient GMM estimator. Hence, the EL framework provides the possibility of using classical-type methods to examine hypotheses for the parameters of interest. See DiCiccio, Hall and Romano (1989) and Owen (1988, 1990, 1991) for a discussion of the method of EL. Qin and Lawless (1994) also discuss some simulation evidence that indicates that the MELE may represent an improvement over the efficient GMM estimator. In the light of Qin and Lawless's (1994) and Altonji and Segal's (1996) Monte Carlo evidence, the EL method offers a potentially useful alternative and asymptotically first-order equivalent approach to GMM estimation.

Empirical likelihood appears to have been largely ignored by econometricians. A relevant related paper is that of Back and Brown (1993), which, however, does not make explicit reference to the literature on EL. More recently, Imbens (1997) proposes the use of an estimator, which is essentially the MELE of Qin and Lawless (1994) and associated test statistics. Imbens, Spady and Johnson (1998) use an information-theoretic approach also for the independently and identically distributed case and suggest an estimator and test statistics which are also asymptotically first-order equivalent to those based on EL (Qin and Lawless (1994)) and GMM (Hansen (1982)).

However, the application of EL and related information-theoretic approaches to time-series DGPs is relatively limited. A notable exception is Kitamura and Stutzer (1997), which uses an approach based on an empirical Kullback–Leibler information criterion that yields estimators first-order equivalent to efficient GMM estimation. Kitamura and Stutzer's (1997) information-theoretic estimation method specialises to that of Imbens, Spady and Johnson (1998) for independent and identically distributed DGPs. As will be seen below, for time-series DGPs, Kitamura and Stutzer's (1997) method and efficient GMM estimation are asymptotically equivalent to estimation based on a suitably smoothed EL function. Smith (1997), by adapting the approach of Chesher and Smith (1997) from the parametric context, introduces a class of semiparametric likelihood criteria which includes the criteria of EL, Kitamura and Stutzer (1997) and Imbens, Spady and Johnson (1998) as special cases.

The emphasis in the statistical literature, however, has tended to be on inference for the parameters of interest rather than issues of misspecification. A major concern of this chapter is to discuss *misspecification* test statistics based on EL criteria for moment conditions. These tests mimic the classical tests in an obvious way. A typical approach in the econometric literature to the construction of misspecification tests is based on using a quadratic form in estimated sample analogues of assumed or implicit population moment conditions, which is examined to ascertain whether or not the sample moments differ significantly from the corresponding theoretical moment conditions (see Newey (1985a, 1985b)). We show that a suitable test, which shares the asymptotic properties of its GMM counterpart, may be based on an *empirical likelihood ratio* (ELR) statistic.

Section 2 briefly reviews GMM estimation and introduces EL estimation in the context of time-series data. A modified EL estimation procedure is introduced that results in consistent and asymptotically efficient estimators. We also present an efficient estimator for the stationary distribution of the time-series DGP, which might prove useful in examining parametric distributional hypotheses. ELR and other classical-type tests for over-identifying moment conditions which have the requisite central chi-squared distribution are obtained in section 3, together with tests for additional moment and parametric restrictions. Section 4 discusses the application of the EL method to testing non-nested hypotheses. Various proofs are given in the Appendix.

2   Empirical likelihood estimation

2.1   Generalised method of moments estimation

Consider the strictly stationary process $\{x_t\}_{t=-\infty}^{\infty}$. Suppose there exists a unique value θ_0 of the p-vector of parameters θ which lies in a compact parameter space $\Theta \subseteq \mathcal{R}^p$ such that the following $r \geq p$ moment conditions hold:

$$E_\mu\{\mathbf{g}(\mathbf{x}_t; \theta_0)\} = \mathbf{0}, \quad t = 0, \pm 1, \ldots, \tag{1}$$

where $E_\mu\{.\}$ denotes expectation taken with respect to the true but unknown distribution or probability measure μ. For economy of notation but without loss of generality, we will deliberately suppress any dependence of the moment vector $\mathbf{g}(\mathbf{x}_t; \theta_0)$ on lagged values $\mathbf{x}_{t-s}$, $s = 1, 2, \ldots$, and current and lagged values of exogenous variables.

Given observations $\{\mathbf{x}_t\}_{t=1}^{T}$, the *optimal* GMM estimator (Hansen (1982)) $\hat{\theta}_T$ is defined by

$$\hat{\theta}_T \equiv \arg\min_{\theta \in \Theta} T^{-1} \sum_{t=1}^{T} \mathbf{g}(\mathbf{x}_t; \theta)' \hat{\mathbf{V}}_T^{-1} \sum_{t=1}^{T} \mathbf{g}(\mathbf{x}_t; \theta), \tag{2}$$

where $\hat{\mathbf{V}}_T$ is a positive semi-definite consistent estimator for the asymptotic variance matrix $\mathbf{V}$ of the random vector $T^{-1/2} \sum_{t=1}^{T} \mathbf{g}(\mathbf{x}_t; \theta_0)$ which is assumed to be positive definite; namely

$$\mathbf{V} \equiv \lim_{T \to \infty} \mathrm{Var} \left\{ T^{-1/2} \sum_{t=1}^{T} \mathbf{g}(\mathbf{x}_t; \theta_0) \right\}. \tag{3}$$

See *inter alia* Andrews (1991) and Newey and West (1987) for positive semi-definite consistent estimation of asymptotic variance matrices.

Under suitable conditions and (1), it may be shown that

$$T^{1/2}(\hat{\theta}_T - \theta_0) \Rightarrow N[\mathbf{0}, (\mathbf{G}'\mathbf{V}^{-1}\mathbf{G})^{-1}],$$

where '$\Rightarrow$' indicates *weak convergence*, $\mathbf{G} \equiv E_\mu\{\nabla_\theta' \mathbf{g}(\mathbf{x}; \theta_0)\}$, which is assumed to have full column rank, and $\nabla_\theta \equiv \partial/\partial\theta$; see Hansen (1982).

2.2   Empirical likelihood estimation

Define the space of probability measures

$$\mathcal{P}(\theta) = \{P : E_P\{\mathbf{g}(\mathbf{x}; \theta)\} = \mathbf{0}\},$$

where $E_P\{.\}$ denotes expectation taken with respect to the probability measure P, which is assumed absolutely continuous with respect to the measure μ. Consider obtaining the maximum likelihood estimator for $dP(\theta)/d\mu$; that is, maximise $E_\mu\{\ln[dP(\theta)/d\mu]\}$ subject to $E_P\{1\} = 1$ (namely, that P is a probability measure) and $E_P\{\mathbf{g}(\mathbf{x}; \theta)\} = \mathbf{0}$.[2] It is straightforward to show that the solution is given by $dP(\theta)/d\mu = [1 + \phi'\mathbf{g}(\mathbf{x}; \theta)]^{-1}$, where ϕ is a vector of Lagrange multipliers associated with the constraint $E_P\{\mathbf{g}(\mathbf{x}; \theta)\} = \mathbf{0}$. Consequently, it may be seen that $dP(\theta)/d\mu = 1$, that is, $P(\theta) = \mu$, if and only if $\phi = \mathbf{0}$. Moreover, given the uniqueness of θ_0 for $E_\mu\{\mathbf{g}(\mathbf{x}; \theta_0)\} = \mathbf{0}$, we have that $P(\theta_0) = \mu$. Note that dropping the constraint $E_P\{\mathbf{g}(\mathbf{x}; \theta)\} = \mathbf{0}$ results in $dP(\theta)/d\mu = 1$.

Given observations $\{\mathbf{x}_t\}_{t=1}^{T}$, the appropriate empirical counterparts to $dP(\theta)/d\mu$ and $d\mu$ are, respectively, $dP_t(\theta)/d\mu_t = [1 + \phi'\mathbf{g}(\mathbf{x}_t; \theta)]^{-1}$ and $d\mu_t = T^{-1}$, $t = 1, \ldots, T$. Therefore, $dP_t(\theta) = T^{-1}[1 + \phi'\mathbf{g}(\mathbf{x}_t; \theta)]^{-1}$, $t = 1, \ldots, T$. For $P_t(\theta)$, $t = 1, \ldots, T$, to define a probability measure we also require $dP_t(\theta) \geq 0$, $t = 1, \ldots, T$, and $\sum_{t=1}^{T} dP_t(\theta) = T^{-1} \sum_{t=1}^{T} [1 + \phi'\mathbf{g}(\mathbf{x}_t; \theta)]^{-1} = 1$. The empirical measures $\{dP_t(\theta)\}_{t=1}^{T}$ may then be used to construct a *semi-parametric* likelihood function for the observations $\{\mathbf{x}_t\}_{t=1}^{T}$. Hence, the log *empirical likelihood* (EL) criterion is given by

---

[2] In this exposition, we ignore the requirement that $dP(\theta)/d\mu \geq 0$.

$$-T \ln T - \sum_{t=1}^{T} \ln[1 + \phi' \mathbf{g}(\mathbf{x}_t; \theta)].$$

This and the above discussion suggest basing an estimation procedure for θ_0 by finding the saddle-point of the criterion $-T \ln T - \sum_{t=1}^{T} \ln[1 + \phi' \mathbf{g}(\mathbf{x}_t; \theta)]$ or, equivalently, the log EL criterion

$$Q_T(\theta, \phi) \equiv \sum_{t=1}^{T} \ln[1 + \phi' \mathbf{g}(\mathbf{x}_t; \theta)]. \tag{4}$$

Consequently, the estimated vector of Lagrange multipliers $\phi_T(\theta)$ associated with the constraint $T^{-1} \sum_{t=1}^{T} [1 + \phi' \mathbf{g}(\mathbf{x}_t; \theta)]^{-1} \mathbf{g}(\mathbf{x}_t; \theta) = \mathbf{0}$ for given θ is given by

$$\phi_T(\theta) = \arg\max_{\phi} Q_T(\theta, \phi),$$

and the corresponding maximum EL estimator (MELE) θ_T by

$$\theta_T = \arg\min_{\theta \in \Theta} \max_{\phi} Q_T(\theta, \phi). \tag{5}$$

Denote $\phi_T \equiv \phi_T(\theta_T)$.

Although the consistency of the saddle-point estimator ϕ_T and the MELE θ_T for $\mathbf{0}$ and θ_0 respectively may be shown by a similar method to the Proof of Lemma 1 given below, the MELE θ_T of (5) based on $Q_T(\theta, \phi)$ of (4) is in general inefficient relative to the GMM estimator $\hat{\theta}_T$ of (2); cf. the Proof of Theorem 1 below. See also Kitamura and Stutzer (1997). In particular, the MELE θ_T and Lagrange multiplier estimator ϕ_T are asymptotically correlated if the moment indicators $\{\mathbf{g}(\mathbf{x}_t; \theta_0)\}_{t=-\infty}^{\infty}$ are serially correlated. Consequently, there is additional information from the moment conditions, $E_\mu\{\mathbf{g}(\mathbf{x}_t; \theta_0)\} = \mathbf{0}$, $t = 0, \pm 1, \ldots$, which is currently ignored and which may usefully be exploited. However, when, for example, the DGP for $\{\mathbf{x}_t\}_{t=-\infty}^{\infty}$ is independently and identically distributed or $\{\mathbf{g}(\mathbf{x}_t; \theta_0)\}_{t=-\infty}^{\infty}$ is a martingale difference process, then θ_T is asymptotically relatively efficient; cf. *inter alia* Qin and Lawless (1994). In this case, θ_T and ϕ_T are asymptotically uncorrelated.

2.3   Efficient maximum empirical likelihood estimation

The inefficiency of the MELE θ_T of (5) relative to the GMM estimator $\hat{\theta}_T$ of (2) is caused by the log EL criterion function $Q_T(\theta, \phi)$ of (4) implicitly imposing an inefficient metric. In effect, $Q_T(\theta, \phi)$ of (4) ignores any serial correlation among the vectors $\{\mathbf{g}(\mathbf{x}_t; \theta)\}_{t=-\infty}^{\infty}$. In order to remedy this difficulty, consider the *smoothed* moment indicators

$$\mathbf{g}_{tT}^{\omega}(\theta) \equiv \sum_{s=-m(T)}^{m(T)} \omega(s; m(T))\mathbf{g}(\mathbf{x}_{t-s}; \theta),$$

with the weights $\{\omega(s; m(T))\}$ acting to take into account any serial correlation among the vectors $\{\mathbf{g}(\mathbf{x}_t; \theta)\}_{t=-\infty}^{\infty}$; cf. section 2.2. The weights $\{\omega(s; m(T))\}$ are chosen so that $\omega(s; m(T)) \geq 0$, $s = -m(T), \ldots, m(T)$, and $\sum_{s=-m(T)}^{m(T)} \omega(s; m(T)) = 1$. We define the lead and lag truncation parameter $m(T)$ such that $m(T) = o(T^{1/2})$; cf. Andrews (1991). Moreover, we choose the weights $\{\omega(s; m(T))\}$ such that $E_\mu\{\mathbf{g}_{tT}^{\omega}(\theta)\} = \mathbf{0} \Leftrightarrow E_\mu\{\mathbf{g}(\mathbf{x}_t; \theta)\} = \mathbf{0}$, $t = 0, \pm 1, \ldots$ Hence, we may reformulate the moment conditions (1) equivalently as

$$E_\mu\{\mathbf{g}_{tT}^{\omega}(\theta_0)\} = \mathbf{0}, \quad t = 0, \pm 1, \ldots \tag{6}$$

Kitamura and Stutzer (1997, equation (8), p. 865) propose the weights $\omega(s; m(T)) = 1/(2m(T) + 1)$, $s = -m(T), \ldots, m(T)$, which give rise to the Bartlett kernel in the estimation of the variance matrix $\mathbf{V}$ of (3); see below (10).

The smoothed log EL criterion function corresponding to the redefined moment conditions (6) is given by

$$\mathcal{R}_T(\theta, \phi) \equiv \sum_{t=1}^{T} \ln[1 + \phi' \mathbf{g}_{tT}^{\omega}(\theta)]. \tag{7}$$

The criterion $\mathcal{R}_T(\theta, \phi)$ of (7) may be thought of as being constructed by redefining the empirical measures $\{dP_t(\theta)\}_{t=1}^{T}$ as

$$\pi_t(\theta, \phi) \equiv T^{-1}[1 + \phi' \mathbf{g}_{tT}^{\omega}(\theta)]^{-1}, \quad t = 1, \ldots, T; \tag{8}$$

cf. section 2.2.[3] Note that it is necessary to ensure $\pi_t(\theta, \phi) \geq 0$, $t = 1, \ldots, T$, and $\sum_{t=1}^{T} \pi_t(\theta, \phi) = 1$.[4] Smoothing the moment indicators

---

[3] Consider the following optimisation problem: maximise with respect to $dP_t(\theta)$, $t = 1, \ldots, T$, the empirical likelihood $\sum_{t=1}^{T} \ln_t(\theta)$ subject to the restrictions $\sum_{t=1}^{T} dP_t(\theta) = 1$, $dP_t(\theta) \geq 0$, $t = 1, \ldots, T$, and the empirical moment condition

$$\sum_{t=1}^{T} dP_t(\theta)\mathbf{g}_{tT}^{\omega}(\theta) = \mathbf{0}.$$

Ignoring for presentational purposes the inequality constraints $dP_t(\theta) \geq 0$, $t = 1, \ldots, T$, the Lagrangean is

$$\sum_{t=1}^{T} \ln dP_t(\theta) + \phi' \sum_{t=1}^{T} dP_t(\theta)\mathbf{g}_{tT}^{\omega}(\theta) + \varphi \left(1 - \sum_{t=1}^{T} dP_t(\theta)\right).$$

It is straightforwardly shown that the solution is given by

$$dP_t(\theta) = T^{-1}[1 + \phi' \mathbf{g}_{tT}^{\omega}(\theta)], \quad t = 1, \ldots, T.$$

[4] Alternatively, the redefinition $\pi_t(\theta, \phi)/\sum_{t=1}^{T} \pi_t(\theta, \phi)$, $t = 1, \ldots, T$, guarantees summation to unity.

$\{\mathbf{g}(\mathbf{x}_t; \theta)\}_{t=1}^{T}$ using the weights $\{\omega(s; m(T))\}$ to take account of their potential serial correlation renders the implicit metric imposed by the smoothed log EL criterion of (7) equal to the required metric $\mathbf{V}$ of (3).

In a likewise manner to that of section 2.2, the Lagrange multiplier estimator $\hat{\phi}_T(\theta)$ for given θ is defined by

$$\hat{\phi}_T(\theta) \equiv \arg\max_{\phi} \mathcal{R}_T(\theta, \phi),$$

and the corresponding efficient maximum empirical likelihood estimator (EMELE) $\hat{\theta}_T$ by

$$\hat{\theta}_T \equiv \arg\min_{\theta \in \Theta} \max_{\phi} \mathcal{R}_T(\theta, \phi); \tag{9}$$

write $\hat{\phi}_T \equiv \hat{\phi}_T(\hat{\theta}_T).$[5] We have deliberately used the same notation $\hat{\theta}_T$ in (9) for the EMELE as that for the optimal GMM estimator of (2) because, as will be seen in Theorem 1 below, the EMELE (9), although not numerically identical, shares the same first-order asymptotic properties as the efficient GMM estimator of (2).

We may prove

Lemma 1 *(Consistency of the EMELE $\hat{\theta}_T$ and Lagrange multiplier estimator $\hat{\phi}_T$.) Under (1), the EMELE $\hat{\theta}_T$ of (9) is a consistent estimator for θ_0 and $\hat{\phi}_T \rightarrow^P \mathbf{0}$.*

Defining $\eta(T) \equiv \sum_{s=-m(T)}^{m(T)} \omega(s; m(T))^2$, we may prove the following theorem, which demonstrates the first-order equivalence of the EMELE $\hat{\theta}_T$ with the optimal GMM estimator of (2).

Theorem 1 *(Limit distribution of the EMELE $\hat{\theta}_T$ and Lagrange multiplier estimator $\hat{\phi}_T$.) Under (1),*

$$T^{1/2} \begin{pmatrix} \eta(T)\hat{\phi}_T \\ \hat{\theta}_T - \theta_0 \end{pmatrix}$$

$$\Rightarrow N\left(\begin{pmatrix} \mathbf{0} \\ \mathbf{0} \end{pmatrix}, \begin{pmatrix} \mathbf{V}^{-1} - \mathbf{V}^{-1}\mathbf{G}(\mathbf{G}'\mathbf{V}^{-1}\mathbf{G})^{-1}\mathbf{G}'\mathbf{V}^{-1} & \mathbf{0}' \\ \mathbf{0} & (\mathbf{G}'\mathbf{V}^{-1}\mathbf{G})^{-1} \end{pmatrix} \right).$$

---

[5] The empirical measures $\pi_t(\hat{\theta}_T, \hat{\phi}_T)$, $t = 1, \ldots, T$, may be regarded as *implied probabilities* for the stationary distribution of $\{\mathbf{x}_t\}_{t=-\infty}^{\infty}$ (see Back and Brown (1993)). See section 2.4.

From Theorem 1, we see that the Lagrange multiplier estimator $\hat{\phi}_T$ is asymptotically uncorrelated with the EMELE $\hat{\theta}_T$, which ensures that the moment conditions (1) are used efficiently in constructing the EMELE; see section 2.2.

In the course of the proof of Theorem 1, we require that

$$\mathbf{V}_T \equiv \sum_{s=-2m(T)}^{2m(T)} \omega^*(s; m(T))\mathbf{C}(s) \to^P \mathbf{V},$$

where the (infeasible) sample autocovariances $\mathbf{C}(s) \equiv T^{-1}\sum_{t=s+1}^{T} \mathbf{g}(\mathbf{x}_t; \theta_0)\times \mathbf{g}(\mathbf{x}_{t-s}; \theta_0)'$, $s \geq 0$, and $\mathbf{C}(-s) = \mathbf{C}(s)'$, $s = -2m(T), \ldots, 2m(T)$. The weights $\{\omega^*(s; m(T))\}$ obey the relations

$$\omega^*(s; m(T)) \equiv (1/\eta(T)) \sum_{r=-m(T)-s}^{m(T)} \omega(r+s; m(T))\omega(r; m(T)), s \leq 0;$$

$$\equiv (1/\eta(T)) \sum_{r=-m(T)}^{m(T)-s} \omega(r+s; m(T))\omega(r; m(T)), s \geq 0.$$

$$(10)$$

Note that $\omega^*(s; m(T)) \geq 0$, $\omega^*(0; m(T)) = 1$ and $\omega^*(s; m(T)) = \omega^*(-s; m(T))$, $s = -2m(T), \ldots, 2m(T)$. Moreover, we require that the boundedness condition of Andrews (1991, (2.6), p. 821) $\lim_{T\to\infty}\sum_{s=-2m(T)}^{2m(T)} \omega^*(s; m(T))^2 < \infty$ is satisfied. Hence, the weights $\{\omega(s; m(T))\}$ give rise to the (infeasible) positive semi-definite consistent estimator $\mathbf{V}_T$ for $\mathbf{V}$. A particular example of the sequence of weights $\{\omega(s; m(T))\}$ is the flat kernel defined by $\omega(s; m(T)) = 1/(2m(T)+1)$, $s = -m(T), \ldots, m(T)$, which results in the Bartlett-type kernel $\omega^*(s; m(T)) = 1 - |s|/(2m(T)+1)$, $s = -2m(T), \ldots, 2m(T)$, with $\eta(T) = 1/(2m(T)+1)$; see Newey and West (1987) and Kitamura and Stutzer (1997, equation (8), p. 865). For other examples, see Andrews (1991).

A feasible positive semi-definite consistent estimator for $\mathbf{V}$ of (3) may therefore be defined as

$$\hat{\mathbf{V}}_T \equiv \sum_{s=-2m(T)}^{2m(T)} \omega^*(s; m(T))\hat{\mathbf{C}}(s), \tag{11}$$

$\hat{\mathbf{C}}(s) = T^{-1}\sum_{t=s+1}^{T} \mathbf{g}(\mathbf{x}_t; \hat{\theta}_T)\mathbf{g}(\mathbf{x}_{t-s}; \hat{\theta}_T)'$, $s \geq 0$, and $\hat{\mathbf{C}}(-s) = \hat{\mathbf{C}}(s)'$, $s = -2m(T), \ldots, 2m(T)$, and the weights $\{\omega^*(s; m(T))\}$ are defined in (10) above. Note that an alternative positive semi-definite consistent estimator to $\hat{\mathbf{V}}_T$ is output as minus $(T\eta(T))^{-1}$ times the (θ, θ) component of the Hessian of $\mathcal{R}_T(\theta, \phi)$ of (7) evaluated at $(\hat{\theta}_T, \hat{\phi}_T)$.

2.4 Efficient cumulative distribution function estimation

The information contained in the moment conditions $E_\mu\{\mathbf{g}(\mathbf{x}_t; \theta_0)\} = \mathbf{0}$, $t = 0, \pm 1, \ldots$, of (1) may be exploited to provide a more efficient estimator of the stationary distribution μ of the process $\{\mathbf{x}_t\}_{t=-\infty}^{\infty}$ than the empirical distribution function $\mu_T(\mathbf{x}) \equiv T^{-1} \sum_{t=1}^{T} 1(\mathbf{x}_t \leq \mathbf{x})$, where $1(.)$ denotes an indicator function, that is, $1(\mathbf{x}_t \leq \mathbf{x}) = 1$ if $\mathbf{x}_t \leq \mathbf{x}$, 0 otherwise, $t = 1, \ldots, T$. Consider the *empirical likelihood cumulative distribution function* (ELCDF) estimator based on the estimated probabilities $\pi_t(\hat{\theta}_T, \hat{\phi}_T)$, $t = 1, \ldots, T$, from (8):

$$\hat{\mu}_T(\mathbf{x}) \equiv \sum_{t=1}^{T} \left(\sum_{r=-m(T)}^{m(T)} \omega(r; m(T)) 1(\mathbf{x}_{t-r} \leq \mathbf{x}) \right) \pi_t(\hat{\theta}_T, \hat{\phi}_T). \quad (12)$$

Theorem 2 *(Limit distribution of the ELCDF estimator $\hat{\mu}_T(\mathbf{x})$.)* *Under (1), the ELCDF estimator $\hat{\mu}_T(\mathbf{x})$ of (12) has limiting distribution given by*

$$T^{1/2}(\hat{\mu}_T(\mathbf{x}) - \mu(\mathbf{x})) \Rightarrow N(0, \omega^2),$$

where

$$\omega^2 \equiv \sigma^2 - \mathbf{B}'(\mathbf{V}^{-1} - \mathbf{V}^{-1}\mathbf{G}(\mathbf{G}'\mathbf{V}^{-1}\mathbf{G})^{-1}\mathbf{G}'\mathbf{V}^{-1})\mathbf{B},$$

$$\mathbf{B} \equiv \sum_{s=-\infty}^{\infty} E_\mu\{1(\mathbf{x}_t \leq \mathbf{x})\mathbf{g}(\mathbf{x}_{t-s}; \theta_0)\}$$

and

$$\sigma^2 \equiv \sum_{s=-\infty}^{\infty} \left(E_\mu\{1(\mathbf{x}_t \leq \mathbf{x})1(\mathbf{x}_{t-s} \leq \mathbf{x})\} - \mu(\mathbf{x})^2 \right).$$

The empirical distribution function $\mu_T(\mathbf{x})$ has a limiting distribution described by

$$T^{1/2}(\mu_T(\mathbf{x}) - \mu(\mathbf{x})) \Rightarrow N(0, \sigma^2).$$

Hence, the ELCDF estimator $\hat{\mu}_T(\mathbf{x})$ is more efficient. Moreover, it may be straightforwardly seen that it dominates other estimators that incorporate the information in the moment conditions $E_\mu\{\mathbf{g}(\mathbf{x}_t; \theta_0)\} = \mathbf{0}$, $t = 0, \pm 1, \ldots$, of (1).

The various components in the variance ω^2 may be consistently estimated by

$$\hat{\sigma}^2 \equiv \sum_{s=-2m(T)}^{2m(T)} \omega^*(s; m(T))\hat{\sigma}^2(s),$$

where $\hat{\sigma}^2(s) \equiv T^{-1} \sum_{t=s+1}^{T} \left(1(\mathbf{x}_t \leq \mathbf{x})1(\mathbf{x}_{t-s} \leq \mathbf{x}) - \mu_T(\mathbf{x})^2\right)$, $s \geq 0$, $\hat{\sigma}^2(-s) = \hat{\sigma}^2(s)$, $s = -2m(T), \ldots, 2m(T)$,

$$\hat{\mathbf{B}} \equiv \sum_{s=-2m(T)}^{2m(T)} \omega^*(s; m(T))\hat{\mathbf{B}}(s),$$

where $\hat{\mathbf{B}}(s) \equiv T^{-1} \sum_{t=\max(1,s+1)}^{\min(T,T+s)} 1(\mathbf{x}_t \leq \mathbf{x})\mathbf{g}(\mathbf{x}_{t-s}; \hat{\theta}_T)$, $s = -2m(T), \ldots,$ $2m(T)$, $\hat{\mathbf{V}}_T$ is given in (11) and

$$\hat{\mathbf{G}}_T \equiv T^{-1} \sum_{t=1}^{T} \nabla'_\theta \mathbf{g}(\mathbf{x}_t; \hat{\theta}_T). \tag{13}$$

Alternatively, $\mathbf{G}$ may be estimated consistently by $T^{-1} \sum_{t=1}^{T} \nabla'_\theta \mathbf{g}^\omega_{tT}(\hat{\theta}_T)$.

3   Empirical likelihood inference

3.1   Tests for over-identifying moment conditions

In order to gauge the validity of the moment conditions $E_\mu\{\mathbf{g}(\mathbf{x}_t; \theta_0)\} = \mathbf{0}$, $t = 0, \pm 1, \ldots$, of (1), Hansen (1982) suggested the statistic

$$\mathcal{G}_T \equiv T^{-1} \sum_{t=1}^{T} \mathbf{g}(\mathbf{x}_t; \hat{\theta}_T)' \hat{\mathbf{V}}_T^{-1} \sum_{t=1}^{T} \mathbf{g}(\mathbf{x}_t; \hat{\theta}_T), \tag{14}$$

which may be shown under the validity of (1) to possess a limiting chi-squared distribution with $(r - p)$ degrees of freedom.

In the context of the smoothed log EL criterion (7), we might think of the validity of the moment conditions (1) as corresponding to the parametric restrictions $\phi = \mathbf{0}$. As will soon become evident, this viewpoint allows us to define straightforward classical-type tests for the validity of the moment conditions (1) based directly on consideration of the hypothesis $\phi = \mathbf{0}$ in the smoothed log EL criterion $\mathcal{R}_T(\theta, \phi)$ of (7). However, it should be emphasised that the parametric hypothesis $\phi = \mathbf{0}$ is equivalent to that of the validity of the moment conditions (1).

Firstly, we consider a likelihood ratio test based on the smoothed log EL criterion $\mathcal{R}_T(\theta, \phi)$ of (7). Under $\phi = \mathbf{0}$, $\mathcal{R}_T(\theta, \mathbf{0}) = 0$. When $\phi \neq \mathbf{0}$, the estimated smoothed log EL criterion is evaluated at $(\hat{\theta}_T, \hat{\phi}_T)$, namely $\mathcal{R}_T(\hat{\theta}_T, \hat{\phi}_T)$. From the classical viewpoint then, the difference between estimated smoothed log EL criteria may be used to define an empirical likelihood ratio (ELR) statistic for testing $\phi = \mathbf{0}$ or, rather, the over-identifying moment conditions $E_\mu\{\mathbf{g}(\mathbf{x}_t; \theta_0)\} = \mathbf{0}$, $t = 0, \pm 1, \ldots$, of (1); namely

$$\mathcal{ELR}^\phi_T \equiv 2\eta(T)\mathcal{R}_T(\hat{\theta}_T, \hat{\phi}_T). \tag{15}$$

Theorem 3 *(Limit distribution of the ELR statistic for over-identifying moment conditions.) Under (1), the ELR statistic $\mathcal{ELR}_T^\phi$ of (15) has a limiting chi-squared distribution with $(r - p)$ degrees of freedom.*

Secondly, by analogy with the classical Wald test for $\phi = 0$, an EL Wald statistic for the over-identifying moment conditions (1) is defined in terms of the Lagrange multiplier estimator $\hat{\phi}_T$; namely

$$\mathcal{EW}_T^\phi \equiv T\eta(T)^2 \hat{\phi}_T' \hat{\mathbf{V}}_T \hat{\phi}_T, \tag{16}$$

where $\hat{\mathbf{V}}_T$ is defined in (11).

Proposition 1 *(Limit distribution of the EL Wald statistic for over-identifying moment conditions.) Under (1), the EL Wald statistic $\mathcal{EW}_T^\phi$ of (16) has a limiting chi-squared distribution with $(r - p)$ degrees of freedom.*

To define a classical score test for $\phi = 0$ based on the smoothed log EL criterion $\mathcal{R}_T(\theta, \phi)$ raises a particular difficulty; namely, when ϕ is set equal to 0 the parameter vector θ is no longer identified. This class of problem has been considered by Davies (1977, 1987) in the classical and other contexts. For a recent treatment of this problem, see Andrews and Ploberger (1994). To circumvent this difficulty, consider a score statistic based on the first-order derivatives of the smoothed log EL criterion $\mathcal{R}_T(\theta, \phi)$ evaluated at $\hat{\theta}_T$ and 0, the former of which could be regarded as using the least favourable choice of estimator for θ_0. The score vector associated with the smoothed log EL criterion $\mathcal{R}_T(\theta, \phi)$ is defined by

$$\mathbf{S}_T \equiv \sum_{t=1}^{T} \pi_t(\theta, \phi) \begin{pmatrix} \mathbf{g}_{tT}^\omega(\theta) \\ \nabla_\theta \mathbf{g}_{tT}^\omega(\theta)'\phi \end{pmatrix},$$

where $\pi_t(\theta, \phi)$, $t = 1, \ldots, T$, are given in (8). Now, $\mathbf{S}_T$ evaluated at $\hat{\theta}_T$ and 0, $\hat{\mathbf{S}}_T$, has second block equal to a vector of zeroes. Also, $\pi_t(\hat{\theta}_T, 0) = T^{-1}$, $t = 1, \ldots, T$. Hence, the EL score statistic is given by

$$\mathcal{ES}_T^\phi \equiv T\hat{\mathbf{S}}_T' \begin{pmatrix} \hat{\mathbf{V}}_T & \hat{\mathbf{G}}_T \\ \hat{\mathbf{G}}_T' & 0 \end{pmatrix}^{-1} \hat{\mathbf{S}}_T$$

$$= T^{-1} \sum_{t=1}^{T} \mathbf{g}_{tT}^\omega(\hat{\theta}_T)' \left(\hat{\mathbf{V}}_T^{-1} - \hat{\mathbf{V}}_T^{-1} \hat{\mathbf{G}}_T (\hat{\mathbf{G}}_T' \hat{\mathbf{V}}_T^{-1} \hat{\mathbf{G}}_T)^{-1} \hat{\mathbf{G}}_T' \hat{\mathbf{V}}_T^{-1} \right)$$

$$\times \sum_{t=1}^{T} \mathbf{g}_{tT}^\omega(\hat{\theta}_T), \tag{17}$$

where $\hat{\mathbf{G}}_T$ and $\hat{\mathbf{V}}_T$ are defined in (13) and (11) respectively.

Proposition 2 *(Limit distribution of the EL score statistic for over-identifying moment conditions.)* Under (1), the EL score statistic $\mathcal{ES}_T^\phi$ of (17) has a limiting chi-squared distribution with $(r - p)$ degrees of freedom.

Because the EMELE $\hat{\theta}_T$ of (9) is first-order equivalent to the optimal GMM estimator of (2), the EMELE asymptotically obeys the optimal GMM estimator's first-order conditions; see Proof of Proposition 2. Hence, an equivalent score-type statistic may be based on

$$T^{-1} \sum_{t=1}^{T} \mathbf{g}_{tT}^\omega(\hat{\theta}_T)' \hat{\mathbf{V}}_T^{-1} \sum_{t=1}^{T} \mathbf{g}_{tT}^\omega(\hat{\theta}_T)$$

$$= T^{-1} \sum_{t=1}^{T} \mathbf{g}(\mathbf{x}_t; \hat{\theta}_T)' \hat{\mathbf{V}}_T^{-1} \sum_{t=1}^{T} \mathbf{g}(\mathbf{x}_t; \hat{\theta}_T) + o_P(1);$$

the latter statistic being the GMM statistic $\mathcal{G}_T$ of (14) using $\hat{\theta}_T$ of (9). Moreover, the EL Wald statistic and the GMM statistic $\mathcal{G}_T$ are first-order equivalent as $T^{1/2}\eta(T)\hat{\phi}_T = \mathbf{V}^{-1}T^{-1/2}\sum_{t=1}^{T}\mathbf{g}(\mathbf{x}_t; \hat{\theta}_T) + o_P(1)$; that is, $\mathcal{EW}_T^\phi = \mathcal{G}_T + o_P(1)$. Moreover, from the proofs of Theorem 1 and Propositions 1 and 2, the ELR, EL Wald and EL score statistics are all first-order equivalent. Therefore, the classical-type EL statistics above offer a potentially useful alternative class of tests for the over-identifying moment conditions (1). Although not discussed here, other first-order equivalent tests based on the $\mathcal{C}(\alpha)$ principle may also be defined in a parallel fashion; see *inter alia* Neyman (1959) and Smith (1987).

3.2   Tests for additional moment conditions

Typically, it may be of interest to examine whether an additional s-vector of moments also has zero mean and, thus, might be usefully incorporated to improve inferences on the vector θ_0; namely

$$E_\mu\{\mathbf{h}(\mathbf{x}_t; \theta_0)\} = \mathbf{0}, \quad t = 0, \pm 1, \ldots. \tag{18}$$

The approach due to Newey (1985a, 1985b) would set up a conditional moment test based on a quadratic form in the estimated sample moments $T^{-1/2}\sum_{t=1}^{T}\mathbf{h}(\mathbf{x}_t; \hat{\theta}_T)$ using as metric the inverse of the asymptotic variance matrix of $T^{-1/2}\sum_{t=1}^{T}\mathbf{h}(\mathbf{x}_t; \hat{\theta}_T)$.

However, similarly to the ELR test for over-identifying moment conditions given in (15), we may define the log EL criterion appropriate for the incorporation of the additional moments $E_\mu\{\mathbf{h}(\mathbf{x}_t; \theta_0)\} = \mathbf{0}$, $t = 0, \pm 1, \ldots$, of (18); namely

$$\mathcal{R}_T^*(\theta, \phi, \psi) \equiv \sum_{t=1}^{T} \ln[1 + \phi' \mathbf{g}_{tT}^{\omega}(\theta) + \psi' \mathbf{h}_{tT}^{\omega}(\theta)], \qquad (19)$$

where $\mathbf{h}_{tT}^{\omega}(\theta) \equiv \sum_{s=-m(T)}^{m(T)} \omega(s; m(T)) \mathbf{h}(\mathbf{x}_{t-s}; \theta)$. The Lagrange multiplier estimators corresponding to $\mathcal{R}_T^*(\theta, \phi, \psi)$ of (19) are given by

$$(\tilde{\phi}_T(\theta), \tilde{\psi}_T(\theta)) = \arg\max_{\phi, \psi} \mathcal{R}_T^*(\theta, \phi, \psi),$$

and the EMELE under the moment conditions (1) and (18) is defined by

$$\tilde{\theta}_T = \arg\min_{\theta \in \Theta} \max_{\phi, \psi} \mathcal{R}_T^*(\theta, \phi, \psi).$$

Define $\tilde{\phi}_T \equiv \tilde{\phi}_T(\tilde{\theta}_T)$ and $\tilde{\psi}_T \equiv \tilde{\psi}_T(\tilde{\theta}_T)$.

Similarly to the classical interpretation of the ELR, EL Wald and EL score statistics in section 3.1 for the over-identifying moment conditions (1), we may construct tests of the additional moment conditions $E_\mu\{\mathbf{h}(\mathbf{x}_t; \theta_0)\} = \mathbf{0}$, $t = 0, \pm 1, \ldots$, of (18), by considering EL-based tests for the parametric hypothesis $\psi = \mathbf{0}$ in the smoothed EL criterion $\mathcal{R}_T^*(\theta, \phi, \psi)$ of (19).

Firstly, consider the difference of ELR statistics under (1), (18) and (1) respectively, which, as $\mathcal{R}_T(\theta, \phi) = \mathcal{R}_T^*(\theta, \phi, \mathbf{0})$, corresponds to an ELR test for $\psi = \mathbf{0}$; namely

$$\mathcal{ELR}_T \equiv \mathcal{ELR}_T^{\phi,\psi} - \mathcal{ELR}_T^{\phi}$$

$$= 2\eta(T)(\mathcal{R}_T^*(\tilde{\theta}_T, \tilde{\phi}_T, \tilde{\psi}_T) - \mathcal{R}_T^*(\hat{\theta}_T, \hat{\phi}_T, \mathbf{0})). \qquad (20)$$

Therefore

Theorem 4 *(Limiting distribution of the ELR statistic for additional moment restrictions.) Under (1) and (18), the ELR statistic $\mathcal{ELR}_T$ of (20) has a limiting chi-squared distribution with s degrees of freedom.*

If one were interested in the full vector of moment conditions (1) and (18), one obtains the statistic $\mathcal{ELR}_T^{\phi,\psi} = 2\eta(T)\mathcal{R}_T^*(\tilde{\theta}_T, \tilde{\phi}_T, \tilde{\psi}_T)$ (see (15)), which has a limiting chi-squared distribution with $(r + s) - p$ degrees of freedom; see section 3.1 and Hansen (1982).

Secondly, we may also define an EL Wald statistic for $\psi = \mathbf{0}$ or the additional moment restrictions (18) in an obvious way. Define the $(r + s, s)$ matrix $\mathbf{S}_\psi$ to select the elements of ψ from the vector $(\phi', \psi')'$; that is, $\mathbf{S}_\psi'(\phi', \psi')' = \psi$. The asymptotic variance matrix of the vector $T^{-1/2} \sum_{t=1}^{T} (\mathbf{g}(\mathbf{x}_t; \theta_0)', \mathbf{h}(\mathbf{x}_t; \theta_0)')'$ is denoted by

$$\mathbf{V}_* \equiv \lim_{T \to \infty} \text{Var} \left\{ T^{-1/2} \sum_{t=1}^{T} \left(\mathbf{g}(\mathbf{x}_t; \theta_0)', \mathbf{h}(\mathbf{x}_t; \theta_0)' \right)' \right\},$$

which is assumed positive definite. A positive semi-definite consistent estimator $\tilde{\mathbf{V}}_{*T}$ for $\mathbf{V}_*$ may be defined similarly to $\hat{\mathbf{V}}_T$ of (11) after appropriate substitution of the estimators $\hat{\theta}_T$, $\hat{\phi}_T$ and $\tilde{\psi}_T$. Similarly, $\tilde{\mathbf{G}}_{*T}$ is a consistent estimator for $\mathbf{G}_* \equiv E_\mu\{(\nabla_\theta \mathbf{g}(\mathbf{x}_t; \theta_0)', \nabla_\theta \mathbf{h}(\mathbf{x}_t; \theta_0)')'\}$ based on $\hat{\theta}_T$, $\hat{\phi}_T$ and $\tilde{\psi}_T$ (see (13)). The EL Wald statistic for the additional moment conditions is then defined as[6]

$$\mathcal{EW}_T \equiv T\eta(T)^2 \tilde{\psi}_T'(\mathbf{S}_\psi'(\tilde{\mathbf{V}}_{*T}^{-1} - \tilde{\mathbf{V}}_{*T}^{-1}\tilde{\mathbf{G}}_{*T}$$

$$\times (\tilde{\mathbf{G}}_{*T}'\tilde{\mathbf{V}}_{*T}^{-1}\tilde{\mathbf{G}}_{*T})^{-1}\tilde{\mathbf{G}}_{*T}'\tilde{\mathbf{V}}_{*T}^{-1})\mathbf{S}_\psi)^{-1}\tilde{\psi}_T'. \quad (21)$$

Therefore

Proposition 3 *(Limiting distribution of the EL Wald statistic for additional moment restrictions.) Under (1) and (18), the EL Wald statistic $\mathcal{EW}_T$ of (21) has a limiting chi-squared distribution with s degrees of freedom.*

The classical-type score test for $\psi = \mathbf{0}$ based on the smoothed log EL criterion $\mathcal{R}_T^*(\theta, \phi, \psi)$ is constructed in a standard manner using the score from $\mathcal{R}_T^*(\theta, \phi, \psi)$ evaluated at the estimators $(\hat{\theta}_T, \hat{\phi}_T, \mathbf{0})$. The score vector of the smoothed log EL criterion $\mathcal{R}_T^*(\theta, \phi, \psi)$ is

$$\mathbf{S}_{*T} \equiv \sum_{t=1}^{T} \pi_t^*(\theta, \phi, \psi) \begin{pmatrix} \mathbf{g}_{tT}^\omega(\theta) \\ \mathbf{h}_{tT}^\omega(\theta) \\ \nabla_\theta \mathbf{g}_{tT}^\omega(\theta)'\phi + \nabla_\theta \mathbf{h}_{tT}^\omega(\theta)'\psi \end{pmatrix}, \quad (22)$$

where

$$\pi_t^*(\theta, \phi, \psi) \equiv T^{-1}[1 + \phi'\mathbf{g}_{tT}^\omega(\theta) + \psi'\mathbf{h}_{tT}^\omega(\theta)]^{-1}, \quad t = 1, \ldots, T;$$

see $\pi_t(\theta, \phi)$, $t = 1, \ldots, T$, of (8). Thus, from (22), we see that the score vector $\mathbf{S}_{*T}$ evaluated at $(\hat{\theta}_T, \hat{\phi}_T, \mathbf{0})$, $\hat{\mathbf{S}}_{*T}$, has zeros in its first and last blocks from the first-order conditions determining $\hat{\theta}_T$ and $\hat{\phi}_T$. Therefore, noting $\pi_t^*(\theta, \phi, \mathbf{0}) = \pi_t(\theta, \phi)$, $t = 1, \ldots, T$, the EL score statistic for $\psi = \mathbf{0}$ for the additional moment conditions is given by

---

[6] The (s, s) matrix $\mathbf{S}_\psi'(\mathbf{V}_*^{-1} - \mathbf{V}_*^{-1}\mathbf{G}_*(\mathbf{G}_*'\mathbf{V}_*^{-1}\mathbf{G}_*)^{-1}\mathbf{G}_*'\mathbf{V}_*^{-1})\mathbf{S}_\psi$ is positive definite as the $(r + s, s + p)$ matrix $(\mathbf{S}_\psi, \mathbf{G}_*)$ is full column rank.

$$\mathcal{ES}_T \equiv T\hat{\mathbf{S}}'_{*T} \begin{pmatrix} \hat{\mathbf{V}}_{*T} & -\hat{\mathbf{G}}_{*T} \\ -\hat{\mathbf{G}}'_{*T} & 0 \end{pmatrix}^{-1} \hat{\mathbf{S}}_{*T}, \qquad (23)$$

$$= T\sum_{t=1}^{T}\pi_t(\hat{\theta}_T, \hat{\phi}_T)\mathbf{h}_{tT}^{\omega}(\hat{\theta}_T)'\mathbf{S}'_{\psi}$$

$$\times \left(\hat{\mathbf{V}}_{*T}^{-1} - \hat{\mathbf{V}}_{*T}^{-1}\hat{\mathbf{G}}_{*T}(\hat{\mathbf{G}}'_{*T}\hat{\mathbf{V}}_{*T}^{-1}\hat{\mathbf{G}}_{*T})^{-1}\hat{\mathbf{G}}'_{*T}\hat{\mathbf{V}}_{*T}^{-1}\right)\mathbf{S}_{\psi}$$

$$\times \sum_{t=1}^{T}\pi_t(\hat{\theta}_T, \hat{\phi}_T)\mathbf{h}_{tT}^{\omega}(\hat{\theta}_T),$$

where

$$\hat{\mathbf{G}}_{*T} \equiv T^{-1}\sum_{t=1}^{T}(\nabla_{\theta}\mathbf{g}(\mathbf{x}_t; \hat{\theta}_T)', \nabla_{\theta}\mathbf{h}(\mathbf{x}_t; \hat{\theta}_T)')'$$

or $T^{-1}\sum_{t-1}^{T}(\nabla_{\theta}\mathbf{g}_{tT}^{\omega}(\hat{\theta}_T)', \nabla_{\theta}\mathbf{h}_{tT}^{\omega}(\hat{\theta}_T)')'$ (see $\hat{\mathbf{G}}_T$ of (13)) and $\hat{\mathbf{V}}_{*T}$ denotes a positive semi-definite consistent estimator for $\mathbf{V}_*$ based on the estimators $\hat{\theta}_T$ and $\hat{\phi}_T$ (see $\hat{\mathbf{V}}_T$ of (11)).

Proposition 4 *(Limiting distribution of the EL score statistic for additional moment restrictions.) Under (1) and (18), the EL score statistic $\mathcal{ES}_T$ of (23) has a limiting chi-squared distribution with s degrees of freedom.*

Other statistics asymptotically equivalent to the above EL-based statistics may be defined. For example, a minimum chi-squared statistic is given by

$$\mathcal{MC}_T = T\eta(T)^2\left((\tilde{\phi}_T - \hat{\phi}_T)'\tilde{\psi}'_T\right)\hat{\mathbf{V}}_{*T}\left((\tilde{\phi}_T - \hat{\phi}_T)'\tilde{\psi}'_T\right)'. \qquad (24)$$

The proofs of Theorem 4 and Propositions 3 and 4 show that the ELR, EL Wald, EL score and EL minimum chi-squared statistics of (20), (21), (23) and (24), respectively, are all first-order equivalent. It also immediately follows from the expression of the ELR statistic $\mathcal{ELR}_T$ of (20) as the difference of the ELR statistics, $\mathcal{ELR}_T^{\phi,\psi}$ and $\mathcal{ELR}_T^{\phi}$, that equivalent statistics may be obtained as the difference of EL Wald and score statistics; namely $\mathcal{EW}_T^{\phi,\psi} - \mathcal{EW}_T^{\phi}$ and $\mathcal{ES}_T^{\phi,\psi} - \mathcal{ES}_T^{\phi}$, respectively. Furthermore, given the discussion in section 3.1 concerning the equivalence of those EL-based statistics with the GMM statistic $\mathcal{G}_T$ of (14), the statistics of section 3.2 are equivalent to the difference of estimated GMM criteria and thus the GMM statistic for additional moment restrictions (see Newey (1985a, 1985b)). A final point to note is that, under the moment conditions (1) and (18), all of the statistics of section 3.2 above are asymptotically independent of those of section 3.1, a property also displayed by the classical tests for a sequence of nested hypotheses; see *inter alia* Aitchison (1962) and Sargan (1980).

3.3   Empirical likelihood specification tests

The limiting distribution results given in section 3.2 may be suitably adapted to allow various classical-type specification (likelihood ratio, Lagrange multiplier and Wald) tests on the parameter vector θ to be defined. Consider the following parametric null hypothesis expressed in *constraint equation* form which includes many forms of parametric restrictions:

$$H_0 : \mathbf{h}(\theta_0) = \mathbf{0}, \tag{25}$$

where $\mathbf{h}(.)$ is a known s-vector of functions that are continuously differentiable. We assume that the derivative matrix $\mathbf{H} = \nabla_\theta \mathbf{h}(\theta_0)'$ is full column rank s.[7]

We may integrate the parametric restrictions $H_0 : \mathbf{h}(\theta_0) = \mathbf{0}$ of (25) into the framework of section 3.2 by recalling that the weights $\{\omega(s; m(T))\}$ obey $\sum_{s=-m(T)}^{m(T)} \omega(s; m(T)) = 1$. Therefore, the corresponding smoothed log EL criterion incorporating the parametric restrictions (25) is

$$\mathcal{R}_T^*(\theta, \phi, \psi) \equiv \sum_{t=1}^{T} \ln[1 + \phi' \mathbf{g}_{tT}^\omega(\theta) + \psi' \mathbf{h}(\theta)], \tag{26}$$

with associated score vector

$$\mathbf{S}_{*T} \equiv \sum_{t=1}^{T} \pi_t^*(\theta, \phi, \psi) \begin{pmatrix} \mathbf{g}_{tT}^\omega(\theta) \\ \mathbf{h}(\theta) \\ \nabla_\theta \mathbf{g}_{tT}^\omega(\theta)' \phi + \nabla_\theta \mathbf{h}(\theta)' \psi \end{pmatrix},$$

where, now, we define

$$\pi_t^*(\theta, \phi, \psi) \equiv T^{-1}[1 + \phi' \mathbf{g}_{tT}^\omega(\theta) + \psi' \mathbf{h}(\theta)].$$

[7] The methods described below may be adapted for other types of constraints; namely, *freedom equation* (Seber (1964)), $H_0 : \theta_0 = \theta(\alpha_0)$, *mixed form* (Gouriéroux and Monfort (1989)), $H_0 : \mathbf{q}(\theta_0, \alpha_0) = \mathbf{0}$, and *mixed implicit* and *constraint equation* (Szroeter (1983)), $H_0 : \mathbf{q}(\theta_0, \alpha_0) = \mathbf{0}, \mathbf{r}(\alpha_0) = \mathbf{0}$, restrictions.

Denoting the EMELE and Lagrange multiplier estimators based on $\mathcal{R}_T^*(\theta, \phi, \psi)$ of (26) by $\tilde\theta_T$, $\tilde\phi_T$ and $\tilde\psi_T$, respectively, we see that $\tilde\theta_T$ satisfies $\mathbf{h}(\tilde\theta_T) = \mathbf{0}$ by recalling $\sum_{t=1}^{T} \pi_t^*(\tilde\theta_T, \tilde\phi_T, \tilde\psi_T) = 1$. Therefore, $\pi_t^*(\tilde\theta_T, \tilde\phi_T, \tilde\psi_T) = \pi_t(\tilde\theta_T, \tilde\phi_T)$, $t = 1, \ldots, T$, and $\mathcal{R}_T^*(\tilde\theta_T, \tilde\phi_T, \tilde\psi_T) = \mathcal{R}_T(\tilde\theta_T, \tilde\phi_T)$.

It is straightforward to demonstrate the consistency of the estimators $(\tilde\theta_T, \tilde\phi_T, \tilde\psi_T)$ for $(\theta_0, \mathbf{0}, \mathbf{0})$ under $E_\mu\{\mathbf{g}(\mathbf{x}_t; \theta_0)\} = \mathbf{0}$, $t = 0, \pm 1, \ldots$, of (1) and $H_0 : \mathbf{h}(\theta_0) = \mathbf{0}$ of (25); see Lemma 1. Moreover, the limiting distribution of the EMELE and Lagrange multiplier estimators $\tilde\theta_T$, $\tilde\phi_T$ and $\tilde\psi_T$ may be derived along similar lines to Theorem 1; namely,

Theorem 5 *(Limiting distribution of the EMELE $\tilde\theta_T$ and Lagrange multiplier estimators $\tilde\phi_T$ and $\tilde\psi_T$.) Under (1) and (25), the EMELE $\tilde\theta_T$ and Lagrange multiplier estimators $\tilde\phi_T$ and $\tilde\psi_T$ have limiting distribution given by*

$$
T^{1/2} \begin{pmatrix} \eta(T)\tilde\phi_T \\ \tilde\psi_T \\ (\tilde\theta_T - \theta_0) \end{pmatrix}
$$

$$
\Rightarrow N\left(\begin{pmatrix} \mathbf{0} \\ \mathbf{0} \\ \mathbf{0} \end{pmatrix}, \begin{pmatrix} \mathbf{V}^{-1} - \mathbf{V}^{-1}\mathbf{G}\mathbf{N}\mathbf{G}'\mathbf{V}^{-1} & \mathbf{P} & \mathbf{0} \\ \mathbf{P}' & \left[\mathbf{H}'(\mathbf{G}'\mathbf{V}^{-1}\mathbf{G})^{-1}\mathbf{H}\right]^{-1} & \mathbf{0} \\ \mathbf{0}' & \mathbf{0}' & \mathbf{N} \end{pmatrix} \right),
$$

where

$$
\mathbf{N} \equiv ((\mathbf{G}'\mathbf{V}^{-1}\mathbf{G})^{-1} - (\mathbf{G}'\mathbf{V}^{-1}\mathbf{G})^{-1}\mathbf{H}\left[\mathbf{H}'(\mathbf{G}'\mathbf{V}^{-1}\mathbf{G})^{-1}\mathbf{H}\right]^{-1}
$$
$$
\times \mathbf{H}'(\mathbf{G}'\mathbf{V}^{-1}\mathbf{G})^{-1}),
$$

$$
\mathbf{P} \equiv \mathbf{V}^{-1}\mathbf{G}(\mathbf{G}'\mathbf{V}^{-1}\mathbf{G})^{-1}\mathbf{H}\left[\mathbf{H}'(\mathbf{G}'\mathbf{V}^{-1}\mathbf{G})^{-1}\mathbf{H}\right]^{-1}.
$$

The corresponding ELR and EL Wald statistics become

$$
\mathcal{ELR}_T \equiv 2\eta(T)(\mathcal{R}_T(\hat\theta_T, \hat\phi_T) - \mathcal{R}_T(\tilde\theta_T, \tilde\phi_T)), \tag{27}
$$

$$
\mathcal{EW}_T \equiv T\tilde\psi_T'\hat{\mathbf{H}}_T'(\hat{\mathbf{G}}_T'\hat{\mathbf{V}}_T^{-1}\hat{\mathbf{G}}_T)^{-1}\hat{\mathbf{H}}_T\tilde\psi_T; \tag{28}
$$

see section 3.2. As the first and last blocks of the score vector $\mathbf{S}_{*T}$ estimated at $(\hat\theta_T, \hat\phi_T, \mathbf{0})$, $\hat{\mathbf{S}}_{*T}$, are zero, the EL score statistic

$$\mathcal{ES}_T \equiv T\hat{\mathbf{S}}_{*T}' \begin{pmatrix} \hat{\mathbf{V}}_T & \mathbf{0} & -\hat{\mathbf{G}}_T \\ \mathbf{0}' & 0 & -\hat{\mathbf{H}}_T \\ -\hat{\mathbf{G}}_T' & -\hat{\mathbf{H}}_T' & 0 \end{pmatrix}^{-1} \hat{\mathbf{S}}_{*T}$$

$$= T\mathbf{h}(\hat{\theta}_T)' \left(\hat{\mathbf{H}}_T' \left(\hat{\mathbf{G}}_T' \hat{\mathbf{V}}_T^{-1} \hat{\mathbf{G}}_T \right)^{-1} \hat{\mathbf{H}}_T \right)^{-1} \mathbf{h}(\hat{\theta}_T), \tag{29}$$

where $\hat{\mathbf{V}}_T$ and $\hat{\mathbf{G}}_T$ are defined in (11) and (13), respectively, and $\hat{\mathbf{H}}_T \equiv \nabla_\theta \mathbf{h}(\hat{\theta}_T)'$. The forms of the EL Wald (28) and EL score (29) statistics are, respectively, those of Lagrange multiplier and Wald statistics in the GMM framework.

Proposition 5 *(Limiting distribution of EL statistics for parametric restrictions.) Under (1) and (25), the EL statistics $\mathcal{ELR}_T$, $\mathcal{EW}_T$ and $\mathcal{ES}_T$ statistics of (27), (28) and (29), respectively, each have limiting chi-squared distributions with s degrees of freedom.*

As the EMELE $\hat{\theta}_T$ is first-order equivalent to the efficient GMM estimator, not only are all three statistics $\mathcal{ELR}_T$, $\mathcal{EW}_T$ and $\mathcal{ES}_T$ asymptotically first-order equivalent (see Proof of Proposition 5) but they are equivalent to GMM tests for $H_0 : \mathbf{h}(\theta_0) = \mathbf{0}$ of (25); see (29). The Proof of Proposition 5 also shows that the following minimum chi-squared statistics are first-order equivalent to $\mathcal{ELR}_T$, $\mathcal{EW}_T$ and $\mathcal{ES}_T$:

$$\mathcal{MC}_T^\phi = T\eta(T)^2(\tilde{\phi}_T - \hat{\phi}_T)'\hat{\mathbf{V}}_T(\tilde{\phi}_T - \hat{\phi}_T),$$

$$\mathcal{MC}_T^\theta = T(\tilde{\theta}_T - \hat{\theta}_T)'\hat{\mathbf{G}}_T'\hat{\mathbf{V}}_T^{-1}\hat{\mathbf{G}}_T(\tilde{\theta}_T - \hat{\theta}_T),$$

as is the statistic $T\eta(T)^2(\tilde{\phi}_T'\tilde{\mathbf{V}}_T\tilde{\phi}_T - \hat{\phi}_T'\hat{\mathbf{V}}_T\hat{\phi}_T)$. Moreover, differences of EL Wald and score statistics for $\phi = \mathbf{0}$, $\psi = \mathbf{0}$ and $\phi = \mathbf{0}$ are also equivalent to the above statistics from the structure of the statistic $\mathcal{ELR}_T$ (27); see section 3.2.

4   Empirical likelihood non-nested tests

Denote the model embodied in the moment conditions $E_\mu\{\mathbf{g}(\mathbf{x}_t; \theta_0)\} = \mathbf{0}$, $t = 0, \pm 1, \ldots$, of (1) by H_g. Consider an alternative model H_h based on the assumed moment conditions

$$E_\mu\{\mathbf{h}(\mathbf{x}_t; \beta_0)\} = \mathbf{0}, \ t = 0, \pm 1, \ldots. \tag{30}$$

We denote the smoothed log EL function under H_h of (30) by

$$\mathcal{R}_T^h(\beta, \delta) \equiv \sum_{t=1}^{T} \ln[1 + \delta' \mathbf{h}_{tT}^{\omega}(\beta)], \tag{31}$$

where $\mathbf{h}_{tT}^{\omega}(\beta) \equiv \sum_{s=-m(T)}^{m(T)} \omega(s; m(T)) \mathbf{h}(\mathbf{x}_{t-s}; \beta)$. For convenience of exposition, the weights and lead and lag truncation parameter have been chosen identical to those under H_g; namely $\{\omega(s; m(T))\}$ and $m(T)$ of section 2.3. Correspondingly, we define the Lagrange multiplier estimator by

$$\hat{\delta}_T(\beta) \equiv \arg\max_{\delta} \mathcal{R}_T^h(\beta, \delta)$$

and the EMELE under H_h of (30) by

$$\hat{\beta}_T \equiv \arg\min_{\beta \in B} \max_{\delta} \mathcal{R}_T^h(\beta, \delta), \tag{32}$$

where B is a compact set; we denote $\hat{\delta}_T \equiv \hat{\delta}_T(\hat{\beta}_T)$.

Under H_g of (1), the asymptotic *pseudo-true value* (PTV) of the Lagrange multiplier estimator $\hat{\delta}_T$ is defined *via*

$$\delta_*(\beta) = \arg\max_{\delta} \lim_{T \to \infty} E_\mu \{\ln[1 + \delta' \mathbf{h}_{tT}^{\omega}(\beta)]\}$$

and that for the EMELE $\hat{\beta}_T$ as

$$\beta_* = \arg\min_{\beta \in B} \max_{\delta} \lim_{T \to \infty} E_\mu \{\ln[1 + \delta' \mathbf{h}_{tT}^{\omega}(\beta)]\};$$

we write $\delta_* = \delta_*(\beta_*)$. Therefore, by a similar argument to Lemma 1, under H_g of (1),

$$\hat{\beta}_T \to^P \beta_*, \quad \hat{\delta}_T \to^P \delta_*.$$

In order to avoid the difficulty of observational equivalence between the smoothed log EL criteria under H_g and H_h, it is assumed that $\lim_{T \to \infty} E_\mu \{\ln[1 + \delta_*' \mathbf{h}_{tT}^{\omega}(\beta_*)]\} > 0$. Hence, $\delta_* \neq \mathbf{0}$.[8]

The usual approach to constructing Cox-type (1961, 1962) tests of H_g of (1) against H_h of (30) involves the contrast of consistent estimators under H_g of the probability limit of the requisite criterion function under H_h evaluated at the corresponding estimator PTV; see Smith (1992, equation (2.3), p. 973). That is, for the smoothed EL criterion (31), $\lim_{T \to \infty} E_\mu \{\ln[1 + \delta_*' \mathbf{h}_{tT}^{\omega}(\beta_*)]\}$. Clearly, the smoothed log EL criterion (31) evaluated at the estimators $(\hat{\beta}_T, \hat{\delta}_T)$, $T^{-1} \mathcal{R}_T^h(\hat{\beta}_T, \hat{\delta}_T)$ provides one such consistent estimator. In order to provide another consistent estimator to contrast with $T^{-1} \mathcal{R}_T^h(\hat{\beta}_T, \hat{\delta}_T)$, recall that the empirical measures $\pi_t(\hat{\theta}_T, \hat{\phi}_T) = T^{-1}(1 + o_p(1))$, $t = 1, \ldots, T$. Hence, consider the alternative smoothed log EL criterion function

---

[8] As in the Proof of Lemma 1, the minimising PTV $\delta_*(\beta)$ is unique for given β.

$$\mathcal{R}_T^{h*}(\beta, \delta) = \sum_{t=1}^{T} \pi_t(\hat{\theta}_T, \hat{\phi}_T) \ln[1 + \delta' \mathbf{h}_{tT}^{\omega}(\beta)], \tag{33}$$

and denote the corresponding optimisers by $\tilde{\beta}_T$ and $\tilde{\delta}_T$. Therefore, as $(\hat{\theta}_T, \hat{\phi}_T)$ are consistent for $(\theta_0, \mathbf{0})$ under H_g, $(\tilde{\beta}_T, \tilde{\delta}_T)$ are consistent for (β_*, δ_*) and an alternative consistent estimator for $\lim_{T\to\infty} E_\mu\{\ln[1+\delta_*' \mathbf{h}_{tT}^{\omega}(\beta_*)]\}$ is obtained by evaluation of (33) at $(\tilde{\beta}_T, \tilde{\delta}_T)$:

$$\mathcal{R}_T^{h*}(\tilde{\beta}_T, \tilde{\delta}_T) = \sum_{t=1}^{T} \pi_t(\hat{\theta}_T, \hat{\phi}_T) \ln[1 + \tilde{\delta}_T' \mathbf{h}_{tT}^{\omega}(\tilde{\beta}_T)].$$

Consequently, an EL likelihood ratio Cox-type statistic for H_g against H_h is based on the contrast between the optimised smoothed log EL criteria, $T^{-1}\mathcal{R}_T^{h}(\hat{\beta}_T, \hat{\delta}_T)$ of (31) and $\mathcal{R}_T^{h*}(\tilde{\beta}_T, \tilde{\delta}_T)$ of (33); namely

$$\mathcal{C}_T(H_g|H_h) = T^{1/2}\eta(T)(T^{-1}\mathcal{R}_T^{h}(\hat{\beta}_T, \hat{\delta}_T) - \mathcal{R}_T^{h*}(\tilde{\beta}_T, \tilde{\delta}_T)). \tag{34}$$

Theorem 6 *(Limiting distribution of the Cox-type statistic.) Under (1), the Cox statistic $\mathcal{C}_T(H_g|H_h)$ of (34) has a limiting $N(0, \sigma^2)$ distribution where*

$$\sigma^2 \equiv \xi_*'(\mathbf{V}^{-1} - \mathbf{V}^{-1}\mathbf{G}(\mathbf{G}'\mathbf{V}^{-1}\mathbf{G})^{-1}\mathbf{G}'\mathbf{V}^{-1})\xi_*,$$

$$\xi_* \equiv \lim_{T\to\infty} E_\mu\{\ln[1 + \delta_*' \mathbf{h}_{tT}^{\omega}(\beta_*)]\mathbf{g}_{tT}^{\omega}(\theta_0)\},$$

and σ^2 is assumed non-zero.

The asymptotic variance σ^2 may be consistently estimated under H_g by

$$\hat{\sigma}_T^2 \equiv \hat{\xi}_T'\left(\hat{\mathbf{V}}_T^{-1} - \hat{\mathbf{V}}_T^{-1}\hat{\mathbf{G}}_T(\hat{\mathbf{G}}_T'\hat{\mathbf{V}}_T^{-1}\hat{\mathbf{G}}_T)^{-1}\hat{\mathbf{G}}_T'\hat{\mathbf{V}}_T^{-1}\right)\hat{\xi}_T,$$

where

$$\hat{\xi}_T \equiv T^{-1}\sum_{t=1}^{T} \ln[1 + \hat{\delta}_T' \mathbf{h}_{tT}^{\omega}(\hat{\beta}_T)]\mathbf{g}_{tT}^{\omega}(\hat{\theta}_T) \tag{35}$$

and $\hat{\mathbf{V}}_T$ and $\hat{\mathbf{G}}_T$ are described in (11) and (13) respectively.

The Proof of Theorem 6 suggests the alternative first-order equivalent linearised Cox-type statistic:

$$\mathcal{LC}_T(H_g|H_h) = \hat{\xi}_T' T^{1/2}\eta(T)\hat{\phi}_T, \tag{36}$$

where $\hat{\xi}_T$ is defined in (35) (see Smith (1992), section 2.1, pp. 974–976).

Corollary 1 *(Limiting distribution of the linearised Cox-type statistic.) Under (1), the linearised Cox statistic $\mathcal{LC}_T(H_g|H_h)$ of (36) has a limiting $N(0, \sigma^2)$ distribution where σ^2, defined in Theorem 6, is assumed non-zero.*

Because $T^{1/2}\eta(T)\hat{\phi}_T = \mathbf{V}^{-1}T^{-1/2}\sum_{t=1}^{T}\mathbf{g}(\mathbf{x}_t; \hat{\theta}_T) + o_p(1)$, the form of the linearised statistic $\mathcal{LC}_T(H_g|H_h)$ emphasises that non-nested tests of competing hypotheses expressed in moment form are particular linear combinations of the estimated sample moment vector under the null hypothesis as this vector represents the sole information feasible and available for inference purposes (see Smith (1992)).

A simplified form of EL likelihood ratio Cox-type statistic evaluates the criterion $\mathcal{R}_T^{h*}(\beta, \delta)$ at $(\hat{\beta}_T, \hat{\delta}_T)$ and is first-order equivalent to the Cox statistics, $\mathcal{C}_T(H_g|H_h)$ of (34) and $\mathcal{LC}_T(H_g|H_h)$ of (36); namely

$$SC_T(H_g|H_h) = T^{1/2}\eta(T)\Big(T^{-1}\mathcal{R}_T^h(\hat{\beta}_T, \hat{\delta}_T) - \mathcal{R}_T^{h*}(\hat{\beta}_T, \hat{\delta}_T)\Big). \qquad (37)$$

Proposition 6 *(Limiting distribution of the simplified Cox-type statistic.) Under (1), the simplified Cox statistic $SC_T(H_g|H_h)$ of (37) has a limiting $N(0, \sigma^2)$ distribution where σ^2, defined in Theorem 6, is assumed non-zero.*

Appendix

Proof of Lemma 1

Define $\mathcal{M}_T(\theta, \phi) \equiv E_\mu\{\ln[1 + \phi'\mathbf{g}_{tT}^\omega(\theta)]\}$, where, from (1) and (6), $E_\mu\{\mathbf{g}_{tT}^\omega(\theta)\} = \mathbf{0} \Leftrightarrow \theta = \theta_0$. Now, $E_\mu\{\mathbf{g}_{tT}^\omega(\theta)\mathbf{g}_{tT}^\omega(\theta)'\}$ is positive definite if $\{\mathbf{g}(\mathbf{x}_t; \theta)\}_{t=-\infty}^{\infty}$ is a *non-defective* process; that is, there exists no sequence of non-zero r-vectors $\{\mathbf{a}_{m,s}\}_{s=-m}^{m}$ such that $\sum_{s=-m}^{m}\mathbf{a}_{m,s}'\mathbf{g}(\mathbf{x}_{t-s}; \theta)$ is a degenerate random variable for some $m = 0, 1, \ldots$. By Chesher and Smith (1997, Lemma, p. 643), the matrix of second derivatives of $\mathcal{M}_T(\theta, \phi)$ with respect to ϕ, $-E_\mu\{[1 + \phi'\mathbf{g}_{tT}^\omega(\theta)]^{-2}\mathbf{g}_{tT}^\omega(\theta)\mathbf{g}_{tT}^\omega(\theta)'\}$, is negative definite. Define

$$\phi_T(\theta) \equiv \arg\max_{\phi} \mathcal{M}_T(\theta, \phi).$$

Hence, $\phi_T(\theta)$ satisfies the first-order conditions

$$E_\mu\{[1 + \phi'\mathbf{g}_{tT}^\omega(\theta)]^{-1}\mathbf{g}_{tT}^\omega(\theta)\} = \mathbf{0}.$$

Therefore, it follows from Chesher and Smith (1997, Lemma and Proof of Theorem 1, p. 643) that the maximiser $\phi_T(\theta)$ is unique. Consequently, as θ_0 uniquely satisfies the moment conditions (1), and, thus, (6), $\phi_T(\theta_0) = \mathbf{0}$ and $\phi_T(\theta) \neq \mathbf{0}$, $\theta \neq \theta_0$.

Now, $0 = \mathcal{M}_T(\theta, \phi_T(\theta_0)) \leq \mathcal{M}_T(\theta, \phi_T(\theta))$, $\theta \neq \theta_0$. Moreover, $0 = \mathcal{M}_T(\theta, \phi_T(\theta_0)) < \mathcal{M}_T(\theta, \phi_T(\theta))$, $\theta \neq \theta_0$ because $\phi_T(\theta)$ is a unique maximiser of $\mathcal{M}_T(\theta, \phi)$. Therefore, θ_0 is the unique minimiser of $\mathcal{M}_T(\theta, \phi_T(\theta))$; namely

$$\theta_0 \equiv \arg\min_{\theta \in \Theta} \mathcal{M}_T(\theta, \phi_T(\theta)),$$

and $\mathcal{M}_T(\theta_0, \phi_T(\theta_0)) = 0$.

Define a δ-neighbourhood of θ_0, $\mathcal{N}_\delta(\theta_0)$, and a sequence of open δ_j-neighbourhoods, $\mathcal{N}_{\delta_j}(\theta_j)$, $\theta_j \in \Theta$, $j = 1, \ldots, J$, such that $\cup_{j=1}^{J} \mathcal{N}_{\delta_j}(\theta_j)$ covers $\Theta - \mathcal{N}_\delta(\theta_0)$. From continuity and the Dominated Convergence Theorem

$$E_\mu \left\{ \inf_{\theta' \in \mathcal{N}_{\delta_j}(\theta_j)} \ln[1 + \phi_T(\theta')' \mathbf{g}_{tT}^\omega(\theta')] \right\} = 2v_j > 0, \quad j = 1, \ldots, J.$$

A point-wise double array WLLN gives:

$$\Pr \left\{ T^{-1} \sum_{t=1}^{T} \inf_{\theta' \in \mathcal{N}_{\delta_j}(\theta_j)} \ln[1 + \phi_T(\theta')' \mathbf{g}_{tT}^\omega(\theta')] < v_j \right\} < \epsilon/2J,$$

$$j = 1, \ldots, J.$$

Hence,

$$\Pr \left\{ \inf_{\theta' \in \Theta - \mathcal{N}_\delta(\theta_0)} T^{-1} \sum_{t=1}^{T} \ln[1 + \phi_T(\theta')' \mathbf{g}_{tT}^\omega(\theta')] < v \right\} < \epsilon/2,$$

where $v = \min_j v_j$. The saddle-point maximisation property of $\hat{\phi}_T(.)$ implies

$$\Pr \left\{ \inf_{\theta' \in \Theta - \mathcal{N}_\delta(\theta_0)} T^{-1} \sum_{t=1}^{T} \ln[1 + \hat{\phi}_T(\theta')' \mathbf{g}_{tT}^\omega(\theta')] < v \right\} < \epsilon/2. \quad (A.1)$$

Now, by concavity

$$\ln[1 + \hat{\phi}_T(\theta_0)' T^{-1} \sum_{t=1}^{T} \mathbf{g}_{tT}^\omega(\theta_0)] \geq T^{-1} \sum_{t=1}^{T} \ln[1 + \hat{\phi}_T(\theta_0)' \mathbf{g}_{tT}^\omega(\theta_0)] \geq 0.$$

As $T^{-1} \sum_{t=1}^{T} \mathbf{g}_{tT}^\omega(\theta_0) = T^{-1} \sum_{t=1}^{T} \mathbf{g}(\mathbf{x}_t; \theta_0) + o_P(1) \rightarrow^P \mathbf{0}$, we have $\hat{\phi}_T(\theta_0) \rightarrow^P \mathbf{0}$ and, thus, $T^{-1} \sum_{t=1}^{T} \ln[1 + \hat{\phi}_T(\theta_0)' \mathbf{g}_{tT}^\omega(\theta_0)] \rightarrow^P 0$. Therefore

$$\Pr \left\{ T^{-1} \sum_{t=1}^{T} \ln[1 + \hat{\phi}_T(\theta_0)' \mathbf{g}_{tT}^\omega(\theta_0)] > v/2 \right\} < \epsilon/2. \quad (A.2)$$

Consider the event

$$\left\{ T^{-1} \sum_{t=1}^{T} \ln[1 + \hat{\phi}_T(\theta_0)' \mathbf{g}_{tT}^{\omega}(\theta_0)] \right.$$

$$\left. < \inf_{\theta' \in \Theta - \mathcal{N}_\delta(\theta_0)} T^{-1} \sum_{t=1}^{T} \ln[1 + \hat{\phi}_T(\theta')' \mathbf{g}_{tT}^{\omega}(\theta')] \right\}.$$

Therefore, $\hat{\theta}_T \in \mathcal{N}_\delta(\theta_0)$. Hence, combining (A.1) and (A.2), we have

$$\Pr\{\hat{\theta}_T \in \mathcal{N}_\delta(\theta_0)\} > 1 - \epsilon,$$

which yields the required result. ■

Proof of Theorem 1

Consider the first-order conditions determining $\hat{\theta}_T$ and $\hat{\phi}_T$

$$\sum_{t=1}^{T} \pi_t(\hat{\theta}_T, \hat{\phi}_T) \begin{pmatrix} \mathbf{g}_{tT}^{\omega}(\hat{\theta}_T) \\ \nabla_\theta \mathbf{g}_{tT}^{\omega}(\hat{\theta}_T)' \hat{\phi}_T \end{pmatrix} = \begin{pmatrix} \mathbf{0} \\ \mathbf{0} \end{pmatrix}. \tag{A.3}$$

Now, as $\sum_{s=-m(T)}^{m(T)} \omega(s; m(T)) = 1$, $\omega(s; m(T)) = O(m(T)^{-1})$. Moreover,

$$T^{-1} \sum_{t=1}^{T} \nabla_\theta \mathbf{g}_{tT}^{\omega}(\theta_0)'$$

$$= T^{-1} \sum_{t=1}^{T} \nabla_\theta \mathbf{g}(\mathbf{x}_t; \theta_0)' - T^{-1} \sum_{t=1}^{T} \left(\sum_{s=t}^{m(T)} \omega(s; m(T)) \right) \nabla_\theta \mathbf{g}(\mathbf{x}_t; \theta_0)'$$

$$- T^{-1} \sum_{t=T-m(T)+1}^{T} \left(\sum_{s=-m(T)}^{t-T} \omega(s; m(T)) \right) \nabla_\theta \mathbf{g}(\mathbf{x}_t; \theta_0)'$$

$$= T^{-1} \sum_{t=1}^{T} \nabla_\theta \mathbf{g}(\mathbf{x}_t; \theta_0)' + O_P(m(T)/T),$$

noting that, for example, $\sum_{s=t}^{m(T)} \omega(s; m(T)) = O(1)$ and $m(T)^{-1} \sum_{t=1}^{m(T)} \times \nabla_\theta \mathbf{g}(\mathbf{x}_{t-s}; \theta_0)' = O_P(1)$. Therefore, a first-order Taylor series expansion of (A.3) about θ_0 and $\mathbf{0}$ yields

$$\begin{pmatrix} \mathbf{0} \\ \mathbf{0} \end{pmatrix} = \begin{pmatrix} T^{-1/2} \sum_{t=1}^{T} \mathbf{g}_{tT}^{\omega}(\theta_0) \\ \mathbf{0} \end{pmatrix} + \begin{pmatrix} -\mathbf{V} & \mathbf{G} \\ \mathbf{G}' & \mathbf{0} \end{pmatrix} T^{1/2} \begin{pmatrix} \eta(T)\hat{\phi}_T \\ \hat{\theta}_T - \theta_0 \end{pmatrix} + o_P(1).$$

Moreover, by a similar argument to that above,

$$T^{-1/2} \sum_{t=1}^{T} \mathbf{g}_{tT}^{\omega}(\theta_0) = T^{-1/2} \sum_{t=1}^{T} \mathbf{g}(\mathbf{x}_t; \theta_0) + O_P((m(T)/T)^{1/2}).$$

Therefore

$$T^{1/2}(\hat{\theta}_T - \theta_0) = -(\mathbf{G}'\mathbf{V}^{-1}\mathbf{G})^{-1}\mathbf{G}'\mathbf{V}^{-1}T^{-1/2} \sum_{t=1}^{T} \mathbf{g}(\mathbf{x}_t; \theta_0) + o_P(1),$$

(A.4)

$$T^{1/2}\eta(T)\hat{\phi}_T = (\mathbf{V}^{-1} - \mathbf{V}^{-1}\mathbf{G}(\mathbf{G}'\mathbf{V}^{-1}\mathbf{G})^{-1}\mathbf{G}'\mathbf{V}^{-1})T^{-1/2}$$

$$\times \sum_{t=1}^{T} \mathbf{g}(\mathbf{x}_t; \theta_0) + o_P(1).$$

(A.5)

Hence, from (A.4) and (A.5), the result of the theorem follows from the CLT $T^{-1/2} \sum_{t=1}^{T} \mathbf{g}(\mathbf{x}_t; \theta_0) \Rightarrow N(\mathbf{0}, \mathbf{V})$. ∎

Proof of Theorem 2

Consider a first-order Taylor series expansion of $T^{1/2}(\hat{\mu}_T(\mathbf{x}) - \mu(\mathbf{x}))$ about θ_0 and $\mathbf{0}$:

$$T^{1/2}(\hat{\mu}_T(\mathbf{x}) - \mu(\mathbf{x})) = T^{1/2}(\mu_T(\mathbf{x}) - \mu(\mathbf{x}))$$

$$- \mathbf{B}'T^{1/2}\eta(T)\hat{\phi}_T + o_P(1).$$

We have made use of the approximations

$$T^{-1/2} \sum_{t=1}^{T} \sum_{r=-m(T)}^{m(T)} \omega(r; m(T))1(\mathbf{x}_{t-r} \leq \mathbf{x})$$

$$= T^{-1/2} \sum_{t=1}^{T} 1(\mathbf{x}_t \leq \mathbf{x}) + o_P(1),$$

and

$$\left((T\eta(T))^{-1} \sum_{t=1}^{T} \sum_{r=-m(T)}^{m(T)} \omega(r; m(T))1(\mathbf{x}_{t-r} \leq \mathbf{x})\mathbf{g}_{tT}^{\omega}(\theta_0)'\right) = \mathbf{B}' + o_P(1);$$

see the Proof of Theorem 1. As

$$T^{-1/2} \sum_{t=1}^{T} \begin{pmatrix} 1(\mathbf{x}_t \leq \mathbf{x}) - \mu(\mathbf{x}) \\ \mathbf{g}(\mathbf{x}_t; \theta_0) \end{pmatrix} \Rightarrow N\left(\begin{pmatrix} 0 \\ \mathbf{0} \end{pmatrix}, \begin{pmatrix} \sigma^2 & \mathbf{B}' \\ \mathbf{B} & \mathbf{V} \end{pmatrix}\right).$$

Therefore, from (A.5),

$$T^{1/2}(\hat{\mu}_T(\mathbf{x}) - \mu(\mathbf{x}))$$

$$= (1, \quad -\mathbf{B}'(\mathbf{V}^{-1} - \mathbf{V}^{-1}\mathbf{G}(\mathbf{G}'\mathbf{V}^{-1}\mathbf{G})^{-1}\mathbf{G}'\mathbf{V}^{-1}))$$

$$\times T^{-1/2} \sum_{t=1}^{T} \begin{pmatrix} 1(\mathbf{x}_t \leq \mathbf{x}) - \mu(\mathbf{x}) \\ \mathbf{g}(\mathbf{x}_t; \theta_0) \end{pmatrix} + o_P(1),$$

and, hence, the result follows. ∎

Proof of Theorem 3

A second-order Taylor series expansion of $\mathcal{R}_T(\theta_0, \mathbf{0}) = 0$ about $\hat{\theta}_T$ and $\hat{\phi}_T$ gives

$$0 = \eta(T)\mathcal{R}_T(\hat{\theta}_T, \hat{\phi}_T) + (1/2)T\left(\eta(T)\hat{\phi}_T' \quad (\hat{\theta}_T - \theta_0)'\right)$$

$$\times \begin{pmatrix} -\mathbf{V} & \mathbf{G} \\ \mathbf{G}' & \mathbf{0} \end{pmatrix} \begin{pmatrix} \eta(T)\hat{\phi}_T \\ (\hat{\theta}_T - \theta_0) \end{pmatrix} + o_P(1). \tag{A.6}$$

After substitution from (A.4) and (A.5) into (A.6) and noting $\mathbf{G}'T^{1/2}\eta(T)\hat{\phi}_T = o_P(1)$, we obtain

$$2\eta(T)\mathcal{R}_T(\hat{\theta}_T, \hat{\phi}_T) = T\eta(T)^2\hat{\phi}_T'\mathbf{V}\hat{\phi}_T + o_P(1)$$

$$= T^{-1/2} \sum_{t=1}^{T} \mathbf{g}(\mathbf{x}_t; \theta_0)'[\mathbf{V}^{-1} - \mathbf{V}^{-1}\mathbf{G}$$

$$\times (\mathbf{G}'\mathbf{V}^{-1}\mathbf{G})^{-1}\mathbf{G}'\mathbf{V}^{-1}]T^{-1/2}$$

$$\times \sum_{t=1}^{T} \mathbf{g}(\mathbf{x}_t; \theta_0) + o_P(1), \tag{A.7}$$

yielding the required result. ∎

Proof of Proposition 1

Follows directly from the expansion (A.7). ∎

Proof of Proposition 2

From (A.5), $T^{1/2}\eta(T)\hat{\phi}_T = \mathbf{V}^{-1}T^{-1/2}\sum_{t=1}^{T}\mathbf{g}(\mathbf{x}_t; \hat{\theta}_T) + o_P(1)$. Moreover, similarly to the Proof of Theorem 1, $T^{-1/2}\sum_{t=1}^{T}\mathbf{g}_{tT}^\omega(\hat{\theta}_T) = T^{-1/2}\sum_{t=1}^{T}\mathbf{g}(\mathbf{x}_t; \hat{\theta}_T) + o_P(1)$. The result follows because the first-order

conditions determining the optimal GMM estimator imply that
$\hat{\mathbf{G}}_T'\hat{\mathbf{V}}_T^{-1}T^{-1/2}\sum_{t=1}^{T}\mathbf{g}_{tT}^{\omega}(\hat{\theta}_T) = o_P(1)$.   ∎

Proof of Theorem 4

A Taylor series expansion for $\mathcal{R}_T^*(\tilde{\theta}_T, \tilde{\phi}_T, \tilde{\psi}_T)$ similar to that in (A.7) for $\mathcal{R}_T(\tilde{\theta}_T, \tilde{\phi}_T)$ results in

$$2\eta(T)\mathcal{R}_T^*(\tilde{\theta}_T, \tilde{\phi}_T, \tilde{\psi}_T) = T\eta(T)^2\big(\tilde{\phi}_T'\quad \tilde{\psi}_T'\big)\mathbf{V}_*\begin{pmatrix}\tilde{\phi}_T\\\tilde{\psi}_T\end{pmatrix} + o_P(1)$$

$$= T^{-1}\sum_{t-1}^{T}\big(\mathbf{g}(\mathbf{x}_t; \theta_0)', \mathbf{h}(\mathbf{x}_t; \theta_0)'\big)\mathbf{A}_*$$

$$\times \sum_{t=1}^{T}\begin{pmatrix}\mathbf{g}(\mathbf{x}_t; \theta_0)\\\mathbf{h}(\mathbf{x}_t; \theta_0)\end{pmatrix} + o_P(1), \qquad (A.8)$$

where $\mathbf{A}_* \equiv \mathbf{V}_*^{-1} - \mathbf{V}_*^{-1}\mathbf{G}_*(\mathbf{G}_*'\mathbf{V}_*^{-1}\mathbf{G}_*)^{-1}\mathbf{G}_*'\mathbf{V}_*^{-1}$, $\mathbf{G}_* \equiv \big(\mathbf{G}'\quad \mathbf{H}'\big)'$, $\mathbf{H} \equiv E_\mu\{\nabla_\theta'\mathbf{h}(\mathbf{x}; \theta_0)\}$ and $\mathbf{V}_* \equiv \lim_{T\to\infty}\mathrm{Var}\{T^{-1/2}\sum_{t=1}^{T}\big(\mathbf{g}(\mathbf{x}_t; \theta_0)', \mathbf{h}(\mathbf{x}_t; \theta_0)'\big)'\}$. Hence

$$2\eta(T)\{\mathcal{R}_T^*(\tilde{\theta}_T, \tilde{\phi}_T, \tilde{\psi}_T) - \mathcal{R}_T^*(\hat{\theta}_T, \hat{\phi}_T, \mathbf{0})\}$$

$$= T^{-1}\sum_{t=1}^{T}\big(\mathbf{g}(\mathbf{x}_t; \theta_0)', \mathbf{h}(\mathbf{x}_t; \theta_0)'\big)(\mathbf{A}_* - \mathbf{A})$$

$$\times \sum_{t=1}^{T}\begin{pmatrix}\mathbf{g}(\mathbf{x}_t; \theta_0)\\\mathbf{h}(\mathbf{x}_t; \theta_0)\end{pmatrix} + o_P(1), \qquad (A.9)$$

where $\mathbf{A} \equiv \mathbf{S}[\mathbf{V}^{-1} - \mathbf{V}^{-1}\mathbf{G}(\mathbf{G}'\mathbf{V}^{-1}\mathbf{G})^{-1}\mathbf{G}'\mathbf{V}^{-1}]\mathbf{S}'$ and $\mathbf{S}$ is a selection matrix such that $\mathbf{S}'\big(\mathbf{g}(\mathbf{x}_t; \theta_0)', \mathbf{h}(\mathbf{x}_t; \theta_0)'\big)' = \mathbf{g}(\mathbf{x}_t; \theta_0)$. Note that $\mathbf{V} = \mathbf{S}'\mathbf{V}_*\mathbf{S}$ and $\mathbf{S}'\mathbf{G}_* = \mathbf{G}$. Now

$$\mathbf{V}_*[\mathbf{A}_* - \mathbf{A}]\mathbf{V}_*[\mathbf{A}_* - \mathbf{A}]\mathbf{V}_* = \mathbf{V}_*[\mathbf{A}_* - \mathbf{A}]\mathbf{V}_*$$

as $\mathbf{A}_*\mathbf{V}_*\mathbf{A}_* = \mathbf{A}_*$ and $\mathbf{A}\mathbf{V}\mathbf{A}_* = \mathbf{A}$. Therefore, Proposition 2 follows from Rao and Mitra (1971, Theorem 9.2.1, p. 171) with degrees of freedom given by

$$tr\{\mathbf{V}_*[\mathbf{A}_* - \mathbf{A}]\} = tr\{\mathbf{V}_*\mathbf{A}_*\} - tr\{\mathbf{V}_*\mathbf{A}\}$$

$$= (r + s - p) - (r - p) = s. \qquad ∎$$

Proof of Proposition 3

Firstly, we have from (A.5) that

$$T^{1/2}\eta(T)\big(\tilde{\phi}_T' \quad \tilde{\psi}_T'\big)' = \mathbf{A}_* T^{-1/2} \sum_{t=1}^{T}\big(\mathbf{g}(\mathbf{x}_t;\theta_0)',\mathbf{h}(\mathbf{x}_t;\theta_0)'\big)' + o_P(1).$$

(A.10)

Combining (A.5) and (A.8) yields the intermediate result that the EL minimum chi-squared statistic $\mathcal{MC}_T$ of (24)

$$T\eta(T)^2\big((\tilde{\phi}_T - \hat{\phi}_T)' \quad \tilde{\psi}_T'\big)\hat{\mathbf{V}}_*\big((\tilde{\phi}_T - \hat{\phi}_T)' \quad \tilde{\psi}_T'\big)'$$

$$= T^{-1}\sum_{t=1}^{T}\big(\mathbf{g}(\mathbf{x}_t;\theta_0)',\mathbf{h}(\mathbf{x}_t;\theta_0)'\big)'(\mathbf{A}_* - \mathbf{A})$$

$$\times \sum_{t=1}^{T}\big(\mathbf{g}(\mathbf{x}_t;\theta_0)',\mathbf{h}(\mathbf{x}_t;\theta_0)'\big) + o_P(1),$$

(A.11)

which, therefore, from (A.7), is asymptotically equivalent to the difference of ELR statistics (20).

Now,

$$\begin{pmatrix} \mathbf{V}_* & -\mathbf{G}_* \\ -\mathbf{G}_*' & \mathbf{0} \end{pmatrix}^{-1}$$

$$= \begin{pmatrix} \mathbf{V}_*^{-1} - \mathbf{V}_*^{-1}\mathbf{G}_*(\mathbf{G}_*'\mathbf{V}_*^{-1}\mathbf{G}_*)^{-1}\mathbf{G}_*'\mathbf{V}_*^{-1} & -\mathbf{V}_*^{-1}\mathbf{G}_*(\mathbf{G}_*'\mathbf{V}_*^{-1}\mathbf{G}_*)^{-1} \\ -(\mathbf{G}_*'\mathbf{V}_*^{-1}\mathbf{G}_*)^{-1}\mathbf{G}_*'\mathbf{V}_*^{-1} & -(\mathbf{G}_*'\mathbf{V}_*^{-1}\mathbf{G}_*)^{-1} \end{pmatrix}.$$

Define the $(r+s+p,s)$ selection matrix $\mathbf{S}_{*\psi}$ such that $\mathbf{S}_{*\psi}'(\phi',\psi',\theta')' = \psi$. Therefore, the EL Wald statistic $\mathcal{EW}_T$ of (21) may be expressed as

$$\mathcal{EW}_T = T \begin{pmatrix} \eta(T)(\tilde{\phi}_T - \hat{\phi}_T) \\ \eta(T)\tilde{\psi}_T \\ (\tilde{\theta}_T - \hat{\theta}_T) \end{pmatrix}' \mathbf{S}_{*\psi}\left(\mathbf{S}_{*\psi}'\begin{pmatrix} \mathbf{V}_* & -\mathbf{G}_* \\ -\mathbf{G}_*' & \mathbf{0} \end{pmatrix}^{-1}\mathbf{S}_{*\psi}\right)^{-1}$$

$$\times \mathbf{S}_{*\psi}'\begin{pmatrix} \eta(T)(\tilde{\phi}_T - \hat{\phi}_T) \\ \eta(T)\tilde{\psi}_T \\ (\tilde{\theta}_T - \hat{\theta}_T) \end{pmatrix} + o_P(1).$$

A Taylor series expansion of the score at $(\tilde{\theta}_T, \tilde{\phi}_T, \tilde{\psi}_T)$ about the score at $(\hat{\theta}_T, \hat{\phi}_T, \mathbf{0})$, $\hat{\mathbf{S}}_{*T}$ (see (22)), yields

$$T^{1/2}\hat{\mathbf{S}}_{*T} = -\begin{pmatrix} \mathbf{V}_* & -\mathbf{G}_* \\ -\mathbf{G}'_* & \mathbf{0} \end{pmatrix} T^{1/2} \begin{pmatrix} \eta(T)(\tilde{\phi}_T - \hat{\phi}_T) \\ \eta(T)\tilde{\psi}_T \\ (\tilde{\theta}_T - \hat{\theta}_T) \end{pmatrix} + o_P(1),$$

$$\text{(A.12)}$$

noting $\quad \mathbf{G}'_* T^{1/2}\eta(T)\big(\tilde{\phi}'_T \quad \tilde{\psi}'_T\big)' = o_P(1)\quad$ and $\quad \mathbf{G}' T^{1/2}\eta(T)\hat{\phi}_T = o_P(1)$. Hence,

$$T^{1/2}\begin{pmatrix} \eta(T)(\tilde{\phi}_T - \hat{\phi}_T) \\ \eta(T)\tilde{\psi}_T \\ (\tilde{\theta}_T - \hat{\theta}_T) \end{pmatrix} = -\begin{pmatrix} \mathbf{V}_* & -\mathbf{G}_* \\ -\mathbf{G}'_* & \mathbf{0} \end{pmatrix}^{-1} T^{1/2}\hat{\mathbf{S}}_{*T} + o_P(1).$$

Therefore, noting that $\hat{\mathbf{S}}_{*T} = \mathbf{S}_{*\psi}\sum_{t=1}^{T}\pi_t(\hat{\theta}_T, \hat{\phi}_T)\mathbf{h}^{\omega}_{tT}(\hat{\theta}_T)$,

$$\mathcal{E}\mathcal{W}_T = T\hat{\mathbf{S}}'_{*T}\begin{pmatrix} \mathbf{V}_* & -\mathbf{G}_* \\ -\mathbf{G}'_* & \mathbf{0} \end{pmatrix}^{-1} \hat{\mathbf{S}}_{*T} + o_P(1)$$

$$= \mathcal{E}\mathcal{S}_T + o_P(1). \tag{A.13}$$

Substituting into (A.13) for $T^{1/2}\hat{\mathbf{S}}_{*T}$ from (A.12) and again recalling $\mathbf{G}'_* T^{1/2}\eta(T)(\tilde{\phi}_T{}' \quad \tilde{\psi}'_T)' = o_P(1)\quad$ and $\quad \mathbf{G}' T^{1/2}\eta(T)\hat{\phi}_T = o_P(1)\quad$ yields (A.11) apart from asymptotically negligible terms. ∎

Proof of Proposition 4

This result is immediate from (A.13). ∎

Proof of Theorem 5

Consider the first-order conditions determining $(\tilde{\theta}_T, \tilde{\phi}_T, \tilde{\psi}_T)$:

$$\sum_{t=1}^{T}\pi_t(\tilde{\theta}_T, \tilde{\phi}_T)\begin{pmatrix} \mathbf{g}^{\omega}_{tT}(\tilde{\theta}_T) \\ \mathbf{h}(\tilde{\theta}_T) \\ \nabla_{\theta}\mathbf{g}^{\omega}_{tT}(\tilde{\theta}_T)'\tilde{\phi}_T + \tilde{\mathbf{H}}_T\tilde{\psi}_T \end{pmatrix} = \begin{pmatrix} \mathbf{0} \\ \mathbf{0} \\ \mathbf{0} \end{pmatrix}. \tag{A.14}$$

Because $\mathbf{h}(\theta_0) = \mathbf{0}$, a first-order Taylor series expansion of (A.14) about $(\theta_0, \mathbf{0}, \mathbf{0})$ yields

$$
\begin{pmatrix} \mathbf{0} \\ \mathbf{0} \\ \mathbf{0} \end{pmatrix} = \begin{pmatrix} T^{-1/2} \sum_{t=1}^{T} \mathbf{g}_{tT}^{\omega}(\theta_0) \\ \mathbf{0} \\ \mathbf{0} \end{pmatrix}
$$

$$
+ \begin{pmatrix} -\mathbf{V} & \mathbf{0} & \mathbf{G} \\ \mathbf{0}' & \mathbf{0} & \mathbf{H}' \\ \mathbf{G}' & \mathbf{H} & \mathbf{0} \end{pmatrix} T^{1/2} \begin{pmatrix} \eta(T)\tilde{\phi}_T \\ \tilde{\psi}_T \\ (\tilde{\theta}_T - \theta_0) \end{pmatrix} + o_P(1).
$$

Therefore

$$
T^{1/2}(\tilde{\theta}_T - \theta_0) = -\mathbf{N}\mathbf{G}'\mathbf{V}^{-1}T^{-1/2}\sum_{t=1}^{T}\mathbf{g}(\mathbf{x}_t; \theta_0) + o_P(1), \qquad (A.15)
$$

$$
T^{1/2}\eta(T)\tilde{\phi}_T = \left(\mathbf{V}^{-1} - \mathbf{V}^{-1}\mathbf{G}\mathbf{N}\mathbf{G}'\mathbf{V}^{-1}\right)T^{-1/2}\sum_{t=1}^{T}\mathbf{g}(\mathbf{x}_t; \theta_0) + o_P(1),
$$

$$
(A.16)
$$

$$
T^{1/2}\tilde{\psi}_T = \mathbf{P}'T^{-1/2}\sum_{t=1}^{T}\mathbf{g}(\mathbf{x}_t; \theta_0) + o_P(1). \quad\blacksquare \qquad (A.17)
$$

Proof of Proposition 5

A Taylor series expansion for $\mathcal{R}_T(\tilde{\theta}_T, \tilde{\phi}_T)$ about $(\theta_0, \mathbf{0}, \mathbf{0})$ results in

$$
2\eta(T)\mathcal{R}_T(\tilde{\theta}_T, \tilde{\phi}_T) = T\eta(T)^2\tilde{\phi}_T'\mathbf{V}\tilde{\phi}_T + o_P(1). \qquad (A.18)
$$

Combining (A.7) and (A.18):

$$
2\eta(T)(\mathcal{R}_T(\tilde{\theta}_T, \tilde{\phi}_T) - \mathcal{R}_T(\hat{\theta}_T, \hat{\phi}_T))
$$

$$
= T\eta(T)^2(\tilde{\phi}_T'\mathbf{V}\tilde{\phi}_T - \hat{\phi}_T'\mathbf{V}\hat{\phi}_T) + o_P(1)
$$

$$
= T^{-1/2}\sum_{t=1}^{T}\mathbf{g}(\mathbf{x}_t; \theta_0)'\mathbf{P}[\mathbf{H}'(\mathbf{G}'\mathbf{V}^{-1}\mathbf{G})^{-1}\mathbf{H}]\mathbf{P}'T^{-1/2}
$$

$$
\times \sum_{t=1}^{T}\mathbf{g}(\mathbf{x}_t; \theta_0) + o_P(1)
$$

$$
= T\tilde{\psi}_T'\mathbf{H}'(\mathbf{G}'\mathbf{V}^{-1}\mathbf{G})^{-1}\mathbf{H}\tilde{\psi}_T + o_P(1);
$$

the second equality following from (A.5) and (A.16) and the third from (A.17). From (A.4) and (A.17),

$$T^{1/2}\mathbf{h}(\hat\theta_T) = -\mathbf{H}'(\mathbf{G}'\mathbf{V}^{-1}\mathbf{G})^{-1}\mathbf{H}T^{1/2}\tilde\psi_T + o_P(1).$$

We also note that, from (A.4), (A.15) and (A.17),

$$T^{1/2}(\tilde\theta_T - \hat\theta_T) = (\mathbf{G}'\mathbf{V}^{-1}\mathbf{G})^{-1}\mathbf{H}T^{1/2}\tilde\psi_T + o_P(1),$$

and, from (A.5), (A.16) and (A.17),

$$T^{1/2}\eta(T)(\tilde\phi_T - \hat\phi_T) = \mathbf{V}^{-1}\mathbf{G}(\mathbf{G}'\mathbf{V}^{-1}\mathbf{G})^{-1}\mathbf{H}T^{1/2}\tilde\psi_T + o_P(1). \quad\blacksquare$$

Proof of Theorem 6

From the first-order conditions determining $(\hat\beta_T, \hat\delta_T)$, a first-order Taylor series expansion about $(\theta_0, \mathbf{0})$ and $(\hat\beta_T, \hat\delta_T)$ for the optimised criterion $\mathcal{R}_T^{h*}(\tilde\beta_T, \tilde\delta_T)$ yields

$$T^{1/2}\eta(T)\Big(T^{-1}\mathcal{R}_T^{h}(\hat\beta_T, \hat\delta_T) - \mathcal{R}_T^{h*}(\tilde\beta_T, \tilde\delta_T)\Big)$$

$$= \Big(T^{-1}\sum_{t=1}^{T}\ln[1 + \hat\delta_T'\mathbf{h}_{tT}^{\omega}(\hat\beta_T)]\mathbf{g}_{tT}^{\omega}(\theta_0)'\Big)T^{1/2}\eta(T)\hat\phi_T + o_P(1)$$

$$= \xi_*'T^{1/2}\eta(T)\hat\phi_T + o_P(1). \quad\blacksquare$$

Proof of Corollary 1

Immediate from that of Theorem 6. $\quad\blacksquare$

Proof of Proposition 6

A first-order Taylor series expansion of the statistic $T^{1/2}\eta(T)$ $(\mathcal{R}_T^{h}(\hat\beta_T, \hat\delta_T) - \mathcal{R}_T^{h*}(\tilde\beta_T, \tilde\delta_T))$ about $(\theta_0, \mathbf{0})$ yields an identical expansion to that in the Proof of Theorem 6. $\quad\blacksquare$

References

Aitchison, J. (1962), 'Large-Sample Restricted Parametric Tests', *Journal of the Royal Statistical Society (Series B)*, 24: 234–250.

Altonji, J.G. and L.M. Segal (1996), 'Small Sample Bias in GMM Estimation of Covariance Structures', *Journal of Business and Economic Statistics*, 14(3): 353–366.

Andrews, D.W.K. (1991), 'Heteroskedasticity and Autocorrelation Consistent Covariance Matrix Estimation', *Econometrica*, 59: 817–858.

Andrews, D.W.K. and W. Ploberger (1994), 'Optimal Tests When a Nuisance Parameter is Present Only under the alternative', *Econometrica*, 62: 1383–1414.

Back, K. and D.P. Brown (1993), 'Implied Probabilities in GMM Estimators', *Econometrica*, 61: 971–975.

Chesher, A. and R.J. Smith (1997), 'Likelihood Ratio Specification Tests', *Econometrica*, 65: 627–646.

Cox, D.R. (1961), 'Tests of Separate Families of Hypotheses', *Proceedings of the Fourth Berkeley Symposium on Mathematical Statistics*, 1: 105–123.

(1962), 'Further Results on Tests of Separate Families of Hypotheses', *Journal of the Royal Statistical Society (Series B)*, 24: 406–424.

Davies, R.B. (1977), 'Hypothesis Testing When a Parameter is Present Only under the Alternative', *Biometrika*, 64: 247–254.

(1987), 'Hypothesis Testing When a Parameter is Present Only under the Alternative', *Biometrika*, 74: 33–43.

DiCiccio, T.J., P. Hall and J.P. Romano (1989), 'Comparison of Parametric and Empirical Likelihood Functions', *Biometrika*, 76: 465–476.

Gouriéroux, C. and A. Monfort (1989), 'A General Framework for Testing a Null Hypothesis in a "Mixed Form"', *Econometric Theory*, 5: 63–82.

Hansen, L.P. (1982), 'Large Sample Properties of Generalized Method of Moments Estimators', *Econometrica*, 50: 1029–1054.

Imbens, G.W. (1997), 'One-Step Estimators for Over-Identified Generalized Method of Moments Models', *Review of Economic Studies*, 64: 359–383.

Imbens, G.W., R.H. Spady and P. Johnson (1998), 'Information Theoretic Approaches to Inference in Moment Condition Models', *Econometrica*, 66: 333–357.

Kitamura, Y. and M. Stutzer (1997), 'An Information-Theoretic Alternative to Generalized Method of Moments Estimation', *Econometrica*, 65: 861–874.

Newey, W.K. (1985a), 'Maximum Likelihood Specification Testing and Conditional Moment Tests', *Econometrica*, 53: 1047–1070.

(1985b), 'Generalized Method of Moments Specification Testing', *Journal of Econometrics*, 29: 229–256.

Newey, W.K. and K.D. West (1987), 'A Simple, Positive Semi-Definite Heteroskedasticity and Autocorrelation Consistent Covariance Matrix', *Econometrica*, 55: 703–708.

Neyman, J. (1959), 'Optimal Asymptotic Tests of Composite Statistical Hypotheses', in U. Grenander (ed.), *Probability and Statistics*, New York: Wiley.

Owen, A.B. (1988), 'Empirical Likelihood Ratio Confidence Intervals for a Single Functional', *Biometrika*, 75: 237–249.

(1990), 'Empirical Likelihood Confidence Regions', *Annals of Statistics*, 18: 90–120.

(1991), 'Empirical Likelihood for Linear Models', *Annals of Statistics*, 19: 1725–1747.

Qin, J. and J. Lawless (1994), 'Empirical Likelihood and General Estimating Equations', *Annals of Statistics*, 22: 300–325.

Rao, C.R. and S.K. Mitra (1971), *Generalized Inverse of Matrices and Its Applications*, New York: Wiley.

Sargan, J.D. (1980), 'Some Tests of Dynamic Specification for a Single Equation', *Econometrica*, 48: 879–897.

Seber, G.A.F. (1964), 'The Linear Hypothesis and Large Sample Theory', *Annals of Mathematical Statistics*, 35: 773–779.

Smith, R.J. (1987), 'Alternative Asymptotically Optimal Tests and Their Application to Dynamic Specification', *Review of Economic Studies*, 54: 665–680.

(1992), 'Non-Nested Tests for Competing Models Estimated by Generalized Method of Moments', *Econometrica*, 60: 973–980.

(1997), 'Alternative Semi-Parametric Likelihood Approaches to Generalized Method of Moments Estimation', *Economic Journal*, 107: 503–519.

Szroeter, J. (1983), 'Generalized Wald Methods for Testing Nonlinear Implicit and Overidentifying Restrictions', *Econometrica*, 51: 335–353.

5 Efficiency and robustness in a geometrical perspective

Russell Davidson

1 Introduction

The aim of this chapter is to construct a general geometrical setting, based on Hilbert space, in which one may study various estimation techniques, in particular with respect to efficiency and robustness. Given the sort of data one wishes to study, such as continuous, discrete, etc., the set of data-generation processes (DGPs) capable of generating data of that sort is given the structure of a Hilbert manifold. Statistical *models* will be treated as submanifolds of this underlying manifold.

Geometrical methods are frequently used in the study of statistical inference. One important strand of the literature is presented in Amari (1990), whose numerous earlier papers were inspired by some very abstract work of Chentsov (1972) and led to the concept of a *statistical manifold*. Other review papers and books in this tradition include Barndorff-Nielsen, Cox and Reid (1986), Kass (1989), Murray and Rice (1993), and Barndorff-Nielsen and Cox (1994). Most of this work makes use of finite-dimensional differential manifolds, which are usually representations of models in the exponential family.

Infinite-dimensional Hilbert space methods are extensively used in another strand of literature, for which the most suitable recent reference is Small and McLeish (1994). This book contains numerous references to the original papers on which it builds. In this work, random variables are represented as elements of Hilbert space, and different probability measures (that is, different DGPs) correspond to different inner products on the Hilbert space. However, no manifold structure is imposed on the set of inner products, so that the set of DGPs, rather than the set of random

This research was supported, in part, by grants from the Social Sciences and Humanities Research Council of Canada. It is loosely based on unpublished joint work with Stanley E. Zin, to whom I am grateful for many useful discussions.

151

variables, is not given a geometrical interpretation. Nevertheless, Small and McLeish's approach provides most of the geometrical elements used in this chapter.

Davidson and MacKinnon (1987) introduced infinite-dimensional statistical manifolds, with Hilbert manifold structure, in a manner similar to that used by Dawid (1975, 1977). Infinite-dimensional differential manifolds are less frequently encountered than finite-dimensional ones, but see Lang (1972) for an excellent account. The use of infinite-dimensional manifolds avoids the need to limit attention to models in the exponential family. In this chapter, that Hilbert space representation is extended, and adapted for use in the context of asymptotic theory.

In this chapter, *estimators* are defined in such a way as to correspond to elements of the *tangent spaces* to the statistical manifold at DGPs belonging to the manifold. In fact, an interpretation of these tangent spaces is given as the space of random variables with zero mean and finite variance under the DGP at which the space is tangent. Since a tangent space to a Hilbert manifold is itself a Hilbert space, it can, under this interpretation, be identified with the subspace of Small and McLeish's Hilbert space corresponding to zero-mean random variables.

The principal focus in this chapter is on estimators defined by the *method of estimating functions*, as proposed by Godambe (1960). This method is essentially equivalent to the method known in the econometrics literature as the *generalised method of moments*, introduced by Hansen (1982). With little effort, the results given in this chapter can be extended to Manski's (1983) closest empirical distribution class of estimators. The efficiency and/or robustness of an estimator is always treated relative to a statistical *model*, treated as a Hilbert submanifold. Since estimators estimate *parameters*, they are defined relative to a *parameter-defining mapping* defined on the model. A *parameterised model* is just the pair consisting of the model and the parameter-defining mapping.

A major result of the chapter is that the tangent space to the underlying statistical Hilbert manifold at a DGP belonging to a parameterised model is the direct sum of three mutually orthogonal subspaces. The model, being a Hilbert submanifold, has its own tangent space at any DGP in it, this being a subspace of the full tangent space. The first of the three subspaces is just the orthogonal complement of the tangent space to the model. The other two are therefore complementary subspaces of the model tangent space. Of these, one is the tangent space to the subset of the model for which the model parameters do not vary, and the other, orthogonal to it, turns out to be the finite-dimensional space in which (asymptotically) *efficient* estimators are located.

Robustness of an estimator with respect to a given model is interpreted as meaning that the estimator is root-n consistent for all DGPs in the model. The property of root-n consistency is shown to have a geometrical interpretation according to which the tangents that represent the estimator are orthogonal to the second subspace described above, the one that is tangent to the space over which the parameters do not vary. Quite generally, a root-n consistent estimator can be made efficient at any given DGP by projecting it orthogonally in Hilbert space on to the finite-dimensional third subspace. Such orthogonal projections can be achieved by making use of a particular privileged basis of the third subspace, a basis that is easy to characterise in terms of Godambe's estimating functions.

In the next section, the Hilbert manifold of DGPs is constructed, and it is shown how to adapt it for use with asymptotic theory. Then, in section 3, estimators are defined in a geometrical context, as also the concepts of efficiency and robustness of estimators. The main results pertaining to the three-subspace decomposition of the tangent space are proved in this section. Section 4 is an interlude of examples and illustrations, and in section 5 the results are specialised to estimators defined by estimating functions and the generalised method of moments. In section 6, the linear regression model is used as the simplest example in which the results of section 5 can be deployed, and a non-trivial application of orthogonal projection is given. Finally, concluding comments are found in section 7.

2   Data-generation processes in Hilbert space

In Davidson and MacKinnon (1987) a Hilbert space representation was introduced for the set of data-generation processes (DGPs) that could have generated a given data set. The representation used here is a slight generalisation of that presented there, in that we will not restrict ourselves to samples of i.i.d. random variables.

First, it is assumed that the DGPs we are concerned with are defined on a measure space $(\Omega, \mathcal{F})$. A DGP corresponds to a probability measure, P say, defined on this space. Observed data, $y^n \equiv \{y_t\}_{t=1}^n$, say, for a sample of size n, are interpreted as realisations of random variables on $(\Omega, \mathcal{F})$. Thus, if each observation has m components (there are m simultaneously observed dependent variables), then for each $t = 1, 2, \ldots, n$ there exists a mapping $Y_t : \Omega \to \mathbb{R}^m$, and for each sample size $n = 1, 2, \ldots$ a mapping $Y^n : \Omega \to \mathbb{R}^{nm}$, where Y_t and Y^n are, respectively, the random variable for observation t and the random variable for a complete sample of size n.

Their stochastic properties are given by the probability measure P, or, equivalently, by the measure that P induces on $\mathbb{R}^{mn}$ by the mapping Y^n.

A *model*, for a given sample size n, will be thought of as a set of DGPs, that is, as a set of probability measures on $\mathbb{R}^{mn}$. We assume that there exists a *carrier measure* P_0^n on $\mathbb{R}^{mn}$ such that the measures associated with all DGPs in the model are absolutely continuous with respect to it. By the Radon–Nikodym theorem, this ensures for each DGP in the model the existence of a probability density for the random variable Y^n.

Consider now one single DGP in the model, and denote the density of Y^n by $L^n : \mathbb{R}^{mn} \to \mathbb{R}$. Since this is the joint density of the Y_t, $t = 1, \ldots, n$, it can be factorised as follows:

$$L^n(y_1, \ldots, y_n) = \prod_{t=1}^{n} L_t(y_t \mid y_{t-1}, \ldots, y_1), \tag{1}$$

where L_t denotes the density of the t'th observation, Y_t, conditional on all the observations before it in the ordering $\{1, 2, \ldots, n\}$, that is, the observations 1 through $t - 1$.

We may now make contact with the representation given in Davidson and MacKinnon (1987), by considering not the density (1) but its square root. Analogously to (1), we write

$$\psi^n(y_1, \ldots, y_n) = \prod_{t=1}^{n} \psi_t(y_t \mid y_{t-1}, \ldots, y_1), \tag{2}$$

where $L^n(y_1, \ldots, y_n) = (\psi^n(y_1, \ldots, y_n))^2$, with a similar relation between $L_t(\cdot)$ and $\psi_t(\cdot)$, $t = 1, \ldots, n$. By construction, ψ^n belongs to the Hilbert space $L^2(\mathbb{R}^{mn}, P_0^n)$, in fact to the *unit sphere* of that space, since the integral of the square of ψ^n with respect to $dy^n \equiv dy_1 dy_2 \ldots dy_n$ equals one. We write $\mathcal{H}^n$ for this unit sphere.

Usually we choose ψ^n and the ψ_t to be the non-negative square roots of L^n and the L_t, but this is not necessary. Indeed, in Hilbert space, it is impossible to limit oneself to non-negative square root densities, since the non-negative cone in an infinite-dimensional Hilbert space has an empty interior, and thus does not have a manifold structure. A consequence of this is that we cannot represent a given DGP *uniquely* in Hilbert space, but this does not matter for anything in this chapter. Hilbert space, on the other hand, is the natural setting for mean-square convergence, and has the considerable advantage that the information matrix – to be defined later – is a smooth tensor in this representation. This would not be so if we used, for instance, the log of the density in place of the square root density.

It is clear from (2) that a convenient way to deal with arbitrary sample sizes is to consider infinite sequences of *contributions* $\{\psi_t\}_{t=1}^{\infty}$. For any given sample size n, the joint square root density of the n observations is given by (2). For a given infinite sequence to define a DGP for each n, it is necessary and sufficient that

$$\int |\psi_t(y_t \mid y_{t-1}, \ldots, y_1)|^2 \, dy_t = 1 \tag{3}$$

for all possible values of the conditioning variables $y_1, \ldots, y_{t-1}$. We denote by $\mathbb{S}$ the set of sequences satisfying these conditions, and consider $\mathbb{S}$ as the space of DGPs for asymptotic theory, since, given any element of $\mathbb{S}$, a proper probability density can be defined for arbitrary sample size. A *model*, for the purposes of asymptotic theory, will thus be a subset of $\mathbb{S}$.

Consider first, for a given n, the *tangent space* to the unit sphere $\mathcal{H}^n$ at some DGP $\psi^n \in \mathcal{H}^n$. A tangent at ψ^n is associated with a smooth *curve* in $\mathcal{H}^n$ through ψ^n. Such a curve is a one-parameter family of DGPs that includes ψ^n. Let the curve be denoted by $\psi^n(\varepsilon)$, $\varepsilon \in \,]-1, 1[$, and $\psi^n(0) = \psi^n$. The tangent to this curve at ψ^n is then represented by the derivative of $\psi^n(\varepsilon)$ at $\varepsilon = 0$. The appropriate derivative in Hilbert space is a mean-square derivative, $(\psi^n)' \in L^2(\mathbb{R}^{mn}, P_0^n)$, say, that satisfies

$$\lim_{\varepsilon \to 0} \left\| \frac{1}{\varepsilon}(\psi^n(\varepsilon) - \psi^n(0)) - (\psi^n)' \right\| = 0, \tag{4}$$

where $\| \cdot \|$ is the Hilbert space norm in $\mathcal{H}^n$.

Consider next a curve in $\mathbb{S}$ through the point $\psi \equiv \{\psi_t\}_{t=1}^{\infty}$. Denote the curve by $\psi(\varepsilon)$, and, for each n, we have a curve in $\mathcal{H}^n$ given by

$$\psi^n(\varepsilon) = \prod_{t=1}^{n} \psi_t(\varepsilon).$$

In order to define the tangent to the curve $\psi(\varepsilon)$, and for the purposes of asymptotic theory more generally, it is more convenient to consider not the sequence $\{\psi^n(\varepsilon)\}$ for a fixed ε, but rather the sequence

$$\{\psi^n(n^{-1/2}\varepsilon)\}_{n=1}^{\infty}.$$

On differentiating with respect to ε at $\varepsilon = 0$, this gives the following representation for the tangent to $\psi(\varepsilon)$ at ψ:

$$\{n^{-1/2}(\psi^n)'\}_{n=1}^{\infty}, \tag{5}$$

where each $(\psi^n)'$ is defined as in (4).

The reason for the factor of $n^{-1/2}$ is that we can now define the norm of the sequence (5), and thus the norm of the tangent ψ' to $\psi(\varepsilon)$ at ψ by the formula

$$\|\psi'\| = \lim_{n \to \infty} \|n^{-1/2}(\psi^n)'\|_{\mathcal{H}^n}, \tag{6}$$

where the norm of each $(\psi^n)'$ is calculated in the Hilbert space corresponding to sample size n. The limit in (6) will be shown shortly to exist in a wide variety of circumstances. Without the factor of $n^{-1/2}$, this would not be the case. Another way to see why the factor is useful is to note that its use converts the curve $\psi(\varepsilon)$ into what Davidson and MacKinnon (1993) call a *drifting DGP*, in the sense of a Pitman drift.

Note that there is no obvious way to embed the contributions $\psi_t(\varepsilon)$ in a Hilbert space or manifold, and there is therefore no direct way to compute their derivatives with respect to ε. An appropriate indirect way is as follows. Recall that ψ^n with a superscript refers to a product of contributions, while ψ_t with a subscript refers to a single contribution. Then define derivatives ψ'_t recursively by the relations

$$\psi'_1 = (\psi^1)', \qquad \psi^{t-1}\psi'_t = (\psi^t)' - \psi_t(\psi^{t-1})'. \tag{7}$$

For values of $(y_1, \ldots, y_{t-1})$ for which ψ^{t-1} vanishes, ψ'_t is arbitrarily set equal to zero. It should be clear that, whenever the $\psi_t(\varepsilon)$ can be differentiated in any useful sense, the derivatives will satisfy (7). With that definition, it is clear that the tangent ψ' can be represented by the infinite sequence of contributions, $\{\psi'_t\}_{t=1}^{\infty}$, such that, for each n,

$$\frac{(\psi^n)'}{\psi^n} = \sum_{t=1}^{n} \frac{\psi'_t}{\psi_t}. \tag{8}$$

The construction of the tangent space at the DGP $\psi \in \mathbb{S}$ as a Hilbert space is almost complete. Tangents are represented by infinite sequences of contributions satisfying (8), with the norm (6). The final step, needed so that (6) should be positive definite, is to identify tangents of zero norm with the actual zero tangent, defined as an infinite sequence of zero contributions. In this way, the Hilbert space that we consider is the space of equivalence classes of infinite sequences of contributions satisfying (8), two sequences being equivalent if the difference between them is a sequence of zero norm using the norm (6). It will be clear shortly that the different elements of equivalence classes so defined are *asymptotically equivalent* in the usual sense of asymptotic theory. The Hilbert space thus defined, the space of tangents to $\mathbb{S}$ at the DGP ψ, will be denoted as $T_S(\psi)$.

It is now possible to give a statistical interpretation of the space $T_S(\psi)$. Consider a curve $\psi(\varepsilon)$ and suppose that, for each n and for all admissible values of $y^n \equiv (y_1, \ldots, y_n)$, $\psi^n(\varepsilon; y^n)$ is non-zero, so that $\log |\psi^n(\varepsilon; y^n)|$ exists everywhere. We remarked above that the curve corresponds to a one-parameter family of DGPs, and it is clear that $\ell^n(\varepsilon, y^n) \equiv 2 \log |\psi^n(\varepsilon; y^n)|$ is the log-likelihood function corresponding to this one-parameter family. Further, $\ell_t(\varepsilon; y^t) \equiv 2 \log |\psi_t(\varepsilon; y^t)|$ is just the contribution to ℓ^n from observation t, and

$$\ell^n(\varepsilon; y^n) = \sum_{t=1}^{n} \ell_t(\varepsilon; y^t). \tag{9}$$

Assuming now that ℓ^n, ℓ_t and ψ_t can be differentiated with respect to ε, we see that, by (8),

$$\sum_{t=1}^{n} \frac{\partial \ell_t}{\partial \varepsilon}(0) = \frac{\partial \ell^n}{\partial \varepsilon}(0) = 2 \frac{(\psi^n)'}{\psi^n} = 2 \sum_{t=1}^{n} \frac{\psi_t'}{\psi_t}. \tag{10}$$

The expression second from the left above is the gradient of the log-likelihood of the one-parameter family at $\varepsilon = 0$, and, as such, its expectation under the DGP ψ^n is zero. In Hilbert space, this result corresponds to a simple orthogonality property, as follows. The expectation of each expression in (10), since the square of ψ^n is the density of y^n, can be written as

$$2 \int \frac{(\psi^n)'}{\psi^n} (\psi^n)^2 \, dy^n = 2 \int (\psi^n)' \psi^n \, dy^n, \tag{11}$$

and the right-hand side of this can be seen to be zero when the normalisation relation

$$\int (\psi^n)^2(\varepsilon) \, dy^n = 1,$$

which holds for all admissible ε, is differentiated with respect to ε and evaluated at $\varepsilon = 0$ to yield

$$\int (\psi^n)' \psi^n \, dy^n = 0, \tag{12}$$

which just says that the inner product in $L^2(\mathbb{R}^{mn}, P_0^n)$ of $(\psi^n)'$ and ψ^n is zero, so that $(\psi^n)'$ and ψ^n are orthogonal. Geometrically, this just says that a radius of the unit sphere – ψ^n – is orthogonal to a tangent to that sphere – $(\psi^n)'$.

From (3), it follows that a result like (12) holds for each contribution:

$$\int \psi_t' \psi_t \, dy_t = 0,$$

which, in terms of ℓ_t, becomes

$$\int \frac{\partial \ell_t}{\partial \varepsilon}(0; y^t) \, \exp(\ell_t(0; y^t)) \, dy_t = E\left(\frac{\partial \ell_t}{\partial \varepsilon}(0; y^t) \,\middle|\, y^{t-1}\right) = 0.$$

The second equation above implies the well-known result that the sequence

$$\left\{\sum_{t=1}^{n} \frac{\partial \ell_t}{\partial \varepsilon}(0)\right\}_{n=1}^{\infty}$$

is a *martingale* under ψ.

Now consider the norm of the tangent ψ', as given by (6). In order to calculate it, we need the norms, in $L^2(\mathbb{R}^{mn}, P_0^n)$, of the tangents $(\psi^n)'$. These norms are given by the formula

$$\|(\psi^n)'\|^2 = \int ((\psi^n)')^2 \, dy^n = \int \left(\frac{(\psi^n)'}{\psi^n}\right)^2 (\psi^n)^2 \, dy^n$$

$$= E_{\psi^n}\left(\left[\sum_{t=1}^{n} \frac{\partial \ell_t}{\partial \varepsilon}(0)\right]^2\right), \tag{13}$$

where the last equality follows from (10). The martingale property allows (13) to be simplified to

$$\sum_{t=1}^{n} E_{\psi^t}\left(\left[\frac{\partial \ell_t}{\partial \varepsilon}(0)\right]^2\right). \tag{14}$$

From (6), the squared norm of ψ' is

$$\lim_{n\to\infty} n^{-1} \sum_{t=1}^{n} E_{\psi^t}\left(\left[\frac{\partial \ell_t}{\partial \varepsilon}(0)\right]^2\right),$$

where the limit exists under mild regularity conditions allowing a law of large numbers to be applied. This limit can be interpreted as the limiting (asymptotic) *variance* under ψ of the sequence

$$\left\{n^{-1/2} \sum_{t=1}^{n} \frac{\partial \ell_t}{\partial \varepsilon}(0)\right\}_{n=1}^{\infty}. \tag{15}$$

Although (15) is derived from a triangular martingale array rather than being a martingale, we will refer to sequences like (15) as martingales, by a slight abuse of terminology. Exactly similar considerations allow us to express the inner product of two tangents $(\psi^1)'$ and $(\psi^2)'$ in $T_S(\psi)$ as the limit of the covariance of the two random variables

$$n^{-1/2} \sum_{t=1}^{n} \frac{\partial \ell_t^1}{\partial \varepsilon^1} (\varepsilon^1 = 0) \quad \text{and} \quad n^{-1/2} \sum_{t=1}^{n} \frac{\partial \ell_t^2}{\partial \varepsilon^2} (\varepsilon^2 = 0),$$

in obvious notation.

The above considerations lead to an intuitive understanding of the Hilbert space $T_S(\psi)$ we have constructed. It is the space of equivalence classes of asymptotically equivalent sequences of random variables of the form

$$h = \left\{ n^{-1/2} \sum_{t=1}^{n} h_t \right\}_{n=1}^{\infty},$$

where

$$E_\psi(h_t \mid h_1, \ldots, h_{t-1}) = 0, \quad t = 1, 2, \ldots,$$
$$E_\psi(h_t^2) = \eta_t < \infty, \quad t = 1, 2, \ldots, \tag{16}$$

and $n^{-1} \sum_{t=1}^{n} \eta_t$ converges as $n \to \infty$ to a finite limiting variance.

The squared norm $\|h\|^2$ of such a sequence is the limiting variance, and the inner product $\langle h^1, h^2 \rangle$ of two such sequences is the limiting covariance of

$$n^{-1/2} \sum_{t=1}^{n} h_t^1 \quad \text{and} \quad n^{-1/2} \sum_{t=1}^{n} h_t^2. \tag{17}$$

The construction depends heavily on the martingale property. On account of the variety of central-limit theorems applicable to martingales (see for instance McLeish (1974)), this property also justifies considering limiting *normal* random variables to which sequences like (17) tend as $n \to \infty$.

The choice of the particular Hilbert space structure just constructed so as to define the tangent space at ψ confers a Hilbert manifold structure on the set $\mathbb{S}$ itself. It is not the aim of the present chapter to conduct a full investigation of this structure, since all the remaining analysis of the chapter will be local, and so just a few remarks will be made. It is clear that it would be necessary to group the elements of $\mathbb{S}$ into equivalence classes of DGPs with asymptotically equivalent properties. The regularity conditions (16) implicitly restrict the sorts of DGPs admitted into $\mathbb{S}$. These are not so strong as those imposed by Hansen (1982), who worked in a stationary ergodic framework. Methods of the sort used in White and

Domowitz (1984) and White (1985) are presumably appropriate for determining just what restrictions are implicit in the present treatment.

3   Efficiency and robustness in Hilbert space

All procedures of estimation or inference treated here will be situated in the context of a particular model, that is, a subset of the set $\mathbb{S}$ introduced in the preceding section. If $\mathbb{M}$ denotes such a model, it is almost always interesting to define some parameters for it. A *parameterised model* will therefore be a pair, of the form $(\mathbb{M}, \boldsymbol{\theta})$, where the mapping $\boldsymbol{\theta} : \mathbb{M} \rightarrow \Theta$ is termed a *parameter-defining mapping*. The set Θ is a finite-dimensional parameter space, a subset of $\mathbb{R}^{k}$ for some positive integer k. A *parameterisation* would go the other way, associating a DGP to each parameter vector in Θ.

Models that can be estimated by maximum likelihood constitute a very straightforward class. They are special in that a parameterisation does exist for them: for each admissible parameter vector, and for each sample size, the likelihood function gives a probability density for the dependent variables, which is precisely what we mean by a DGP. The image of the parameterisation is the model, and the parameter-defining mapping is the inverse of the parameterisation. Note that the inverse will not exist if the parameterisation is not one-to-one. In such cases, the model parameters are not identified. A convenient way to impose identification of all the parameters we consider, not just in the context of maximum likelihood models, is to require the existence of a parameter-defining mapping.

In more general circumstances, a given parameter vector corresponds to an infinite number of DGPs. A simple case is that of a linear regression model

$$y_t = X_t \boldsymbol{\beta} + u_t, \quad E(u_t) = 0, \quad E(u_t^2) = \tau^2, \tag{18}$$

in which the distribution of the error terms is not specified past the first two moments. Any mean-zero error distribution with finite variance can be used in combination with a fixed parameter vector $\boldsymbol{\beta}$ and variance τ^2. Clearly, there is an infinite number of such error distributions.

In order to benefit from the Hilbert space structure introduced in the preceding section, it will be desirable to consider only models $\mathbb{M}$ that are *closed submanifolds* of $\mathbb{S}$. Locally, in a neighbourhood of a DGP $\psi \in \mathbb{M}$, this just means that, if we consider the subset of tangents at ψ generated by curves that lie entirely in the subset $\mathbb{M}$, this subset, denoted by $T_M(\psi)$, should be a closed subspace of the full tangent space $T_S(\psi)$.

If this condition is satisfied, then another regularity condition needed for the rest of the development can be imposed on the parameter-defining mappings that may be used with $\mathbb{M}$. It is that such a mapping must be a *submersion* (see, for instance, Lang (1972)). Among the consequences of this technical condition is that, if θ denotes the parameter-defining mapping, open neighbourhoods of ψ in $\mathbb{M}$ are mapped by θ into open sets of the parameter space Θ. This avoids redundant parameters: if, for instance, one parameter, θ_1 say, was always just twice another parameter, θ_2, all points in the image of θ would satisfy $\theta_1 = 2\theta_2$, and so the image could not be an open set. Another consequence, more important for what follows, is that $T_M(\psi)$ can be expressed as the direct sum of two orthogonal subspaces, the first, possibly infinite-dimensional, corresponding to tangents to curves along which the parameters defined by θ are constant, and the second the orthogonal complement of the first, and necessarily of finite dimension k, where k is the number of parameters defined by θ. A maximum likelihood model is itself of dimension k, and so the first of these orthogonal subspaces contains only the zero element of $T_M(\psi)$. In general, the first of the subspaces, that for which the parameters are constant, will be denoted as $T_M(\psi, \theta)$, and the second as $E(\psi, \theta)$. These two subspaces, together with their orthogonal complement in $T_M(\psi)$, comprise the three subspace decomposition of $T_M(\psi)$ alluded to in the introduction.

An *estimator* of the parameters of a given parameterised model is a sequence of random k-vectors $\hat{\theta}^n$ which, for each n, are defined solely in terms of the random variable Y^n of which any data set of size n is a realisation. Thus $\hat{\theta}^n$ maps from $\mathbb{R}^{mn}$ to a parameter space Θ. The estimator characterised by the sequence $\{\hat{\theta}^n\}$ will be written as just $\hat{\theta}$. The above definition clearly contains many useless estimators; usually we will be interested only in consistent estimators. The property of consistency can be expressed as follows. For each DGP $\psi \in \mathbb{M}$, we must have

$$\operatorname*{plim}_{\substack{\psi \\ n \to \infty}} \hat{\theta}^n = \theta(\psi).$$

The notation means that the probability limit is calculated under the DGP ψ, and that the limit is what is given by the parameter-defining mapping θ for that DGP.

Most root-n consistent estimators correspond to vectors of tangents at each point of the model for which they are defined. Consider a DGP ψ in a parameterised model $(\mathbb{M}, \theta)$, and let $\theta(\psi) = \theta_0$ be the parameter vector for ψ. Then, for a root-n consistent estimator $\hat{\theta}$, construct the vector sequence with typical element

$$s_t \equiv t(\hat{\theta}^t - \theta_0) - (t - 1)(\hat{\theta}^{t-1} - \theta_0). \tag{19}$$

Clearly

$$n^{1/2}(\hat{\theta}^n - \theta_0) = n^{-1/2} \sum_{t=1}^{n} s_t.$$

The components of $\{s_t\}$ may not exactly satisfy the conditions (16), but they will usually be asymptotically equivalent to sequences that do. Since such asymptotically equivalent sequences are identified in our Hilbert space structure, the estimator $\hat{\theta}$ can be associated with the vector of tangents at ψ defined by the equivalence classes containing the components of $\{s_t\}$. In fact, all estimators that are asymptotically equivalent to $\hat{\theta}$ are associated with the same vector of tangents.

A simple illustration may be helpful here. The OLS estimator of the regression model (18) satisfies the relation

$$n^{1/2}(\hat{\beta}^n - \beta_0) = \left(n^{-1} \sum_{t=1}^{N} X_t' X_t\right)^{-1} n^{-1/2} \sum_{t=1}^{n} X_t' u_t \tag{20}$$

when the true parameter vector is β_0. Under standard regularity conditions, $n^{-1} \sum_{t=1}^{n} X_t^{\top} X_t$ tends to a non-random, symmetric, positive definite limiting matrix A, say. Thus the sequence with typical element (20) is asymptotically equivalent to the sequence

$$\hat{s} \equiv \left\{ n^{-1/2} \sum_{t=1}^{n} A^{-1} X_t' u_t \right\}_{n=1}^{\infty},$$

which clearly obeys the requirements of (16).

If the parameter space Θ is k-dimensional, we may denote the k tangents corresponding to $\hat{\theta}$ at ψ by the vector $\hat{s}$, with typical element $\hat{s}_i$, $i = 1, \ldots, k$. It follows from the interpretation of the Hilbert space norm of a tangent as a variance that the $k \times k$ matrix with typical element $\langle \hat{s}_i, \hat{s}_j \rangle$ is the asymptotic covariance matrix of $\hat{\theta}$, that is,

$$\lim_{n \to \infty} \mathrm{Var}(n^{1/2}(\hat{\theta}^n - \theta_0)). \tag{21}$$

The notion of *robustness* used in this chapter can be defined as follows. Suppose we have two parameterised models $(\mathbb{M}_0, \theta_0)$ and $(\mathbb{M}_1, \theta_1)$, where θ_0 and θ_1 map into the same parameter space Θ, such that $\mathbb{M}_0 \subseteq \mathbb{M}_1$ and $\theta_0(\psi) = \theta_1(\psi)$ for all $\psi \in \mathbb{M}_0$. Then a consistent estimator $\hat{\theta}$ of the parameters of the first model is said to be *robust* with respect to the second if it is also consistent for the second model. (Note that, since $\theta_0 : \mathbb{R}^{mn} \to \Theta$, it satisfies our definition of an estimator of $(\mathbb{M}_1, \theta_1)$.) Thus the OLS estimator of the regression model (18) restricted so as to have normal errors is robust with respect to the full model (18) with arbitrary error distribution satisfying the conditions on the first two moments.

It may happen that the 'unrestricted' model $\mathbb{M}_1$ has more parameters than the 'restricted' model $\mathbb{M}_0$. The above definition may still be used by limiting the parameter-defining mapping θ_1 to its projection on to those parameters that do appear in $(\mathbb{M}_0, \theta_0)$. For instance, the unrestricted regression

$$y_t = X_t\beta + Z_t\gamma + u_t \qquad (22)$$

contains the restricted regression

$$y_t = X_t\beta + u_t \qquad (23)$$

as a special case, but has more parameters. In order to see if an estimator for (23) is robust with respect to (22), one just forgets about the γ parameters for model (22). It then follows by standard arguments that the OLS estimator of (23) is robust with respect to (22) if and only if $\operatorname{plim}_{n\to\infty} n^{-1} \sum_{t=1}^{n} Z_t' X_t = \mathbf{0}$.

Robustness is often thought to entail a cost in terms of the *efficiency* of an estimator. One of the chief aims of this chapter is to make explicit the trade-off between these two desirable features. Before we can do so, we need a geometrical characterisation of efficiency. As with robustness, efficiency will always be defined with respect to a given parameterised model $(\mathbb{M}, \theta)$. A root-n consistent estimator $\hat{\theta}$ is *efficient* for $(\mathbb{M}, \theta)$ at a DGP $\psi \in \mathbb{M}$ if no other root-n consistent estimator $\check{\theta}$ for $(\mathbb{M}, \theta)$ has smaller asymptotic variance under ψ. Specifically, the difference between the asymptotic covariance matrix of $\check{\theta}$, given by (21), and that for $\hat{\theta}$ is a positive semi-definite matrix. The geometrical characterisation of efficiency is given by the following theorem.

Theorem 1 *Under the regularity assumed so far, the root-n consistent estimator $\hat{\theta}$ is efficient for the parameterised model $(\mathbb{M}, \theta)$ at a DGP $\psi \in \mathbb{M}$ if and only if the tangents $\hat{s}_i$, $i = 1, \ldots, k$, associated with $\hat{\theta}$ belong to the space $E(\psi, \theta)$.*

In order to prove this theorem, we will develop in a series of lemmas a number of properties of root-n consistent estimators. First, note that, if the condition of the theorem is true, the $\hat{s}_i$, $i = 1, \ldots, k$, span the k-dimensional space $E(\psi, \theta)$, since any linear dependence of the $\hat{s}_i$ would imply that the model parameters were not independent, contrary to the assumption that the parameter-defining mapping is a submersion.

Lemma 1 *The tangents $\check{s}_i$, $i = 1, \ldots, k$, associated with a root-n consistent estimator $\check{\theta}$ of the parameterised model $(\mathbb{M}, \theta)$ at a DGP $\psi \in \mathbb{M}$ are orthogonal to the space $T_M(\psi, \theta)$.*

164   **Russell Davidson**

Proof If $T_M(\psi, \theta)$ consists only of the zero tangent, the lemma is trivial. Otherwise, consider a curve in M through ψ such that, for all points $\psi(\varepsilon)$ on the curve, $\theta(\psi(\varepsilon)) = \theta(\psi)$. The tangent ψ' to this curve belongs to $T_M(\psi, \theta)$ by definition, and any element of $T_M(\psi, \theta)$ can be generated by such a curve. Then, for all admissible ε, the expectation of $\hat{\theta}^n$ under $\psi(\varepsilon)$ tends to $\theta_0 \equiv \theta(\psi)$ as $n \to \infty$.

Suppose that the curve is expressed in terms of contributions $\ell_t(\varepsilon)$, as in (9), and that the tangents $\check{s}_i$ correspond to components $\check{s}_{ti}$ satisfying (16). Then we have

$$0 = E_{\psi(\varepsilon)}(\check{s}_{ti}(y^t) \mid y^{t-1}) = \int \exp(\ell_t(\varepsilon; y^t))\, \check{s}_{ti}(y^t)\, dy_t.$$

From (19), it is clear that, since $\theta(\psi(\varepsilon))$ is independent of ε, so too is $\check{s}_{ti}$ along the curve $\psi(\varepsilon)$. Thus differentiating with respect to ε and evaluating at $\varepsilon = 0$ gives

$$\int \exp(\ell_t(0; y^t)) \frac{\partial \ell_t}{\partial \varepsilon}(0; y^t)\, \check{s}_{ti}(y^t)\, dy_t = E_\psi\left(\frac{\partial \ell_t}{\partial \varepsilon}(0; y^t)\, \check{s}_{ti}(y^t) \,\middle|\, y^{t-1} \right)$$

$$= 0.$$

Thus the random variables $\partial \ell_t / \partial \varepsilon(0)$ and $\check{s}_{ti}$ have zero covariance at ψ conditional on y^{t-1}. By the martingale property (compare (14)), this implies that the unconditional covariance of $n^{-1/2} \sum_{t=1}^n \partial \ell_t / \partial \varepsilon(0)$ and $n^{-1/2} \sum_{t=1}^n \check{s}_{ti}$ is zero, and so, letting $n \to \infty$ gives

$$\lim_{n\to\infty} E_\psi\left(n^{-1/2} \sum_{t=1}^n \frac{\partial \ell_t}{\partial \varepsilon}(0, y^n)\, n^{1/2}(\hat{\theta}^n(y^n) - \theta_0) \right) = 0. \tag{24}$$

Since the left-hand side of this is the limiting covariance of $n^{1/2}(\hat{\theta}^n - \theta_0)$ and $n^{-1/2} \sum_{t=1}^n (\partial \ell_t / \partial \varepsilon)$ under ψ, the typical element of (24) becomes

$$\langle \psi', \check{s}_i \rangle = 0.$$

Since ψ' is an arbitrary element of $T_M(\psi, \theta)$, this completes the proof. ∎

Lemma 1 shows that any $\check{s}_i$ can be expressed as the sum of a component in $E(\psi, \theta)$ and a component in the orthogonal complement of $T_M(\psi)$ in $T_S(\psi)$. The two terms of this sum are themselves orthogonal. According to Theorem 1, the second term must vanish for an efficient estimator. In fact, the efficient estimator will turn out to be asymptotically unique.

For the next lemma, for each $j = 1, \ldots, k$, consider any curve $\psi_j(\varepsilon)$ in $\mathbb{M}$ that satisfies the relation

$$\theta(\psi_j(\varepsilon)) = \theta_0 + \varepsilon e_j, \qquad (25)$$

where e_j is a k-vector all the components of which are zero except for component j, which equals one. The existence of such curves is once more guaranteed by the requirement that θ be a submersion.

Lemma 2 *For any root-n consistent estimator $\check{\theta}$ characterised at the DGP ψ in the parameterised model $(\mathbb{M}, \theta)$ by the tangents $\check{s}_i$, $i = 1, \ldots, k$, and for any curve $\psi_j(\varepsilon)$ satisfying (25), the inner product $\langle \psi_j', \check{s}_i \rangle = \delta_{ij}$.*

Proof Suppose as in the proof of Lemma 1 that the $\check{s}_i$ correspond to components $\check{s}_{ti}$ satisfying (16). From (19) and (25) it follows that $\partial \check{s}_{ti}/\partial \varepsilon = \delta_{ij}$ along $\psi_j(\varepsilon)$. Letting $\psi_j(\varepsilon)$ be expressed in terms of contributions $(\ell_j)_t(\varepsilon)$, then, by exactly the same arguments as in the proof of Lemma 1, for $i = 1, \ldots, k$, we see that

$$E_\psi \left(\frac{\partial(\ell_j)_t}{\partial \varepsilon}(0; y^t) \, \check{s}_{ti}(y^t) \, \middle| \, y^{t-1} \right) = \delta_{ij}.$$

This implies that $\langle \psi_j', \check{s}_i \rangle = \delta_{ij}$, as required. ∎

Lemma 3 *At each DGP ψ in the parameterised model $(\mathbb{M}, \theta)$, there exist unique tangents $\hat{s}_i$, $i = 1, \ldots, k$ in the space $E(\psi, \theta)$ such that for any root-n consistent estimator $\check{\theta}$ characterised at ψ by the tangents $\check{s}_i$, $i = 1, \ldots, k$, $\check{s}_i = \hat{s}_i + v_i$, where v_i belongs to the orthogonal complement of $T_M(\psi)$ in $T_S(\psi)$. Similarly, for all $j = 1, \ldots, k$ and for any curve $\psi_j(\varepsilon)$ satisfying (25), there exist unique tangents σ_j in $E(\psi, \theta)$ such that $\psi_j' = \sigma_j + w_j$, where w_j belongs to $T_M(\psi, \theta)$.*

Proof For any $\check{\theta}$, we know from Lemma 1 that $\check{s}_i$ can be expressed as a sum of a tangent in $E(\psi, \theta)$ and some v_i in the orthogonal complement of $T_M(\psi)$ in $T_S(\psi)$. This decomposition is unique, because it is orthogonal. Thus we may choose an arbitrary estimator $\check{\theta}$ and *define* the $\hat{s}_i$ by $\check{s}_i = \hat{s}_i + v_i$. Similarly, for any given set of curves $\psi_j(\varepsilon)$ satisfying (25), since the ψ_j' lie in $T_M(\psi)$, we may *define* the tangents σ_j by $\psi_j' = \sigma_j + w_j$, $\sigma_j \in E(\psi, \theta)$, $w_j \in T_M(\psi, \theta)$. Clearly the σ_j span $E(\psi, \theta)$.

By Lemma 2, we have

$$\delta_{ij} = \langle \psi_j', \check{s}_i \rangle = \langle \sigma_j + w_j, \hat{s}_i + v_i \rangle = \langle \sigma_j, \hat{s}_i \rangle, \qquad (26)$$

since v_i, being orthogonal to $T_M(\psi)$, is orthogonal to both σ_j and w_j, and w_j, being orthogonal to $E(\psi, \theta)$, is orthogonal to $\hat{s}_i$.

Consider any other root-n consistent estimator characterised by tangents $\tilde{s}_i$ such that $\tilde{s}_i = t_i + u_i$, $t_i \in E(\psi, \theta)$, u_i orthogonal to t_i. Then (26) applies to the $\tilde{s}_i$, and so

$$\langle \sigma_j, t_i \rangle = \delta_{ij}.$$

Since the σ_j span $E(\psi, \theta)$, and the t_i and the $\hat{s}_i$ belong to $E(\psi, \theta)$ and have the same inner products with the basis vectors σ_j, we have $t_i = \hat{s}_i$, and so the $\hat{s}_i$ are unique, as claimed. The uniqueness of the σ_j follows by an exactly similar argument starting from any other set of curves satisfying (25). ∎

Since all the tangents in the above lemma can be represented by martingales, the results of the lemma can be expressed in terms of contributions, as follows:

$$E_\psi(\hat{s}_{ti}(y^t) v_{ti}(y^t) | y^{t-1}) = 0, \text{ and}$$

$$E_\psi(\sigma_{tj}(y^t) w_{tj}(y^t) | y^{t-1}) = 0.$$

The relations

$$\langle \sigma_j, \hat{s}_i \rangle = \delta_{ij} \tag{27}$$

can be expressed by saying that the σ_j and the $\hat{s}_i$ constitute a pair of *dual bases* for $E(\psi, \theta)$. This property also implies that the $k \times k$ matrix with typical element $\langle \hat{s}_i, \hat{s}_j \rangle$ is the inverse of the matrix with typical element $\langle \sigma_i, \sigma_j \rangle$. Since the former matrix is the asymptotic covariance matrix of the estimator θ, the latter can be thought of as performing the role of the asymptotic *information matrix* – in a maximum likelihood model, it would be the asymptotic information matrix in the usual sense. Since the scalar product is a smooth tensor on Hilbert space or a Hilbert manifold, it is seen that the information matrix is smooth in our Hilbert space construction.

The proof of Theorem 1 can now be finished easily. Any estimator $\hat{\theta}$ satisfying the condition of the theorem is characterised by tangents lying in $E(\psi, \theta)$, which, by the uniqueness given by Lemma 3, must be the $\hat{s}_i$ of that lemma. Any other estimator $\check{\theta}$ has associated tangents of the form $\hat{s}_i + v_i$. Since all the $\hat{s}_i$ are orthogonal to all the v_i, the asymptotic covariance matrix of $\check{\theta}$ equals the matrix of inner products of the $\hat{s}_i$ plus the matrix of inner products of the v_i. Since all of these matrices are covariance matrices, they are all positive semi-definite, and so the difference between the asymptotic covariance matrix of $\check{\theta}$ and that of $\hat{\theta}$ is positive semi-definite, as required. ∎

4 Examples and illustrations

As a textbook example, consider the linear regression model (18) with normal errors. Since asymptotic theory is hardly necessary to treat this model, we can consider a finite sample size n. The model can be written in matrix notation as follows:

$$y = X\beta + u, \tag{18}$$

where y and u are $n \times 1$, X is $n \times k$, and β is $k \times 1$. We also consider the model (22):

$$y = X\beta + Z\gamma + u. \tag{22}$$

As we saw, the OLS estimator for (18) is not robust with respect to (22) if $Z'X$ is non-zero. However the OLS estimator for (22), restricted to the parameters β, is consistent, but not efficient, for (18). The OLS estimator from (18) is

$$\hat{\beta} \equiv (X'X)^{-1}X'y,$$

and the estimator of β from (22) is

$$\check{\beta} \equiv (X'M_ZX)^{-1}X'M_Zy, \tag{28}$$

where $M_Z \equiv I - Z(Z'Z)^{-1}Z'$ is the orthogonal projection on to the orthogonal complement of the span of the extra regressors Z. It is easy to show that (see, for instance, Davidson and MacKinnon (1993), chapter 11)

$$\check{\beta} - \hat{\beta} = (X'M_ZX)^{-1}X'M_ZM_Xy, \tag{29}$$

with M_X defined similarly to M_Z.

When (18) is specified with normal errors, the model is finite-dimensional, $k + 1$-dimensional in fact, if τ^2 is allowed to vary. Since the log-likelihood of the model is

$$\ell(\beta, \tau^2) = -\frac{n}{2}\log 2\pi\tau^2 - \frac{1}{2\tau^2}\|y - X\beta\|^2,$$

the tangents to the curves along which just one component of β varies are represented by the k-vector of zero-mean random variables

$$\sigma \equiv n^{-1/2}\frac{1}{\tau^2}X'u. \tag{30}$$

The only way to vary the DGP without changing the parameter vector $\boldsymbol{\beta}$ is to vary the error variance. Thus the space $T_M(\psi, \boldsymbol{\beta})$ is one-dimensional in this case, and is generated by the tangent represented by

$$n^{-1/2}\frac{\partial \ell}{\partial \tau^2} = n^{-1/2}\frac{1}{2\tau^2}\sum_{t=1}^{n}\left(\frac{u^2}{\tau^2} - 1\right), \tag{31}$$

which has zero covariance with all the components of (30). This means that these components lie in $E(\psi, \boldsymbol{\beta})$, thereby justifying the notation $\boldsymbol{\sigma}$.

The OLS estimator $\hat{\boldsymbol{\beta}}$ is associated with the tangents

$$\hat{\boldsymbol{s}} \equiv (n^{-1}\boldsymbol{X}'\boldsymbol{X})^{-1}n^{-1/2}\boldsymbol{X}'\boldsymbol{u}, \tag{32}$$

which are seen immediately to be linear combinations of the components of $\boldsymbol{\sigma}$ in (30). The tangents $\hat{\boldsymbol{s}}$ therefore also lie in $E(\psi, \boldsymbol{\beta})$ and so $\hat{\boldsymbol{\beta}}$ is seen to be asymptotically efficient. Note also that the matrix of inner products of the components of $\boldsymbol{\sigma}$ and $\hat{\boldsymbol{s}}$ is the expectation of

$$n^{-1/2}\frac{1}{\tau^2}\boldsymbol{X}'\boldsymbol{u}\,n^{-1/2}\boldsymbol{u}'\boldsymbol{X}(n^{-1}\boldsymbol{X}'\boldsymbol{X})^{-1} = \boldsymbol{I},$$

confirming the dual basis property (27).

The tangents corresponding to the estimator (28) are seen, from (29), to be

$$\check{\boldsymbol{s}} = \hat{\boldsymbol{s}} + (n^{-1}\boldsymbol{X}'\boldsymbol{M}_Z\boldsymbol{X})^{-1}n^{-1/2}\boldsymbol{X}'\boldsymbol{M}_Z\boldsymbol{M}_X\boldsymbol{u}.$$

It is simple to check that the covariances of the second term of this with the components of (32) are zero, as also with (31), which represents the tangent that generates $T_M(\psi, \boldsymbol{\beta})$. Thus this second term represents a tangent orthogonal to all of $T_M(\psi)$, as required by the theory of the preceding section.

As a slightly less trivial example, consider again the regression model (18), without imposing the normality of the error terms. The OLS estimator is of course *robust* for any model at all that satisfies the regression equation with zero-mean errors, but it is interesting to enquire under what conditions it is also efficient.

Consider a parameterised model $(M, \boldsymbol{\beta})$ the DGPs of which satisfy (18), but do not necessarily have normal errors. The OLS estimator is still characterised by the tangents (32), and its robustness implies, by Lemma 1, that these tangents are orthogonal to $T_M(\psi, \boldsymbol{\beta})$ for all $\psi \in M$. Consequently, the estimator is efficient at a given ψ if M is large enough to contain the tangents (32) in its tangent space $T_M(\psi)$ at ψ, since then, being orthogonal to $T_M(\psi, \boldsymbol{\beta})$, they must belong to $E(\psi, \boldsymbol{\beta})$. Although it is difficult to state a precise condition that will guarantee this property, intuitively it can be seen that the model must include the case of normal errors.

It can be checked that, if the model specifies the error distribution, up to a scale factor, then *only* normal errors are compatible with the efficiency of the OLS estimator. Suppose that the error density, scaled to have unit variance, is denoted by f. Then the log-density of observation t of the model (18) is

$$\log\left(\frac{1}{\tau}f\left(\frac{y_t - X_t\beta}{\tau}\right)\right).$$

The tangent corresponding to a variation of β_i is then represented by

$$-\frac{1}{\tau}n^{-1/2}\sum_{t=1}^{n}X_{ti}\frac{f'(e_t)}{f(e_t)},$$

where $e_t \equiv (y_t - X_t\beta)/\tau$. If the tangents $\hat{s}$ given by (32) are linear combinations of those above, for $i = 1, \ldots, k$, then it is necessary that

$$\frac{f'(e_t)}{f(e_t)} = ce_t, \tag{33}$$

for some constant c independent of t. The general solution to the differential equation (33) is

$$f(e) = C\exp(ce^2/2),$$

(C another constant) and, since this density must have mean zero and unit variance, it must be the standard normal density, with $C = (2\pi)^{-1/2}$, and $c = -1$.

In general, if one wishes to improve the precision of a parameter estimate, more information of some sort is necessary. Such information may take the form of the true value of some other parameter, or the true nature of the error density, or the like. When models are considered as sets of DGPs, this sort of information corresponds to a *reduction* of the model size, since only DGPs satisfying the constraints imposed by the new information can belong to the model. Then efficiency gains are possible because estimators that would not have been robust with respect to the original model may be so for the reduced model. In some circumstances, though, this is not so, in which case the extra information is uninformative concerning the parameters.

These general considerations can be illustrated geometrically. Consider figure 5.1, which represents the space $E(\psi, \theta)$ for some parameterised model as a two-dimensional space, with $\theta = [\beta : \gamma]$. The origin corresponds to the DGP ψ, at which it is supposed that $\beta = \beta_0$, $\gamma = 0$. The

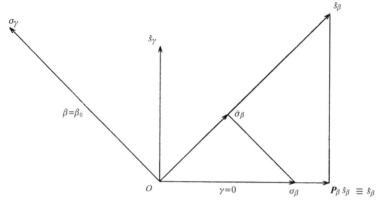

Figure 5.1 Efficiency gain from added information

dual bases $\{\hat{s}_\beta, \hat{s}_\gamma\}$ and $\{\sigma_\beta, \sigma_\gamma\}$ are drawn, and it can be seen that $\hat{s}_\beta$ is orthogonal to σ_γ, and $\hat{s}_\gamma$ to σ_β. The tangent σ_γ gives the direction in which only γ varies, and so it is labelled $\beta = \beta_0$. Similarly, σ_β is labelled $\gamma = 0$.

Now suppose that we are provided with the information that $\gamma = 0$. The model must now be restricted to DGPs that satisfy that property. The two-dimensional $E(\psi, \theta)$ depicted in the figure is reduced to the one-dimensional line in the direction of σ_β, that being the direction in which γ remains constant at zero. But $\hat{s}_\beta$ does not belong to the one-dimensional $E(\psi, \beta)$, and so is no longer efficient for the constrained model. The efficient estimator for that model is obtained by projecting $\hat{s}_\beta$ orthogonally on to the direction of σ_β, using the projection denoted by $\boldsymbol{P}_\beta$ in the figure. This gives rise to a new consistent estimator associated with $\tilde{s}_\beta \equiv \boldsymbol{P}_\beta \hat{s}_\beta$. Since $\tilde{s}_\beta$ is obtained from $\hat{s}_\beta$ by an orthogonal projection, it is of smaller norm or, in statistical terms, of smaller asymptotic variance. In addition, the orthogonal projection means that $\tilde{s}_\beta$ has the same inner product with σ_β as does $\hat{s}_\beta$, and so it satisfies the condition of Lemma 2 for a consistent estimator. The result of Lemma 1 is also seen to be satisfied: the inefficient estimator $\hat{s}_\beta$ for the constrained model equals the efficient estimator $\tilde{s}_\beta$ plus something orthogonal to the constrained model.

If γ is a 'nuisance' parameter, the value of which is used only to improve the precision of the estimate of β, then it could have been left out of the parameter-defining mapping of the original, unreduced, model. If so, the omission of γ once more leads to a one-dimensional $E(\psi, \beta)$, but this time in the direction of $\hat{s}_\beta$. This is because $E(\psi, \beta)$ must be orthogonal to all directions in which β does not vary, now *including* the direction of σ_γ. This time, it is σ_β that is projected orthogonally on to the direction of $\hat{s}_\beta$ to yield $\bar{\sigma}_\beta$, which replaces σ_β for the model with γ dropped. This orthogonal projection, which means that $\bar{\sigma}_\beta$ has smaller norm than σ_β, corresponds to a reduction in information about β. Notice that the *estimator* $\hat{s}_\beta$ is unchanged whether or not γ is dropped. The information gain moving from $\bar{\sigma}_\beta$ to σ_β is not realised so long as β and γ are estimated jointly, and is realised only when information about γ is available.

If σ_β and σ_γ were orthogonal, so would be $\hat{s}_\beta$ and $\hat{s}_\gamma$, and the directions of σ_β and $\hat{s}_\beta$ would coincide, as would those of σ_γ and $\hat{s}_\gamma$. Redrawing figure 5.1 to reflect this state of affairs shows that information about γ no longer leads to any gain in the precision of the estimate of β. This is perfectly intuitive, since the orthogonality means that the asymptotic covariance matrix of the parameter estimates is diagonal.

A simple example of such orthogonality is provided by the linear regression model (18) with normal errors, for which the tangents (30) corresponding to variation of the parameters β of the regression function are orthogonal to the tangent (31), which corresponds to variation of τ^2. As is well known, knowledge of the value of the error variance is uninformative about β. In much the same way, it was seen above that if normal errors are not assumed in (18), then, if it were learnt that the errors were in fact normal, this new information would not lead to any gain as regards estimation of β, since the OLS estimator remains efficient for normal errors.

5   Estimating functions and GMM

The generalised method of moments (GMM) was proposed by Hansen (1982), apparently without knowledge of a very similar method proposed by Godambe (1960); see also Godambe and Thompson (1989) and Godambe (1991). It is convenient to refer to Godambe's method as the *method of estimating functions*. Both approaches start from what in the estimating function context are called *elementary zero functions*, which are functions – at least one for each observation of the sample – of both data and parameters. When these functions are evaluated at the correct values for any given DGP, their expectation under that DGP is zero. The simplest example is, as usual, the linear regression model (18), for which the elementary zero functions are the $y_t - X_t\beta$, one for each observation t.

Specifying a set of elementary zero functions is very similar to specifying a model and a parameter-defining mapping. Suppose that, for each observation t, the elementary zero functions are written as $f_t(y^t, \theta)$, where, as before, the argument $y^t \in \mathbb{R}^{mt}$ corresponds to the observed data in observations 1 through t, and θ is a k-vector of parameters. The p-vector-valued function f_t will usually depend on explanatory variables (covariates), hence the index t. The natural way to proceed is to specify the model as the set of those DGPs ψ for which there exists a unique parameter vector $\boldsymbol{\theta}$ such that $E_\psi(f_t(Y^t, \boldsymbol{\theta})) = 0$. (Recall that Y^t is the random variable of which observations 1 through t are a realisation.) The parameter-defining mapping then maps ψ to this unique $\boldsymbol{\theta}$.

The above way of defining a parameterised model needs to be qualified somewhat, for a number of reasons. The first is that, in order to perform inference, it is necessary to be able to estimate not only the parameter vector $\boldsymbol{\theta}$, but also the asymptotic covariance matrix of the estimator $\hat{\boldsymbol{\theta}}$, and, for this, one needs the existence of higher moments. It would therefore be preferable to limit the model to those DGPs for which those higher moments exist.

The second reason reveals a difficulty that arises whenever a model, parameter-defining mapping or estimation method makes use of *moments*, that is expectations. It is that, in any commonly used stochastic topology, including the one used here based on Hilbert space norms (see Billingsley (1968, 1979)), expectations of unbounded random variables are not continuous functions of the DGP under which they are calculated. For instance, even the smallest admixture of the Cauchy distribution with the normal is enough to destroy the existence of the first moment. The unfortunate consequence is that, if a model is defined by moments, it will not be a smooth submanifold of the overall set of DGPs, $\mathbb{S}$.

The lack of continuity of moments is a problem for establishing appropriate regularity conditions in many contexts, not just the geometrical one. For present purposes, the easiest solution is just to require that the elementary zero functions $f_t(y^t, \boldsymbol{\theta})$ should be bounded functions of y^t. Of course, this assumption excludes most interesting models, even the linear regression model, but, since the emphasis of this chapter is geometrical, it does not seem worthwhile to look further for more suitable regularity conditions. In particular, imposing the existence of moments on a model is not informative about that model's parameters. This can be seen by considering a very simple problem, namely that of estimating the mean of a set of scalar i.i.d. observations. If these observations may take values anywhere in an unbounded set, then the set of DGPs defined by requiring that the observations be i.i.d. drawings from a distribution for which the mean exists is not a smooth submanifold of $\mathbb{S}$. However, the set is *dense* in such a submanifold. To see why, consider the Hilbert space $L^2(\mathbb{R})$ in which the unit sphere represents all univariate densities defined on $\mathbb{R}$. Then, for ψ in this unit sphere, the mean of the density to which ψ corresponds, if it exists, is

$$\int_{-\infty}^{\infty} |\psi(y)|^2 y \, dy. \tag{34}$$

The integral above defines an unbounded quadratic operator on $L^2(\mathbb{R})$, the domain of which is dense in $L^2(\mathbb{R})$. In other words, the densities for which the mean exists are dense in the unit sphere of $L^2(\mathbb{R})$. It is straightforward to extend this univariate result to the asymptotic Hilbert space $\mathbb{S}$.

Clearly the model implicitly defined by the problem of estimating the mean is just the set of all i.i.d. sequences, and this set does constitute a smooth submanifold because the requirement that all the observations be i.i.d. can be expressed by the relations $\psi_t = \psi$, for some ψ independent of $t = 1, \ldots$, and these relations are trivially continuously differentiable in the Hilbert space norm of $L^2(\mathbb{R})$. The set of DGPs in this model for which the mean actually exists is a dense set, so that its closure is the full submanifold. However, any information gain that could lead to increased precision of the estimate of the mean must involve, as we saw above, a reduction in the dimension of the model. Since we have seen that imposing a finite mean does not reduce the dimension, no information gain is possible from the knowledge that the mean exists.

Any expectation can be expressed as an integral similar to (34), and can therefore be used to define an unbounded operator on the Hilbert spaces for finite samples. Thus the argument above generalises to all models defined using the expectations of unbounded random variables, and so, for the purposes of geometrical discussions of efficiency and robustness, we must limit ourselves to models defined in terms of the expectations of bounded random variables, for instance, variables obtained by censoring unbounded variables above some suitably high threshold.

Suppose then that we define a parameterised model $(\mathbb{M}, \theta)$ by a set of elementary zero functions given by the components of the p-vector $f_t(y^t, \theta)$, as above. Suppose further that the parameter-defining mapping θ thus implicitly defined is in fact defined for all $\psi \in \mathbb{M}$, so that the identification condition is satisfied, and that θ is a submersion, as we required earlier. Consider any $\psi \in \mathbb{M}$ and suppose that $\theta(\psi) = \theta_0$. Then, for each component f_{ti}, $i = 1, \ldots, p$, of f_t, $E_\psi(f_{ti}(Y^t, \theta_0)) = 0$, and so in some circumstances it may be that the sequence

$$n^{-1/2} \sum_{t=1}^{n} \sum_{i=1}^{p} a_{ti}(y^{t-1}) f_{ti}(y^t, \theta_0) \tag{35}$$

represents a vector of tangents at ψ, where the $a_{ti}(y^{t-1})$ are predetermined at t, and such that $\lim_{n \to \infty} n^{-1} \sum_{t=1}^{n} \sum_{i=1}^{p} E_\psi(a_{ti}^2)$ is finite. This may equally well not be so, because, since only the *unconditional* expectations of the zero functions must vanish, the sequence may not be a martingale,

as required by the first equation of (16). For the moment, we suppose that
the martingale property is satisfied. Then we have:

Lemma 4 *For a parameterised model* $(\mathbb{M}, \boldsymbol{\theta})$ *defined by a set of
elementary zero functions* $f_t(y^t, \boldsymbol{\theta})$ *obeying the above regularity conditions
and such that, for all* $\psi \in \mathbb{M}$, *the sequence (35) is a martingale, the tangents represented by the components of (35) are orthogonal to* $T_M(\psi, \boldsymbol{\theta})$,
the space of tangents at ψ *that correspond to curves within the model along
which the parameters are constant at* $\boldsymbol{\theta}_0$.

Proof As in the proof of Lemma 1, consider a curve $\psi(\varepsilon)$ in
$T_M(\psi, \boldsymbol{\theta})$, represented by the log-density contributions $\ell_t(\varepsilon)$. Then, as in
Lemma 1,

$$\int f_{ti}(y^t, \boldsymbol{\theta}_0) \frac{\partial \ell_t}{\partial \varepsilon}(\varepsilon; y^t) \exp(\ell_t(\varepsilon; y^t)) \, dy_t = 0. \tag{36}$$

On multiplying by a_t, the martingale property implies the result.   ∎

Lemma 4 is the geometrical expression of the fact that, under suitable
regularity conditions, the parameters $\boldsymbol{\theta}$ can be consistently estimated by
solving any k linearly and functionally independent equations of the form

$$\sum_{t=1}^{n} \sum_{i=1}^{p} a_{ti}(Y^{t-1}) f_{ti}(Y^t, \hat{\boldsymbol{\theta}}) = 0, \tag{37}$$

where the a_{ti}, $t = 1, \ldots, n$, $i = 1, \ldots, p$, are predetermined at t. Standard
arguments based on a short Taylor expansion (see, for instance,
Davidson and MacKinnon (1993), chapter 17) show that, asymptotically,
the components of the sequence $n^{1/2}(\hat{\boldsymbol{\theta}} - \boldsymbol{\theta}_0)$ are linear combinations of
the tangents represented by

$$n^{-1/2} \sum_{t=1}^{n} \sum_{i=1}^{p} a_{ti}(y^{t-1}) f_{ti}(y^t, \boldsymbol{\theta}_0), \tag{38}$$

provided that a law of large numbers can be applied to the sequences

$$\left\{ \frac{\partial f_{ti}}{\partial \theta_j}(Y^t, \boldsymbol{\theta}_0) \right\}_{t=1}^{\infty}.$$

Although this point will not be developed here, regularity conditions like
these are the algebraic counterparts of the geometrical regularity conditions, involving identifiability and the submersion property, discussed
above. For further discussion, see Newey and McFadden (1994).

Just as with the tangents $\breve{s}_i$ used in Lemma 1, the tangents (38) can be expressed as the sum of two orthogonal components, one in the k-dimensional space $E(\psi, \theta)$, and the other orthogonal to the model M. The first component corresponds to the asymptotically efficient estimator, and so, in order to find an efficient estimator, we wish to *project* the tangents (38) orthogonally on to $E(\psi, \theta)$. Intuitively, this orthogonal projection is on to the model M itself, since the tangents are already orthogonal to $T_M(\psi, \theta)$, the orthogonal complement of $E(\psi, \theta)$ in the tangent space to the model M.

We can perform the orthogonal projection by expressing the unique tangents $\sigma_j, j = 1, \ldots, k$, defined in Lemma 3, in the form (38). As seen in the proof of that lemma, we can compute the inner product of any tangent of the form (38) with σ_j by considering a curve satisfying (25), since the tangent to such a curve equals σ_j plus a component orthogonal to everything like (38). These inner products are given by the following lemma.

Lemma 5 *For a parameterised model (M, θ) defined by a set of elementary zero functions $f_t(y^t, \theta)$ obeying the regularity conditions of Lemma 4, the tangent σ_j at DGP $\psi \in M$ corresponding to component $j = 1, \ldots, k$ of θ can be represented by the sequence of contributions*

$$\sigma_{tj} \equiv \sum_{i=1}^{p} \sigma_{tij} f_{ti}(\theta_0). \tag{39}$$

Further, for all $i = 1, \ldots, p, j = 1, \ldots, k$,

$$E_\psi(\sigma_{tj} f_{ti}(\theta_0) \, g \mid y^{t-1}) = -E_\psi\left(\frac{\partial f_{ti}}{\partial \theta_j}(\theta_0) \,\middle|\, y^{t-1}\right). \tag{40}$$

If the covariance matrix of $f_t(y^t, \theta_0)$ under ψ, conditional on y^{t-1}, is $\Omega_t(y^{t-1})$, then

$$\sigma_{tij}(y^{t-1}) = -\sum_{l=1}^{p} (\Omega_t^{-1}(y^{t-1}))_{il} E_\psi\left(\frac{\partial f_{tl}}{\partial \theta_j}(y^t) \,\middle|\, y^{t-1}\right). \tag{41}$$

Proof The first statement of the lemma, (39), simply requires the equations that define the asymptotically efficient estimator to take the general form (37). For this to be false, there would need to exist consistent estimators defined by equations that did not take this form. But the model is defined by the expectations of the elementary zero functions, and expectations of non-linear functions of these will not in general be zero. Thus a consistent estimator cannot be defined using non-linear functions of the elementary zero functions, and so (39) is true.

For (40), consider, as in Lemma 2, a curve $\psi_j(\varepsilon)$ in M satisfying (25). Then we have, for $i = 1, \ldots, p$, $j = 1, \ldots, k$, $t = 1, \ldots$, and all admissible ε,

$$\int \exp((\ell_j)_t(y^t; \varepsilon)) f_{ti}(y^t, \theta_0 + \varepsilon e_j) \, dy_t = 0,$$

and so, on differentiating with respect to ε, and setting $\varepsilon = 0$, we get

$$E_\psi \left(\frac{\partial(\ell_j)_t(0)}{\partial \varepsilon} f_{ti}(\theta_0) \,\middle|\, y^{t-1} \right) = -E_\psi \left(\frac{\partial f_{ti}}{\partial \theta_j}(\theta_0) \,\middle|\, y^{t-1} \right).$$

By Lemma 3 and the remark following it, we may replace $\partial(\ell_j)_t(0)/\partial \varepsilon$ in the left-hand side above by the contribution σ_{tj}, thus yielding (40).

Substituting the expression for σ_{tj} in (39) into (40) gives

$$\sum_{l=1}^{p} \sigma_{tlj} E_\psi(f_{tl}(\theta_0) f_{ti}(\theta_0) | y^{t-1}) = -E_\psi \left(\frac{\partial f_{ti}}{\partial \theta_j}(\theta_0) \,\middle|\, y^{t-1} \right),$$

from which (41) follows, since by definition

$$(\boldsymbol{\Omega}_t)_{li} = E_\psi(f_{tl}(\theta_0) f_{ti}(\theta_0) | y^{t-1}). \quad \blacksquare$$

The following theorem now follows immediately from Lemma 5.

Theorem 2 *Let the parameterised model* $(\mathsf{M}, \boldsymbol{\theta})$ *be defined by means of the set of bounded elementary zero functions* $\boldsymbol{f}_t(y^t, \boldsymbol{\theta})$ *with the restriction that, for all* $\psi \in \mathsf{M}$, *the sequences* $f_{ti}(Y^t, \theta_0)$, $i = 1, \ldots, p$, *satisfy the conditions of (16) under* ψ. *Define the sequences of random variables* σ_{ti} *by (39), with the coefficients* $\sigma_{tij}(y^{t-1})$, *predetermined at* t, *given by (41). Then the estimator* $\hat{\boldsymbol{\theta}}$ *obtained by solving the equations*

$$\sum_{t=1}^{n} \sum_{i=1}^{p} \sigma_{tij}(Y^{t-1}) f_{ti}(Y^t, \hat{\boldsymbol{\theta}}) = 0, \tag{42}$$

for $j = 1, \ldots, k$, *is asymptotically efficient for* $(\mathsf{M}, \boldsymbol{\theta})$.

Proof As mentioned above, $\hat{\boldsymbol{\theta}}$ can be expressed asymptotically as a linear combination of the tangents (38) with the a_{ti} replaced by σ_{tij}. By Lemma 5, these tangents belong to $E(\psi, \boldsymbol{\theta})$ for all $\psi \in \mathsf{M}$. By Theorem 1, $\hat{\boldsymbol{\theta}}$ is asymptotically efficient. $\quad \blacksquare$

The conditions (16) are quite essential for Theorem 2, in particular the martingale condition. However, if the elementary zero functions do not satisfy that condition, it is often possible to find linear combinations, $g_t(y^t, \theta)$ of the $f_s(y^s, \theta)$, $s = 1, \ldots, t$, that do. The transformation from the f_t to the g_t is analogous to the transformation used to estimate models by GLS rather than OLS.

For instance, suppose that there is just one elementary zero function $f_t(\theta)$ per observation (that is, $p = 1$), and denote the covariance matrix of the f_t, for sample size n, by the $n \times n$ matrix V. V may depend on θ, and possibly on other parameters as well, such as autocorrelation coefficients. Let ϕ denote the complete set of parameters, and let ϕ_0 be the parameter values for the DGP ψ. In addition, since we are interested in the conditional covariance structure, V_{ts}, if $t \geq s$, may depend on Y^{s-1}.

Then if the lower-triangular matrix $P(\phi)$ is such that $P^\top(\phi)P(\phi) = V^{-1}(\phi)$, we form the vector of zero functions $g(\phi) = P(\phi)f(\theta)$, where f is $n \times 1$, with typical element f_t. Note that $P_{ts}(\phi)$ is non-zero only if $t \geq s$, and in that case it may depend on y^{s-1}. The covariance matrix of $g(\phi)$ is then just the identity matrix, and the martingale condition is satisfied.

In order to obtain the optimal estimating equations, we use the relation

$$E_\psi\left(\frac{\partial g_t}{\partial \phi_j}(y^t, \phi_0) \,\middle|\, y^{t-1}\right) = \sum_{s=1}^{t} P_{ts}(y^{s-1}, \phi)E_\psi\left(\frac{\partial f_s}{\partial \phi_j}(y^s, \theta_0) \,\middle|\, y^{s-1}\right),$$

which holds since

$$E_\psi\left(\frac{\partial P_{ts}}{\partial \phi_j}(y^{s-1}, \phi)f_s(y^s, \theta_0) \,\middle|\, y^{s-1}\right)$$

$$= \frac{\partial P_{ts}}{\partial \phi_j}(y^{s-1}, \phi)E_\psi(f_s(y^s, \theta_0) \,|\, y^{s-1}) = 0.$$

Thus the equations that define the asymptotically efficient estimator are obtained from (42) with g_t in place of f_{ti} (the index i is omitted since we have assumed that $p = 1$), and σ_{t1j} is defined by (41) with g in place of f. Because $p = 1$, Ω_t is just a scalar, equal to one, since the covariance matrix of g is the identity matrix. Putting all this together gives as the estimating equation

$$\sum_{t=1}^{n}\sum_{s=1}^{n} E_{\hat{\psi}}\left(\frac{\partial f_t}{\partial \phi_j}(\hat{\phi}) \,\middle|\, Y^{t-1}\right)V(\hat{\phi})f_s(Y^s, \hat{\phi}) = 0. \tag{43}$$

The notation is intended to indicate that the conditional expectation of $\partial f_t/\partial \phi_j$ must be estimated in some manner – we need not specify details, since many procedures exist. The result (43) is standard in the estimating functions literature, and can be found, for instance, in Godambe (1960) and Godambe and Thompson (1989).

All of the results of this section can be extended quite simply to the sort of model usually found in the context of the generalised method of moments. Such models are still defined in terms of elementary zero functions $f_t(y^t, \theta)$, but the requirement that these have zero mean is strengthened so as to require that their means conditional on some set of random variables be zero.

More formally, let $\mathcal{F}_t$, $t = 1, \ldots$, be a nested set of sigma-algebras, with $\mathcal{F}_{t-1} \subseteq \mathcal{F}_t$, and such that $Y^t \in \mathcal{F}_t$. Then the condition on the zero functions becomes

$$E_\psi(f_{ti}(Y^t, \theta_0) \mid \mathcal{F}_{t-1}) = 0,$$

where as usual $\theta_0 = \theta(\psi)$, $t = 1, \ldots$, and $i = 1, \ldots, p$. An equivalent way of expressing the condition is to require that, for all random variables $h_{t-1} \in \mathcal{F}_{t-1}$, the unconditional expectation of $h_{t-1} f_{ti}(\theta_0)$ be zero. Lemma 5 can be applied to all of these new zero functions, and it follows that (40) and (41) are now true with the expectations conditional on $\mathcal{F}_{t-1}$ rather than just on Y^{t-1}.

In addition, Theorem 2 continues to hold with the σ_{tij} defined by the modified (41). This result is most often expressed in terms of the *optimal instruments* for GMM estimation (see, for instance, Davidson and MacKinnon (1993), chapter 17).

6   The linear regression model

Despite its simplicity, the linear regression model (18) can be used to illustrate most of the theory of the preceding section. The elementary zero functions, one per observation, are given by

$$f_t(y_t, \beta) = y_t - X_t\beta. \tag{44}$$

In order to use (41), we compute $\partial f_t / \partial \beta_j = -X_{tj}$. Thus, if the f_t are homoskedastic, and provided that $X_{tj} \in \mathcal{F}_{t-1}$, it follows from Theorem 2 that solving the estimating equations

$$\sum_{t=1}^n X_{tj}(y_t - X_t\beta) = 0, \quad j = 1, \ldots, k,$$

yields an asymptotically efficient estimator, namely the OLS estimator, as required by the Gauss–Markov theorem. In case of heteroskedasticity, if $E((y_t - X_t\beta)^2) = \tau_t^2$, the estimating equations are

$$\sum_{t=1}^{n} \frac{1}{\tau_t^2} X_{tj}(y_t - X_t\beta) = 0,$$

and they yield the Aitken GLS estimator. If the explanatory variables X_t are endogenous and do not belong to $\mathcal{F}_{t-1}$, then the estimating equations are, assuming homoskedasticity,

$$\sum_{t=1}^{n} E(X_{tj} \mid \mathcal{F}_{t-1})(y_t - X_t\beta) = 0.$$

In simultaneous equations models, the expectations of endogenous explanatory variables can be expressed in terms of exogenous instrumental variables: the equation above then defines an instrumental variables estimator with optimal instruments.

It is clear that, if the model M includes heteroskedastic as well as homoskedastic DGPs, then there will be no estimator that is at the same time robust with respect to the whole model and efficient at every DGP in the model, unless there is a way of consistently estimating the variances τ_t^2. This will be the case whenever feasible GLS can be used, but not more generally.

In section 4, it was seen that, in regression models in which the error density is specified, the OLS estimator is efficient only if that density is normal. It is of interest to see if an efficiency gain with respect to OLS can be realised when the density is not normal, but is nonetheless of unknown form. We will now derive an estimator that can be used with homoskedastic errors, is robust against non-normal error densities, and is more efficient than OLS in some cases of non-normality. This estimator, which was recently proposed by Im (1996) using arguments somewhat different from those here, can be derived directly using the theory of the preceding section.

We rename the zero function (44) as $u_t(y_t, \beta)$, and introduce a new zero function and a new parameter by the relation

$$v_t(y_t, \beta, \tau^2) = u_t^2(y_t, \beta) - \tau^2,$$

where the homoskedasticity assumption is made explicit in terms of the error variance τ^2. It will also be assumed that the v_t are homoskedastic, and that the expectation of $u_t v_t$ does not depend on t. If this last assumption does not hold, the estimator we are about to derive is still robust, but is no longer efficient.

Analogously to (39), tangents that span the efficient space for the present model can be defined by the contributions

$$\sigma_{ti} = a_{ti}u_t + b_{ti}v_t, \quad i = 1, \ldots, k, \text{ and}$$
$$\sigma_{t\tau} = a_{t\tau}u_t + b_{t\tau}v_t, \tag{45}$$

where a_{ti}, b_{ti}, $a_{t\tau}$ and $b_{t\tau}$ are exogenous or predetermined at t. Now by (40) we have

$$E(\sigma_{ti}u_t) = -E\left(\frac{\partial u_t}{\partial \beta_i}\right) = X_{ti},$$

$$E(\sigma_{ti}v_t) = -E\left(\frac{\partial v_t}{\partial \beta_i}\right) = 2E(X_{ti}u_t) = 0,$$

$$E(\sigma_{t\tau}u_t) = -E\left(\frac{\partial u_t}{\partial \tau^2}\right) = 0, \text{ and}$$

$$E(\sigma_{t\tau}v_t) = -E\left(\frac{\partial v_t}{\partial \tau^2}\right) = 1.$$

Thus, on substituting the definitions (45) into the above, we obtain the following equations for the a_{ti}, etc.:

$$a_{ti}\tau^2 + b_{ti}\gamma = X_{ti};$$

$$a_{ti}\gamma + b_{ti}\kappa = 0;$$

$$a_{t\tau}\tau^2 + b_{t\tau}\gamma = 0;$$

$$a_{t\tau}\gamma + b_{t\tau}\kappa = 1,$$

where $\gamma \equiv E(u_t^3)$ and $\kappa \equiv E(u_t^4) - \tau^4$ are independent of t by assumption, and equal 0 and $2\tau^4$ under normality. Letting $\delta = \tau^2 - \gamma^2/\kappa$, we find that

$$\delta a_{ti} = X_{ti}, \quad \delta b_{ti} = -(\gamma/\kappa)X_{ti}, \quad \delta a_{t\tau} = -\gamma/\kappa, \quad \delta b_{t\tau} = \tau^2/\kappa.$$

Thus, according to Theorem 2, the estimating equations for $\boldsymbol{\beta}$ are

$$\sum_{t=1}^{n} X_{ti}\left(u_t - \frac{\gamma}{\kappa}(u_t^2 - \tau^2)\right) = 0. \tag{46}$$

If γ is known to be zero, that is, if the error density is not skewed, these equations give the OLS estimator. Otherwise, γ can be consistently estimated by $n^{-1}\sum_{t=1}^{n}\hat{u}_t^3$, and κ by $n^{-1}\sum_{t=1}^{n}\hat{u}_t^4 - \hat{\tau}^4$, where $\hat{u}_t$ and $\hat{\tau}^2$ can be obtained by, for example, OLS.

The procedure suggested by Im (1996) makes use of the artificial regression

$$y_t = X_t\boldsymbol{\beta} + (\hat{u}_t^2 - \hat{\tau}^2)\theta + \text{residual},$$

where θ is an auxiliary parameter. A little algebra shows that the OLS estimate of β from this is the solution of (46). Im shows, both theoretically and by Monte Carlo simulation, that his estimator, which he calls RALS (for residuals augmented least squares) is more efficient than OLS when the error terms are skewed. In fact, he goes further and, by introducing at third zero function

$$w_t(y_t, \beta, \tau^2, \gamma) = u_t^3(y_t, \beta) - 3\tau^2 u_t - \gamma,$$

in which γ, as defined above, becomes an explicit parameter, shows that further efficiency gains relative to OLS are available if the errors have non-normal kurtosis. The approach of the preceding paragraph can again be used to derive the explicit form of this estimator. As Im points out, estimators of this sort are constructed in the spirit of adaptive estimation (see, for instance, Newey (1988)).

7   Concluding remarks

In this chapter, geometrical characterisations have been given of efficiency and robustness for estimators of model parameters, with special reference to estimators defined by the method of estimating functions and/or the generalised method of moments. It has been shown that, when a parameterised model is considered as a Hilbert manifold in an underlying space of DGPs, the tangent space at any DGP of the model can be expressed as the direct sum of three mutually orthogonal subspaces. Consistent estimators of the model parameters all have the same component in one of these subspaces, which is finite-dimensional, with dimension equal to the number of parameters. This space contains the asymptotically efficient estimator. Inefficient estimators also have a non-vanishing component in the orthogonal complement of the tangent space to the model, and they thus lose efficiency by including random variation in directions excluded by the specification of the model.

Information about parameters is represented geometrically by tangents that lie within the tangent space to the model. There is a unique tangent in the finite-dimensional efficient subspace that corresponds to the variation of each parameter, and the tangent to any curve along which that parameter alone varies is the sum of this unique tangent and a component in the tangent subspace in which the model parameters do not vary. These information tangents form a basis of the efficient subspace that is dual to that provided by the efficient estimators.

Efficient estimating equations for model parameters can be obtained by projecting arbitrary root-n consistent estimators on to the efficient subspace. Lemma 5 provides a simple method of performing this sort of projection. As seen in the example of the RALS estimator, the projection can often be implemented by an artificial regression. More generally, as shown in Davidson and MacKinnon (1990) in the context of fully parameterised models, artificial regressions can be used in many one-step efficient estimation procedures that are equivalent to projection on to the efficient subspace. The theory of this chapter suggests that artificial regressions can be developed to perform such projections in greater generality.

One-step estimators of a seemingly different sort have been proposed recently by Imbens (1997), and it is claimed that their finite-sample properties are substantially better than those of conventional, asymptotically efficient, GMM estimators. Although these estimators are not implemented by artificial regression, they are of course the result of implicit projection on to the efficient subspace. Another asymptotically efficient estimation method with finite-sample properties different from those of GMM has been proposed by Kitamura and Stutzer (1997), based on minimisation of the Kullback–Leibler information criterion. It seems probable that this minimisation is another asymptotically equivalent way of projecting on to the efficient subspace.

It is hoped that the geometrical construction laid out in this chapter will serve as a unified framework for the discussion of asymptotic efficiency and robustness.

References

Amari, S. (1990), *Differential-Geometrical Methods in Statistics*, 2nd edn, Lecture Notes in Statistics No. 28, Berlin: Springer Verlag.

Barndoff-Nielsen, O.E. and D.R. Cox (1994), *Inference and Asymptotics*, Monographs on Statistics and Applied Probability No. 52, London: Chapman & Hall.

Barndorff-Nielsen, O.E., D.R. Cox and N. Reid (1986), 'The Role of Differential Geometry in Statistical Theory', *International Statistical Review*, 54: 83–96.

Billingsley, P. (1968), *Convergence of Probability Measures*, New York: John Wiley.

(1979), *Probability and Measure*, New York: John Wiley.

Chentsov, N.N. (1972), *Statistical Decision Rules and Optimal Inference* (in Russian), Moscow: Nauka. English translation (1982), *Translations of Mathematical Monographs*, vol. 53, Providence, RI: American Mathematical Society.

Davidson, R. and J.G. MacKinnon (1987), 'Implicit Alternatives and the Local Power of Test Statistics', *Econometrica*, 55: 1305–1329.

(1990), 'Specification Tests Based on Artificial Regressions', *Journal of the American Statistical Association*, 85: 220–227.

(1993), *Estimation and Inference in Econometrics*, New York: Oxford.

Dawid, A.P. (1975), Discussion of B. Efron (1975), 'Defining the Curvature of a Statistical Problem', *Annals of Statistics*, 3: 1189–1242.

(1977), 'Further Comments on a Paper by Bradley Efron', *Annals of Statistics*, 5: 1249.

Godambe, V.P. (1960), 'An Optimum Property of Regular Maximum Likelihood Estimation', *Annals of Mathematical Statistics*, 31: 1208–1212.

(ed.) (1991), *Estimating Functions*, Oxford: Clarendon Press.

Godambe, V.P. and M.E. Thompson (1989), 'An Extension of Quasi-likelihood Estimation' (with discussion), *Journal of Statistical Planning and Inference*, 22: 137–172.

Hansen, L.P. (1982), 'Large Sample Properties of Generalized Method of Moments Estimators', *Econometrica*, 50: 1029–1054.

Im, Kyung So (1996), 'Least Square Approach to Non-Normal Disturbances', DAE Working Paper No. 9603, University of Cambridge.

Imbens, G.W. (1997), 'One-Step Estimators for Over-Identified Generalized Method of Moments Models', *Review of Economic Studies*, 64: 359–383.

Kass, R.E. (1989), 'The Geometry of Asymptotic Inference (with Discussion)', *Statistical Science*, 4: 187–263.

Kitamura, Y. and M. Stutzer (1997), 'An Information-Theoretic Alternative to Generalized Method of Moments Estimation', *Econometrica*, 65: 861–874.

Lang, S. (1972), *Differential Manifolds*, Reading, Mass.: Addison-Wesley; reprinted 1985.

McLeish, D.L. (1974), 'Dependent Central Limit Theorems and Invariance Principles', *Annals of Probability*, 2: 620–628.

Manski, C.F. (1983), 'Closest Empirical Distribution Estimation', *Econometrica*, 51: 305–320.

Murray, M.K. and J.W. Rice (1993), *Differential Geometry and Statistics*, Monographs on Statistics and Applied Probability No. 48, London: Chapman & Hall.

Newey, W.K. (1988), 'Adaptive Estimation of Non-Linear Models', *Journal of Econometrics*, 38: 301–339.

Newey, W.K. and D. McFadden (1994), 'Estimation in Large Samples', in D. McFadden and R.F. Engle (eds.), *Handbook of Econometrics*, vol. 4, Amsterdam: North-Holland.

Small, C.G. and D.L. McLeish (1994), *Hilbert Space Methods in Probability and Statistical Inference*, New York: Wiley-Interscience.

White, H. (1985), *Asymptotic Theory for Econometricians*, New York: Academic Press.

White, H. and I. Domowitz (1984), 'Nonlinear Regression with Dependent Observations', *Econometrica*, 52: 143–161.

6 Measuring earnings differentials with frontier functions and Rao distances

Uwe Jensen

1 Introduction

In a seminal paper Rao (1945) introduced the concept of 'Geodesic Distance' (or 'Rao Distance') into statistics. This concept has important theoretical properties and is based on the demanding differential-geometrical approach to statistics. These mathematical requirements and difficulties in its application are responsible for the low level of familiarity by econometricians with this generalisation of the well-known Mahalanobis distance. Econometricians require some detailed knowledge of Riemannian geometry to gain a complete understanding of Rao distances. Section 2 provides a short introduction to the necessary theory on Rao distances, hyperbolic curvature, isocircles and Rao distance tests.

Since their original development in the paper by Aigner and Chu (1968), frontier functions have served almost exclusively for estimating production and cost functions consistently with an economic theory of optimising behaviour. In section 3 of this chapter, an extended human capital model is estimated as a stochastic earnings frontier with data from the German socio-economic panel. This provides a deeper interpretation of the deviations of observed income from estimated income. Distinguishing between 'potential human capital' and 'active human capital ' accounts for the partial failure of human capital models when estimated as average functions.

There has been a tendency in Germany for the number of years of education attained to increase, in part owing to the combination of an

Thanks for helpful comments to Günter Coenen, Gerd Hansen, Christof Helberger, Norbert Janz, Stefan Mittnik, Marc Paolella, Wolfgang Wetzel and the participants of the Workshop on Applied Econometrics in Berlin and the Workshop on Applications of Differential Geometry to Econometrics in Florence. All remaining errors are my own.

apprenticeship with university studies. Büchel and Helberger (1995) call this combination an inefficient 'insurance strategy' pursued mainly by children from low-income and low-education families because of low efficiency or high risk-aversion. The authors observe that the strategy is not rewarded by an expected increase in income or a smaller probability of being unemployed, although this result is contentious. The concepts of Rao distance and earnings frontiers are then combined in section 4 and applied to the analysis of the pecuniary consequences of this strategy of education choice.

2   Rao distances

This section gives a short introduction to the Rao distance theory neces-sary for the economic application in section 4. See Jensen (1995) for more detail and references.

2.1   Derivation of the Rao distance

Let Ω be a sample space, $\mathcal{A}$ a σ-algebra of subsets of Ω and $P : \mathcal{A} \to [0, 1]$ a probability measure. The random variable X has a density function $p(x, \theta)$ with an n-dimensional parameter $\theta = (\theta_1, \theta_2, \ldots, \theta_n)$ and $\theta \in \Theta$. The parameter space Θ is an open subset of $\mathbf{R}^n$. Then,

$$S = \{p(x, \theta) \mid \theta \in \Theta\} \tag{1}$$

is a statistical model.

Example 1   If X follows a normal distribution with

$$(\theta_1, \theta_2) = (\mu, \sigma), \qquad \Theta = \{(\mu, \sigma) \mid \mu \in \mathbf{R}, \sigma > 0\}, \tag{2}$$

we identify the family of all normal distributions and the set of all points p on the upper real half-plane. But this identification does not mean that the family of normal distributions is geometrically flat. A distance should quantify how difficult it is to discriminate between two distributions and, because, for instance, $N(\mu_1, 0.1)$ and $N(\mu_2, 0.1)$ can be discriminated more easily than $N(\mu_1, 10)$ and $N(\mu_2, 10)$, this surface should be curved.

It is assumed therefore that an n-parametric family of distributions behaves only locally like $\mathbf{R}^n$, so that its potential curvature can be analysed. Such a generalisation of a real space is called an n-dimensional manifold. Then, local coordinates are transferred from $\Theta \subseteq \mathbf{R}^n$ to open neighbourhoods of the points on the n-manifold. In the example of the 2-parameter normal distribution, we could take (μ, σ) for this purpose.

These coordinates can be changed by admissible (smooth) transformations being three times continuously differentiable and having a non-singular functional determinant. In this way, S is equipped with a differentiable structure and S is called a differentiable n-manifold.

With the definition

$$\partial_i l(x, \theta) := \frac{\partial}{\partial \theta_i} \ln p(x, \theta) \tag{3}$$

a statistical model is called regular if the following regularity conditions (known from the Cramer–Rao inequality) hold:

1. $\forall\, \theta \in \Theta$ and $\forall\, x \in \Omega$, $p(x, \theta) > 0$
2. $\forall\, \theta \in \Theta$, the n components of the score function

$$(\partial_1 l(x, \theta), \partial_2 l(x, \theta), \ldots, \partial_n l(x, \theta)) \tag{4}$$

   are linearly independent
3. For $r = 3$, $i = 1, 2, \ldots, n$ and $\forall\, \theta \in \Theta$, $E[\partial_i l(x, \theta)]^r < \infty$
4. For all functions $f(x, \theta)$ used in the following,

$$\frac{\partial}{\partial \theta_i} \int f(x, \theta)\, dP = \int \frac{\partial}{\partial \theta_i} f(x, \theta)\, dP. \tag{5}$$

In the sequel, we will inspect only regular statistical models that are differentiable n-dimensional manifolds, which will be called statistical models or n-manifolds for short. The examples used in this chapter are the normal statistical model (see Example 1) and the inverse Gaussian model:

Example 2 $X \sim IG(\mu, \lambda)$ with

$$p(x; \lambda, \mu) = \sqrt{\frac{\lambda}{2\pi x^3}} \exp\left(\frac{-\lambda(x - \mu)^2}{2\mu^2 x}\right) I_{(0,\infty)}(x) \tag{6}$$

and

$$(\theta_1, \theta_2) = (\mu, \lambda), \qquad \Theta = \{(\mu, \lambda) \mid \mu, \lambda > 0\}. \tag{7}$$

The regularity conditions are partly responsible for the restricted applicability of Rao distances, because distributions outside the exponential family cannot be analysed with this concept.

The n linearly independent vectors (see regularity condition 2) $\partial_i l(x, \theta)$ measuring relative density changes are taken as a basis for the n-dimensional vector space $T_\theta^{(1)}$, the so-called 1-representation of the tangent space. Then, the inner product

$$g_{ij}(\theta) = \langle \partial_i l(x, \theta), \partial_j l(x, \theta) \rangle = E[\partial_i l(x, \theta) \, \partial_j l(x, \theta)] \tag{8}$$

is formed from the basis of $T_\theta^{(1)}$ by averaging out x. Because of

$$E[\partial_i l(x, \theta)] = 0 \qquad \text{for} \qquad i = 1, 2, \ldots, n, \tag{9}$$

we have

$$g_{ij}(\theta) = \text{Cov}[\partial_i l(x, \theta), \partial_j l(x, \theta)]. \tag{10}$$

Of course, $g_{ij}(\theta)$ is the Fisher information.

Since this $(n \times n)$-matrix is defined for every point $p \in S$, it is a matrix field $(g_{ij}(\theta))$. This matrix field is a Riemannian metric tensor, i.e. a tensor of order two with positive definite matrices and the property that the arc-length defined below (the Rao distance) is an invariant. See, if necessary, an introduction on tensor calculus, e.g. Kay (1988).

The main diagonal provides the lengths of the basis vectors:

$$|\partial_i l(x, \theta)|^2 = \langle \partial_i l(x, \theta), \partial_i l(x, \theta) \rangle = g_{ii}(\theta) = \text{Var}\,(\partial_i l(x, \theta)). \tag{11}$$

Beside the main diagonal, we find the necessary information on the angles α_{ij} of the basis vectors:

$$\cos \alpha_{ij} = \frac{\langle \partial_i l(x, \theta), \partial_j l(x, \theta) \rangle}{|\partial_i l(x, 0)||\partial_j l(x, 0)|} = \frac{g_{ij}(\theta)}{\sqrt{g_{ii}(\theta)\,g_{jj}(\theta)}}$$

$$= \text{Corr}\,(\partial_i l(x, \theta), \partial_j l(x, \theta)). \tag{12}$$

Example 3 For $X \sim N(\mu, \sigma^2)$, the Fisher information is found to be

$$(g_{ij}(\theta)) = \frac{1}{\sigma^2} \begin{pmatrix} 1 & 0 \\ 0 & 2 \end{pmatrix}. \tag{13}$$

Since $g_{12}(\theta) = 0$, the coordinate vectors of the coordinate system $\theta = (\mu, \sigma)$ are orthogonal for all $p \in S$, but the lengths of the coordinate vectors depend on σ. Therefore, (μ, σ) is not a Cartesian coordinate system.

For $X \sim IG(\mu, \lambda)$

$$(g_{ij}(\theta)) = \begin{pmatrix} \dfrac{\lambda}{\mu^3} & 0 \\ 0 & \dfrac{1}{2\lambda^2} \end{pmatrix}. \tag{14}$$

Once again, the coordinate vectors of the coordinate system $\theta = (\mu, \lambda)$ are orthogonal for all $p \in S$, but their lengths depend on θ; with

$\xi := (E[X], Std[X]) = (\mu, \sqrt{(\mu^3/\lambda)})$, even the angles of the coordinate vectors depend on ξ.

Now let $C_\lambda = \{c_\lambda \mid \lambda \in \Lambda\}$ be the set of all curves lying completely in S and connecting two distributions F_1 and F_2 represented by parameter values θ_1 and θ_2. With $t_1 < t_2$, $c_\lambda(t_1) = \theta_1$ and $c_\lambda(t_2) = \theta_2$, the Rao distance (or geodesic distance or Riemannian distance) is the minimum arc-length of all these curves:

$$d(F_1, F_2) = \min_{c_\lambda \in C_\Lambda} \int_{t_1}^{t_2} \sqrt{\sum_{i=1}^{n} \sum_{j=1}^{n} g_{ij}(\theta(t)) \frac{d\theta_i(t)}{dt} \frac{d\theta_j(t)}{dt}} \, dt. \qquad (15)$$

$d(F_1, F_2)$ is a mathematical distance and – since the Fisher information is a Riemannian metric tensor – it is invariant for all non-singular differentiable transformations of Θ and Ω.

2.2   Calculation of Rao distances

In this chapter, Rao distances will be applied only to two-parameter statistical families. The calculation of Rao distances in the one-parameter case is presented in Jensen (1995). For n-parameter families with $n \geq 2$, some results on the curvature of manifolds are necessary. Curvature measures are necessary for geometrical intuition and for the classification of statistical distributions.

In order to determine the curves with minimum length between two points on S, we first have to 'connect' the tangent spaces. An affine connection is a bilinear map on a Cartesian product of vector fields $V(S) \times V(S) \to V(S)$ providing the directional derivation of vector fields. There is an infinite number of possible affine connections, but there is only one for which the movement of vectors from one tangent space to another is an isometry (preserving all distances and angles) and the Christoffel symbols (see below) are symmetric. This connection is called the Levi–Civita connection. By choosing a specific connection on a manifold, specific curves – called geodesics – are distinguished to be generalisations of the straight lines in $\mathbf{R}^n$. If the Levi–Civita connection has been chosen, these geodesics locally show the shortest way (in S) between any two points on S. In $\mathbf{R}^n$, the geodesics are the straight lines. If a different connection is selected (e.g. the exponential connection distinguishing one-parametric exponential families as geodesics; see Efron (1975) and Amari (1985)), this leads in general to non-Riemannian geometry and the geodesics are no longer distance minimising.

An affine connection can be defined with the help of the n^3 Christoffel symbols of the first kind

$$\Gamma_{ijk} = \frac{1}{2}\left(\frac{\partial}{\partial\theta_i}g_{jk}(\theta) + \frac{\partial}{\partial\theta_j}g_{ki}(\theta) - \frac{\partial}{\partial\theta_k}g_{ij}(\theta)\right). \tag{16}$$

The Christoffel symbol of the second kind

$$\Gamma_{ij}^k = \sum_{m=1}^{n}\Gamma_{ijm}\,g^{mk} \quad \text{for} \quad i,j,k = 1,2,\ldots,n, \tag{17}$$

is the first auxiliary quantity, where $g^{mk}(\theta)$ is the inverse matrix of the metric tensor $g_{mk}(\theta)$. The use of lower and upper indices has tensorial reasons (see Kay (1988)).

The Riemannian tensor of the second kind is a tensor of order 4 with n^4 components

$$R_{ijk}^l = \frac{\partial}{\partial\theta_j}\Gamma_{ik}^l - \frac{\partial}{\partial\theta_k}\Gamma_{ij}^l + \sum_{m=1}^{n}\Gamma_{ik}^m\Gamma_{mj}^l - \sum_{m=1}^{n}\Gamma_{ij}^m\Gamma_{mk}^l, \tag{18}$$

and the Riemannian tensor of the first kind is also a tensor of order 4:

$$R_{ijkl} = \sum_{m=1}^{n}R_{jkl}^m\,g_{mi}. \tag{19}$$

Both tensors consist of second derivatives of the metric tensor (measuring curvature). For $n = 2$, only one component of the Riemannian tensor of the first kind is independent from the rest and not identically zero:

$$R_{1212} = R_{2121} = -R_{1221} = -R_{2112}. \tag{20}$$

Finally, for a 2-manifold, the sectional curvature (or mean Gaussian curvature) is

$$K = \frac{R_{1212}}{g_{11}\,g_{22} - g_{12}^2} \tag{21}$$

and is identical with the Gaussian curvature of surfaces in $\mathbf{R}^3$. K is an invariant. An n-manifold S is said to be of constant curvature if K is constant for all $p \in S$. S is said to be flat if K vanishes for all p. Two manifolds with constant sectional curvature are locally isometric iff their sectional curvatures are identical. The curvature is called parabolic if $K = 0$, it is called elliptic if $K > 0$, and it is called hyperbolic if $K < 0$. In $\mathbf{R}^3$, the plane is a standard example for a surface with constant $K = 0$. The sphere is the typical example for a surface with constant elliptic curvature ($K = 1/r^2 > 0$ with radius r). Hyperbolic curvature can be seen on parts of the torus (the tyre of a bicycle). The inner side (facing the spokes) shows hyperbolic curvature, the outer side (facing the road) is elliptically curved. In the neighbourhood of hyperbolic points, tangent planes always cut the surface.

It may be appropriate to remark that the curvature measures discussed here are not identical with the 'statistical curvature' introduced by Efron (1975), which is the curvature of embedding of a submanifold (known as Euler–Schouten curvature) in non-Riemannian geometry (see Amari (1985) and Lauritzen (1987)).

Example 4   The sectional curvature of the 2-manifolds of the normal distributions and the inverse Gaussian distributions is $K = -0.5$. This means that both manifolds are of the same constant hyperbolic curvature – independent of the parameterisation (see Amari (1985, pp. 7 and 30) and Lauritzen (1987)).

Many standard statistical distributions lead to manifolds with constant negative sectional curvature (see Jensen (1995)). This calls for deeper knowledge of hyperbolic geometry, which is rather unfamiliar for most econometricians.

Any Riemannian 2-manifold with positive (not necessarily constant) sectional curvature can be embedded isometrically in $\mathbf{R}^3$. Comparable results are not available for 2-manifolds with hyperbolic curvature, because no embedded complete surface in $\mathbf{R}^3$ can have constant negative curvature (a metric space is called complete if any Cauchy sequence converges). Any surface in $\mathbf{R}^3$ with constant negative curvature must have singularities.

That is why the Poincaré model is used in most cases for the distorted representation of 2-manifolds with constant hyperbolic curvature in $\mathbf{R}^2$. For $K = -1$ (the hyperbolic analogue of the unit sphere, statistically represented by the $t(3)$-distribution), the set of points is the upper half-plane without the abscissa and the (distorted) geodesics are all semicircles with centre on the abscissa and all straight lines orthogonal to the abscissa (see Millman and Parker (1991)).

The derivation of the Rao distance for a 2-manifold with constant hyperbolic curvature now consists of a transformation of its metric to the Poincaré metric

$$ds^2 = \frac{(d\mu^*)^2 + (d\sigma^*)^2}{(\sigma^*)^2}, \tag{22}$$

which is the so-called first fundamental form of the 2-manifold with constant $K = -1$. This manifold is known to have the Möbius distance

$$d(F_1, F_2) = 2 \tanh^{-1}\left(\sqrt{\frac{(\mu_1^* - \mu_2^*)^2 + (\sigma_1^* - \sigma_2^*)^2}{(\mu_1^* - \mu_2^*)^2 + (\sigma_1^* + \sigma_2^*)^2}}\right) \tag{23}$$

as Rao distance (see Burbea and Rao (1982)).

Example 5 The metric of the 2-manifold of normal distributions with $\theta = (\mu, \sigma)$ is

$$ds_{NV}^2 = \frac{(d\mu)^2 + 2(d\sigma)^2}{\sigma^2}. \tag{24}$$

The Rao distance between $N(\mu_1, \sigma_1)$ and $N(\mu_2, \sigma_2)$ follows as

$$d(F_1, F_2) = 2\sqrt{2} \tanh^{-1}\left(\sqrt{\frac{(\mu_1 - \mu_2)^2 + 2(\sigma_1 - \sigma_2)^2}{(\mu_1 - \mu_2)^2 + 2(\sigma_1 + \sigma_2)^2}}\right) \tag{25}$$

(Atkinson and Mitchell (1981, pp. 352ff)), whereas the Rao distance between two inverse Gaussian distributions $IG(\lambda_1, \mu_1)$ and $IG(\lambda_2, \mu_2)$ is

$$d(F_1, F_2)$$

$$= 2\sqrt{2} \tanh^{-1}\left(\sqrt{\frac{2\left(\sqrt{1/\mu_2} - \sqrt{1/\mu_1}\right)^2 + \left(\sqrt{1/\lambda_2} - \sqrt{1/\lambda_1}\right)^2}{2\left(\sqrt{1/\mu_2} - \sqrt{1/\mu_1}\right)^2 + \left(\sqrt{1/\lambda_2} + \sqrt{1/\lambda_1}\right)^2}}\right) \tag{26}$$

(Villarroya and Oller (1991)).

See Jensen (1995) for more results on Rao distances in 2-manifolds and for some results and many problems in multivariate distributions.

2.3   Isocircles

An isocircle on a 2-manifold S is the set of all points $p \in S$ having constant distance $d > 0$ from a 'centre' $p_0 \in S$. This generalisation of the circle in Euclidean space can be very useful in two-parameter applications of Rao distances (see section 4).

Example 6 For the calculation of the isocircle with fixed 'radius' $d > 0$ and 'centre' (μ_1, σ_1) for the two-parameter normal distribution, (25) has to be solved for μ_2 and σ_2. For improved readability, we write

$$A = \left[\tanh\left(\frac{d}{2\sqrt{2}}\right) \right]^2, \quad m = \mu_1, \quad \mu = \mu_2, \quad s = \sigma_1, \quad \sigma = \sigma_2$$

(27)

with $0 \le A < 1$ and obtain

$$\sigma_{1,2} = \frac{1+A}{1-A} s \pm \sqrt{\frac{4As^2}{(1-A)^2} - \frac{(m-\mu)^2}{2}}.$$

(28)

σ is maximal (minimal) for $m = \mu$ and the extreme values of μ are

$$\mu_{\max,\min} = m \pm \frac{\sqrt{8A}}{1-A} s.$$

(29)

Figures 6.1 and 6.2 show various isocircles.
1. A shift in μ-direction does not change the isocircle, because the metric tensor depends only on σ.
2. A shift in σ-direction does not change the form (which is always the same within the distribution family) but does change either the Euclidean volume of the isocircle or the relative position of the 'centre'.
   (a) The isocircle for $d = 1$ and $(m, s) = (0, 0.1)$ has the same form as the isocircle for $d = 1$ and $(m, s) = (0, 1)$ in figure 6.1, but is much smaller because the distances increase with decreasing σ. Dividing all the coordinates by 10 would restore the original Euclidean volume because the decreasing volume was created by the distorted representation of the hyperbolic surface in $\mathbf{R}^2$.
   (b) Calculating the isocircle for $(m, s) = (0, 0.1)$ with constant Euclidean volume provides an isocircle of the same form with $d = 3.862$, where the 'centre' has been shifted away from the Euclidean centre (see figure 6.2). Note that the distance between any distribution and the μ-axis is infinity.
3. Variation of the 'radius' d leads to the isocircles in figure 6.1: the form is identical but the size varies.

Example 7   For the inverse Gaussian distribution with 'centre' $(\mu_1, \lambda_1) = (m, s)$, we choose the abbreviations

$$A := \left[\tanh\left(\frac{d}{2\sqrt{2}}\right) \right]^2, \quad \mu := \mu_2, \quad \lambda := \lambda_2$$

(30)

and the isocircle follows to be

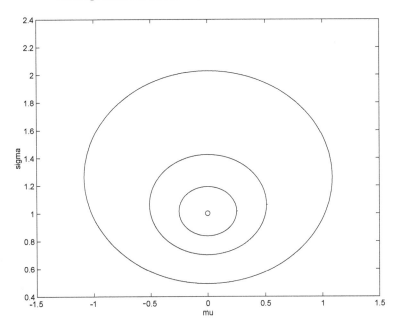

Figure 6.1 Isocircles, normal distribution, $d = 0.25, 0.52, 1$

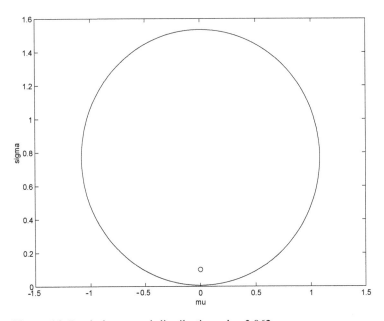

Figure 6.2 Isocircle, normal distribution, $d = 3.862$

$$\lambda_{1,2} = \left(\frac{1+A}{(1-A)\sqrt{s}} \pm 2\sqrt{2} \sqrt{\frac{2A}{(1-A)^2 s} - \left(\sqrt{\frac{1}{m}} - \sqrt{\frac{1}{\mu}} \right)^2} \right)^{-2},$$

(31)

where

$$\lambda_{\max,\min} \quad \text{for} \quad m = \mu \quad \mu_{\max,\min} = \left(\sqrt{\frac{1}{m}} \pm \frac{\sqrt{2A}}{(1-A)\sqrt{s}} \right)^{-2}.$$

(32)

2.4   Rao distance tests

The parameter values defining the distributions for which the Rao distances are to be calculated are generally unknown. Hence, the parameter values and the Rao distances must be estimated. If the n-dimensional parameters θ_1 and θ_2 of an n-parameter family have been estimated by maximum likelihood (ML) from independent random samples, the invariance property of ML estimation provides an estimate of the required Rao distance:

$$\hat{d}_{ML}(\theta_1, \theta_2) = d(\hat{\theta}_{1,ML}, \hat{\theta}_{2,ML}).$$

(33)

Distance measures and tests are closely related. Therefore, it is not surprising to see that it is possible to construct tests from (estimated) distances. For a density function $p(x, \theta)$ with parameter vector θ, the general test problem

$$H_0 : g(\theta) = 0 \quad \text{versus} \quad H_1 : g(\theta) \neq 0$$

(34)

is considered where g is a smooth function. The null hypothesis selects a subset of the parameter space Θ (a submanifold of the manifold S).

$$\Theta_{H_0} = \{\theta \in \Theta \mid g(\theta) = 0\}.$$

(35)

Given a sample $X_1, \ldots, X_m$ from $p(x, \theta)$, the Rao distance between $\hat{\theta}$ and Θ_{H_0} is defined as:

$$d(\hat{\theta}, \Theta_{H_0}) = \inf\{d(\hat{\theta}, \theta) \mid \theta \in \Theta_{H_0}\}.$$

(36)

If $\Theta_{H_0} \neq \emptyset$, the infimum exists because $d(\cdot, \cdot) \geq 0$. Then, a critical region

$$C = \{(X_1, \ldots, X_m) \mid d(\hat{\theta}(X), \Theta_{H_0}) > u^*\}$$

(37)

is defined with a constant u^* depending on the significance level of the test.

The minimisation in (36) and the derivation of the test statistic may be difficult, but the idea behind a (Rao) distance test is extremely simple. The null hypothesis is rejected if the distance (weighted with the sample size) between the estimated distribution and the distribution under H_0 is too big. In some standard test problems, Rao distance tests are equivalent to classical t, χ^2 or F tests (see the survey in Jensen (1995)). In addition, when testing for two or more parameters, the following theorems can provide a useful and easy alternative to the explicit derivation of the individual test statistic.

Theorem 1 *(Burbea and Oller (1989), pp. 13f) Let S be a regular n-parametric family of density functions. Let $X_1, \ldots, X_m$ be a random sample of size m from $p_0 \in S$. Let $\tilde{p}_m$ be a consistent sequence of critical points of the log-likelihood function. Then*

$$md^2(p_0, \tilde{p}_m) \xrightarrow{L} Z \sim \chi^2(n). \tag{38}$$

Theorem 2 *(Burbea and Oller (1989), p. 14) Let S be a regular n-parametric family of density functions. Let $X_1, \ldots, X_m$ and $Y_1, \ldots, Y_l$ be two independent random samples of size m and l, respectively, obtained from $p_0 \in S$. Let $\tilde{p}_m$ and $\tilde{p}_l$ be two consistent sequences of critical points of the log-likelihood functions. Then*

$$\frac{ml}{m+l} d^2(\tilde{p}_m, \tilde{p}_l) \xrightarrow{L} Z \sim \chi^2(n). \tag{39}$$

Example 8 Consider two independent samples of size m_1 and m_2 from $N(\mu_1, \sigma_1^2)$ and $N(\mu_2, \sigma_2^2)$ and the test problem

$$H_0 : (\mu_1, \sigma_1) = (\mu_2, \sigma_2) \quad \text{versus} \quad H_1 : (\mu_1, \sigma_1) \neq (\mu_2, \sigma_2). \tag{40}$$

A Rao distance test is easily derived with the help of Theorem 2. The critical region is

$$C = \left\{ U = \frac{m_1 m_2}{m_1 + m_2} d^2((\hat{\mu}_1, \hat{\sigma}_1), (\hat{\mu}_2, \hat{\sigma}_2)) \,\middle|\, U > u^* \right\}, \tag{41}$$

where $d(\cdot, \cdot)$ is taken from (25), $P(U > u^* \mid H_0) = \alpha$ and $U \sim \chi^2(2)$ asymptotically under H_0.

Testing

$$H_0 : (\mu, \sigma) = (\mu_0, \sigma_0) \quad \text{versus} \quad H_1 : (\mu, \sigma) \neq (\mu_0, \sigma_0) \tag{42}$$

Theorem 1 can be applied to derive the critical region

$$C = \{U = md^2((\hat{\mu}, \hat{\sigma}), (\mu_0, \sigma_0)) \mid U > u^*\}, \tag{43}$$

where $P(U > u^* \mid H_0) = \alpha$ and $U \sim \chi^2(2)$ asymptotically under H_0.

Villarroya and Oller (1991) extensively analyse Rao distance tests for the inverse Gaussian distribution – with very satisfactory results. Two-parameter test problems can be treated with Theorems 1 and 2 and the distance (26) as in the previous example.

3   Earnings frontiers

We now turn to consider the estimation of a human capital model as a stochastic earnings frontier. In the first subsection, we look at the basic human capital model for explaining individual income. In subsection 3.2, the data taken from the German socio-economic panel are described. The subsequent subsection provides essential information on stochastic frontier models in general. In subsection 3.4, the earnings frontier function is derived as an extended human capital model with imperfect information on the employees' side. The costs for this imperfection are measured by the inefficiency terms of the frontier model. Subsection 3.5 presents the estimation results and the economic implications in detail. The final subsection discusses the relative advantages and limitations of the approach.

3.1   Human capital theory

Since the pathbreaking work of Mincer (1958) and Becker (1964), human capital theory has been the most popular approach for explaining individual income. Schooling is seen as an investment in human capital because it means renouncing present consumption for higher future income by increasing the individual's resources. The basic model derived by Mincer (1974) is

$$LI = \beta_0 + \beta_1 S + \beta_2 E + \beta_3 E^2 + v, \quad \beta_0, \beta_1, \beta_2 > 0, \quad \beta_3 < 0, \tag{44}$$

where LI is the natural logarithm of individual wage income, S is schooling (years of education) and E is experience (age-education-6).

For all the success and broad applicability of this approach, it has limitations. Even in extended human capital models the portion of unexplained variance remains persistently near 50 per cent of the total variance and this has led to a debate about the reasons for this partial failure. This discussion has been very fruitful for econometrics but has not yet resolved the empirical problems of human capital models (see Wagner (1981)).

The number of exogenous variables will be heavily augmented in this chapter, as in many other papers. However, in addition, we apply a frontier function model to explain the deviations between estimated and empirical earnings. The idea behind adopting this approach is simply that human capital models can explain only potential income, whereas actual income achieved depends on the individual's search for an appropriate job.

3.2   The data from the socio-economic panel

The data are taken from the tenth wave of the German socio-economic panel (SOEP). After a detailed data analysis, the twenty-four variables presented below have been selected following the recommendations for the extension of the basic human capital model given by various authors (see e.g. Becker (1964), Brinkmann (1981), Griliches (1977) or Hübler (1984)). The 13,179 individuals were reduced to $n = 1,334$ full-time employees, workers or public servants throughout the year 1992 who provided information on all the required variables.

The endogenous variable LI is the natural Logarithm of gross wage Income in 1992 including all extra payments. The exogenous variables are:

1. Schooling:
   (a) QUUN: Dummy: 1 for **QU**alification for **UN**iversity entrance
       – 0 for lower education
2. Professional **TR**aining:
   (a) TRAP: Dummy: 1 for **AP**prenticeship, technical schools, health schools, etc.
   (b) TRPS: Dummy: 1 for **P**ublic **S**ervice education
       Both 0 for no professional training
3. **ST**udies:
   (a) STTC: Dummy: 1 for **T**echnical **C**ollege
   (b) STUN: Dummy: 1 for **UN**iversity
       Both 0 for no studies
4. Experience:
   (a) AGE1: **AGE** in years divided by 10
   (b) AGE2: **AGE**1 squared
5. On-the-**J**ob-**T**raining:
   (a) JTNO: Dummy: 1 for '**NO** interest in on-the-job-training'
   (b) JTNC: Dummy: 1 for 'No interest in on-the-job-training at one's own **C**ost'

6. Health:
   (a) SAHL: **SA**tisfaction with one's own **H**ealth and **L**ife – values on an integer scale ranging from 0 (no) to 20 (yes) – an indicator for physical and emotional health
7. Gifts, predisposition:
   (a) FATH: Status of the job of the **FATH**er – values on an integer scale ranging from 0 to 1.868 – the Wegener scale provided by the SOEP divided by 1000
8. Ability:
   (a) PCHA: **P**robability of **CHA**nging the occupation in the near future – values on an integer scale ranging from 1 (yes) to 4 (no) – an indicator for 'being in the right place'
   (b) PDET: **P**robability of **DET**erioration in the same firm in the near future – values on an integer scale ranging from 1 (yes) to 4 (no) – an indicator for 'being on the right level'
   (c) SATW: **SAT**isfaction with **W**ork – values on an integer scale ranging from 0 (no) to 10 (yes)
9. Demographic variables:
   (a) MALE: Dummy: 1 for **MALE** – 0 for female
   (b) MARR: Dummy: Marital status: 1 for **MARR**ied (including those living separated), divorced and widowed – 0 for unmarried
   (c) RESI: Size of the **RESI**dence constructed from the Boustedt type of residence provided by the SOEP – 0: centre or outskirts of cities with more than 500,000 inhabitants ... – 6: towns with fewer than 2,000 inhabitants
10. Job characteristics:
    (a) SIZE: **SIZE** of the firm: Number of employees divided by 1000
    (b) i. EMPL: Dummy: 1 for salaried **EMPL**oyees
         ii. SERV: Dummy: 1 for public **SERV**ants
         Both 0 for workers
    (c) STAT: **STAT**us of the job – values on an integer scale ranging from 0.2 to 1.731 – the Wegener scale provided by the SOEP divided by 1000
11. Working time:
    (a) HOUR: Weekly working **HOUR**s including overtime
12. **SENI**ority:
    (a) SENI: Years of affiliation to the firm
13. **PROP**erty:
    (a) PROP: Interest and dividend income in 1992 divided by 1000

Unfortunately, some interesting information is not provided by the SOEP. One has to be satisfied with proxy variables for health status, predisposition, ability and the region of residence. Furthermore, the variables for health status, ability and the region of residence have been measured on ordinal scales but are treated as quantitative variables. It is to be hoped that the estimation results are not overly biased by these inaccuracies. On the other hand, the choice of the dummy variables for schooling (instead of years of education) and of age (instead of age-education-6) for experience is deliberate and deserves some explanation.

I agree with researchers like Helberger (1988) who find it problematic to take the years of education as proxy for education. First, pupils repeating a school year or students changing subject, studying for an excessively long time or breaking off their studies certainly do not augment their human capital according to the theory. Secondly, information on the actual years of education is not available and one has to fix theoretical values for different types of schooling. Dummies and theoretically fixed years are not affected by the problems mentioned above, but both are affected in different ways by the 'insurance strategy' mentioned in section 1.

The decision to use dummy variables is motivated by the fact that years of education cannot discriminate between the yield of one year of apprenticeship and that of one year at university, whereas dummy variable parameters provide interesting information on the yield of different types of education (see subsection 3.5 and section 4). The decision to take age as a proxy for experience (instead of age-education-6) is based on the similarity of the latter with the seniority variable.

Becker (1964) mentioned that the search for information is also a very important human capital investment. This suggestion has not been employed here because it is difficult to quantify; nevertheless, in section 3.4 we will see a fruitful way to capture it indirectly.

3.3   The stochastic frontier model

A production function gives the maximum possible output that can be produced from given input quantities. Ever since the seminal paper by Aigner and Chu (1968), a range of production functions have been estimated as frontier functions consistent with the economic theory of optimising behaviour. In the following, we will concentrate on the stochastic frontier model of Aigner et al. (1977) and Meeusen and van den Broeck (1977). See Greene (1993) for a discussion of the alternatives. A stochastic Cobb–Douglas production frontier is

$$y_i = \alpha + \sum_{j=1}^{k} \beta_j x_{ij} + e_i, \quad e_i = v_i - u_i, \quad u_i \geq 0, \quad i = 1, \ldots, n,$$

(45)

where y_i is output in logs and x_{ij} are inputs in logs. Then, $\hat{y}_i$ is estimated maximum possible output. The composite error term e_i consists of the technical inefficiency u_i of individual number i (in logs), which follows a one-sided distribution, and a symmetric part v_i representing statistical noise. v_i and u_i are assumed to be independent.

The v_i are assumed to follow a normal distribution. The authors employ the half-normal and exponential distributions for the u_i, whereas Stevenson (1980) proposes the truncated normal distribution. Greene (1989) has developed the econometric computer package LIMDEP, which estimates all versions of this model by direct maximisation of the likelihood function.

3.4   The earnings frontier

What do we gain by estimating the earnings function not as an average function but as a frontier function? Why is it sensible? Following Daneshvary et al. (1992), it is assumed that wages LI depend upon personal characteristics H augmenting human capital stock, job characteristics C and information I on labour market conditions, the wage distribution and job search methods. Individuals stop their search when a wage offer exceeds the reservation wage LI_r. For any set of H and C and perfect information I^*, a potential maximum attainable wage LI^* exists. We estimate $LI = LI(H, C, I)$ as a stochastic earnings frontier (45) where $y = LI$ is empirical gross wage income in logs and x is the vector of twenty-four variables presented in subsection 3.2.

Then,

$$\widehat{LI}_i = LI_i^*$$

(46)

is the estimated maximum possible income and the inefficiency term

$$\hat{u}_i = \widehat{LI}_i - LI_i$$

(47)

is interpreted as the cost of imperfect information becoming apparent in the underemployment or overeducation of individual number i. We distinguish between the underemployed 'potential human capital' produced through the education process and the 'active human capital' used as a factor of production (see Mäding (1981)).

The return from estimating an earnings frontier instead of the average function

$$y_i = \alpha + \sum_{j=1}^{k} \beta_j x_{ij} + v_i, \quad i = 1, \ldots, n \tag{48}$$

with standard assumptions arises from the interpretation of a significant part of the deviations of empirical income from estimated income. Furthermore, the earnings frontier takes account of the important but difficult to measure component of human capital consisting of 'search for information'.

3.5   Results

Estimation has been carried out using LIMDEP, with all three inefficiency distributions mentioned in subsection 3.3. In the exponential case, the estimation procedure did not converge. The truncated normal distribution

$$u_i \sim truncN(\mu_u, \sigma_u^2) \tag{49}$$

and its special case for $\mu_u = 0$, the half-normal distribution

$$u_i \sim |N(0, \sigma_u^2)|, \tag{50}$$

provided very similar results and an insignificant μ_u in (50). So, the results with specification (51) are presented in the following. LIMDEP takes the OLS regression coefficients as starting values for an iterative procedure combining the DFP algorithm and the method of steepest descent. The estimation results are given in table 6.1.

The OLS regression has an adjusted R^2 of 0.6016. One could argue that this is sufficient for a cross-section data set, especially if compared with the empirical success of extended human capital models in general (see section 3.1). However, 40 per cent unexplained variance leaves some scope for improvement.

It can be seen that the step from OLS to the frontier does not turn the results upside down. The coefficients and t-ratios change marginally. The benefit of the frontier model lies in the interpretation of the deviations of the observations from the estimated function (see below). To begin with, the frontier coefficients and t-ratios will be examined carefully. The OLS results can be analysed in a similar way if 'maximum possible income' is replaced by 'average income'.

Table 6.1. *Estimation results*

Estimation method		OLS		Frontier	
Adjusted R^2		0.6016			
	Variable	Coefficient	t-ratio	Coefficient	t-ratio
	Constant	8.56200	56.498	8.85160	59.988
1 a	QUUN	0.07614	2.665	0.07559	2.507
2 a	TRAP	0.05908	2.709	0.05502	2.594
b	TRPS	0.07315	1.876	0.08549	2.251
3 a	STTC	0.10015	2.347	0.09697	2.043
b	STUN	0.23441	5.978	0.24188	6.213
4 a	AGE1	0.54392	8.638	0.50281	7.941
b	AGE2	−0.05877	−8.061	−0.05441	−7.319
5 a	JTNO	−0.05795	−2.979	−0.04884	−2.580
b	JTNC	−0.06603	−4.120	−0.06969	−4.345
6 a	SAHL	−0.00221	−0.716	−0.00199	−0.614
7 a	FATH	0.01115	0.432	0.00310	0.119
8 a	PCHA	0.04106	2.792	0.03921	2.913
b	PDET	−0.04315	−2.938	−0.04041	−2.752
c	SATW	0.01688	3.337	0.01621	3.375
9 a	MALE	0.20714	10.898	0.20679	10.862
b	MARR	0.08087	3.433	0.07253	2.983
c	RESI	−0.00783	−2.058	−0.00714	−1.888
10 a	SIZE	0.00989	6.298	0.00931	5.605
b i	EMPL	0.09566	4.533	0.09640	4.741
b ii	SERV	−0.12591	−3.557	−0.13828	−3.825
c	STAT	0.35893	9.904	0.35701	11.180
11 a	HOUR	0.01084	9.213	0.01212	13.381
12 a	SENI	0.00540	5.363	0.00514	5.063
13 a	PROP	0.00655	4.041	0.00699	4.138
	σ_u/σ_v			1.52190	12.571
	$\sqrt{\sigma_u^2+\sigma_v^2}$			0.35832	37.601

The step from the average function to the frontier increases the constant, which is (and should be) highly significant. The interpretation of the dummy variable coefficients is straightforward; if we rewrite equation (45) as

$$INC_i = \exp(\alpha) \cdot \prod_{j=1}^{k} \exp(\beta_j x_{ij}) \cdot \exp(v_i) \cdot \exp(-u_i),$$

$$u_i \geq 0, \quad i = 1, \ldots, n \tag{51}$$

with the untransformed gross wage income *INC*, this implies that studying at the university means, for instance, multiplying maximum possible gross wage income without any study by the factor $\exp(0.24188) = 1.2736$. Being male implies multiplying female maximum possible gross wage income by the factor $\exp(0.20679) = 1.2297$.

The health proxy SAHL in 6 and the predisposition proxy FATH in 7 show very insignificant coefficients. Naturally, the insignificance could originate in poor suitability of the proxy variables, but employees are perhaps neither healthy nor satisfied with their health and life when they are working 'on the frontier'. The irrelevance of predisposition for explaining income is in agreement with earlier results on this question.

The rest of the variables are weakly to highly significant and show expected signs. The maximum possible income is greater
- with higher education (1–3b).
- with higher experience (= age) (4) with the well-known concavity of the influence of experience on income.
- with interest in on-the-job-training (5a,b).
- for individuals who will not change their occupation in the near future and who are satisfied with their work (8a,c). These people seem to be able to accomplish the tasks their job demands.
- for individuals who fear – at the time of estimation – some deterioration in their prospects in the near future (8b). In the present position, their actual human capital stock may be overcharged.
- for men (9a).
- for individuals who are or have been married (9b). Part of this effect may be due to the payment system in the public service, but it could also be that being married is highly correlated with hardly measurable parts of human capital stock such as trustworthiness or a sense of responsibility that are appreciated by employers. Many employers hire married persons by preference because of this supposed or actual correlation.
- in places with more inhabitants (9c).
- in firms with more employees (10a). This could be interpreted from an efficiency wage viewpoint. Because these firms have higher costs for the motivation and monitoring of their employees they give income incentives to increase the efficiency of their employees and to prevent shirking because idlers must fear being dismissed even more from this high-income firm (see e.g. Franz (1994)).
- for salaried employees than for workers, whereas public servants have the lowest maximum possible income (10b). Public servants have to pay the price for the various non-income contributions such as, for example, the greater security of their jobs.

- for jobs with higher status (10c).
- with higher working time (11).
- with increasing years of affiliation to the firm (12). It is possible that some firms try to eliminate shirking by rewarding efficient workers with delay so that idlers again have to fear being dismissed even more because of the loss of the subsequent payments (seniority hypothesis).
- with higher property (13). Individuals with higher income today are likely to have had a higher income in the past, which has led to higher property wealth.

Now the frontier specific results will be examined. The high significance of the ratio

$$\lambda = \frac{\sigma_u}{\sigma_v} \tag{52}$$

means that the variation of the inefficiency terms u_i in relation to the variation of the noise v_i is reasonably large. $\lambda = 0$ would lead to the simple OLS model because there are no inefficient individuals in this case.

Note that σ_u is not the standard deviation of u because of definition (50). From the estimated coefficients in the last two lines of table 6.1 we can calculate $\sigma_u = 0.2995$ and $\sigma_v = 0.1968$. This leads to the estimates for the mean and standard deviation of u

$$E(u) = \sqrt{\frac{2}{\pi}}\sigma_u = 0.2389 \quad \text{and} \quad Std(u) = \sqrt{\frac{\pi-2}{\pi}}\sigma_u = 0.1805 \tag{53}$$

(see e.g. Aigner et al. (1977)). Combining $E(u)$ with equation (51), we see for example that on average individuals receive only $\exp(-0.2389) \cdot 100 = 78.75\%$ of the maximum possible income.

3.6   Assessment of the approach

Now the benefit of estimating an earnings frontier instead of an average function mentioned in subsection 3.4 can be seen. The frontier model includes the important but hardly measurable human capital investment 'search for information' and it explains an essential part of the deviations of empirical income from estimated income. The extended human capital model explains potential income sufficiently, but individuals do not obtain their maximum possible income because of imperfect information on labour market conditions, the wage distribution, and job search methods. The more or less underemployed 'potential human capital' produced through the education process is distinguished critically from the 'active human capital' used as a factor of production. In the OLS approach, we simply interpret inefficiency as misspecification.

What are the limits of the extended human capital model underlying both the OLS and the frontier approach? First of all, there are the data problems mentioned in subsection 3.2, including a possible selection bias because of the systematic elimination of many individuals from the data set and a possible bias because of the inclusion of many exogenous variables that could be highly correlated (see Griliches (1977)).

The standard assumptions of human capital models, such as the complete entrance of schooling efforts into working productivity, will certainly be violated. Unemployment and other limitations on the labour demand side were excluded. The monetary and social costs of migration and search for information were left out of consideration. Because of these omissions, all conclusions have to be viewed with caution.

As for the reasons for income inefficiency, the frontier analysis concentrated on imperfect information on the employees' side. There are certainly further causes for this sort of inefficiency. Employers often are not sufficiently informed about the potential human capital of their employees or applicants, and, if they do know, they are not able to relate individual skills to the tasks available. This is another classic criticism of human capital models (see e.g. Klein (1994)), but this information problem could certainly be included in the frontier model presented above.

What arguments could be put forward for applying the standard OLS approach instead of the frontier approach? Many researchers are perhaps interested only in estimating average income, not in estimating maximum possible income. This reservation is meaningless as long as the model lacks a sensible job search variable, which is not available. By simply mixing up inefficiency and white noise, OLS does not solve the problem.

4 Differentials in earnings and inefficiency

In this section, Rao distances are applied to the earnings frontier problem presented above.

4.1 Earnings differentials

We now want to consider the issue raised by Büchel and Helberger (1995) when criticising the 'insurance strategy' discussed in section 1. One first idea would be to isolate this effect by constructing three new dummy variables:

- TRAPN: Dummy: 1 only for apprenticeship, etc. and No university study
- STUNN: Dummy: 1 only for university study and No apprenticeship, etc.
- INSU: Dummy: 1 only for the **INSU**rance strategy

Substituting these variables for TRAP and STUN in the earnings frontier of section 3 and re-estimating the function yields minimal changes in the frontier results and an INSU parameter that is smaller than but not significantly different from the STUNN (or STUN) parameter.

Rather than analysing point estimates, which focus only on central tendencies, it will be more useful to consider instead the entire income distribution of some sample subgroups constructed from the dummy variables in section 3. The standard approach of applying inequality measures for the comparison of these income distributions will not be adopted in the following, however, since we are interested in earnings differentials rather than in the interpretation of, for instance, Gini coefficients.

In recent years, the kernel density estimation of income distributions has become more and more popular (see e.g. DiNardo *et al.* (1996)) because it is still an open question which theoretical distribution is best. Unfortunately, this nonparametric approach cannot be applied here because of limited sample sizes in some subgroups. So, some choice has to be made as to a suitable income distribution. The Pearson family is often applicable but is intractable in many respects and this is why the inverse Gaussian distribution for income and the normal distribution for log income were chosen, given that they performed satisfactorily. In these cases, it is possible to examine the subgroup distributions in (μ, σ)-plots or $(\mu, 1/\lambda)$-plots, which is much more informative than looking at the densities themselves. Furthermore, Rao distances and isocircles (see section 2) can be applied for an intuitive understanding and for tests in these plots. Finally, a Rao distance analysis with the log-normal distribution for income would not differ from the analysis with the normal distribution for log income because of the invariance property of the distance.

Figure 6.3 is the (μ, σ)-plot of estimated normal distributions of log income for some subgroups of individuals having passed through certain courses of education. We can see how mean and variance of income increase with increasing the additional qualification of apprentices. It can also be seen that university study and the insurance strategy differ in distribution although not so much in mean. The mean difference is in fact insignificant, but the Rao distance test (40) shows that these

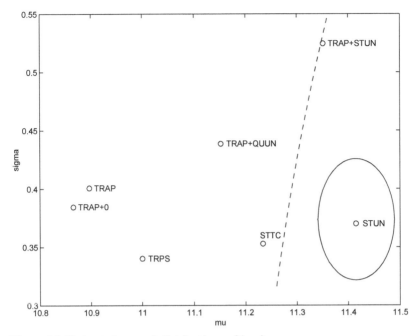

Figure 6.3 Estimated normal distributions of log income

distributions are significantly different with $\alpha = 0.06$, mainly due to the difference in variances.

Dealing with the mean and variance of (log) income in (μ, σ)-plots, an obvious idea is to exploit the analogy with a simple yield–risk analysis in asset theory. We assume
- that individuals judge different types of schooling A_i by their income distributions represented by expected incomes μ_i and 'risk' σ_i,
- that the rest of the economic environment is irrelevant for the choice of the optimal A^*, and
- that a preference function $\psi(\mu, \sigma)$ exists for the selection of A^*.

Taking $\psi(\mu, \sigma) = \mu - (\sigma^2/2)$ with indifference curves $\sigma = \sqrt{2\mu - c}$, the decision according to the (μ, σ)-rule is consistent with the Bernoulli principle. Of course, there are limitations to the analogy between asset allocation decisions and decisions on courses of education, for instance because – in the latter problem – it is difficult to include costs and because a 'true' portfolio analysis is not applicable given that it is virtually impossible to diversify education risks (Helberger (1997)).

Interpreting income variance as risk, we see that the 'insured' have the highest risk! Figure 6.3 shows the indifference curve I going through

INSU. It is interesting to know if STUN could also lie on I, in other words whether or not it might nevertheless be rational to choose the insurance strategy (if these two courses of education are 'true' alternatives for the individual). This can be tested by the Rao distance test (42), where (μ_0, σ_0) is an unknown point on I. For known sample size and significance level $\alpha = 0.05$, the critical Rao distance can be determined and the corresponding isocircle can be plotted as in figure 6.3. Because this isocircle does not intersect I, the null hypothesis that STUN lies on I can be rejected. This result could also be achieved by drawing a Rao distance confidence band around I, which can be constructed by moving an appropriate isocircle along I. This confidence band deviates from I for growing σ because of the distorted representation of the hyperbolic surface in $\mathbf{R}^2$. See subsection 2.3 and Jensen (1995) for more details.

Finally, figure 6.4 shows the $(\mu, 1/\lambda)$-plot of estimated inverse Gaussian distributions of income for the same subgroups. The interpretation is slightly more complicated because the vertical axis no longer represents the standard deviation of the distributions (see Example 3 for the reason). That is why some lines of constant standard deviation are

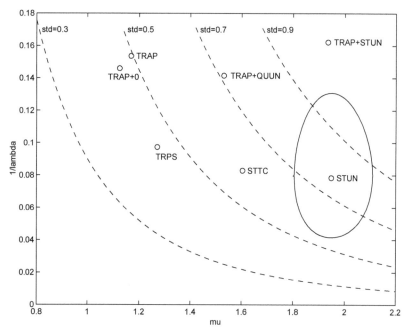

Figure 6.4 Estimated inverse Gaussian distributions of income

added to this plot to compensate for this drawback. Apart from that, the results in the inverse Gaussian case do not differ substantially.

4.2   Inefficiency differentials

The results of subsection 4.1 have made clear – with the help of (μ, σ)-plots and Rao distances – that there are significant differences between the income distribution of university students and that of individuals having followed the insurance strategy. Finally in this subsection, Rao distances and the frontier results from subsection 3.5 on inefficiency will be combined to get even more insight into the financial implications of these courses of education and of the relationship with other sample subgroups. The inefficiency distribution of various subgroups will be analysed to answer questions such as:

● Are low-educated persons very inefficient in finding suitable jobs?
● Are older people more inefficient than younger people?
● Are the 'insured' particularly inefficient?

Unfortunately, the individual inefficiency terms u_i are unobservable (see subsection 3.3), but we have

$$u_i | c_i \sim trunc_0 N(\mu_i^*, \sigma_*^2), \quad \mu_i^* = \frac{-\sigma_u^2 e_i}{\sigma^2} \quad \sigma_* = \frac{\sigma_u \sigma_v}{\sigma} \tag{54}$$

(Jondrow *et al.* (1982)) and, because the Rao distances for $N(\mu_i^*, \sigma_*^2)$ are also Rao distances for $trunc_0 N(\mu_i^*, \sigma_*^2)$, the estimated normal distributions of conditional inefficiency in various sample subgroups can be plotted, as in figure 6.5, with the following additional abbreviations (see subsection 3.2):

● QUU0: lower education than 'qualification for university entrance'
● 1830, 3140, 4150, 5165: age between 18 and 30, ..., 51 and 65
● FEMA: female
● UNMA: unmarried
● WORK: workers

The inefficiency distributions of the age classes make clear that increasing age leads to higher average inefficiency and lower standard deviation of inefficiency. This could be a hint that human capital models need the inclusion of retirement effects. Public servants and those trained for public service show relatively high average inefficiency and low standard deviation. This had to be expected because of the payment system in the public service, and very plausibly the 'insured' are close to these two groups.

On the other hand, university students show relatively low average inefficiency but very high variation. The latter could be due to the

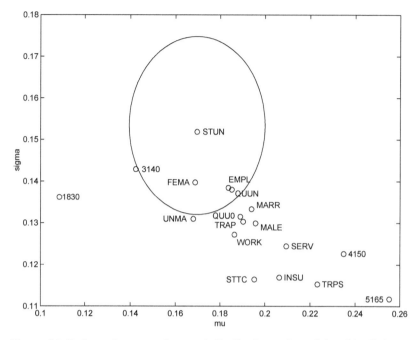

Figure 6.5 Estimated truncated normal distributions of conditional inefficiency

well-known fact that many university graduates do not find suitable jobs. As in the previous subsection, the mean difference between INSU and STUN is clearly insignificant, but the Rao distance test (40) indicates that the distributions depending on μ and σ are significantly different with $\alpha = 0.1$. Finally, the Rao distance test (42) can be applied to construct a confidence region around, for instance, STUN. If (μ_0, σ_0) is an unknown point on the surface, the critical Rao distance can be determined for known sample size and significance level $\alpha = 0.05$, and the corresponding isocircle can be plotted as in figure 6.5.

5   Conclusions

Estimating an extended human capital model as a stochastic earnings frontier has proved to be a fruitful way of explaining potential income and the deviations between empirical and potential income. The partial failure of human capital models when estimated as average functions can thus be explained. The inefficiency terms of the frontier model capture the important but difficult to measure human capital investment in the 'search for information'. Inefficiency turned out to be considerable: the individuals in the sample received only 79 per cent of their maximum possible income on average. Human capital theory is able to explain maximum possible income sufficiently but individuals are inefficient in their job search.

The results of section 4 sustain the judgement of Büchel and Helberger (1995) that the combination of an apprenticeship with university study is an inefficient 'insurance strategy'. Comparing the pecuniary implications of university study STUN and the insurance strategy INSU, it turns out that:

1. the income distributions of STUN and INSU differ significantly;
2. interpreting income variance as risk, the insured have the highest risk of all courses of education in the analysis;
3. the inefficiency distributions of STUN and INSU differ significantly;
4. the name 'insurance strategy' is justified in that the inefficiency distribution of INSU is very similar to that in public service (high average inefficiency, low variance).

At least for the present data set, the second and the fourth items mean that the insurance strategy is poor and costly.

It has been shown that the application of Rao distances is straightforward if one is willing to restrict the analysis to the narrow class of distributions allowing explicit analytic calculation of the necessary distance formula. Rao distances and isocircles are very helpful tools in an intuitive comparison of distributions, especially in two-parameter families. Rao distance tests are based on simple geometrical ideas and – in combination with isocircles – they make it possible graphically to solve test problems such as the test for a (μ, σ)-pair lying on an indifference curve.

References

Aigner, D.J. and S.-F. Chu (1968), 'On Estimating the Industry Production Function', *American Economic Review*, 58: 826–839.

Aigner, D.J., C.A.K. Lovell and P. Schmidt (1977), 'Formulation and Estimation of Stochastic Frontier Production Function Models', *Journal of Econometrics*, 6: 21–37.

Amari, S.I. (1985), *Differential-Geometrical Methods in Statistics*, New York: Springer Verlag.

Atkinson, C. and A.F.S. Mitchell (1981), 'Rao's Distance Measure', *Sankhyā A*, 43: 345–365.

Becker, G.S. (1964), *Human Capital*, New York: NBER.

Brinkmann, G. (1981), 'Die Einkommensfunktion und ihre Testbarkeit', in W. Clement (ed.), *Konzept und Kritik des Humankapitalansatzes*, Berlin: Duncker & Humblot, pp. 87–116.

Büchel, F. and C. Helberger (1995), 'Bildungsnachfrage als Versicherungs-strategie', *Mitteilungen aus der Arbeitsmarkt- und Berufsforschung*, 1/95: 32–42.

Burbea, J. and J.M. Oller (1989), 'On Rao Distance Asymptotic Distribution', Universitat de Barcelona.

Burbea, J. and C.R. Rao (1982), 'Entropy Differential Metric, Distance and Divergence Measures in Probability Spaces: A Unified Approach', *Journal of Multivariate Analysis*, 12: 575–596.

Daneshvary, N., H.W. Herzog, R.A. Hofler and A.M. Schlottmann (1992), 'Job Search and Immigrant Assimilation: An Earnings Frontier Approach', *Review of Economics and Statistics*, 74: 482–492.

DiNardo, J., N.M. Fortin and T. Lemieux (1996), 'Labour Market Institutions and the Distribution of Wages, 1973–1992: A Semiparametric Approach', *Econometrica*, 64: 1001–1044.

Efron, B. (1975), 'Defining the Curvature of a Statistical Problem (with Applications to Second Order Efficiency)', *Annals of Statistics*, 3: 1189–1242.

Franz, W. (1994), *Arbeitsmarktökonomik*, 2nd edn, Berlin: Springer.

Greene, W.H. (1989), *LIMDEP*, New York: Econometric Software.

(1993), 'The Econometric Approach to Efficiency Analysis', in H.O. Fried, C.A.K. Lovell and S.S. Schmidt (eds.), *The Measurement of Productive Efficiency*, New York: Oxford University Press, pp. 68–119.

Griliches, Z. (1977), 'Estimating the Returns to Schooling: Some Econometric Problems', *Econometrica*, 45: 1–22.

Helberger, C. (1988), 'Eine Überprüfung der Linearitätsannahme der Humankapitaltheorie', in H.-J. Bodenhöfer (ed.), *Bildung, Beruf, Arbeitsmarkt*, Berlin: Duncker & Humblot, pp. 151–170.

(1997), personal communication.

Hübler, O. (1984), 'Zur empirischen Überprüfung alternativer Theorien der Verteilung von Arbeitseinkommen', in L. Bellmann, K. Gerlach and O. Hübler, (eds.), *Lohnstruktur in der Bundesrepublik Deutschland*, Frankfurt: Campus, pp. 17–189.

Jensen, U. (1995), 'A Review of the Derivation and Calculation of Rao Distances with an Application to Portfolio Theory', in G.S. Maddala, P.C.B. Phillips and T.N. Srinivasan (eds.), *Advances in Econometrics and Quantitative Economics*, Oxford: Blackwell, pp. 413–462.

Jondrow, J., C.A.K. Lovell, I.S. Materov and P. Schmidt (1982), 'On the Estimation of Technical Inefficiency in the Stochastic Frontier Production Function Model', *Journal of Econometrics*, 19: 233–238.

Kay, D.C. (1988), *Tensor Calculus*, Auckland: Schaum, McGraw-Hill.

Klein, T. (1994), 'Die Einkommenskarriere von Hochschulabsolventen', *Mitteilungen aus der Arbeitsmarkt- und Berufsforschung*, 3/94: 205–211.

Lauritzen, S.L. (1987), 'Statistical Manifolds', in S.I. Amari, O.E. Barndorff-Nielsen, R.E. Kass, S.L. Lauritzen and C.R. Rao (eds.), *Differential Geometry in Statistical Inference*, Hayward, Calif.: Institute of Mathematical Statistics, pp. 163–216.

Mäding, H. (1981), 'Humankapitalbildung zwischen Bildungs- und Arbeitsmarktpolitik', in W. Clement (ed.), *Konzept und Kritik des Humankapitalansatzes*, Berlin: Duncker & Humblot, pp. 117–140.

Meeusen, W. and J. van den Broeck (1977), 'Efficiency Estimation from Cobb–Douglas Production Functions with Composed Error', *International Economic Review*, 18: 435–444.

Millman, R.S. and G.D. Parker (1991), *Geometry – A Metric Approach with Models*, 2nd edn, New York: Springer Verlag.

Mincer, J. (1958), 'Investment in Human Capital and Personal Income Distribution', *Journal of Political Economy*, 66: 281–302.

——— (1974), *Schooling, Experience and Earnings*, New York: NBER.

Rao, C.R. (1945), 'Information and the Accuracy Attainable in the Estimation of Statistical Parameters', *Bulletin of the Calcutta Mathematical Society*, 37: 81–91. Also in S. Kotz and N.L. Johnson, *Breakthroughs in Statistics*, vol. 1, New York: Springer Verlag (1992), pp. 235–247.

Stevenson, R.E. (1980), 'Likelihood Functions for Generalized Stochastic Frontier Estimation', *Journal of Econometrics*, 13: 57–66.

Villarroya, A. and J.M. Oller (1991), 'Statistical Tests for the Inverse Gaussian Distribution Based on Rao Distance', Department of Statistics, University of Barcelona.

Wagner, M. (1981) 'Unerklärte Varianz – Zur Forschungsstrategie der mikro-ökonomischen Humankapitaltheorie', in W. Clement (ed.), *Konzept und Kritik des Humankapitalansatzes*, Berlin: Duncker & Humblot, pp. 165–184.

7 First-order optimal predictive densities

J.M. Corcuera and F. Giummolè

1 Introduction

Consider a vector of observations $x = (x_1, \ldots, x_n)$, not necessarily independent, that corresponds to a random variable X having a distribution that depends on an unknown parameter θ. We suppose that the sample size n is large enough to allow asymptotic approximations.

The aim is to predict the value of an as yet unobserved random variable Y, with a distribution related to that of the data. In general, X and Y have different distributions and are dependent. The conditional density of Y given X is assumed to belong to a regular parametric model

$$\mathcal{P}^x = \{p(y; \theta|x), \ \theta \in \Theta\},$$

where $p(y; \theta|x)$ are densities with respect to some reference measure μ, σ-finite in $\mathbb{R}^p$, and Θ is an open set in $\mathbb{R}^k$.

If possible, we operate with a prior reduction of the problem. Let z be a minimal *predictive sufficient statistic* of the data, that is, z is a minimal sufficient statistic among those that satisfy

$$p(y; \theta|x) = p(y; \theta|z).$$

Then, without loss of information, we can write z instead of x. We also assume that there exists a decomposition $z = (\hat{\theta}, a)$, where $\hat{\theta}$ is the maximum likelihood estimator for θ and a is an *ancillary statistic*, that is, distribution constant, at least up to certain order. According to the conditional principle, the values of a are kept fixed as the sample varies, so that we can denote the densities in $\mathcal{P}^x$ as

$$p(y; \theta|\hat{\theta}), \quad \theta \in \Theta.$$

This work was partially supported by EU HCOM, contract ERB CHRX CT94 0499.

2   Different approaches to the problem

It is possible to predict Y by using a *point value predictor* $g(X)$. In order to compare different point value predictors, it is necessary to specify a loss function as a measure of the error. In the case of Y and $g(X)$ being square integrable variables, we have

$$E_\theta\big((Y - g(X))^2\big) = E_\theta\big((Y - E_\theta(Y|X))^2\big)$$
$$+ E_\theta\big((E_\theta(Y|X) - g(X))^2\big).$$

Thus, if we use the mean square error to measure the goodness of a prediction, the best predictor $g(X)$ is the one that minimises

$$E_\theta\big((E_\theta(Y|X) - g(X))^2\big).$$

Notice that we cannot choose $E_\theta(Y|X)$ as the optimal predictor, since it depends on the unknown value of the parameter θ. If Y and X are independent, the optimal predictor is then the best estimate for $E_\theta(Y)$. Anyway, a point prediction does not give any information about the 'likelihood' of values of Y different from the prediction itself.

Another way to solve the problem is based on *prediction limits* or *intervals*, that is functions $c_\alpha(X)$ such that

$$P_\theta\big\{Y < c_\alpha(X)\big\} = \alpha.$$

Exact prediction limits can be found by means of pivotal quantities (functions that depend on Y and X, whose distribution is independent of θ), or we can look for an approximate solution with an order of approximation that depends on the sample size. One of the problems with this method is that there is not an obvious generalisation to the multivariate case.

Another possibility, which we are going to develop throughout the chapter, consists of finding an optimal *predictive density*, $\hat{p}(y|x)$, that is as close as possible, in some sense, to the true conditional density of Y given $X = x$. We need then to specify a loss function between densities.

3   The form of the optimal solutions

We can use an *estimative density* $p(y; \tilde{\theta}|\hat{\theta})$, obtained by substituting the unknown parameter θ with a suitable estimator $\tilde{\theta}$. Anyway, there could be a predictive density outside the model $\mathcal{P}^x$ that is closer than any estimative density to the true one, $p(y; \theta_0|\hat{\theta})$.

Example 1 Let $X_1, \ldots, X_n$ and Y be independent random variables with the same normal distribution $N(\mu, \sigma^2)$, σ^2 fixed. It is known that the estimative density

$$\phi(y - \bar{x}; \sigma^2)$$

($\phi(\cdot, \sigma^2)$ denotes the density function of a Gaussian random variable with zero mean and variance σ^2) does not provide good prediction intervals for Y. Instead,

$$\phi\left(y - \bar{x}; \sigma^2\left(1 + \frac{1}{n}\right)\right)$$

gives exact prediction intervals, since

$$Y - \bar{X} \sim N\left(0, \sigma^2\left(1 + \frac{1}{n}\right)\right).$$

Notice that this density, for each x, does not belong to the original parametric model of Y. As we shall see in Example 3, this density is closer than the estimative density to the true one, in a precise sense.

Let us consider a regular parametric model of dimension $r > k$ that contains $\mathcal{P}$ (from now on we will not indicate the dependence of the model on the data):

$$\mathcal{M} = \{p(y; \omega|\hat{\theta}), \ \omega \in \Omega\},$$

where Ω is an open set in $\mathbb{R}^r$ and Θ a k-dimensional submanifold of Ω. In $\mathcal{M}$ we choose a coordinate system $\omega = (\theta, s)$, where θ^i, $i = 1, \ldots, k$, are the old coordinates in $\mathcal{P}$ and s^I, $I = k+1, \ldots, r$, the new ones in $\mathcal{M}$. We also take $s = 0$ for the points in $\mathcal{P}$ and θ and s orthogonal in $\mathcal{P}$. We use indices $A, B, C \ldots$ for the components of the coordinate system $\omega = (\theta, s)$ in the enlarged model $\mathcal{M}$, $i, j, k \ldots$ for those in the original family $\mathcal{P}$ and $I, J, K \ldots$ for the components of s.

Every density in $\mathcal{M}$ admits the formal expansion

$$p(y; \theta, s|\hat{\theta}) = p(y; \theta|\hat{\theta}) + p(y; \theta|\hat{\theta})s^I h_I(y; \theta|\hat{\theta}) + \cdots,$$

where

$$h_I(y; \theta|\hat{\theta}) = \partial_I \log p(y; \theta, s|\hat{\theta})|_{s=0}, \quad I = k+1, \ldots, r,$$

and we use the repeated index convention.

We consider in $\mathcal{M}$ predictive densities of the form

$$\hat{p}(y|x) = p(y; \hat{\omega}|\hat{\theta}) = p(y; \hat{\theta}, \hat{s}|\hat{\theta}),$$

with $\hat{s}(\hat{\theta})$ a smooth function of $\hat{\theta}$ of order n^{-1}, so that

$$\hat{s}(\hat{\theta}) = \frac{1}{n}\bar{s}(\hat{\theta}) + o_p(n^{-1}).$$

The aim is then to find a predictive density in $\mathcal{M}$,

$$\hat{p}(y|x) = p(y; \hat{\theta}|\hat{\theta})\left(1 + \frac{1}{n}\bar{s}^I(\hat{\theta})h_I(y; \hat{\theta}|\hat{\theta})\right) + o_p(n^{-1}), \qquad (1)$$

that minimises, uniformly in θ, the leading term in the asymptotic expansion of the *risk*,

$$E_\theta\left[L\Big(\hat{p}(y|x), p(y; \theta|\hat{\theta})\Big)\right],$$

where L is a loss function to be specified and the expectation is calculated keeping the value of the ancillary statistic a fixed.

4 A measure of the discrepancy between densities

We consider a very general class of loss functions called *divergences*. Given a fixed regular parametric model

$$\mathcal{M} = \{p(y; \omega), \ \omega \in \Omega\},$$

we can use any smooth function

$$\varphi : \Omega \times \Omega \to [0, \infty),$$

such that

$$\varphi(\omega, \omega') = 0 \iff \omega = \omega',$$

to measure the discrepancy between two points in $\mathcal{M}$.

The condition of minimum in the diagonal can be expressed by

$$\not\phi_{i;}(\omega) = 0, \quad \forall \omega \in \Omega, \qquad (2)$$

and

$$\not\phi_{ij;}(\omega) \quad \text{is a positive definite matrix,} \quad \forall \omega \in \Omega, \qquad (3)$$

where $\not\phi$ means that φ is calculated in the diagonal and the semicolon indicates the argument with respect to which the derivative is taken.

By repeatedly differentiating expression (2), we obtain the so-called *balance equations* for φ:

$$\not\phi_{ij;}(\omega) + \not\phi_{i;j}(\omega) = 0 \qquad (4)$$

and

$$\not\phi_{ijk;}(\omega) + \not\phi_{ij;k}(\omega) + \not\phi_{ik;j}(\omega) + \not\phi_{i;jk}(\omega) = 0. \qquad (5)$$

It is interesting to observe that similar functions have already been studied by different authors. By changing the sign of φ we obtain a *normalized yoke* (Blæsild (1991)), while φ itself is a smooth *contrast function* (Eguchi (1992)).

Let us now study the geometry that a divergence induces over the manifold where it is defined.

By (2) and (3), we have a metric tensor associated with φ:

$$g_{ij}(\omega) = \phi_{ij;}(\omega). \tag{6}$$

Moreover, φ generates a whole family of affine connections whose coefficients are given by

$$\overset{\beta}{\Gamma}_{ijk} = -\frac{1+\beta}{2}\,\phi_{ij;k} - \frac{1-\beta}{2}\,\phi_{k;ij}, \quad \beta \in \mathbb{R}. \tag{7}$$

In fact, let ξ be another coordinate system for the model $\mathcal{M}$ where φ is defined. Using indices i, j, k for ω and a, b, c for ξ, we can write the Christoffel symbols just defined in the new parameterisation ξ as:

$$\overset{\beta}{\Gamma}_{abc}(\xi) = -\frac{1+\beta}{2}\left(\phi_{ij;k}(\omega)\frac{\partial\omega^i}{\partial\xi^a}\frac{\partial\omega^j}{\partial\xi^b} - \phi_{i;k}(\omega)\frac{\partial^2\omega^i}{\partial\xi^a\partial\xi^b}\right)\frac{\partial\omega^k}{\partial\xi^c}$$

$$-\frac{1-\beta}{2}\left(\phi_{k;ij}(\omega)\frac{\partial\omega^i}{\partial\xi^a}\frac{\partial\omega^j}{\partial\xi^b} - \phi_{k;i}(\omega)\frac{\partial^2\omega^i}{\partial\xi^a\partial\xi^b}\right)\frac{\partial\omega^k}{\partial\xi^c}$$

$$= \left(\overset{\beta}{\Gamma}_{ijk}(\omega)\frac{\partial\omega^i}{\partial\xi^a}\frac{\partial\omega^j}{\partial\xi^b} + g_{ik}(\omega)\frac{\partial^2\omega^i}{\partial\xi^a\partial\xi^b}\right)\frac{\partial\omega^k}{\partial\xi^c},$$

which is exactly the transformation law that characterises the coefficients of an affine connection (Amari (1985), p. 36).

Using (5) and (7), it is easy to see that

$$\phi_{ijk;}(\omega) = \overset{1}{\Gamma}_{ijk} + \overset{1}{\Gamma}_{ikj} + \overset{-1}{\Gamma}_{jki}.$$

Example 2 An α-divergence between two points ω and $\tilde{\omega}$ in $\mathcal{M}$ is defined as follows:

$$\varphi(\tilde{\omega}, \omega) = \int f_\alpha\left(\frac{p(y;\tilde{\omega})}{p(y;\omega)}\right)p(y;\omega)\mu(dy),$$

with

$$f_\alpha(t) = \begin{cases} \dfrac{4}{1-\alpha^2}(1-t^{\frac{1+\alpha}{2}}) & \alpha \neq \pm 1 \\ t \log t & \alpha = 1 \\ -\log t & \alpha = -1. \end{cases}$$

α-divergences include well-known divergences as particular cases. For $\alpha = -1$ we obtain the Kullback–Leibler divergence and for $\alpha = 0$ twice the Hellinger distance.

Suppose $\alpha \neq \pm 1$. If we write $p = p(y; \omega)$, $\tilde{p} = p(y; \tilde{\omega})$, $l = \log p$ and $\tilde{l} = \log \tilde{p}$, under regularity conditions,

$$\varphi_{i;}(\tilde{\omega}, \omega) = \frac{2}{\alpha - 1} \int \left(\frac{\tilde{p}}{p}\right)^{\frac{\alpha-1}{2}} \partial_i \tilde{p} \, \mu(dy),$$

$$\varphi_{i;j}(\tilde{\omega}, \omega) = -\int \left(\frac{\tilde{p}}{p}\right)^{\frac{1+\alpha}{2}} p \, \partial_i \tilde{l} \, \partial_j l \, \mu(dy),$$

$$\varphi_{ij;k}(\tilde{\omega}, \omega) = -\frac{1+\alpha}{2} \int \left(\frac{\tilde{p}}{p}\right)^{\frac{1+\alpha}{2}} p \, \partial_i \tilde{l} \, \partial_j \tilde{l} \, \partial_k l \, \mu(dy)$$

$$- \int \left(\frac{\tilde{p}}{p}\right)^{\frac{1+\alpha}{2}} p \, \partial_i \partial_j \tilde{l} \, \partial_k l \, \mu(dy)$$

$$= -\int \left(\frac{\tilde{p}}{p}\right)^{\frac{1+\alpha}{2}} p \, \partial_k l \left(\partial_i \partial_j \tilde{l} + \frac{1+\alpha}{2} \partial_i \tilde{l} \partial_j \tilde{l}\right) \mu(dy)$$

and, by symmetry,

$$\varphi_{i;jk}(\tilde{\omega}, \omega) = -\int \left(\frac{p}{\tilde{p}}\right)^{\frac{1-\alpha}{2}} \tilde{p} \, \partial_i \tilde{l} \left(\partial_j \partial_k l + \frac{1-\alpha}{2} \partial_j l \partial_k l\right) \mu(dy).$$

By (6) and (4), the metric induced by φ on $\mathcal{M}$ is

$$g_{ij}(\omega) = \varphi_{ij;}(\omega) = -\varphi_{i;j}(\omega) = E_\omega[\partial_i l \partial_j l],$$

which corresponds to the Fisher metric. Moreover,

$$\overset{1}{\Gamma}_{ijk}(\omega) = -\varphi_{ij;k}(\omega) = E_\omega\left[\left(\partial_i \partial_j l + \frac{1+\alpha}{2} \partial_i l \partial_j l\right) \partial_k l\right]$$

and

$$\overset{-1}{\Gamma}_{ijk}(\omega) = -\varphi_{k;ij}(\omega) = E_\omega\left[\left(\partial_i \partial_j l + \frac{1-\alpha}{2} \partial_i l \partial_j l\right) \partial_k l\right].$$

It is immediate to check that the result also holds for $\alpha = \pm 1$. The family of affine connections defined by (7) is then given by

$$\overset{\beta}{\Gamma}_{ijk}(\omega) = E_\omega\left[\left(\partial_i\partial_j l + \frac{1+\alpha\beta}{2}\partial_i\partial_j l\right)\partial_k l\right],\qquad(8)$$

which for $\beta = -1$ are the coefficients of the Amari α-connections (Amari (1985), p. 39).

Since the conditional model $\mathcal{P}$ depends on x, we consider the family of divergences obtained as the data change. This family depends on the data through z and, since the value of a is considered fixed in $z = (\hat\theta, a)$, we write $\varphi^{\hat\theta}$. Similarly, $g_{ij}^{\hat\theta}$ and $\overset{\beta\,\hat\theta}{\Gamma}_{ijk}$ denote the families of metrics and affine connections corresponding to φ.

We can finally say that our purpose is to determine the predictive density in $\mathcal{M}$ of the form (1) that minimises, uniformly in θ, the leading term of the asymptotic expansion of the average divergence

$$E_\theta\left[\varphi^{\hat\theta}(\hat\omega, \omega)\right] - \int \varphi^{\hat\theta}(\hat\omega, \omega)p(\hat\theta; \theta)\,d\hat\theta,$$

where $p(\hat\theta; \theta)$ is the distribution of the maximum likelihood estimator conditioned on the observed value of the ancillary a.

5   The asymptotic risk

From now on, we denote by g and $\overset{\beta}{\Gamma}$, respectively, the metric and family of connections induced by φ in a fixed $\mathcal{M}$.

If $\omega_0 = (\theta_0, 0)$ is the true value of the parameter ω in $\mathcal{M}$, the following result holds:

Proposition 1 *Suppose that $\hat\theta - \theta_0 = O_p(n^{-1/2})$. Then the average divergence from the true distribution $p(y; \omega_0|\hat\theta)$ to a predictive density $p(y; \hat\theta, \hat{s}|\hat\theta)$, is given by*

$$E_{\theta_0}\left[\varphi^{\hat\theta}(\hat\omega, \omega_0)\right] = E_{\theta_0}\left[\varphi^{\hat\theta}((\hat\theta, 0), \omega_0)\right] + \frac{1}{2n^2}g_{IJ}\bar{s}^I\bar{s}^J$$

$$- \frac{1}{2n^2}\overset{-1}{\Gamma}_{ijK}\mathbf{i}^{ij}\bar{s}^K + o(n^{-2}),\qquad(9)$$

where

$$\mathbf{i}^{ij} = \lim_{n\to\infty} nE_{\theta_0}[(\hat\theta - \theta_0)^i(\hat\theta - \theta_0)^j]$$

and $g_{IJ} = g_{IJ}^{\theta_0}(\omega_0)$, $\overset{-1}{\Gamma}_{ijK} = \overset{-1\,\theta_0}{\Gamma}_{ijK}(\omega_0)$ and $\bar{s} = \bar{s}(\theta_0)$.

Proof The asymptotic expansion of $\varphi^{\hat\theta}(\tilde\omega, \omega_0)$ as a function of $\tilde\omega$ in a neighbourhood of ω_0, is

$$\varphi^{\hat{\theta}}(\tilde{\omega}, \omega_0) = \varphi^{\hat{\theta}}(\omega_0) + \varphi^{\hat{\theta}}_{A;}(\omega_0)(\tilde{\omega} - \omega_0)^A$$

$$+ \tfrac{1}{2}\, \varphi^{\hat{\theta}}_{AB;}(\omega_0)(\tilde{\omega} - \omega_0)^A(\tilde{\omega} - \omega_0)^B$$

$$+ \tfrac{1}{6}\, \varphi^{\hat{\theta}}_{ABC;}(\omega_0)(\tilde{\omega} - \omega_0)^A(\tilde{\omega} - \omega_0)^B(\tilde{\omega} - \omega_0)^C$$

$$+ \tfrac{1}{24}\, \varphi^{\hat{\theta}}_{ABCD;}(\omega_0)(\tilde{\omega} - \omega_0)^A(\tilde{\omega} - \omega_0)^B$$

$$\times (\tilde{\omega} - \omega_0)^C(\tilde{\omega} - \omega_0)^D + \cdots.$$

Now, let $\hat{\omega} = (\hat{\theta}, \hat{s})$, with $\hat{s} = O_p(n^{-1})$ and $\hat{\theta} - \theta_0 = O_p(n^{-1/2})$. Taking into account (6) and using the fact that

$$g^{\hat{\theta}}_{iJ}(\omega_0) = 0, \quad \forall i = 1, \ldots, k, \, J = k + 1, \ldots, r, \tag{10}$$

we can write

$$\varphi^{\hat{\theta}}(\hat{\omega}, \omega_0) = \tfrac{1}{2} g^{\hat{\theta}}_{ij}(\hat{\theta} - \theta_0)^i(\hat{\theta} - \theta_0)^j + \tfrac{1}{2} g^{\hat{\theta}}_{IJ} \hat{s}^I \hat{s}^J$$

$$+ \tfrac{1}{6}\, \varphi^{\hat{\theta}}_{ijk;}(\hat{\theta} - \theta_0)^i(\hat{\theta} - \theta_0)^j(\hat{\theta} - \theta_0)^k$$

$$+ \tfrac{1}{2}\, \varphi^{\hat{\theta}}_{ijK;}(\hat{\theta} - \theta_0)^i(\hat{\theta} - \theta_0)^j \hat{s}^K$$

$$+ \tfrac{1}{24}\, \varphi^{\hat{\theta}}_{ijkh;}(\hat{\theta} - \theta_0)^i(\hat{\theta} - \theta_0)^j(\hat{\theta} - \theta_0)^k(\hat{\theta} - \theta_0)^h + o_p(n^{-2}),$$

where the coefficients are calculated in ω_0.

Moreover, by (10) and (4), it holds

$$0 = \partial_i\, \varphi^{\hat{\theta}}_{jK;} = \varphi^{\hat{\theta}}_{ijK;} + \varphi^{\hat{\theta}}_{jK;i}$$

and

$$0 = \partial_j\, \varphi^{\hat{\theta}}_{K;i} = \varphi^{\hat{\theta}}_{jK;i} + \varphi^{\hat{\theta}}_{K;ij}.$$

It is then obvious, using also (7), that

$$\varphi^{\hat{\theta}}_{ijK;} = -\overset{-1}{\Gamma}{}^{\hat{\theta}}_{ijK}.$$

Thus, we can write

$$\varphi^{\hat{\theta}}(\hat{\omega}, \omega_0) = \tfrac{1}{2} g^{\hat{\theta}}_{ij}(\hat{\theta} - \theta_0)^i(\hat{\theta} - \theta_0)^j + \tfrac{1}{2} g^{\hat{\theta}}_{IJ} \hat{s}^I \hat{s}^J$$

$$+ \tfrac{1}{6}\, \varphi^{\hat{\theta}}_{ijk;}(\hat{\theta} - \theta_0)^i(\hat{\theta} - \theta_0)^j(\hat{\theta} - \theta_0)^k$$

$$- \tfrac{1}{2}\overset{-1}{\Gamma}{}^{\hat{\theta}}_{ijK}(\hat{\theta} - \theta_0)^i(\hat{\theta} - \theta_0)^j \hat{s}^K$$

$$+ \tfrac{1}{24}\, \varphi^{\hat{\theta}}_{ijkh;}(\hat{\theta} - \theta_0)^i(\hat{\theta} - \theta_0)^j(\hat{\theta} - \theta_0)^k(\hat{\theta} - \theta_0)^h + o_p(n^{-2}),$$

so that

$$\varphi^{\hat{\theta}}(\hat{\omega}, \omega_0) = \varphi^{\hat{\theta}}((\hat{\theta}, 0), \omega_0) + \tfrac{1}{2}g^{\hat{\theta}}_{IJ}\hat{s}^I \hat{s}^J$$
$$- \tfrac{1}{2}\overset{-\frac{1}{2}}{\Gamma}{}^{\hat{\theta}}_{ijK}(\hat{\theta} - \theta_0)^i(\hat{\theta} - \theta_0)^j \hat{s}^K + o_p(n^{-2}).$$

By taking the expectations and disregarding terms of higher order, we obtain

$$E_{\theta_0}\left[\varphi^{\hat{\theta}}(\hat{\omega}, \omega_0)\right] = E_{\theta_0}\left[\varphi^{\hat{\theta}}((\hat{\theta}, 0), \omega_0)\right] + \tfrac{1}{2}g^{\theta_0}_{IJ}(\omega_0)E_{\theta_0}\left[\hat{s}^I \hat{s}^J\right]$$
$$- \tfrac{1}{2}\overset{-1}{\Gamma}{}^{\theta_0}_{ijK}(\theta_0)E_{\theta_0}\left[(\hat{\theta} - \theta_0)^i(\hat{\theta} - \theta_0)^j \hat{s}^K\right] + o(n^{-2}).$$

Now, since

$$\hat{s}^I(\hat{\theta}) = \frac{\bar{s}^I(\theta_0)}{n} + o_p(n^{-1}),$$

we have

$$E_{\theta_0}\left[\varphi^{\hat{\theta}}(\hat{\omega}, \omega_0)\right] = E_{\theta_0}\left[\varphi^{\hat{\theta}}((\hat{\theta}, 0), \omega_0)\right] + \tfrac{1}{2}g^{\theta_0}_{IJ}(\omega_0)\bar{s}^I(\theta_0)\bar{s}^J(\theta_0)$$
$$- \tfrac{1}{2}\overset{-1}{\Gamma}{}^{\theta_0}_{ijK}(\theta_0)E_{\theta_0}\left[(\hat{\theta} - \theta_0)^i(\hat{\theta} - \theta_0)^j\right]\hat{s}^K(\theta_0) + o(n^{-2}).$$

Finally, putting

$$\mathbf{i}^{ij} = \lim_{n\to\infty} nE_{\theta_0}\left[(\hat{\theta} - \theta_0)^i(\hat{\theta} - \theta_0)^j\right]$$

gives the result. ∎

5.1   The optimal predictive density in the enlarged model

Expression (9) allows us to split the problem of prediction into one of estimation followed by a correction of the estimative density. In the i.i.d. case, when the model is a curved exponential family, the term corresponding to the estimation can be expanded further and different estimative densities can be compared. Here we concentrate on the problem of finding an expression for $\bar{s}$ that gives the optimal correction to the estimative density obtained with the maximum likelihood estimator.

We can easily prove the following result:

Proposition 2   *The optimal choice of $\bar{s}$ is given by*

$$\bar{s}^I_{opt}(\theta_0) = \tfrac{1}{2}\overset{-1}{\Gamma}{}^{\theta_0}_{ij}{}^I(\theta_0, 0)\mathbf{i}^{ij}(\theta_0) + o(n^{-1}). \tag{11}$$

Proof By differentiating (9) with respect to $\bar{s}$ we obtain

$$\bar{s}^I = \tfrac{1}{2}\overset{-1}{\Gamma}_{ijK}g^{KI}\mathbf{i}^{ij} = \tfrac{1}{2}\overset{-1}{\Gamma}{}^{I}_{ij}\mathbf{i}^{ij},$$

which minimises the risk and thus the optimal choice of $\bar{s}$ $((g^{KI})$ is the inverse of (g_{IK}) and we raise and lower indices by multiplying respectively by (g^{KI}) and $(g_{IK}))$. ∎

Notice that $\overset{-1}{\Gamma}_{ijK}$ is in fact a tensor and represents the components of the embedding curvature of $\mathcal{P}$ in the enlarged manifold $\mathcal{M}$. This is easily proved since, if we change the parameterisation in $\mathcal{M}$, using (10), we have

$$\overset{-1}{\Gamma}_{abC}(\xi) = \left(\overset{-1}{\Gamma}_{ijK}(\omega) \frac{\partial \omega^i}{\partial \xi^a} \frac{\partial \omega^j}{\partial \xi^b} + g_{iK}(\omega) \frac{\partial^2 \omega^i}{\partial \xi^a \partial \xi^b} \right) \frac{\partial \omega^K}{\partial \xi^C}$$

$$= \overset{-1}{\Gamma}_{ijK}(\omega) \frac{\partial \omega^i}{\partial \xi^a} \frac{\partial \omega^j}{\partial \xi^b} \frac{\partial \omega^K}{\partial \xi^C},$$

where we used indices a, b, C for the coordinate system ξ and i, j, K for ω.

(1) and (11) allow us to write the asymptotic expression for the optimal predictive density in $\mathcal{M}$:

$$\hat{p}^{\mathcal{M}}(y|x) = p(y; \hat{\theta}|\hat{\theta}) \left[1 + \frac{1}{2n} \mathbf{i}^{ij} \overset{-1}{\Gamma}{}^{\hat{\theta}}_{ij}{}^{I}(\hat{\theta}, 0)(\hat{\theta})h_I(y; \hat{\theta}|\hat{\theta}) \right] + o_p(n^{-1}).$$

$$(12)$$

Of course, this expression depends on $\mathcal{M}$, so that, in general, if we further enlarge the model, we can improve the predictive density (12).

6   A global solution

In this section we want to find sufficient conditions for the existence of an extended manifold $\mathcal{M}$ such that the optimal predictive density in $\mathcal{M}$ is the global solution to the problem of prediction.

In order to do that, we associate with each point θ in $\mathcal{P}$, the vector space that includes all the possible directions in which we can extend the original model.

First of all, the tangent space T_θ to $\mathcal{P}$ in θ can be identified with the linear space generated by

$$\partial_i l(y; \theta|\hat{\theta}) = \frac{\partial l(y; \theta|\hat{\theta})}{\partial \theta^i}, \quad i = 1, \ldots, k,$$

where $l(y; \theta|\hat{\theta}) = \log p(y; \theta|\hat{\theta})$. In T_θ, it is possible to define a scalar product by means of the Fisher information matrix, and a family of affine connections, the Amari α-connections defined in (8).

A vector space containing T_θ,

$$H_\theta = \left\{ h(y) : \int h(y) p(y, \theta|\hat{\theta}) \mu(dy) = 0, \right.$$

$$\left. \int h^2(y) p(y; \theta|\hat{\theta}) \mu(dy) < \infty \right\},$$

can be associated to each point θ in $\mathcal{P}$. H_θ, as a subspace of $L^2(p\,d\mu)$, inherits in a natural way the scalar product

$$\langle h(y), g(y) \rangle = \int h(y) g(y) p(y; \theta|\hat{\theta}) \mu(dy), \quad h, g \in H_\theta.$$

It is immediate to see that this scalar product is compatible with the one given in T_θ by the Fisher information matrix. We refer to

$$\mathcal{H}(\mathcal{P}) = \bigcup_{\theta \in \Theta} H_\theta$$

as the *vector fibre bundle* of $\mathcal{P}$.

Let $h \in \mathcal{H}(\mathcal{P})$ be a vector field such that

$$\partial_a h + \frac{1+\alpha}{2} E(h\partial_a l) + \frac{1-\alpha}{2} h\partial_a l \equiv \overset{\alpha(\mathcal{H})}{\nabla}_{\partial_a l} h \qquad (13)$$

belongs to $\mathcal{H}(\mathcal{P})$. The previous expression could be seen as a covariant derivative in $\mathcal{H}(\mathcal{P})$; anyway its interest here is due to the fact that

$$\langle \overset{\alpha(\mathcal{H})}{\nabla}_{\partial_a l} \partial_b l, \partial_c l \rangle = \overset{\alpha(A)}{\Gamma}_{abc}, \qquad (14)$$

where $\overset{\alpha(A)}{\Gamma}_{abc}$ are the coefficients of the Amari α-connections.

Notice that the geometry given by the Fisher information matrix and the Amari α-connections does not necessarily coincide with that induced by the considered divergence φ. The space M_θ, tangent to $\mathcal{M}$ in the points of the original manifold $\mathcal{P}$, is generated by vectors $\partial_A l(y; \omega|\hat{\theta})|_{s=0}$, $A = 1, \ldots, r$, belonging to H_θ. The divergence induces on $\mathcal{M}$ a metric $g_{AB}(\omega)$ given by (6), which is in general different from the Fisher metric. We also have a family of affine connections or covariant derivatives

$$\overset{\beta(\mathcal{M})}{\nabla}_{\partial_A l(y;\theta|\hat{\theta})} \partial_B l(y; \theta|\hat{\theta}) \equiv \overset{\beta\hat{\theta}}{\Gamma}_{ABC}(\theta) g^{\hat{\theta} CD}(\theta) \partial_D l(y; \theta|\hat{\theta})$$

$$= \overset{\beta\hat{\theta}}{\Gamma}_{AB}{}^D(\theta) \partial_D l(y; \theta|\hat{\theta}),$$

where $\overset{\beta}{\Gamma}_{ABC}$ are given by (7). In general they are not the Christoffel symbols of the Amari α-connections. Since $T_\theta \subset M_\theta$, we have an induced scalar product in T_θ given by g_{ij}, and an induced covariant derivative obtained by projecting the preceding one:

$$\overset{\beta}{\nabla}{}^{(P)}_{\partial_i l(y;\theta|\hat\theta)} \partial_j l(y;\theta|\hat\theta) = \overset{\beta}{\Gamma}{}^{\hat\theta}_{ijh}(\theta) g^{\hat\theta\,hk}(\theta) \partial_k l(y;\theta|\hat\theta) = \overset{\beta}{\Gamma}{}^{\hat\theta\,k}_{ij}(\theta) \partial_k l(y;\theta|\hat\theta).$$

Consider now, for $i, j = 1, \ldots, k$, vectors

$$h^M_{ij} = \overset{-1}{\Gamma}{}^l_{ij} h_l = \overset{-1}{\Gamma}{}^l_{ij} \partial_l = \overset{-1}{\nabla}{}^{(M)}_{\partial_i l} \partial_j l - \overset{-1}{\nabla}{}^{(P)}_{\partial_i l} \partial_j l.$$

They are orthogonal to P and belong to the tangent space to M in P, thus to the vector fibre bundle $\mathcal{H}(P)$. h^M_{ij}'s represent the orthogonal components to P of the -1-covariant derivative induced in M by the divergence φ.

Using the definition of h^M_{ij}, we can rewrite expression (12) of the optimal predictive density in M as

$$\hat{p}^M(y|x) = p(y; \hat\theta|\hat\theta)\left(1 + \frac{1}{2n} h^M_{ij} \mathbf{i}^{ij}\right) + o_p(n^{-1}). \tag{15}$$

We now present an example in which there exists a special orthogonal direction to enlarge the original model P, such that, if the model M contains that direction, the preceding predictive density represents the maximal improvement to an estimative density.

6.1 The case of α-divergences

In this case, the -1-covariant derivatives induced by α-divergences in M and P coincide with Amari α-connections, as we have seen in (8). Moreover, as shown in (14), they can be obtained by projecting (13) over the tangent spaces of M and P.

Let

$$h_{ij} = \overset{\alpha(\mathcal{H})}{\nabla}_{\partial_i l} \partial_j l - \overset{\alpha(A)}{\Gamma}{}^k_{ij} \partial_k l, \qquad \forall i, j = 1, \ldots, k.$$

Notice that, by (14), these vectors are orthogonal to P.

We can now prove the following result, which states the existence of an optimal direction to enlarge the model P.

Proposition 3 *The optimal direction is given by $\mathbf{i}^{ij} h_{ij}$ and the optimal predictive density can be written, up to order n^{-1}, as*

$$\hat{p}(y|x) = p(y; \hat{\theta}|\hat{\theta}) \left[1 + \frac{1}{2n} \mathbf{i}^{ij} \left(\partial_i \partial_j l(y; \hat{\theta}|\hat{\theta}) + \frac{1-\alpha}{2} \partial_i l(y; \hat{\theta}|\hat{\theta}) \partial_j l(y; \hat{\theta}|\hat{\theta}) \right. \right.$$

$$\left. \left. + \frac{1+\alpha}{2} g_{ij}^{\hat{\theta}}(\hat{\theta}) - \overset{\alpha(A)}{\Gamma}{}^k_{ij}(\hat{\theta}) \partial_k l(y; \hat{\theta}|\hat{\theta}) \right) \right].$$

Proof The gain in average divergence obtained by using $\hat{p}^{\mathcal{M}}$ instead of the estimative is

$$E_{\theta_0}[\varphi^{\hat{\theta}}((\hat{\theta}, 0), \omega_0)] - E_{\theta_0}[\varphi^{\hat{\theta}}((\hat{\theta}, \hat{s}_{opt}), \omega_0)]$$

$$= \frac{1}{2n^2} (-g_{IJ}\bar{s}_{opt}^I \bar{s}_{opt}^J + \overset{-1}{\Gamma}_{ijK}\mathbf{i}^{ij}\bar{s}_{opt}^K) + o(n^{-2})$$

$$= \frac{1}{2n^2} (-\tfrac{1}{4}g_{IJ}\overset{-1}{\Gamma}{}^I_{ij}\overset{-1}{\Gamma}{}^J_{kh}\mathbf{i}^{ij}\mathbf{i}^{kh} + \tfrac{1}{2}\overset{-1}{\Gamma}{}^I_{ij}g_{IJ}\overset{-1}{\Gamma}{}^J_{kh}\mathbf{i}^{ij}\mathbf{i}^{kh}) + o(n^{-2})$$

$$= \frac{1}{8n^2} \overset{-1}{\Gamma}{}^I_{ij}\overset{-1}{\Gamma}{}^J_{kh}\mathbf{i}^{ij}\mathbf{i}^{kh}g_{IJ} + o(n^{-2})$$

$$= \frac{1}{8n^2} \| \overset{-1}{\Gamma}{}^I_{ij}\mathbf{i}^{ij}\partial_I l \|^2 + o(n^{-2})$$

$$= \frac{1}{8n^2} \| h_{ij}^{\mathcal{M}}\mathbf{i}^{ij} \|^2 + o(n^{-2}).$$

On the other hand,

$$\langle h_{ij}, \partial_I l \rangle g^{IJ}\partial_J l = \langle \overset{\alpha(\mathcal{H})}{\nabla}_{\partial_i l}\partial_j l, \partial_I l \rangle g^{IJ}\partial_J l$$

$$= \langle \overset{-1(\mathcal{M})}{\nabla}_{\partial_i l}\partial_j l, \partial_I l \rangle g^{IJ}\partial_J l = h_{ij}^{\mathcal{M}}, \quad \forall \mathcal{M} \supset \mathcal{P}$$

and we can write

$$\frac{1}{8n^2} \| h_{ij}^{\mathcal{M}}\mathbf{i}^{ij} \|^2 = \frac{1}{8n^2} \| \mathbf{i}^{ij} \langle h_{ij}, \partial_I l \rangle g^{IJ}\partial_J l \|^2$$

$$= \frac{1}{8n^2} \| \langle h_{ij}\mathbf{i}^{ij}, \partial_I l \rangle g^{IJ}\partial_J l \|^2,$$

which depends only on the projection of $h_{ij}\mathbf{i}^{ij}$ on the tangent space to $\mathcal{M}$ in $\mathcal{P}$. The gain is then maximum if and only if vector $h_{ij}\mathbf{i}^{ij}$ belongs to that space and, in this case, $h_{ij}^{\mathcal{M}}\mathbf{i}^{ij} = h_{ij}\mathbf{i}^{ij}$, since h_{ij} are orthogonal to $\mathcal{P}$. The final expression for the optimal predictive density follows from (13) and the definition of vectors h_{ij}. ∎

7   Examples

In the following examples we always take α-divergences as loss functions.

Example 3   Let $x = (x_1, x_2, \ldots, x_n)$ be a random sample of size n from $X = (X_1, X_2, \ldots, X_n)$ and suppose that we want to predict a value from $Y = (X_{n+1} + X_{n+2} + \cdots + X_{n+m})/m$, where $X_i \sim N(\mu, \sigma^2)$, $i = 1, 2,$ $\ldots$, with σ^2 known.

The maximum likelihood estimator for μ is given by

$$\hat{\mu} = \bar{X} = \frac{\displaystyle\sum_{i=1}^{n} X_i}{n}$$

and it is normally distributed with variance σ^2/n.

Since $Y \sim N(\mu, \sigma^2/m)$, we have that

$$\partial_\mu l = \frac{m(y - \mu)}{\sigma^2} \quad \text{and} \quad \partial_\mu^2 l = -\frac{m}{\sigma^2}.$$

It is also easy to see from (8) that

$$\overset{\alpha}{\Gamma} = 0, \quad \forall \alpha.$$

Then, the optimal predictive density is given by

$$\hat{p}(y|x) = \phi(y - \hat{\mu}, \sigma^2/m)$$

$$\times \left[1 + \frac{(1 - \alpha)m}{4n} \left(\frac{m(y - \hat{\mu})^2}{\sigma^2} - 1 \right) \right] + o_p(n^{-1}),$$

where $\phi(\cdot, \sigma^2)$ denotes the normal density with mean 0 and variance σ^2. $\hat{p}$ can be written in a close form as

$$\hat{p}(y|x) = \phi\left(y - \hat{\mu}, \sigma^2 \left(\frac{1}{m} + \frac{1 - \alpha}{2n} \right) \right).$$

For $\alpha = -1$ it coincides with the exact solution that we obtain from the pivotal statistics

$$\frac{Y - \bar{X}}{\sigma\left(\dfrac{1}{m} + \dfrac{1}{n} \right)^{1/2}}.$$

Example 4   Let $X_0, X_1, \ldots, X_n$ be an autoregressive process of order 1, with $X_0 = 0$ and $X_n | X_{n-1} \sim N(\rho X_{n-1}, \sigma^2)$, where σ^2 is known and $|\rho| < 1$. Suppose that $x = (x_1, x_2, \ldots, x_n)$ and $y = x_{n+1}$.

It is well known that

$$\hat{\rho} = \frac{\sum_{i=1}^{n} X_{i-1} X_i}{\sum_{i=1}^{n+1} X_{i-1}^2}$$

is asymptotically normal with asymptotic variance $1 - \rho^2$. Moreover,

$$\partial_\rho l = \frac{x_n(x_{n+1} - \rho x_n)}{\sigma^2} \quad \text{and} \quad \partial_\rho^2 l = -\frac{x_n^2}{\sigma^2}.$$

Then the optimal predictive density is, up to order n^{-1},

$$\hat{p}(y|x) = \phi(x_{n+1} - \hat{\rho} x_n, \sigma^2)$$

$$\times \left[1 + \frac{1 - \alpha}{4n} \frac{x_n^2 (1 - \hat{\rho}^2)}{\sigma^2} \left(\frac{(x_{n+1} - \hat{\rho} x_n)^2}{\sigma^2} - 1 \right) \right],$$

which can be written in the equivalent form

$$\hat{p}(y|x) = \phi\left(x_{n+1} - \hat{\rho} x_n, \sigma^2 \left(1 + \frac{1 - \alpha}{2n} \frac{(1 - \hat{\rho}^2) x_n^2}{\sigma^2} \right) \right).$$

Example 5 Let $y = (y_1, y_2, \ldots, y_n)$ be an observation from a random vector $Y = (Y_1, Y_2, \ldots, Y_n)$ such that

$$Y_i = \beta_1 x_{i1} + \cdots + \beta_m x_{im} + \epsilon_i, \quad i = 1, \ldots, n.$$

We can write, using matrix notation,

$$Y = X\beta + \epsilon,$$

where:
- $Y = (Y_1, Y_2, \ldots, Y_n)'$;
- $X = (x_{ij})$ is a $n \times m$ non-stochastic matrix of rank $m \leq n$;
- $\epsilon = (\epsilon_1, \epsilon_2, \ldots, \epsilon_n)'$ is distributed as $N(0, \sigma^2 I_n)$, with $\sigma^2 > 0$ known;
- $\beta = (\beta_1, \beta_2, \ldots, \beta_n)'$ is the unknown parameter.

We also assume that

$$(X'X)^{-1} = \frac{\Sigma}{n} + O(n^{-2}),$$

with Σ known.

We want to predict the future observation y_{n+1} from the random variable

$$Y_{n+1} = \beta_1 x_{n+1,1} + \cdots + \beta_m x_{n+1,m} + \epsilon_{n+1} = x'_{n+1}\beta + \epsilon_{n+1},$$

with $x_{n+1} = (x_{n+1,1}, \ldots, x_{n+1,m})'$ known and $\epsilon_{n+1} \sim N(0, \sigma^2)$.

The maximum likelihood estimator for the unknown parameter β coincides with the least square estimator:

$$\hat{\beta} = (X'X)^{-1}X'y.$$

The covariance matrix of $\hat{\beta}$ is

$$\mathrm{Var}(\hat{\beta}) = \sigma^2 (X'X)^{-1},$$

so that $\lim_{n\to\infty} n\mathrm{Var}(\hat{\beta}) = \sigma^2 \Sigma$. Moreover, since $Y_{n+1} \sim N(x'_{n+1}\beta, \sigma^2)$, we have that

$$\partial_i l(y_{n+1}; \beta) = \frac{y_{n+1} - x'_{n+1}\beta}{\sigma^2} x_{n+1,i}$$

and

$$\partial_{ij} l(y_{n+1}; \beta) = -\frac{x_{n+1,i} x_{n+1,j}}{\sigma^2}.$$

Thus, the optimal predictive density for y_{n+1} with respect to an α-divergence, is

$$\hat{p}(y_{n+1}|y) = \phi(y_{n+1} - x'_{n+1}\hat{\beta}, \sigma^2)\left[1 + \frac{1-\alpha}{4n} x'_{n+1}\Sigma x_{n+1} \right.$$

$$\left. \times \left(\frac{(y_{n+1} - x'_{n+1}\hat{\beta})^2}{\sigma^2} - 1 \right) \right] + o_p(n^{-1}),$$

which, up to terms of order n^{-1}, can be written as

$$N\left(x'_{n+1}\hat{\beta}, \left(1 - \frac{1-\alpha}{2n} x'_{n+1}\Sigma x_{n+1} \right)^{-1}\sigma^2 \right).$$

Again, for $\alpha = -1$ we obtain a predictive density that gives exact prediction intervals.

References

Amari, S. (1985), *Differential-Geometrical Methods in Statistics*, Lecture Notes in Statistics No. 28, New York: Springer Verlag.

Blæsild, P. (1991), 'Yokes and Tensors Derived from Yokes', *Annals of the Institute of Statistical Mathematics*, 43(1): 95–113.

Eguchi, S. (1992), 'Geometry of Minimum Contrast', *Hiroshima Math. J.*, 22: 631–647.

8 An alternative comparison of classical tests: assessing the effects of curvature

Kees Jan van Garderen

1 Introduction

The last two decades have seen a rapid growth in the application of differential geometry in statistics. Efron (1975) stimulated much of this research with his definition of statistical curvature and he showed that curvature has serious consequences for statistical inference.

Many papers on the application of differential geometry in statistics go straight into defining all the necessary tools, such as the metric and an affine connection on a manifold, and show how they can be used in statistical analysis. The emphasis is predominantly on asymptotic theory and applications are mainly in estimation, information loss and higher-order efficiency. Barndorff-Nielsen, Cox and Reid (1986) give a very accessible account of the relevant ideas in differential geometry and also provide a historical overview; see also Amari (1985) and Okamoto, Amari and Takeuchi (1991) provide a brief recent summary of main achievements.

This chapter is concerned with the effects of curvature on hypothesis testing. However, our approach differs from the differential geometrical approach mentioned above in a number of ways. First, we give a global analysis, i.e. for the whole of the sample and parameter space, not merely in a neighbourhood of a fixed point such as the true parameter value. Secondly, the analysis is valid for all sample sizes, not just asymptotically. Finally, we are concerned with hypothesis testing, which is less common, and use the partitioning of the sample space into critical region and acceptance region to illustrate our arguments graphically, rather than solely investigating the (analytic) properties of test statistic(s).

More specifically, this chapter investigates the effects of global curvature on the different classical tests: the Lagrange multiplier (LM), Wald, and likelihood ratio (LR) tests, as well as the point optimal (PO) and geodesic tests. Traditional approaches can be found in most econometrics text books, and see Engle (1984) and Buse (1982) for a comparison between the LM, Wald and LR tests using simple diagrams of the log-likelihood. The LR measures the difference in height of the log-likelihood between restricted and unrestricted models, the LM test measures the slope of the log-likelihood at the null, and the Wald measures the distance between the unrestricted MLE and the restricted value under the null directly. In these approaches all three tests appear equally reasonable, a view reinforced by the fact that they are asymptotically equivalent. We shall see that this can be very misleading and that the tests make very different choices in terms of their critical regions. We also consider the global curvature of the model and show that the one-sided LM and PO tests, for instance, are potentially inconsistent for distant alternatives because of their straight critical regions.

Another comparison between the classical tests from a differential geometrical point of view was developed by Kumon and Amari (1983) and Amari (1983); also see Amari (1985, chapter 6). They analysed first-order efficient (most powerful) tests, showed that they are automatically second-order efficient (most powerful), and compared the third-order power loss, i.e. the asymptotic difference between the power of a test and the power envelope. This power loss depends on the curvature of the model at H_0, common to all tests, and the curvature properties of the boundary of the critical region. The LR is shown to have good performance over a 'wide range' of alternatives, the LM test in a range close to H_0, and the Wald test for more distant alternatives, where distance is measured in terms of the geodesic distance to local alternatives.

Other articles on hypothesis testing dealing specifically with curvature include Efron (1975, section 8), Critchley, Marriott and Salmon (1996), Davidson (1992) and Hillier (1990, 1995). Efron (1975) showed that the (local) curvature at H_0 gives a good indication of the performance of the locally most powerful test and concludes that a point optimal test may be preferable if the curvature is larger than $1/8$, as a rough guide. Hillier (1990, 1995) considers the global curvature properties of the model and proposes a measure of global curvature. If the measure is small, then curvature does not pose a serious problem and any of the classical tests will give a reasonable test. Davidson (1992) and Critchley et al. (1996) consider the Wald test and propose alternative geometric solutions to the non-invariance problem of the Wald statistic – a $C(\alpha)$ type test and a geodesic test, respectively – but the two tests must still contend with a number of practical problems.

There are two main approaches in analysing testing procedures. The usual approach is to define the test statistic and evaluate its properties, such as its exact, asymptotic or simulated distribution, and find size and power properties. The second approach is in the tradition of Neyman and Pearson and looks at the partition of the sample space into a critical region (CR) and an acceptance region defined by the test. The two approaches are equivalent in the sense that every statistic induces a partition of the sample space and vice versa, but in practice they are quite different.

This chapter follows the second approach and is therefore closely related to Hillier (1990, 1995); see section 5 below in particular. He uses the change in the PO test CR as a measure of global curvature. We show how curvature also affects the CR of other classical test procedures. This chapter is further related to Kumon and Amari (1983), Amari (1983) and Amari (1985), as mentioned before, who call the boundaries of the CR ancillary manifolds but concentrate on an asymptotic treatment.

It is well known that if the model is a one-parameter linear exponential model, then there exists a uniformly most powerful (UMP) test against one-sided alternatives. Conversely, it is also true that if a UMP test exists, then the model must be a one-parameter linear exponential model, as was shown by Pfanzagl (1968). In Theorem 1 in section 2 we give a new and simple proof of a slightly stronger result, assuming the density belongs to an exponential family of arbitrary, but fixed, dimension.

We will assume throughout the chapter that the models of interest are (curved) exponential models. If the density belongs to a curved exponential family, it means that the dimension of the minimal sufficient statistic is finite and fixed. This allows us to concentrate on the critical region, which is a subset in the sample space of fixed dimension for all sample sizes, rather than on the test statistic (which concentrates the sufficient statistic into a one-dimensional statistic).

A wide variety of models belong to this class of models. In van Garderen (1997a) we motivate the use of curved exponential models and give a variety of examples in econometrics, such as the seemingly unrelated regressions model, the single structural equation model, demand systems, and time-series models, as well as references to other examples in, for instance, continuous time-series models.

Another reason for the assumption is that, since UMP tests do not exist if the model is curved, it seems natural to use a general class of models that includes the one-parameter linear exponential model to determine the effects of curvature. Models close to linear exponential models can then be analysed, as well as models that are very different. Of course, this can be generalised to non-exponential families. Efron (1975) derived a curvature measure based on exponential models and generalised this to arbitrary families of distributions. Many expressions derived here have analogues in terms of derivatives of the likelihood also. We shall not pursue such a generalisation, but the intuition developed here holds more generally. It should be noted that the dimension in such a generalisation is implicitly restricted because only a finite number of derivatives are taken into account and, secondly, these derivatives and their expectations are evaluated at specific points.[1] This leads quite naturally to asymptotic theory in a neighbourhood of a chosen point.

In contrast, we restrict the dimension explicitly from the onset, because we set out to consider the whole of the sample and parameter space and consider finite sample behaviour.

No test exists that is best for all parameter values if the model is curved. Different test procedures achieve good power properties for certain regions of the parameter space (only), or achieve some overall desirable power properties, and some tests do not achieve either. We want to assess the reasonableness of tests based on the shape of the CR.

The LM and PO test give a straight boundary of the critical region regardless of the model curvature, as shown in sections 3 and 4, and thus in effect ignore the curvature of the model. The Wald test does give a curved boundary, but the test statistic is inherently a non-geometric quantity and depends on the parameterisation used (see section 5). A geometric counterpart introduced in section 6, called the geodesic test, also gives a curved boundary, but raises practical and fundamental questions. The analysis of the LR test in section 7 is the most interesting. The LR test gives a curved boundary that trades off the global curvature against the local curvature of the model, and the LR test can be seen as an average of best critical regions in all directions.

If a model is not too curved in the sense of both Efron and Hillier, then any of the tests give a reasonable solution to the non-existence of a uniformly most powerful test. The main conclusion of the present analysis is that if the model is seriously curved then the LR test appears the clear favourite, from both a practical and a theoretical point of view.

Section 8 provides an example and shows the CRs of the different tests when testing for autocorrelation or for a unit root in the first-order autoregressive (AR(1)) model. Section 9 concludes.

---

[1] Unless we regard the derivative as elements of a function space, e.g. the score which can be regarded as a function of the parameters. If the density belongs to an exponential family then there is a finite dimensional basis for the function space of scores. If the density does not belong to an exponential family then this space is infinite dimensional.

2   UMP tests and one-parameter linear exponential models

To test a simple null hypothesis H_0 against a simple alternative H_a we can use the Neyman–Pearson lemma to give a test that is at least as powerful as any other test of the same size.

Neyman–Pearson Lemma (NPL)   *Let $x \in X$ be a random variable of dimension n, with likelihood function $L(x|H_0)$ and $L(x|H_a)$ under the null and alternative hypothesis, respectively. When testing H_0 versus H_a the critical region*

$$BCR = \left\{ x \in X \left| \frac{L(x|H_a)}{L(x|H_0)} \geq c_\alpha \right. \right\}, \tag{1}$$

$c_\alpha \geq 0$, *is most powerful among all tests with the same size* $\alpha = Prob[x \in CR/H_0]$.

The critical value c_α determines the size α. In general, if x is continuous, we can also determine for any α, c_α such that the size of the test is α.

The lemma is very general in the sense that it gives the best critical region (BCR) regardless of the distributions under H_0 and H_a. The hypotheses may for instance be non-nested.

Naturally, the CR (critical region) may change if the alternative changes, or the null for that matter. This implies that a test which is best against one alternative is in general not best against another alternative. Only in special cases will the two tests coincide. If the CR is the same for all elements in the alternative, then this region is called a uniformly most powerful size α region. If the system of CRs has this property for each α, the test is called uniformly most powerful (UMP).

Finally note that the NPL can be used to determine the power envelope, which is the function describing the maximum attainable power for any test at each point under the alternative. The power envelope is found by constructing, for each point in the alternative, the BCR and calculating the power for this alternative. Since this test is at least as powerful as any other test, this power must be on the power envelope.

The BCRs have a particularly simple form in exponential families where the boundary of the CR is orthogonal to the direction from the null to the alternative hypothesis (see Theorem 1 below). An exponential model is a family of distributions with densities that can be written as

$$pdf(x; \eta) = \exp\{\eta' t(x) - \kappa(\eta)\} h(x). \tag{2}$$

This is called the canonical representation with canonical parameter $\eta \in N$, a $k \times 1$ vector, and canonical statistic $t(x) \in T$, a $k \times 1$ vector of random variables. The representation is called minimal if k is the smallest possible integer such that (2) holds. In this case, $t(x)$ is minimal sufficient and has itself an exponential distribution similar to the distribution of x, but with a different $h(\cdot)$ (see Lehmann (1986), Lemma 8, p. 58). Thus,

$$pdf(t; \eta) = \exp\{\eta' t - \kappa(\eta)\} h(t).$$

The minimal sufficiency of t implies that there is no essential loss of information by considering only t, instead of the whole sample x (see, for example, Lehmann (1986), 1.5), and in what follows we shall work directly with the distribution of t itself.

If η is a smooth function of a parameter θ, of dimension $d < k$, then the model is a (k, d)-curved exponential model. In that case, $\eta(\theta)$ describes a curved d-dimensional manifold (e.g. a surface) in N. The parameter θ may originate from the way the model was initially written down, which is not usually in canonical form.[2] k is the dimension of $t(x)$, which is a minimal sufficient statistic, i.e. a statistic of smallest dimension that still contains all information in the sample. The expectation of t is a function of η, which we denote by $\tau(\eta)$. This function is one-to-one and easily derived using the fact that in exponential models

$$\tau(\eta) \equiv E_\eta[t] = \partial\kappa(\eta)/\partial\eta. \tag{3}$$

In curved exponential models, the expectation of t is a function of θ, since $\eta = \eta(\theta)$, and we write $\tau(\theta) \equiv E_\theta[t]$. $\tau(\theta)$ is obtained by substitution

$$\tau(\theta) = E_\theta[t] = \tau(\eta(\theta)). \tag{4}$$

$\tau(\theta)$ is a d-dimensional manifold and can be thought of as lying in the sample space for t. We shall make regular use of (4) and the following expression obtained by the chain rule

$$\frac{\kappa}{\theta} = \frac{\eta'}{\theta} t(\theta). \tag{5}$$

The importance of exponential models is that the dimension of t is constant, regardless of the sample size. In van Garderen (1997a) we prove that curved exponential models can be defined by the property that the number of parameters is smaller than the dimension of a minimal sufficient statistic, even for non-i.i.d. observations. This basically means that the dimension of the problem is finite and fixed. The paper motivates curved exponential models more generally and provides econometric examples.

---

[2] The canonical form is not always the most useful form for economic interpretation or even for distributional derivations, but is very instructive here.

If the densities belong to a one-parameter linear exponential family, then it is easily shown, as in Theorem 1 below, that the CR is the same for all (one-sided) alternatives. Hence, there is a class of models for which a UMP test exists, but the question is whether or not there are any other classes of models with this property. The short answer, under mild regularity conditions, is no. Borges and Pfanzagl (1963) showed that the existence of a UMP test for all sample sizes and all significance levels α implies a one-parameter exponential family. Pfanzagl (1968) extended this result to one level of significance and all (arbitrarily large) sample sizes. Their assumptions include that the family of distributions is mutually absolutely continuous, a property shared by exponential families.

Theorem 1 gives a new simple proof of a slightly more general result, assuming that the density belongs to an exponential family of arbitrary dimension. The dimension of this family is arbitrary but fixed, which means that the dimension of the problem does not increase with the sample size. In the introduction we have already given a number of arguments why the assumption may not be too restrictive. It is also worth noting that in addition to the regularity conditions, which are considered weak (Lehmann (1986), p. 80), Pfanzagl requires that a UMP test exists for arbitrarily large sample sizes. We restrict the dimension by assuming an exponential model from the start, and the existence of a UMP test for one sample size (and one α) then implies the existence of a UMP test for all sample sizes (and all α's).

Theorem 1 *Let the density of x (of dimension n) belong to an exponential family of arbitrary, but fixed dimension k.*
(a) If the model is a one-parameter linear exponential model then a one-sided UMP test exists for all n and α.
(b) If a UMP test exists for one α and one $n \geq k$ then the density is a one-parameter linear exponential model.

Proof   Let η be the $(k \times 1)$ canonical parameter vector and $t(x)$ the $(k \times 1)$ canonical statistic. Using the exponential distribution of the minimal sufficient statistic t, we obtain the BCR for testing $H_0 : \eta = \eta_0$ against $H_a : \eta = \eta_a$ directly from the NPL as

$$BCR = \{t \in T \mid \exp((\eta_a - \eta_0)'t - \kappa(\eta_a) + \kappa(\eta_0)) \geq c_\alpha\} \qquad (6)$$

or simply, by defining $c_\alpha^{(a)} = \ln(c_\alpha) + \kappa(\eta_a) - \kappa(\eta_0)$, as

$$BCR = \{(\eta_a - \eta_0)'t \geq c_\alpha^{(a)}\}. \qquad (7)$$

The boundary of the BCR is a hyperplane of dimension $(k - 1)$ which is orthogonal to $(\eta_a - \eta_0)$. The BCR is determined by the direction of $(\eta_a - \eta_0)$ only. The length of $(\eta_a - \eta_0)$ is irrelevant because $c_\alpha^{(a)}$ is determined by the *size condition*:

$$\text{Prob}[(\eta_a - \eta_0)'t \geq c_\alpha^{(a)} \mid H_0] = \alpha. \tag{8}$$

(a) In a one-parameter linear exponential model the direction of $(\eta_a - 0)$ is constant for all η_a as long as the sign does not change, i.e. a one-sided test in terms of η, since the vector is one-dimensional.[3] The BCR of size α is constant for all alternatives, and, since this holds for all α, the CRs define a UMP test.

(b) If the size α BCR is constant for all η_a, then $(\eta_a - \eta_0)$ must have the same direction for any parameter value η_a in the alternative, since every such vector is orthogonal to the same $(k - 1)$-dimensional hyperplane. Hence the vectors are proportional and $(\eta_a - \eta_0) = \phi(\eta_{a1} - \eta_0)$ for all a and some fixed $a1$. But this constitutes a one-parameter exponential family with ϕ as canonical parameter and $s(x) = (\eta_{a1} - \eta_0)'t$ as canonical statistic. This holds for any α used to construct the BCR. ∎

The statements (a) and (b) follow from simple linear algebra, since a plane determines a normal, and a normal determines a plane, as illustrated in figure 8.1. Note that $(\eta_a - \eta_0)$ is a vector in the parameter space, whereas the boundary of $CR_{(a)}$ is a hyperplane in the sample space. The proof therefore makes use of the duality between the parameter space and the sample space.[4] This explains why the condition $n \geq k$ is necessary in part (b) of the proof. If $n \leq k - 1$, the boundary of the BCR no longer defines a unique normal vector in N (there are fewer than $k - 1$ restrictions on η), but rather a $(k - n + 1)$-dimensional hyperplane.

Part (b) of the proof shows that the alternative does not need to be a continuous line, but may consist of points as long as these points are on

---

[3] η is in general a function of θ. The necessary and sufficient condition for (a) in terms of θ is that the function $\eta(\theta)$ is one-to-one. Sufficiency is immediate and necessity follows from the fact that there would otherwise be two values of θ with the same value of η. We could not sensibly test one value of θ against the other because the two models are essentially the same (observationally equivalent), and the NPL does not define a CR. Note that the condition guarantees likelihood ratio monotonicity in terms of θ.

[4] The duality here is between N and T through the bilinear product $\langle \eta, t \rangle = \eta't = \sum \eta_i t_i$, defined on $N \times T$. This is different from the usual convex duality that is used in the theory of exponential models, which is really between the canonical parameter space and the expectation parameter space, and the dual of $\kappa(\eta)$ is defined through the Legendre transform. See Barndorff-Nielsen (1978).

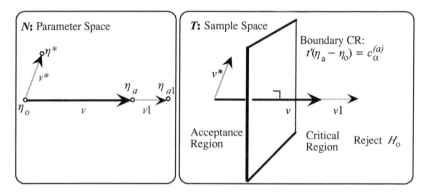

Figure 8.1 Best critical regions

the same line. In fact, we can think of the NPL as defining straightness in a space of distributions even more general than exponential families, as well as straightness in the sample space, since the NPL is valid for all distributions.

The proof also shows a well-known result that if we are testing one linear restriction on the canonical parameter η, we can reparameterise the model to obtain a UMP test (see, for instance, Lehmann (1986)).

Given the regularity conditions in Pfanzagl (1968) or the assumption made here, a UMP test exists if, and only if, the model is one-parameter linear exponential. This is the ideal situation and most practical situations do not fall into this category.

In curved models the NPL cannot be used to give a best test, since no test exists that maximises power against every alternative. We have to use a different approach and compromise power against different alternatives. Different tests compromise in a different way.[5] In what follows we will show how different tests choose different critical regions and, in the spirit of Theorem 1, show that they can be thought of as choosing directions for $(\eta_a - \eta_0)$. The point optimal test chooses an arbitrary 'suitable' point θ from which η_a and the direction follow. The LM, locally most powerful and locally best test choose a direction equal to the gradient of $\eta(\theta)$ at θ_0. The Wald test uses the gradient of $\eta(\theta)$ at point(s) different from θ_0, but this direction is not used to construct a BCR in the

[5] Cox and Hinkley (1974, p. 102) offer three suggestions: (a) pick an arbitrary point and maximise power against this alternative; (b) choose this point close to θ_0 and maximise the power locally near the null hypothesis; and (c) maximise some weighted average of power.

sense that the LM and PO test do. The Wald test introduces a distance concept that is generally not compatible with the model. The geodesic test uses a geometrical notion of distance but there are some theoretical, as well as practical problems, although it does give a test that takes the curvature of the model into account and gives a curved boundary for the CR. The LR test can be viewed as averaging over all possible directions.

3 The point optimal (PO) test

A point optimal test is a direct application of the NPL. It simply chooses a particular parameter point θ^* in the alternative (and a θ_0 under the null if it is composite) and forms the best CR for testing the simple null versus this simple alternative. If we write $\eta_a \equiv \eta^* = \eta(\theta^*)$ and $\eta_0 = \eta(\theta_0)$ in (7), we see immediately that the CR for the PO test equals

$$CR_{PO} = \{(\eta(\theta^*) - \eta(\theta_0))'t \geq c_\alpha^*\}. \tag{9}$$

The CR is determined by the direction of $(\eta^* - \eta_0)$ since the boundary of CR_{PO} is a hyperplane orthogonal to this direction. The size condition determines c_α^*, and hence how far the boundary is translated from zero. It is worth recalling that c_α^* changes with θ^*, depending on the direction and length of $(\eta(\theta^*) - \eta_0)$, so that $c_\alpha^* = c_\alpha(\eta(\theta^*)) = c_\alpha(\theta^*)$. (The LR test indirectly uses (9) in all directions with c_α fixed, as we shall see below.)

Since zero is just an arbitrary point in the sample space, it is more relevant how distant the boundary is from the expectation of t under the null, $\tau(\theta_0)$. We therefore rewrite the CR by defining $\tilde{c}_\alpha^* = c_\alpha^* - (\eta^* - \eta_0)'\tau(\theta_0)$, as

$$CR_{PO} = \{(\eta^* - \eta_0)'(t - \tau(\theta_0)) \geq \tilde{c}_\alpha^*\}, \tag{10}$$

which is shown in figure 8.2. The left-hand frame shows the canonical parameter space N and the canonical manifold $\eta(\theta)$ with the relevant directions determining the PO test. The right-hand frame shows the sample space T and the CRs for two different choices of θ^*. The expectation manifold, $E_\theta[t] = \tau(\theta)$, is superimposed on T.

The left frame shows how the vector $(\eta^* - \eta_0)$ is obtained: choosing θ^* determines a direction and hence a test (choosing θ^{**} is choosing a different direction and a different test). The direction of $(\eta^* - \eta_0)$ depends on θ^* only through $\eta(\theta)$. This has two consequences: the picture and conclusions drawn from it are the same regardless of the parameterisation used (i.e. whether θ is used or some other parameter ϕ), but, on the other hand, a different parameterisation will generally result in a different

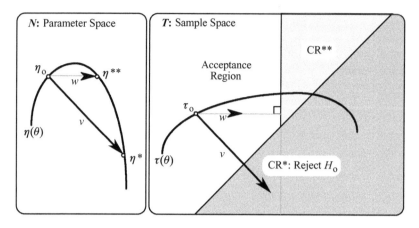

Figure 8.2 Point optimal tests based on the points θ^* and θ^{**}

choice of η^* and hence a different direction. In this sense the test is not invariant under reparameterisations.

The PO test is not as widely applied as the LM, Wald and LR tests, but has been successfully exploited in econometrics, mainly in time-series applications. Early examples are Kadiyala (1970) and Berenblutt and Webb (1973), and later examples include King (1987), Brooks (1993), Silvapulle and King (1993) and Saikkonen and Luukkonen (1993). King and Wu (1994) provide a survey and references, including most of King's own and joint work. Evans and King (1985) derive a PO test for heteroskedasticity.

The test statistic is often quite easy to derive and the main difficulty is determining the critical value. $c_\alpha(\theta^*)$ can in principle be obtained numerically by, for example, Monte Carlo integration. In time-series models the statistic is frequently a ratio of quadratic forms in normal variates and the critical value can be determined by Imhof's (1961) or Davies's (1980) procedure, similar to obtaining the exact DW critical value.

Apart from its simplicity, the test has some other attractions. The power of the test equals the power envelope for at least one parameter point, and we can choose this point based on economic or other external considerations. This freedom, on the other hand, makes the procedure ad hoc, since there is no general principle or optimality consideration to choose the point.

One solution to this arbitrariness is to choose the point closest to the null for which the power equals a pre-set level such as 0.8. This gives the

β-optimal test of Davies (1969) but is often computationally difficult.[6] Other solutions include to choose the maximum or the middle of the θ values, but this determines a direction which depends on the parameterisation used. Using ϕ instead of θ gives a different middle value and consequently $\eta(\theta^*) \neq \eta(\phi^*)$, resulting in different tests. Another problem is that we can easily think of parameterisations $\eta(\theta)$ that give the same η for two different values of θ, disturbing the idea that we can sensibly talk about minima, maxima or middle values.

Figure 8.2 suggests part of the answer. We should be thinking in terms of choosing a direction, taking into account the global properties of the model, rather than choosing a point in an arbitrary parameterisation.

A further question concerning the choice of PO point is whether or not it should be the same regardless of the sample size. The PO test based on θ^* in figure 8.2 is very unattractive for large sample sizes and local alternatives because the boundary of the CR is virtually orthogonal to the BCR based on local alternatives (and to the LR, LM and Wald CRs)! It appears more sensible to choose the point optimal direction for large sample sizes based on (a sequence of) local alternatives which achieve maximal power against local alternatives, since, even for these tests, the power will approach 1 for distant alternatives such as θ^*, provided the model is not too curved.

If the model is very curved then it is possible, because of the straight boundary, that $\tau(\theta)$ curves back into the acceptance region for large values of θ. Put differently, the expectation of t in such a case lies in the acceptance region for values of θ very distant from θ_0. Asymptotically, with independent sampling and $t = (1/n) \sum_{i=1}^{n} t_i$, we have that $t \to \tau(\theta)$ as $n \to \infty$. This means that the test is not globally consistent and, for certain values of the parameter, very different from θ_0, the test accepts the null with probability one.

Returning to the attractions of the PO test, it follows directly from the NPL that the PO test can be applied to non-nested problems, e.g. testing MA versus AR errors as in Silvapulle and King (1993).

Furthermore, if $\eta(\theta)$ is a straight line, then the BCR is constant and the test is UMP, as in Theorem 1. Put differently, if a UMP test exists, then the PO tests will produce it.

Even if a UMP test does not exist, the PO test may still give a satisfactory test. In particular if $\eta(\theta)$ is not too curved and therefore $(\eta(\theta) - \eta_0)$ does not change very much, the BCRs do not change very

---

[6] The β-optimal test may not exist if the power envelope does not reach the pre-specified level such as 0.8.

much either. Hence, the power of any of the PO tests will be close to the power envelope.

If $\eta(\theta)$ is seriously curved and $(\eta(\theta^*) - \eta_0)$ changes a lot for different values of θ^* in the alternative, then the BCRs also change a lot. This means that very different tests are obtained for different choices of θ^*. The test becomes sensitive to the choice of θ^* and this choice gets more important. A small value of θ^* causes a loss of power against alternatives further away from H_0 and vice versa, and, because the boundary of the CR is straight, it may be impossible to get desirable power properties against the whole range of alternatives.

These ideas were developed in detail by Hillier (1990, 1995). He analysed the global behaviour of the BCRs and suggested a measure of the variability of the BCRs based on the probability of the *enveloping region*, which he defined as the union of all possible fixed-size PO critical regions. If the probability of the enveloping region under H_0 is close to α, then the model cannot be very curved, but the model must be globally curved if this probability is much larger than α. It is clear from figure 8.2 that in the two-dimensional case this relates to the maximum possible angle between any two vectors $(\eta^* - \eta_0)$ and $(\eta^{**} - \eta_0)$, which is a measure of the total curvature of $\eta(\theta)$.

This global concept of curvature is different from Efron's statistical curvature, which is the curvature of the model at a particular point. Efron (1975) related his curvature to the *rate* of change of the BCR at H_0, whereas Hillier's global measure relates to the total change in all BCRs. The local measure of curvature, evaluated at θ_0, does, however, give a good indication of the relative performance of the LMP test, as Efron showed. Large curvature leads to poor performance of the LMP test as compared with a PO test. Efron therefore suggested the use of a PO test as an alternative to the LMP test if the model has curvature larger than $1/8$ at H_0, which we shall now discuss.

4   Lagrange multiplier (LM), locally most powerful (LMP) and locally best (LB) test

The locally most powerful (LMP) test is a test that gives maximal power against alternatives in a neighbourhood of the null.[7] Although the NPL gives the BCR for all $\eta_a \neq \eta_0$, it is clear that, if we let $\theta_a \to \theta_0$,

---

[7] A level-α test φ is said to be LMP if, given any other level-α test ϕ, there exists a number ε such that power$_\varphi(\theta) \geq$ power$_\phi(\theta)$ for all alternatives θ in an ε-neighbourhood of θ_0, i.e. $\|\theta - \theta_0\| < \varepsilon$, where $\| \cdot \|$ is some metric. See Lehmann (1986, p. 537).

$(\eta_a - \eta_0) \to 0$, and no CR is defined. The main point of Theorem 1 is, however, that the direction of $(\eta_a - \eta_0)$ determines the CR, not its length (the critical value $c_\alpha = c_\alpha(\theta) = c_\alpha(\eta(\theta))$ absorbs the length because of the size condition). The direction does not change if we divide both sides in (7) by $\|\theta_a - \theta_0\|$ with $\|\cdot\|$ some measure of distance, and we write the BCR as

$$\frac{(\eta(\theta_a) - \eta(\theta_0))'}{\|\theta_a - \theta_0\|} t - \frac{\kappa(\eta(\theta_a)) - \kappa(\eta(\theta_0))}{\|\theta_a - \theta_0\|} \geq \frac{c_\alpha(\theta_a)}{\|\theta_a - \theta_0\|}. \tag{11}$$

We may now let the point θ_a approach θ_0 arbitrarily closely and take the limit as $\theta_a \to \theta_0$ on both sides to obtain the CR

$$CR_{\mathrm{LMP}} = \left\{ \frac{\eta(\theta_0)'}{\theta} t \geq c_\alpha^{**} + \partial\kappa(\theta_0)/\partial\theta \right\}. \tag{12}$$

This shows that the CR of the LMP test is determined by the direction of $\partial\eta(\theta_0)/\partial\theta = \partial\eta(\theta)/\partial\theta|_{\theta=\theta_0}$, the gradient of $\eta(\theta)$ at θ_0. The CR is bounded by a hyperplane orthogonal to $\partial\eta(\theta_0)/\partial\theta$. We can rewrite the CR as in (10), using (4),

$$CR_{\mathrm{LMP}} = \left\{ \frac{\eta(\theta_0)'}{\theta} (t - \tau(\theta_0)) > c_\alpha^{**} \right\}. \tag{13}$$

Figure 8.3 illustrates how the direction and CR are obtained (note that $\partial\eta/\partial\theta \neq \partial\tau/\partial\theta$).[8] The equivalence between the tests will be shown below. If $\eta(\theta)$ is a straight line then $\partial\eta/\partial\theta$ has the same direction as $(\eta^* - \eta_0)$ for any η^* and hence the CR of the LMP test is the same as the CR for any PO test. Thus the LMP test also produces the UMP test if it exists.

Figure 8.3 also illustrates the parameterisation invariance of the test because the direction is the same regardless of which parameter is used. Analytically this follows because

$$[\partial\eta'\partial\phi] = (\partial\theta/\partial\phi)[\partial\eta'/\partial\theta],$$

and the direction $\partial\eta'/\partial\phi$ determined by ϕ is proportional to $\partial\eta'/\partial\theta$ since $(\partial\theta/\partial\phi)$ is 1×1 and the CRs are the same.

If $\eta(\theta)$ is curved, the LMP test gives the same CR regardless of how curved the model is. The LMP uses the direction only at θ_0, essentially ignoring the curvature. Figure 8.3 shows that this can have serious consequences. Since the boundary is straight, it is possible that $\tau(\theta)$ curves

---

[8] Since $\tau(\eta) = \partial\kappa/\partial\eta$, we have by the chain rule $\partial\tau/\partial\theta' = (\partial^2\kappa/\partial\eta\partial\eta')(\partial\eta/\partial\theta') = \Sigma(\partial\eta/\partial\theta')$, where $\Sigma = \mathrm{Cov}(t)$.

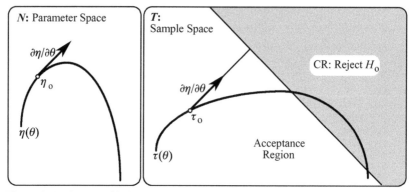

Figure 8.3 The one-sided LM, LMP and LB test

back into the acceptance region for large values of θ and the test is not consistent. Again, with independent sampling and $t = 1/n \sum_{i=1}^{n} t_i$, $t \to \tau(\theta)$ as $n \to \infty$, and the test will accept the null with probability one asymptotically for values of θ very distant from θ_0. This is similar to the PO test but, since the LMP test chooses an extreme direction, the problem may be more serious. Usually the test is globally consistent, but even in less extreme cases we would expect poor power performance away from the null if the model has appreciable global curvature.

The relation between the curvature and performance of the LMP test was pointed out by Efron (1975, section 8). He concluded that, if the curvature at θ_0 is larger than $1/8$, then the performance of the LMP is seriously affected and a PO test should be considered. His measure describes the local curvature at H_0. Figure 8.3 gives the global picture.

The LMP test is derived here as a limiting case of a PO test if we let $\theta \to \theta_0$. The LMP test maximises the slope of the power curve at the null in most cases. A test that maximises the slope of the power is often referred to as a locally best (LB) test. Lehmann (1986, p. 528) gives counter-examples when the two tests are different and sufficient conditions for the two tests are to be the same: if there is a unique level α LB test, then it is the unique LMP test.[9] The LB test can be found directly using a generalised version of the NPL (e.g. Cox and Hinkley (1974), p. 126): the region $w = \{t \in T | f(t) \geq cg(t)\}$ maximises $\int_w f(t)dt$, subject to $\int_w g(t)dt = a$, provided such a c exists. Since the LB test maximises the slope of the power function, we have

---

[9] See also Cox and Hinkley (1974), pp. 107 and 113, for relevant discussions.

$$\max \bar{\theta} \int_w pdf(t; \theta))dt|_{\theta=\theta_0} = \int_w \left[\frac{\eta(\theta_0)'}{\theta}(t - \tau(\theta_0))\right] \exp\{\eta_0' t - \kappa\}dt,$$

$$\text{s.t.} \int_w pdf(t; \theta_0))dt = \alpha \Leftrightarrow \int_w \exp\{\eta_0' t - \kappa\}dt = \alpha,$$

where we have used (3) and the fact that in exponential models we may interchange differentiation and integration. The region w becomes,

$$CR_{LB} = \left\{\frac{\eta(\theta_0)'}{\theta}(t - \tau(\theta_0)) \geq c\right\}, \tag{14}$$

which is equal to (13) with $c = c_\alpha^{**}$.

The Lagrange multiplier (LM) test, or (efficient) score test, is one of the most widely applied tests in econometrics (see Breusch and Pagan (1980), Engle (1984) or Godfrey (1988) and references therein). The general form of the test is to reject for large values of the LM test statistic

$$LM = s(\hat{\theta})' I(\hat{\theta})^{-1} s(\hat{\theta}) \geq c_\alpha, \tag{15}$$

where $s(\hat{\theta})$ is the score statistic $\partial \ell(\hat{\theta}; t)/\partial\theta$, a $d \times 1$ vector, and $I(\hat{\theta})$ is the $d \times d$ information matrix, all evaluated at the restricted MLE $\hat{\theta}(H_0)$. A one-sided version of the LM test if $d = 1$ (ignoring sign) would be to reject for large values of

$$I(\hat{\theta})^{1/2} s(\hat{\theta}) \geq c_\alpha. \tag{16}$$

The restricted MLE in the present case is θ_0 because H_0 is simple. Furthermore, using (5), the score in an exponential model can be written as

$$s(\theta) = \frac{1(t, \eta(\theta))}{\theta} = \frac{\eta'}{\theta}[t - \tau(\theta)]. \tag{17}$$

Substitution gives

$$CR_{LM} = \left\{I(\theta_0)^{-1/2} \frac{\eta(\theta_0)'}{\theta}[t - \tau(\theta_0)] \geq c_\alpha\right\}, \tag{18}$$

which, after pre-multiplication by $I(\theta_0)^{1/2}$, is equal to (13) and (14). Hence, the one-sided version of the LM test in exponential models is equal to the LMP and LB test.

Of course, if $d > 1$ the statistic $(\partial\eta/\partial\theta)$ is $d \times 1$ and needs to be reduced to a one-dimensional test statistic. The LM statistic does this by weighting the elements by the inverse of the Fisher information matrix, which, incidentally, keeps the test parameterisation invariant even if $d > 1$. A different matrix could be chosen to give more weight to particular directions.

5   The Wald test

One of the main attractions of the Wald test is that it requires estimation of the parameters only under the alternative hypothesis. The Wald test is slightly at odds with the other tests discussed in this chapter because the Wald statistic is inherently a non-geometric quantity. The test statistic depends on the algebraic formulation of the restrictions defining the null hypothesis. The main problem with the Wald test is that it uses only the first term in the Taylor expansion of the restriction, and there are uncountably many other restrictions that correspond, up to first order, with the restriction written down. Gregory and Veall (1985) showed that this non-invariance can lead to drastically different conclusions, even in a very simple model. Nevertheless, the Wald test is one of the classic tests and widely applied.

The general form of the Wald statistic for testing

$$H_0 : r(\theta) = 0 \quad \text{versus} \quad H_a : r(\theta) > 0, \tag{19}$$

where $r(\theta)$ describe some non-linear restrictions on θ, is given by

$$w(\hat{\theta}) = r(\hat{\theta})'[R(\hat{\theta})'I(\hat{\theta})^{-1}R(\hat{\theta})]^{-1}r(\hat{\theta}), \quad R(\hat{\theta}) = \frac{r(\theta)}{\theta}\Big|_{\theta=\hat{\theta}}. \tag{20}$$

In section 8 we use the following example to demonstrate a number of problems set out in this section. Since H_0 is simple we may set $\theta_0 = 0$ without loss of generality. There are many ways of writing this restriction in the form (19), but consider,

$$r_b(\theta) = \frac{\exp(b\theta) - 1}{b} = 0, \quad \text{with } R_b(\theta) = \exp(b\theta), \tag{21}$$

which for each value of b gives a different way of writing the restriction. In the limiting case $b \to 0$, (21) reduces to $r_0(\theta) = \theta = 0$. The Wald statistics with $b = 0$ and $b = 1$ are

$$w_{r_0}(\hat{\theta}) = \hat{\theta}^2 I\hat{\theta}, \quad w_{r_1}(\hat{\theta}) = (1 - \exp(\hat{\theta}))^2 I_{\hat{\theta}}, \tag{22}$$

and obviously differ, although they agree in a neighbourhood of H_0.

The Wald test introduces an arbitrary measure of distance on the manifold (the curve $\eta(\theta)$), which is determined by the way the restrictions are formulated. This distance is not an intrinsic quantity, meaning that it depends on the parameterisation used.

Shortcomings of the Wald statistics are well known; see, for example, Gregory and Veall (1985), Breusch and Schmidt (1988), Lafontaine and White (1986), Phillips and Park (1988) and Nelson and Savin (1990). They all show certain properties of the test, such as dependence on the formulation of the restrictions and the possibility of obtaining any numerical value, problems with the size and the power function or approximations to them, but offer limited explanations. We provide an alternative view by considering the CR rather than the test statistic, which is quite revealing.

We turn to the partition of the sample space into acceptance region and critical region that is induced by the one-sided version of the Wald test. First note that the test statistic is a function of the estimator $\hat{\theta}$ only, and that it determines a 'distance' from $\hat{\theta}$ to θ_0, using the distance measure $w_r(\cdot)$.[10] If $\hat{\theta}$ is further than a particular w_r-distance away from θ_0 we reject the null hypothesis, i.e. the test rejects when[11]

$$w_r(\hat{\theta}) \geq c_\alpha^*, \tag{23}$$

where the subscript indicates the dependence on r, the formulation of the restrictions. The critical value c_α^* is generally based on the asymptotic chi-square distribution of $w_r(\hat{\theta})$ under H_0 and does not change with r, which has important adverse consequences in finite samples as we shall see below.

Assume for the moment that $w_r(\cdot)$ is monotonically increasing so that the CR can be expressed directly in terms of $\hat{\theta}$. Let θ_r^* be the critical value in terms of $\hat{\theta}$, which now does depend on r, precisely because c_α^* does not depend on r. The one-sided Wald test rejects for all those observations $t \in T$ for which

$$\hat{\theta}(t) \geq \theta_r^*. \tag{24}$$

We have written $\hat{\theta}(t)$ to make explicit that $\hat{\theta}$ is a function of t. There will be many different values of t that give the same value for $\hat{\theta}$ because the dimension of t is larger than the dimension of θ. The boundary of the CR is determined by all those t in the sample space that give θ_r^* as the MLE, i.e. the boundary is the inverse image of θ_r^*:

$$\text{boundary } CR_{\text{Wald}} = \hat{\theta}^{-1}(\theta_r^*) = \{t \in T \mid \hat{\theta}(t) = \theta_r^*\}. \tag{25}$$

We can determine the inverse image of θ_r^* by solving the first-order conditions for the MLE, as a first step. Following Efron (1978) we denote the set of solutions to the first-order conditions (f.o.c.) by

---

[10] The quotation marks are necessary because $w_r(\cdot)$ is not necessarily a metric monotonically increasing in terms of $\hat{\theta}$. $I_{\hat{\theta}}$ depends on $\hat{\theta}$ and may decrease faster than, for instance, $\hat{\theta}^2$ increases in (22). Of course, if $I_{\hat{\theta}}$ is constant or monotonically increasing then $w_r(\cdot)$ is strictly monotonically increasing.

[11] The PO, LM and LR tests do not always reject if $\hat{\theta}$ is larger than a particular value.

$$\pounds_{\theta^*} = \left\{ t \in T \left| \frac{1(\theta; t)}{\theta} \right|_{\theta=\theta^*} = 0 \right\} : \text{MLE constant (f.o.c.).} \qquad (26)$$

Keeping θ fixed at θ^*, we can solve for t such that (26) holds. Thus $\pounds_{\theta^*}$ is the pre-image of θ^*, plus all values of t satisfying the first-order conditions only. In curved exponential models we have, using (2) and (5),

$$\pounds_{\theta^*} = \left\{ t \in T \left| \frac{\eta(\theta)'}{\theta} (t - \tau(\theta)) \right|_{\theta=\theta^*} = 0 \right\} : \text{MLE constant (f.o.c.).}$$
$$(27)$$

Clearly $t = \tau(\theta^*)$ satisfies (27) and the complete solution consists of a hyperplane in the sample space through $\tau(\theta^*)$ orthogonal to the gradients $\partial\eta(\theta^*)/\partial\theta_i$, $i = 1, \ldots, d$. The hyperplane is thus of dimension $(k - d)$. The straight part of the Wald test CR is illustrated in figure 8.4 for $k = 2$, $d = 1$ and critical value θ_r^*. (The curved part of the boundary is discussed jointly with the geodesic test; see figure 8.6 in particular.)

The boundary is orthogonal to the gradient of $\eta(\theta)$ at θ_r^* for the Wald test, versus θ_0 for the LMP test. Also note that the boundary of the LMP test stretches out infinitely, whereas the boundary of the Wald test is a hyperplane only until it crosses another line of constant MLE. Points where two constant MLE lines cross and give more than one maximum likelihood solution were defined in van Garderen (1995) as critical points, since the MLE is not unique. Beyond such critical points the boundary is curved (see the discussion of the geodesic test below).

Using a different formulation of the restriction, e.g. $r_1(\cdot)$ instead of $r_0(\cdot)$, will result in a different value for θ_r^* and a different CR. Figure 8.4 would apply with the boundary shifted to coincide with $\hat{\theta}^{-1}(t) = \theta_{r1}^*$. Similarly, changing the critical value c_α^* changes θ_r^*.

In principle c_α^* a could, and should, be chosen such that the significance level is exactly α. In practice this is typically too difficult, and asymptotic theory is used to find an approximation. The asymptotic critical value is the same regardless of which $r_b(\cdot)$ is used. Note that the asymptotic critical value is based on θ_r^* close to θ_0, the value under the null. This gives a boundary parallel to the LR and LM statistic, and asymptotically the boundaries are equivalent, defining the same test statistic. For large θ_r^* in a curved model, the boundary is at an angle with the asymptotic boundaries and defines a different statistic. The asymptotic critical value does not take this into account and size and power calculations are suspect in small samples.

It was assumed in figure 8.4 that $w_r(\cdot)$ was monotonically increasing. If the Fisher information $I(\theta)$ is decreasing faster than $[r(\theta)/R(\theta)]^2$ is increasing, then it is possible that $w_r(\cdot)$ is not monotonic, as will be

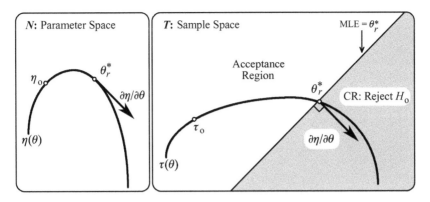

Figure 8.4 Critical region of the one-sided Wald test

demonstrated for testing against the null hypothesis of a unit root test in section 8. This means that $w_r(\cdot)$ is not a proper distance measure and, as a consequence, there are potentially three (or more) values of $\hat{\theta}_i$ for which

$$w_r(\theta_r^*(1)) = w_r(\theta_r^*(2)) = w_r(\theta_r^*(3)) = c_\alpha^*. \qquad (28)$$

The Wald test rejects in that case for values of $\hat{\theta}$ in two unconnected intervals

$$\theta_r^*(1) \le \hat{\theta} \le \theta_r^*(2) \cup \hat{\theta} \ge \theta_r^*(3). \qquad (29)$$

This means that for values of $\hat{\theta}$ between $\theta_r^*(2)$ and $\theta_r^*(3)$ we do not reject, even though they are much larger than $\theta_r^*(1)$, the smallest value for which the test rejects. Instead of the one line in figure 8.4, there are now three lines bounding the CR. This is shown in figure 8.5. Figure 8.5 shows that the Wald test can lead to very unattractive CRs. It also explains why the power function can be non-monotonic, as reported in Nelson and Savin (1990): the probability of rejection is larger for $\theta = \theta_r^*(2)$ than for θ between $\theta_r^*(2)$ and $\theta_r^*(3)$.

The next section discusses a geometrical version of the Wald test and deals with some further issues not related to the non-invariance of the test.

6   A geodesic distance test

The Wald statistic is a non-geometric quantity which defines a 'distance' not compatible with the model. Improvements based on differential geometrical arguments have been proposed by Critchley, Marriott and Salmon (1996) and Davidson (1992); see also Væth (1985). We can define

250   **Kees Jan van Garderen**

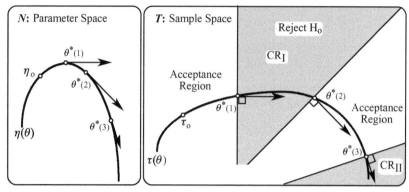

Figure 8.5 Disconnected critical region ($CR_{\mathrm{I}} \cup CR_{\mathrm{II}}$) for non-monotonic Wald statistic

distances on the manifold in a geometric way by defining a metric, with coefficients g_{ij}, and an affine connection, with coefficients Γ_{ij}^m, and determine the geodesic distance on the manifold from $\hat{\theta}$ to θ_0.[12,13] A geodesic on a manifold is the analogue of a straight line in Euclidean space and gives the shortest distance between two points on the manifold, e.g. between $\eta(\hat{\theta})$ and $\eta(\hat{\theta}_0)$ or $\tau(\hat{\theta})$ and $\tau(\theta_0)$, based on the distance defined by the metric, and connection. This distance is the same regardless of the parameterisation. The Fisher information metric is commonly used for g_{ij}, together with the Riemannian (Levi–Civita) connection for Γ_{ij}^m. Rao (1945, 1949) was the first to explore the idea of a geodesic definition of the distance between two distributions (see also Jeffreys (1939), however). We could use this distance for hypothesis testing, as in fact Critchley *et al.* (1996) do. They use the geodesic distance based on the Fisher information metric between $\hat{\theta}$ and θ_0 as test statistic

$$gd(\hat{\theta},\theta_0) = \min_{\theta(x)} \int_0^1 \sqrt{\sum_{i,j=1}^d g_{ij}(\theta(x))\frac{\theta_i(x)}{x}\frac{\theta_j(x)}{x}}dx, \qquad (30)$$

s.t. $\theta(0) = \hat{\theta}$ and $\theta(1) = \theta_0$ (or $\theta(1) = \hat{\theta}$ and $\theta(0) = \theta_0$)

---

[12] The null hypothesis is simple so that θ_0 is known. A composite H_0 complicates the test even further.
[13] If $g_{ij} = g_{ij}(\theta)$ is the metric with inverse g^{ij}, then the Christoffel symbols for the Levi–Civita connection are defined by $\Gamma_{ij}^m = \sum_{l=1}^d \frac{1}{2}g^{ml}((\partial g_{il}/\partial\theta^j) + (\partial g_{lj}/\partial\theta^i) - (\partial g_{ij}/\partial\theta^l))$, which is the unique Riemannian connection (the conventional superscript on $\partial\theta$ denotes a coefficient and is not a power). $g_{ij}(\theta)$ is often the Fisher information metric $g_{ij}(\theta) = i_{ij} = E[\partial\mathbf{l}/\partial\theta_i\partial\mathbf{l}/\partial\theta_j]$.

where the minimum is over all possible curves $\theta(x)$ in Θ that connect $\hat{\theta}$ and θ_0. The test rejects for large values of the geodesic distance

$$gd(\hat{\theta}) = gd(\hat{\theta}, \theta_0) \geq c_\alpha^*, \tag{31}$$

which is exactly like (23) for the Wald test, but now the test statistic is by definition strictly monotonic and it does not depend on the algebraic formulation of the restrictions. Consequently, the test rejects for all $\hat{\theta}(t) \geq \theta_\alpha^*$, as in (24), but the critical value does not depend on r. The boundary has the same shape as the (monotonic) Wald test in figure 8.4, if the correct critical values are used, and is again determined by the inverse image of θ_α^*:

$$\text{boundary } CR_{\text{geodesic}} = \hat{\theta}^{-1}(\theta_\alpha^*) = \{t \in T \mid \hat{\theta}(t) = \theta_\alpha^*\}. \tag{32}$$

Geodesics have been determined for a limited number of distributions. Rao (1987) summarises a number of these geodesic distances in statistical manifolds. These can be used directly to define a geodesic test, but in general they need to be worked out specifically.

This poses a serious practical problem for geodesic tests because solving (30) in higher dimensions requires the solution of the following second-order non-linear differential equation

$$\frac{\partial^2 \theta_m}{\partial x^2} + \sum_{i,j=1}^{d} \Gamma_{ij}^m \frac{\theta_i}{x} \frac{\theta_j}{x} = 0, \quad m = 1, \ldots, d, \tag{33}$$

where Γ_{ij}^m are the Christoffel symbols for the Levi–Civita connection. Equation (33), together with initial conditions $\theta(0) = \theta^*$ and $\partial\theta/\partial x|_{x=0} = v$, defines a unique curve $\theta(x)$ that minimises the distance between $\theta(0)$ and other points on $\theta(x)$.

We do need to determine the initial direction v that will assure that $\theta(x)$ passes through the points θ^* and θ_0. In the general setting of the Wald test, estimation is carried out only under the (unrestricted) alternative, and hence θ_0 is unknown.

Considering these problems, it seems more natural to use the geodesic distance to construct confidence regions, since we can start from $\hat{\theta}$ and determine in each direction v the points in Θ of equal distance to $\hat{\theta}$. These geodesic circles or orbits could be evaluated numerically, and for different distances correspond to different confidence levels. Moolgavkar and Venzon (1987), for instance, construct Wald-type confidence regions using a geodesic distance, although based on a different metric and connection.

In general we can construct many different metrics and connections. In fact, Chentsov (1982) and Amari (1982) introduced a one-parameter

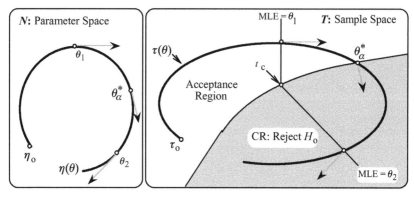

Figure 8.6 The geodesic test

family of so-called α-connections, and different values of α are useful in different contexts.[14] The Riemannian connection used in (30) and (31) corresponds to $\alpha = 0$, which may, or may not, be the most relevant for hypothesis testing.

The geodesic test also poses a fundamental question, namely: should the shortest distance between two distributions be measured as the distance over the manifold, i.e. as curves in N, or, alternatively, as the shortest distance in the embedding space, i.e. straight lines in N?[15] Figure 8.6 shows an extreme case where the manifold curves back to the origin.

Regardless of how close, in terms of η, we get to the origin, we will always reject if $\hat{\theta} \geq \theta_{\alpha}^*$. The test rejects only because it took a long time to get to $\eta(\hat{\theta})$, not because $pdf(t; \theta_0)$ is very different from $pdf(t; \theta_a)$. In economic applications this would mean that we reject a maintained model even though in economic terms there is hardly any difference between the null and the estimated model.

This comparison between models is in contrast with the NPL, where it is the direct distance in the full exponential model that matters. It may therefore be the case that the problem lies, not with the geodesic test in principle, but with the metric and α-connection usually chosen. The Fisher information metric, essentially defined on the manifold, may be useful in applications other than hypothesis testing, but the NPL and figure 8.6 suggest that

[14]The α-connections determine a non-Riemannian geometry and are defined as

$$(\alpha)\Gamma_{ij}^m = \Gamma_{ij}^m + \frac{1-\alpha}{2}\sum_{l=1}^d g^{ml}T_{ij1},$$

where $T_{ij1} = E[\partial \mathbf{l}/\partial \theta_i\, \partial \mathbf{l}/\partial \theta_j\, \partial \mathbf{l}/\partial \theta_1]$, the skewness tensor.
[15] Davidson (1992) raises the same question in his discussion of Critchley *et al.* (1996).

the geodesics in the embedding density give the relevant distances in hypotheses testing, not the geodesics on the manifold.

Decreasing the size of the test does not affect the bottom part of the CR. θ_α^* will increase, but this changes only the top right-hand side of the CR. Under H_0, the additional points so excluded are less likely than the points at the bottom, which is undesirable. Further note that the boundary of the CR in the top right can be orthogonal to the BCR in that direction.

The boundary of the CR consists of two types of points: the inverse image of θ_α^*, i.e. $\hat{\theta}^{-1}(\theta_\alpha^*)$, which gives the straight part of the boundary, mainly on the outside of the ellipse; and those points on the inside, such as t_c, that have two maximum likelihood solutions, one solution on the left and one solution on the right. Such points were called *critical points* in van Garderen (1995) and I investigated the sensitivity of the MLE as t gets closer to critical points, based on the local curvature at $\hat{\theta}$. The same argument applies here, even though the critical points in figure 8.6 are global in nature. The sensitivity for global critical points is only more extreme. Let t_c be a point on the boundary on the inside of the curve $\tau(\theta)$. A small change ε in the observation, from $t_c - \varepsilon/2$ to $t_c + \varepsilon/2$ leads to a huge increase in $\hat{\theta}$, from θ_1 to θ_2. The test statistic suddenly appears highly significant despite the fact that the likelihood of $t_c - \varepsilon$ is virtually the same as the likelihood of $t_c + \varepsilon$ under the null, as well as under the alternative.[16]

This raises another problem for a geodesic or Wald-type test. Since the test statistic is based on an estimator (whether this is the MLE or some other estimator), there are many points t in the sample space giving the same value of the estimator but lending very different support to the null. Observations on the inside of $\tau(\theta)$ in figure 8.6 provide little information about the validity of H_0 or H_a, because the likelihood values under the null and alternative will be very similar. In contrast, observations on the right of the curve $\tau(\theta)$ giving rise to the same value of $\hat{\theta}$ are much more likely under H_a than under H_0 and do provide strong evidence against the null. It is unreasonable to treat points on the inside and on the outside the same.

This implies that the geodesic and Wald tests should be carried out conditional on the relative position of the observation to the manifold and critical point. The tests could, for example, be conditional on the relative distance auxiliary defined in van Garderen (1995). Implementation of such a conditional test is likely to be difficult, with little intuition

---

[16] At t_c the likelihood is exactly the same under H_0 as under H_a, since this equality defines critical points.

why it should be better than the PO, LM or LR test. Furthermore, the traditional Wald computational advantage of having to estimate only under the alternative seems to have been lost in the process.

7   The likelihood ratio test

The PO, LMP and (one-sided) LM test are all determined by particular directions in the canonical parameter space and have flat CR boundaries. As a consequence they have optimal properties in the directions used to construct the test. The LR does not satisfy any such optimality criteria, but performs remarkably well in a range of diverse testing problems. It also tends to perform well against a range of alternatives, whereas the PO and LM test may break down against alternatives that differ from the directions used to construct the test. It is an interesting question why the LR test provides a reasonable solution in such a broad range of testing problems.

Part of the explanation is that the boundary of the LR CR mirrors the global curvature of the model. If the model is flat, the CR boundary is flat, just like the PO and LM boundaries, but if the model is curved the LR boundary reflects this curvature. This relation is, however, not straightforward and is quite interesting in its own right. We will therefore spend some time discussing and explaining the relation between three different elements that determine the curvature of the CR. A further explanation for the performance of the LR test is that it implicitly averages over different alternatives, and we give an interpretation of the LR CR as a 'weighted average of BCRs'.

Because of the issues involved, this section is subdivided as follows. Section 7.1 determines the boundary of the LR test CR, described as a function of the parameter values in the alternative. Section 7.2 discusses how the three aspects referred to above influence the relation between the global curvature of the model and the shape of the CR boundary. Section 7.3 further discusses some of the merits of the trade-off between global and local curvature that the LR makes. This prepares for the interpretation of the LR CR as a 'weighted average of BCRs' given in section 7.4. Finally, in section 7.5, we discuss when the LR test may fail.

7.1   The boundary of the LR CR

The LR test rejects for large values of the LR statistic:

$$\text{LR} = 2 \operatorname*{Sup}_{\theta\,\Theta_a} \ell(\theta; t) - \operatorname*{Sup}_{\theta\,\Theta_o} \ell(\theta; t) \geq c_\alpha. \tag{34}$$

The second maximisation in (34) is not required if the null hypothesis is simple (as assumed throughout this chapter) and the maximum becomes $\ell(\theta_0; t)$. If, moreover, there was only one point in the alternative then the test would be just like a PO test. If there are more points in the alternative, we first have to maximise the likelihood under the alternative and calculate the likelihood ratio using this value of $\hat{\theta}$. The LR test can therefore be broken up into two steps:

(i)   maximise the likelihood to obtain the MLE $\hat{\theta} = \hat{\theta}(t)$,

(ii)   for this value of θ^* (i.e. $\theta^* = \hat{\theta}$) calculate the likelihood ratio

$$\mathrm{LR}_{\theta^*, \theta_0}(t) = 2^*[\ell(\theta^*; t) - \ell(\theta_0; t)]$$

and compare it with the critical value c_α.

Hence, if t^* is a point in the sample space on the *boundary* of the CR, it satisfies two conditions:[17]

$$(i) \quad \hat{\theta}(t^*) = \theta^* \quad \text{and} \quad (ii) \quad \mathrm{LR}_{\theta^*, \theta_0}(t^*) = c_\alpha, \tag{35}$$

where θ^* is fixed at the same value for (i) and (ii). Changing the perspective, we may ask, for each value of $\theta^* \in \Theta$, which t^*'s in the sample space lie on the boundary for that particular value of θ^*. This requires solving for t^* from (i) and (ii) jointly, for fixed θ^*. Thus, we are going to determine all t^* in T satisfying (i) and (ii) as a function of θ^*.

We can determine all t that give θ^* as the MLE, just as we did for the Wald and geodesic tests, by solving the first-order conditions (f.o.c.) for the MLE (see (27)).

$$(i) \quad \frac{\eta(\theta^*)'}{\theta}(t - \tau(\theta^*)) = 0 : \text{MLE constant (f.o.c.)}, \tag{36}$$

which, for a fixed value of θ^*, is a hyperplane through $\tau(\theta^*)$ orthogonal to $\partial \eta / \partial \theta|_{\theta = \theta^*}$.

We have further seen from the PO test that the set of t values for which the likelihood ratio is constant is also a hyperplane, but orthogonal to $(\eta(\theta^*) - \eta_0)$. We have

$$(ii) \quad (\eta(\theta^*) - \eta_0)'t = \tfrac{1}{2}c_\alpha + \kappa(\theta^*) - \kappa(\theta_0) : \text{LR constant}. \tag{37}$$

The 'constant MLE' hyperplane is of dimension $(k - d)$ and the 'constant LR' hyperplane is of dimension $(k - 1)$, and they will intersect since the gradient $\partial \eta / \partial \theta$ at θ^* has a direction different from the vector

---

[17] The boundary of the LR CR can in principle also be determined by substitution of $\theta^* = \hat{\theta}(t)$ and trying to solve $\mathrm{LR}_{\hat{\theta}, \theta_0}(t) = 2[\ell(\hat{\theta}(t); t) - \ell(\theta_0; t)] = c_\alpha$ directly, but explicit formulas for $\hat{\theta}(t)$ are often unavailable.

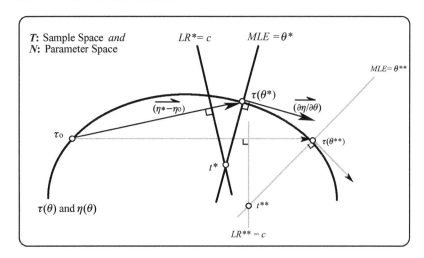

Figure 8.7 The intersection of constant MLE and constant LR lines

$(\eta(\theta^*) - \eta_0)$.[18] The intersection forms part of the boundary of the LR critical region. It is a set in the k-dimensional sample space satisfying $d + 1$ linear restrictions and is thus a $(k - d - 1)$-dimensional hyperplane in T. If $d = k - 1$, this intersection is just a point.

The intersection is shown in figure 8.7, for $k = 2$ and $d = 1$, so (36) and (37) are straight lines intersecting (if at all) in a point. Two values θ^* and θ^{**} are shown. In figure 8.7 we have actually chosen a bivariate normal distribution for t, i.e. $t \sim N(\mu(\theta), I_2)$, because the canonical parameter in this case is equal to the expectation parameter $\eta(\theta) = \tau(\theta) \equiv \mu(\theta)$, and this allows us to depict the parameter and sample space together in one figure. To get a general interpretation, all arrows should be interpreted as vectors from the canonical parameter space, as in figure 8.1.

---

[18] Different directions in the sense that $[(\eta(\theta^*) - \eta_0)]$ cannot be written as a linear combination of the columns of $\partial\eta/\partial\theta$ at θ^*. An exception is a linear exponential model when the gradient is a vector with the same direction as the difference vector for all θ^*. In that case the LR test equals to PO and LM tests and is UMP with a straight boundary of the CR. A second exception is caused by the global curvature of the model. For example, if $k = 2$, $d = 1$ and $\eta(\theta)$ curves back such that two θ values give the same direction of $(\eta(\theta) - \eta_0)$, then there will exist a θ value in between such that the MLE constant line and LR constant line are parallel. No point from the PO tests based on the $\eta(\theta)$ furthest from η_0 is part of the boundary. Finally, the two lines may fail to cross because $\hat{\theta}^{-1}(\theta^*)$ is only a half line, which does not stretch out beyond the critical point. Again, no point from the PO boundary based on this $\hat{\theta}$ is part of the LR boundary.

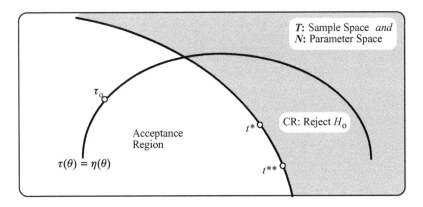

Figure 8.8 The boundary of the LR critical region

All points on the inverse image of θ^* (the MLE $= \theta^*$ line) to the right of t^* have $LR_{\theta^*,\theta_0}(t) > c_\alpha$ and therefore lie in the CR. Similarly, all points to the right of t^{**}, giving θ^{**} as the MLE, fall in the CR also.

The boundary point t^* is determined by fixing θ^* and solving (36) and (37) for this particular value, and likewise t^{**} is determined for θ^{**}. We can repeat this process for all parameter values, generating a curve in the sample space. This curve forms the boundary of the CR, which can thus be described as a function of θ^*. The CR consists of all points in T to the right of this curve. This is shown in figure 8.8.

7.2 Determinants of the shape and location for the LR CR boundary

The boundary of the LR CR clearly reflects the global curvature of the model, and it is instructive to examine this relationship in some detail. The shape and position of the boundary depend on three things: the significance level (through c_α), the distance from $\eta(\theta^*)$ to η_0, and the angle between $(\eta(\theta^*) - \eta_0)$ and the gradient $\partial\eta/\partial\theta$ at θ^*.

First, it is useful to rewrite (36) and (37) by subtracting $(\partial\eta/\partial\theta)'\tau_0$ and $(\eta^* - \eta_0)'\tau_0$, respectively, to obtain

$$\text{(i)} \qquad \frac{\eta(\theta^*)'}{\theta}(t - \tau_0) = \frac{\eta(\theta^*)'}{\theta}(\tau(\theta^*) - \tau_0), \qquad (36')$$

$$\text{(ii)} \quad (\eta(\theta^*) - \eta_0)'(t - \tau_0) = \tfrac{1}{2}c_\alpha + KLI(\eta_0, \eta^*), \qquad (37')$$

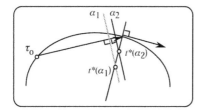 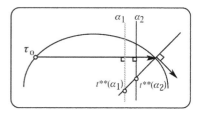

Figure 8.9 The effect of decreasing the significance level from α_1 to α_2

where $KLI(\eta_0, \eta^*)$ is the Kullback–Leibler information (directed) distance from $pdf(t; \eta_0)$ to $pdf(t; \eta^*)$.[19]

The boundary of the LR CR as a function of θ^* is found by solving (36′) and (37′) simultaneously for each $\theta^* \in \Theta$. It is clear that the significance level and the distance from $\eta(\theta^*)$ to η_0, directly affect (37′) and together they determine the position of the constant LR hyperplane. The constant MLE hyperplane is also determined by η^*, via $\tau(\eta(\theta^*))$, as well as by the gradient $\partial\eta(\theta^*)/\partial\theta$. The angle between $(\eta(\theta^*) - \eta_0)$ and the gradient determines where the two hyperplanes intersect. We shall now review their influence on the position and the shape of the boundary more closely.

7.2.1   The significance level

The significance level influences the position of the constant LR line. Decreasing the size of the test increases c_α, which in turn shifts the constant LR lines further to the right, because a larger value of t is required for (37′) to hold. The shift is illustrated in figure 8.9.

Figure 8.10 shows the critical regions for two different significance levels. The boundary shifts away from τ_0 as α decreases and the CR is smaller (reducing the probability of rejecting H_0).

7.2.2   The distance between the null and the alternative

The distance between η_0 and $\eta(\theta^*)$ also determines the position of the constant LR line, as (37′) clearly shows. But, unlike increasing c_α, increasing η^* does not always shift LR^* away from τ_0, because η^* enters on both sides of (37′). Increasing η^* enlarges $(\eta^* - \eta_0)$ on the left-hand

---

[19] $KLI(\eta_0, \eta^*) \equiv E_{\theta_0}[\ln\{L(\eta_0)/L(\eta^*)\}]$ which, for exponential models, equals

$$KLI(\eta_0, \eta^*) = (\eta_0 - \eta^*)'E_{\theta_0}[t] - (\kappa(\eta_0) - \kappa(\eta^*)) = (\eta_0 - \eta^*)'\tau_0 - (\kappa(\eta_0) - \kappa(\eta^*)).$$

(36′) relates to the local curvature of $\eta(\theta)$ through the change in $\partial\eta/\partial\theta$, and to the global curvature of $\tau(\theta)$ through $(\tau(\theta^*) - \tau_0)$. (37′) involves the distance between the null and the $\eta(\theta^*)$ alternative through the terms $(\eta(\theta^*) - \eta_0)$ and $KLI(\eta_0, \eta^*)$, and relates to the global behaviour of $\eta(\theta)$.

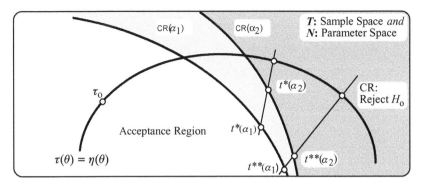

Figure 8.10 The boundary of the LR test for two different significance levels $\alpha_1 > \alpha_2$

side, pulling LR^* towards τ_0, since t needs to be reduced for $(37')$ to hold. But increasing η^* also increases the Kullback–Leibler distance on the right-hand side, pushing LR^* away from τ_0, since t needs to be increased for $(37')$ to hold.

In order to be more specific we need to define the length of $(\eta^* - \eta_0)$ and the distance between τ_0 and LR^*. This can be done in different ways, but we shall simply use Euclidean distance, which suffices for present purposes.[20] We define the distance between τ_0 and LR^* as $\delta(\eta^*) = \|t_m - \tau_0\|$, where t_m is the intersection point of the line through τ_0 in the direction $(\eta^* - \eta_0)$ and the constant LR hyperplane (see figure 8.12). Thus t_m is the point on LR^* closest to τ_0 in Euclidean sense.[21] Since $(t_m - \tau_0)$ is a multiple of $(\eta^* - \eta)$, we have $(\eta^* - \eta)'(t_m - \tau_0) = \|\eta^* - \eta\|\|t_m - \tau_0\|$, and using $(37')$ we obtain

$$\delta(\eta^*) \equiv \|t_m - \tau_0\| = \frac{c_\alpha}{2\|\eta^* - \eta_0\|} + \frac{KLI(\eta_0, \eta^*)}{\|\eta^* - \eta_0\|}. \tag{38}$$

For the normal distribution with identity covariance matrix, as used in figure 8.7, we have $\mu(\theta) = \tau(\theta) = \eta(\theta)$, $KLI(\eta, \eta^*) = \frac{1}{2}\|\eta - \eta^*\|^2$, and (38) reduces to

$$\delta_\alpha(\eta^*) \equiv \|t_m - \tau_0\| = \frac{c_\alpha}{2\|\eta^* - \eta_0\|} + \frac{1}{2}\|\eta^* - \eta_0\|. \tag{39}$$

[20] It is generally more appropriate to use Mahalanobis distance $\|v\| = v'\sum^{-1}v$ in the sample space $(v \in T)$ and $\|w\| = w'\sum w$ in the parameter space $(w \in N)$. This would show, for instance, that the distance δ between τ_0 and LR^* goes to 0 as the number of observations goes to infinity. The current relations are valid for fixed sample sizes and in fixed directions.
[21] But not necessarily in the Mahalanobis sense.

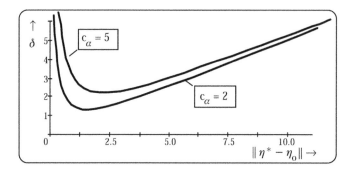

Figure 8.11 The distance of $\delta = \delta_\alpha(\eta^*)$ from τ_0 to the constant LR hyperplane

For distant η^*, the second term in (38) is dominating, and doubling the distance to η^* approximately doubles $\delta(\cdot)$. For η^* close to η_0, the first term in (38) dominates, and now halving the distance approximately doubles the distance $\delta(\cdot)$. For distant alternatives and nearby ones, more extreme observations are required before the null is rejected. Figure 8.11 shows the distance $\delta(\cdot)$ as a function of the length of $(\eta^* - \eta_0)$. Note that the minimum, and where the minimum is attained, increase with c_α.

The critical value c_α is constant regardless of the $(\eta^* - \eta_0)$ direction, with the result that, as θ^* varies, the distances δ from τ_0 to the CR vary, depending on the distance to the alternative. This turns out to be crucial in the implicit power trade-off between different alternatives that the LR test makes.

This concludes the discussion of (37′); the position of the constant LR line is determined by the significance level and length of $(\eta^* - \eta_0)$.

The distance from η^* to η_0 also enters (36′), because it determines τ^* and τ_0. Increasing η^* also increases τ^* and, since τ^* lies on the constant MLE hyperplane, shifts this hyperplane away from τ_0.

Finally, we consider the interaction between (37′) and (36′), and what determines their intersection.

7.2.3   The angle between the difference vector and the gradient

The angle between $(\eta^* - \eta_0)$ and $\partial\eta/\partial\theta|_{\theta=\theta^*}$ determines the angle between the LR^* and the constant MLE hyperplane, and consequently where these planes intersect, i.e. the position of the CR boundary in the sample space. Note that the local behaviour of $\eta(\theta)$ at θ^* only enters in

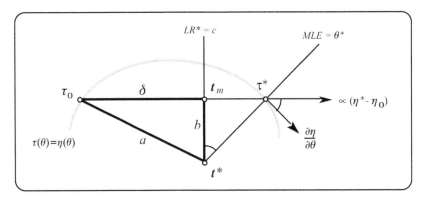

Figure 8.12 The angle between the gradient and the difference vector

(36′) and does not affect (37′), which is essentially determined by the global behaviour. Figure 8.12 illustrates the situation.

For fixed η^* and c_α, the constant LR line is fixed and the gradient determines the intersection with the constant MLE line, and therefore the point t^* on the boundary of the LR CR. The gradient $\partial \eta / \partial \theta |_{\theta = \theta^*}$ represents the local direction of the canonical manifold and $(\eta^* - \eta_0)$ represents the average direction from the null to the alternative. The closer the direction of the gradient is to the average direction, the further the boundary point moves away from the expectation under the null and the point t_m (both $a = \| t^* - \tau_0 \|$ and $b = \| t^* - t_m \|$ increase). The larger the value of b, the larger the proportion of the constant MLE line that falls in the CR.

The two extreme cases are when the gradient is orthogonal to the average direction ($b = 0$ and $a = \delta$) and when the gradient is proportional to the average direction and the two lines are parallel; they either coincide or do not cross at all.

7.3   Discussion

7.3.1

The direct effect of decreasing the significance level is to shift LR^* away from τ_0, but there is also an effect on the shape of the boundary, because shifting out LR^* changes the trade-off between average (global) direction and local direction, but only indirectly through the effects given in subsections 7.3.2 and 7.3.3.

7.3.2

We shall now motivate figure 8.11 and justify the shifting of LR^* away from τ_0 for distant alternatives and alternatives close to H_0, since this is a crucial aspect of the trade-off between different alternatives implicit in the LR test.

The increasing value of δ for distant alternatives solves a classic problem in hypothesis testing illustrated by the following example. Suppose $x \sim N(\mu, 1)$ and we are testing $\mu = 0$ versus $\mu = 10$. If $x = 3$ is observed, then the null hypothesis is rejected because of the size condition. This is quite unreasonable since the value of 3 is so much more unlikely under the alternative than under the null.[22] What the LR test does implicitly is to adjust the critical value for the BCR if the alternative is far away (large power will be attained against distant alternatives regardless; there is little power loss and large size gain), in favour of alternatives closer to H_0 (against which higher power is worth the additional size penalty).

For distributions very similar to η_0 it is also sensible to require observations to be further away from τ_0 before the null is rejected. This avoids including points in the CR that are of little use in discriminating between H_a and H_0, being almost as likely under the null as under the alternative. They contribute to the size of the test without contributing much in terms of power.

7.3.3

The angle between the gradient and the difference vector helps to explain why the boundary is flatter when the model is less curved.

First consider a third type of extreme case (in addition to the directions being orthogonal or parallel), when the angle is, in fact, irrelevant, namely at the point on the expectation manifold where the constant LR line and constant MLE line cross. This is the point where the boundary of the CR crosses the expectation manifold. This point depends on the significance level, however, and for a different α the angle does matter.

For models close to linear exponential models, this crossing point, call it $\tau(\theta_x)$, helps to show why the LR boundary is less curved. The boundary is a function of θ^* and passes through $\tau(\theta_x)$ when $\theta^* = \theta_x$, and as a consequence $b = 0$ in figure 8.12. If the model is not very curved the constant MLE and LR lines are close to being parallel and, as θ^* deviates

---

[22] This criticism applies directly to the PO test. The PO test has a critical value that varies with θ^* such that the size of the test is constant. This means that for a fixed direction the distance to the boundary of the PO CR is constant regardless of the distance to the alternative.

from θ_x, the value of b increases very quickly, despite δ being fairly constant, resulting in a very flat boundary. If the model is exactly linear exponential, then there is only one value θ^* for which the constant MLE and LR lines coincide and this line forms the *straight* boundary of the CR.

If the local (Efron) curvature at θ^* is large, then the gradient changes quickly relative to the average direction. The distance b changes quickly (depending of course on the distance of δ relative to $||t^* - t_m||$) and the boundary is more curved as a result.

7.4   The LR as a 'weighted sum of BCRs'

We are now able to give an interpretation of the LR test as a weighted sum of BCRs or PO tests in the following sense.

For each possible parameter value $\theta^* \in \Theta_a$, we construct the PO test $\{LR_{\theta^*, \theta_0}(t) \geq c_\alpha\} \in T$, in the direction $\eta^* = \eta(\theta^*)$ and take the intersection with the inverse image of the MLE $\theta^*, \hat{\theta}^{-1}(\theta^*) \in T$. The proportion of the inverse image $\hat{\theta}^{-1}(\theta^*)$ that forms part of the CR depends on where the constant LR hyperplane using the same θ^*, $\{LR_{\theta^*, \theta_0}(t) = c_\alpha\}$, intersects the inverse image. The location of the constant LR hyperplane depends on the significance level α (figure 8.9), and varies with the distance between the null and alternative (figure 8.11). For distant (and close) alternatives the hyperplane is more distant from τ_0. The $(k - d - 1)$-dimensional hyperplane of intersection between the inverse image and constant LR plane also depends on the angle between the gradient vector(s) of $\eta(\theta)$ at θ^* (i.e. the tangent space of $\eta(\theta)$ at θ^*) and the average direction vector $(\eta^* - \eta_0)$. If the angle is small, the constant MLE and LR planes are more parallel and the intersection is further away from τ_0, but this also means that a larger proportion of the inverse image of θ^* is part of the CR (figure 8.12).

Each point in the alternative contributes one slice of a BCR, the intersection with the inverse image. The weights refer to the proportion of the slice that is included in the LR CR. An alternative interpretation is thus as a weighted average of constant MLE hyperplanes, but this is simply the other side of the same coin, since we always consider the intersection of the two sets.

If the model is a one-parameter linear exponential then the whole BCR in the direction η^* is taken and the whole inverse image for all $\theta^* \geq \theta_{\text{crit}}$.[23]

---

[23] Thus the test statistic and the estimator determine the same partition of the sample space (define the same orbits in the sample space on which they are constant).

In contrast with the LR tests, the PO and LM tests take the whole BCR in one direction, regardless of the value of the MLE, i.e. the PO test uses only $LR_{\theta^*,\theta_0}(t)$ for one θ^* regardless of $\hat{\theta}$. The Wald and geodesic tests, on the other hand, take the whole inverse image of θ^*, regardless of the value of $LR_{\theta^*,\theta_0}(t)$, as long as θ^* maximises the likelihood and θ^* is larger than θ_{crit}.

7.5   When does the LR test fail?

The discussion so far gives the impression that the LR test is more than just appealing, but we should be cautious. In curved models the maximum power against all alternatives as an optimality criterion is vacuous since no such test exists. We did not define an alternative optimality criterion, but gave a general appreciation of different tests instead. Optimality requirements are not necessarily desirable and can on occasion be viewed as simply restricting the class of tests to be considered. The LMP and PO tests, for example, uniquely satisfy optimality requirements but potential drawbacks are well known and have been exposed in this chapter. The LR test does not satisfy these optimality requirements, and is inadmissible on these criteria, but seems 'reasonable' nevertheless. On the other hand, one would also expect the LR to perform badly in extreme cases, just like the PO, LM and Wald/geodesic tests.

In particular, if the model is globally very curved, we can expect the power function of the LR test to differ substantially from the power envelope. The basic reason is that the power envelope is based on the PO test in each and every direction. When the global curvature of the model is large, these PO tests will define very different CRs and the LR CR must differ substantially from the CRs of these tests (which give the power envelope), since all of them are of size α. The extent to which they are different is measured by Hillier's (1990) global curvature measure – the probability of the enveloping region (ER) under the null. If this probability is large, say 2α, then the ER is much larger than the LR CR, which is always of size α, and we may expect the LR power to be well below the power envelope. Hillier (1995) shows that the LR CR is a proper subset of the ER because the critical value used for the LR test, c_α in (34), is larger than or equal to the maximum of the critical values $c_\alpha(\theta^*)$ in (9), for all PO tests of the same size, i.e. $c_\alpha \geq \max_{\theta^* \in \Theta} c_\alpha(\theta^*)$. Hence, the ER includes every BCR, as well as the LR CR.

In fact, Hillier (1995) shows that the ER is the smallest region that contains all sensible CRs (in the sense that it is the smallest region that includes all proper Bayes procedures of size α). Put differently, in determining a solution to the non-existence of a UMP test, we need to consider only subsets of ER[24] The LR, LM and PO CRs are just particular choices. If Prob[ER] = α, then $ER = CR_{LR} = CR_{LM} = CR_{PO^*}$, for all θ^*, and the three testing principles give the unique optimal test. If Prob[ER] > α, no test exists that is UMP and a trade-off is necessary between power against different alternatives. As Prob[ER] gets larger, there is greater (undesirable) freedom to choose, and maximising power against one particular direction has more serious consequences for power against other alternatives.

A natural counterpart to ER, which could be used to restrict the choice of CR, is the intersection of all BCRs of size α, which we shall call the intersection region (IR). It seems reasonable to require of CRs that they include IR, since it consists of points in T that lie in all possible BCRs, and no BCR would exclude them. By definition every PO test includes IR, and the LM test, being a limiting case, essentially includes IR also.[25] The LR test turns out to include IR in the examples below, but, although this might hold more broadly, it remains to be proved in general.

Note that Prob[IR] could be used as a measure of global curvature also, but since IR can be empty if the model is too curved it provides no additional information on the global curvature beyond this cut-off point. In contrast, Prob[ER] will continue to increase with increasing global curvature and is therefore more useful.

Concluding, we need to choose a CR that is a subset of ER and possibly includes IR. This could be based on a desire to optimise power against particular parameter values, which are of economic interest for instance, or to average power over a range of alternatives (both require additional information on the parameter values). The LR averages in an implicit fashion that may not be appropriate for the situation at hand, but in many cases the LR test will be a convenient choice.

8   Example: testing for autocorrelation and unit roots

This section illustrates the critical regions of different tests when testing for autocorrelation and unit roots in an AR(1) model. An illustration of

---

[24] Note that the Wald/geodesic CR is not in general a subset of ER.

[25] Related to Roy's union-intersection method, we could think of two tests – one based on ER and one on IR. The ER tests would be based on the ER of size α (Prob[ER] can be decreased by decreasing the size on which the BCR is based). This test would exclude part of IR in the examples below. The IR test would be based on the IR of size α (Prob[IR] might be increased by increasing the size on which the BCR is based, but if the model is very curved Prob[IR] might be zero for all significance levels used). In the examples below, the IR test is not a subset of ER, i.e. it includes points that are excluded by all BCRs of size α.

the problems of the Wald test, including the possibility of disconnected parts of the CR, is given at the end of this section.

Consider the AR(1) model with fixed initial value:

$$y_i = \rho y_{i-1} + \varepsilon_i, \quad \varepsilon_i \sim IIN(0, \sigma^2), \quad i = 1, \dots, T, \tag{40}$$

and y_0 fixed. Assuming σ^2 known reduces the model to a (2,1)-curved exponential model, and we set $\sigma^2 = 1$.[26] The canonical parameter η and minimal sufficient statistics t, as in (2), are easily derived and are

$$\eta(\rho) = \begin{pmatrix} -\frac{1}{2}\rho^2 \\ \rho \end{pmatrix}, \quad t(y) \equiv \begin{pmatrix} s \\ d \end{pmatrix} = \begin{pmatrix} \sum_{i=1}^{T} y_{i-1}^2 \\ \sum_{i=1}^{T} y_i y_{i-1} \end{pmatrix}. \tag{41}$$

The expectation of t as a function of ρ, i.e. the expectation manifold $\tau(\rho)$, equals

$$\tau_1(\rho) = E_\rho[s] = y_0^2 S_T(\rho) + \frac{1}{1-\rho^2}(T - S_T(\rho)), \quad |\rho| \neq 1 \tag{42a}$$

$$= y_0^2 T + \frac{1}{2}(T-1)T, \quad |\rho| = 1 \tag{42b}$$

$$\tau_2(\rho) = E_\rho[d] = \rho \tau_1(\rho), \quad \text{all } \rho \tag{43}$$

where $S_T(\rho) \equiv \sum_{i=0}^{T-1} \rho^{2i} = (1 - \rho^{2T})/(1 - \rho^2)$, when $|\rho| \neq 1$.
The maximum likelihood estimator is

$$\hat{\rho} = \frac{d}{s}. \tag{44}$$

It follows trivially from (44) that all d proportional to s by the same factor give the same value for the MLE. Consequently, the lines of constant MLE, (27) and (36), used in the Wald, geodesic and LR test are rays from the origin through $(1, \rho)$.

$$\pounds_{\hat{\rho}} = \{d - \hat{\rho} s = 0\} : \text{MLE constant (f.o.c.)}. \tag{45}$$

The inverse image of $\hat{\rho}$, i.e. $\hat{\rho}^{-1}(\hat{\rho})$, does not continue to the left of the origin, since s is a sum of squares and is always larger than zero. The

---

[26] The model with σ^2 unknown is a (3,2)-curved exponential model and is analysed as such more extensively in van Garderen (1995). Note that σ^2 and ρ are orthogonal in the sense that the (expected, as well as observed) Fisher information matrix is diagonal, which tends to make the assumption of known σ^2 less restrictive.

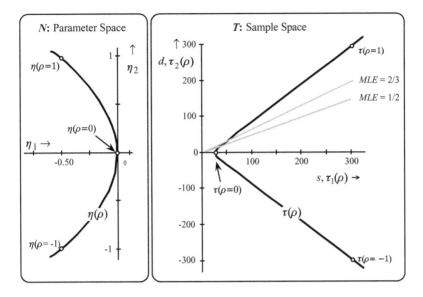

Figure 8.13 Canonical and expectation manifolds for the AR(1) model

origin is the only critical point, because it is the only point in T for which the MLE is not uniquely defined. Note, however, that $\text{Prob}[(s, d) = 0] = 0$.

The canonical and expectation manifolds are shown in figure 8.13, as well as two lines of constant MLE, the inverse image of $\hat{\rho}(t) = 1/2$ and $2/3$, i.e. $\hat{\rho}^{-1}(1/2)$ and $\hat{\rho}^{-1}(2/3)$. Thus all the points on each MLE line give the same value for the MLE and the critical point lies on both lines.

The expected Fisher information on ρ is τ_1 and the observed information equals s.

The different classical tests have the following general forms.

1. The PO test for testing $H_0 : \rho = \rho_0$ against $H_a : \rho = \rho^*$.
   The test rejects for large values of $(\eta^* - \eta_0)'t$ and the CR is

$$CR_{\text{PO}(\rho^*,\rho_0)} = \{-\tfrac{1}{2}((\rho^*)^2 - \rho_0^2)s + (\rho^* - \rho_0)d \geq c_\alpha\}, \tag{46}$$

   regardless of whether ρ^* is larger or smaller than ρ_0.

2. The LM test for testing $H_0 : \rho = \rho_0$ against one-sided alternatives.
   When testing against $H_a : \rho > \rho_0$ ($\rho < \rho_0$), the test rejects for large (small) values of $(\partial \eta(\rho_0)/\partial \rho)'t$ and the CR is

$$CR_{\text{LM}} = \{-\rho_0 s + d \geq c_\alpha\}. \tag{47}$$

When testing against $H_a : \rho < \rho_0$, the inequality sign is reversed and a different critical value, obtained from the left tail of the distribution of $\partial \eta(\rho_0)/\partial \rho' t$, is used.

3. The geodesic/Wald test.

The standard version of the Wald test is analysed at the end of this section. The geodesic version does not require solving the partial differential equation (33), since the manifold is one-dimensional. Consequently, the geodesic test simply rejects if $\hat{\rho} > \rho_\alpha^*$, when $H_a : \rho > \rho_0$ (or $\hat{\rho} < \rho_\alpha^*$ when $H_a : \rho < \rho_0$). This determines a CR above (or below) the inverse image of $\hat{\rho}^{-1}(\rho_\alpha^*)$ and ρ_α^* is such that Prob$[\hat{\rho} > \rho_\alpha^*] = \alpha$.

Note that the inverse image of $\hat{\rho}$ is a ray through the origin, and the boundary of the CR is a straight line as a result. As a consequence of this straight boundary there exists a PO test that coincides with this geodesic test. The intercept of the PO test changes with ρ^* and happens to pass through the origin for particular ρ^*'s in each of the cases considered here. For this value of ρ^*, the PO and geodesic test coincide. Note, however, that $\rho_\alpha^* \neq \rho^*$.

4. The LR test for testing $H_0 : \rho = \rho_0$ against one-sided alternatives.

The points on the boundary of the CR are simultaneously on the constant MLE line and on the constant LR line. As a function of ρ^* and α, they are defined by (see (45) and (46))

$$\text{(i)} \quad d - \rho^* s = 0, : \text{MLE constant,} \tag{48}$$

$$\text{(ii)} \quad (\rho^* - \rho_0)d - \tfrac{1}{2}(\rho^{*2} - \rho_0^2)s = \tfrac{1}{2}c_\alpha : \text{LR constant.} \tag{49}$$

Solving (i) and (ii) simultaneously for s and d in terms of ρ^* and c_α, we obtain

$$s(\rho^*, \alpha) = c_\alpha \frac{1}{(\rho^* - \rho_0)^2}, \quad d(\rho^*, \alpha) = c_\alpha \frac{\rho^*}{(\rho^* - \rho_2)^2}. \tag{50}$$

Note that $s(\rho^*, \alpha)$ and $d(\rho^*, \alpha)$ do not depend on y_0, other than the value of c_α.[27] The effect of $y_0 \neq 0$ is that the expectation manifold shifts to the right.

We now focus on testing for serially uncorrelated observations and testing for a unit root, thus specialising the general formulas given above to: $\rho_0 = 0$ against $\rho_a > 0$, i.e. positive autocorrelation (negative autocorrelation gives the mirror image), and secondly to: $\rho_0 = 1$ against

---

[27] It is also interesting to note that, if $\rho_0 = 0$, the boundary points close to the origin are obtained for large values of ρ^* in (50).

stationary alternatives, $\rho_a < 1$, and explosive alternatives, $\rho_a > 1$. Critical values were obtained by simulation, using 100,000 replications for testing both serial independence and unit roots.[28] To obtain critical values for the one-sided version of the LR test, the signed LR statistic was calculated: $\lambda_{LR}^{\pm} = \text{sign}(\hat{\rho} - \rho_0)\lambda_{LR}$, where $\lambda_{LR} = 2((\hat{\rho} - \rho_0)d - \frac{1}{2}(\hat{\rho}^2 - \rho_0^2)s)$, which is larger than 0 for all s and d.

8.1   Testing for serial correlation

Figure 8.14 shows the PO critical region for testing the null of no serial correlation, $\rho = 0$, against positive autocorrelation, $\rho > 0$, i.e. a one-sided test, using four different values of the PO point.

Comments on figure 8.14
1. $\tau(\rho)$ is the expectation manifold, i.e. the expectation of (s, d) as a function of ρ. For $\rho = 0$ this equals the expectation under H_0, τ_0, and for other values describes the expectation of (s, d) under H_a.
2. The tinted area is the intersection region IR of all BCRs considered here, i.e. the part of the sample space that falls in the CR of all the PO tests.[29] It is a subset of Hillier's enveloping region ER, which, in addition, includes the 'bow tie' shaped area. All the tests, including the LR and geodesic test, have their boundary inside this double conic section, which means that they all have the desirable properties that their CRs are proper subsets of ER, and they include IR.
3. The probabilities on ER and IR were calculated numerically for different nominal values of α, and using the PO points 1, 0.75, 0.5 and 0.25 and the LM test. With $\alpha = 10\%$ we obtained for Hillier's global curvature measure $\delta_{\alpha=0.1} = \text{Prob}[ER] = 15.3\%$, and for the IR region $\text{Prob}[IR] = 5.1\%$. This leaves a fair amount of (undesirable) freedom to choose a CR that includes IR and is a proper subset of ER. This freedom is due to the global curvature of the model and means that global curvature poses a notable problem.

---

[28] For the no-serial correlation case a bivariate approximation is available for (s, d) using that under $H_0 : E[s] = T$, $\text{Var}[s] = 2T$, $E[d] = 0$ and $\text{Cov}[s, d] = 0$. The critical values obtained from this approximation did not seem too far astray, but the union of all BCRs, i.e. the enveloping region, did not include the LR CR, which we know should be a proper subset of the enveloping region.
[29] $\rho^* \in (0, 1]$. Stopping at $\rho^* = 1$ might be sensible but is rather arbitrary. Increasing ρ^* results in a steeper boundary, smaller IR and larger ER. In the limit, the boundary becomes vertical, implying that the ER includes the CR of a test depending on s only, which may be considered undesirable.

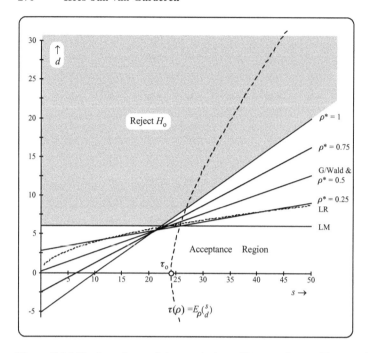

Figure 8.14 Testing for serial correlation. $H_0 : \rho = 0$ vs. $H_a : \rho > 0$. $T = 25$, $y_0 = 0$, $\alpha = 10\%$. Lines correspond to the CR boundaries of four different PO tests using $\rho^* = 0.25, 0.5, 0.75, 1$; the LM test (horizontal); the one-sided LR (dashed); and the G(eodesic)/Wald test (equal to $PO_{\rho^*=0.5}$). τ_0 is the expectation of $(s, d)'$ when $\rho = 0$, i.e. under H_0, and $\tau(\rho)$ (dashed) is the expectation manifold, i.e. the expectation of $(s, d)'$ for values of ρ under the alternative. The grey area is the intersection region. $\text{Prob}[IR] = 5\%$, $\text{Prob}[ER] = 15\%$

4. Figure 8.14 also illustrates the LM test as a limiting PO test as $\rho^* \to 0$. The critical region in this case depends only on d, but note that the variance is assumed known ($\sigma^2 = 1$).
5. The geodesic/Wald test rejects if $\hat{\rho} > 0.25 (= \rho^*_\alpha)$ and coincides with the PO test based on 0.5 (illustrating the obvious point made earlier that $\rho^*_\alpha \neq \rho^*$).
6. The LR boundary lies between the G/Wald and LM boundaries, for large values of s and d below the Wald and above the LM boundaries and vice versa for small s and d. The LR test is actually very close to the PO test with $\rho^* = 0.25$, being slightly above it for central values of s and below it elsewhere. This value for the PO point is the average of the two PO points that generate the Wald test and the limiting value that generates the LM test, but this is coincidental.

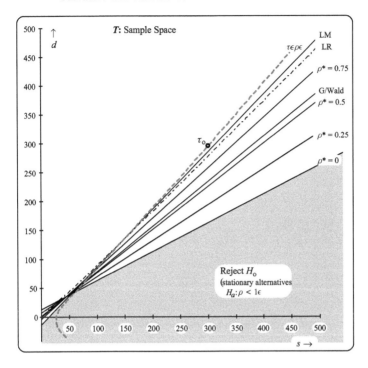

Figure 8.15 Testing for a unit root. $H_0 : \rho = 1$ vs. $H_a : \rho < 1$. $T = 25$, $y_0 = 0$, $\alpha = 10\%$. Lines correspond to the CR boundaries of four different PO tests using $\rho^* = 0, 0.25, 0.5, 0.75$; the LM test; the one-sided LR (dashed); and the G(eodesic)/Wald test. τ_0 is the expectation of (s, d) under H_0, and $\tau(\rho)$ (dashed) is the expectation manifold. $\text{Prob}[IR] = 2\%$, $\text{Prob}[ER] = 19\%$

8.2 Testing for a unit root

Figure 8.15 shows the boundaries of different CRs for testing the null of a random walk, $\rho = 1$, against stationary alternatives, $\rho < 1$. Figure 8.16 shows the different CR's boundaries for testing the random walk hypothesis versus explosive alternatives.

Comments on figures 8.15 and 8.16
1. All the CRs in figures 8.15 and 8.16 are again proper subsets of the relevant ERs, and include the IRs.
2. The figures give the impression that the IR is smaller in the stationary case than in the explosive case, but this is not true in terms of their probability content, which shows, in fact, the reverse. Thus care needs to be taken when making direct comparisons of IR and ER in different

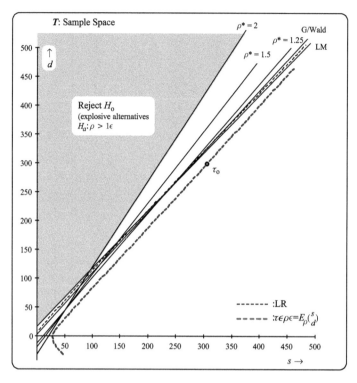

Figure 8.16 Testing for a unit root against explosive alternatives. $H_0 : \rho = 1$ vs. $H_a : \rho > 1$. $T = 25$, $y_0 = 0$, $\alpha = 10\%$. Lines correspond to the CR boundaries of three different PO tests using $\rho^* = 1.25$, 1.5, 2; the LM test; the one-sided LR (dashed); and the G(eodesic)/Wald test. τ_0 is the expectation of (s, d) under H_0, and $\tau(\rho)$ (dashed) is the expectation manifold. Prob[IR] $< 0.1\%$, Prob[ER] $= 25\%$

testing problems. The IR and ER *probabilities* serve the purpose of allowing such a comparison. They were calculated for both cases, and can be compared with the serial correlation case discussed earlier.

For stationary alternatives we used the LM test and the PO tests based on $\rho^* = 0.75, 0.5, 0.25$ and 0, making it comparable with the serial correlation case. With $\alpha = 10\%$ we obtained for Hillier's $\delta_{\alpha=0.1} = $ Prob[ER] $= 19.2\%$ and for Prob[IR] $= 1.7\%$. We see that there is much greater freedom for choosing a CR, and global curvature poses a much more serious problem for unit root testing than for testing for serial correlation. For explosive alternatives we used the LM test and the PO tests based on $\rho^* = 1.25, 1.5$ and 2. With

$\alpha = 10\%$ we   obtained $\delta_{\alpha=0.1} = \text{Prob}[ER] = 25.5\%$,   and Prob$[IR] < 0.1\%$.

It should be noted that $\rho^* = 2$ is much further away from $\rho_0 = 1$ than $\rho^* = 0$, in terms of, for instance, the Kullback–Leibler or Jeffreys distance.[30] The point $\rho^* = 1.156$ on the explosive side is the same Jeffreys distance away from 1 as $\rho^* = 0$ on the stable side. Hence, we further calculated the probabilities using the LM test and the PO tests based on $\rho^* = 1.05$ and $\rho^* = 1.156$, and obtained $\delta_{\alpha=0.1} = \text{Prob}[ER] = 19.0\%$ and Prob$[IR] = 2.2\%$, which is very similar to the results for stationary alternatives.

Irrespective of the question of which points should be included, global curvature poses a much more serious problem for testing unit roots than for testing serial correlation.[31]

3. The boundary for the LM test against stationary (one-sided) alternatives is of course parallel to the boundary for the LM test against explosive alternatives, since they are based on the same test statistic. The test against stationary alternatives uses the left tail, and the test against explosive alternatives uses the right tail of the distribution.

4. The geodesic/Wald test rejects for $\hat{\rho} < 0.79$, when testing against stationary alternatives, and rejects for $\hat{\rho} > 1.04$, when testing against explosive alternatives.

   One explanation for this asymmetry round 1 is that the distribution of $\hat{\rho}$ is heavily skewed to the left. Another explanation, related to a point made earlier, is that the distribution of the canonical statistic (s, d) changes much quicker when $\rho > 1$ than for $\rho < 1$. Considering the mean of s and d, for instance, ρ needs to be increased by 1 to change expectation from $(0,0)$ to $(300,300)$, whereas an increase by less than 0.04 on the explosive side achieves the same change. Similarly, the Fisher information on ρ, which equals $\tau(\rho)$, increases much faster for $\rho > 1$ than for $\rho < 1$. We are better able to distinguish the null distribution from distributions with $\rho > 1$ than for $\rho < 1$.

5. The LR boundaries for the unit roots test case are much less curved than for the serial correlation case and are almost straight lines. The boundaries again lie between the Wald and LM boundaries, but are much closer to the LM boundary. In fact, it is difficult to distinguish between the LM and LR boundaries for large sections.

---

[30] Pertaining to the discussion in section 7, Prob$[ER]$ takes no account of the distance from null to alternative.

[31] Van Garderen (1997b) calculates the exact Efron curvature for stable, unit root and explosive values of ρ. The curvature increases dramatically as ρ approaches the explosive region.

8.3   The Wald test

We conclude this section by illustrating a number of problems with the Wald test, in particular when testing for a unit root against stationary alternatives. The Wald test depends on the formulation of the restrictions. We use the class of restrictions (22) and choose different values of b to make a comparison.

$$r(\rho) = (\exp\{b(\rho - \rho_0)\} - 1)/b, \tag{51}$$

$$R(\rho) = \partial r(\rho)/\partial \rho = \exp\{b(\rho - \rho_0)\}. \tag{52}$$

The information matrix (1×1) in this case is equal to $\tau_1(\rho)$ and the Wald statistic is

$$w_r(\hat{\rho}) = \left(\frac{\exp\{b(\hat{\rho} - \rho_0)\} - 1}{b}\right)^2 \tau_1(\hat{\rho}). \tag{53}$$

The information matrix is increasing in $\rho > 0$ since $\tau_1(\rho)$ is increasing when $\rho > 0$. The Wald statistic $w_r(\cdot)$ is therefore monotonically increasing when testing $H_0 : \rho = \rho_0$ against $H_a : \rho > \rho_0$. By the same token, $\tau_1(\rho)$ is decreasing as $\rho \downarrow 0$ and the Wald statistic need not be monotonic.

This non-monotonicity is shown in figure 8.17, when testing for a unit root $H_a : \rho = 1$ against $H_a : \rho < 1$. The three curves correspond to three different values of b. We know from before that the geodesic version of the Wald test with the correct size, rejects if $\hat{\rho} < 0.79$ (at 10% significance level) and we use this value for comparison. Figure 8.17 also illustrates that we can obtain any value for the test statistic we like by varying the choice of b. For $\hat{\rho} = 0.79$, the test statistics take the values 0.66, 1.01 and 1.59 for $b = 7.5$, 5 and 2.5 respectively. This implies that using the same critical value for all three values of b can lead to very different conclusions and is clearly inappropriate (as pointed out by Breusch and Schmidt (1985) and Lafontaine and White (1986)).

Instead of using a common critical value, we could choose a critical value such that the value of ρ closest to 1, for which the tests reject, is 0.79. This is also illustrated in figure 8.17. For $b = 2.5$ this actually gives a size-adjusted monotonic version of the Wald test, and coincides therefore with the geodesic test. This is not the case for $b = 5$ or 7.5, which illustrate the situation where the test determines two unconnected parts of the CR. Taking $b = 5$ for example, the test rejects for $w_5 > 1.01$, which corresponds to rejecting if

$$\hat{\rho} < -0.22 \quad \text{or} \quad 0.35 < \hat{\rho} < 0.79, \tag{54}$$

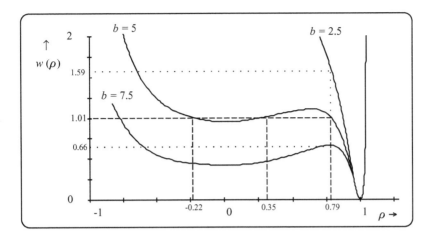

Figure 8.17 The Wald test for three values of b (2.5, 5 and 7). The test with $b = 5$ and critical value 1.01 rejects if $\hat{\rho} = 0.79$

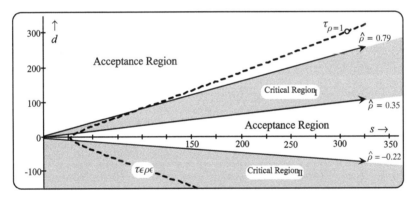

Figure 8.18 Disconnected critical region of the Wald test for a unit root based on equation (53) with $b = 5$. $\tau_{\rho=1}$ is the expectation of (s, d) under H_0. $T = 25$, $y_0 = 0$

but does not reject for values of $\hat{\rho}$ between -0.22 and 0.35. The resulting CR is shown in figure 8.18 and is very unattractive indeed.

9   Conclusion

In this chapter we have presented a review of classical tests very different from traditional treatments. Traditional approaches are concerned with explaining and justifying the choice of test statistics and deriving their properties. From this viewpoint questions about correct critical values and appropriate approximations to their distributions are important. Whether we can easily find the correct critical value is also important from a practical point of view but is irrelevant in answering questions about the 'optimal' or desirable properties of a test. Optimality considerations apply whether the test is carried out at a 1% or a 10% significance level.

The LM, Wald and LR tests are asymptotically equivalent and this gives the impression that choosing a test is merely a question of which test is most convenient. Being aware of the approximate nature of this result, effort is often put into making sure that particular choices are appropriate in particular situations, and determining the right finite sample critical values and power functions or higher-order corrections to improve results for finite samples more generally.

Asymptotic considerations can also go astray because of their local nature. A sequence of local alternatives, for instance, cannot reveal the power properties for alternatives quite different from the null. It may be thought that distinguishing the null from local alternatives is harder than for alternatives further away, and hence that only local properties matter asymptotically. The figures presented here illustrate that this can be very misleading because the classical tests behave very differently for distant alternatives.

This chapter shows that the choice of test (statistic) is a matter of convenience only if the model is not seriously curved. If the model is appreciably curved then the different tests imply very different critical regions.

The PO test and LM test give a straight boundary of the CR and cannot guarantee global consistency. The PO test further depends on the parameterisation of the model and, because of the size condition, ignores the distance to η^*, which can lead to (inappropriate) high power against (less relevant) distant alternatives. Choosing the same direction regardless of the sample size gives an inferior test in large samples also. The LM test is asymptotically superior to the PO test in most cases and is invariant under reparameterisations. The LM test can be seen, however, as an extreme case of a PO test and the power of the LM test is more easily affected by curvature of the model and is likely to have inferior power properties to the PO test in small samples, especially if the local curvature at H_0 is large.

The Wald test gives a curved boundary but the numerical value of the test statistic depends on the algebraic formulation of the restrictions. The geometric version of the Wald test, the geodesic test, raises a number of practical problems as well as a number of fundamental questions that apply directly to the Wald test also. The geodesic distance on the manifold is arguably not the right definition of distance for hypothesis testing and the geodesic distance in the larger embedding manifold provides a better idea of departure from the null. The fact that the geodesic and Wald test is solely a function of the estimator means that the boundary always consists of the inverse image of the estimator at the critical value, $\hat{\theta}^{-1}(\theta^*)$ in the sample space. This raises two problems: first, there are many different t such that $\hat{\theta}(t) = \theta^*$, which lends very different support to the (non-)validity of H_0 so that the test should be carried out conditionally; secondly, the boundary of the CR can be orthogonal to the BCR based on the direction from $\eta(\theta_0)$ to $\eta(\theta^*)$, since this (average) direction can be orthogonal to the gradient of $\eta(\theta)$ at θ^* on which $\hat{\theta}_{\text{mle}}^{-1}(\theta^*)$ is based, if the model is very curved globally. Furthermore, the geodesic/Wald CR is not in general a proper subset of the ER and does not always include the IR.

All these problems are a direct consequence of the curvature of the model. No test exists that is best in every direction. Choosing one particular direction, like the PO and LM tests, gives maximum power in that direction, but no guarantee of reasonable properties in different directions. One first needs to investigate the curvature properties of the model. Ideally, we would like a test with a curved boundary that takes into account the curvature of the model and gives reasonable power in all possible directions.

One solution would be to take the intersection of all BCRs against all possible alternatives such that the overall size is α, i.e. a weighted version of all possible PO tests. The problem is how to choose the weights or critical values associated with each parameter point. If all the significance levels are equal, then this is the enveloping region of Hillier (1990) adjusted for size and is related to Roy's union-intersection method, but this CR does not generally include the IR.

We could also specify a weighting function reflecting the importance of different parameter values, e.g. based on external or prior information on the parameter values, since the ER ignores the distance of different alternatives from the null. Specifying a weighting function objectively and determining appropriate critical values raise practical as well as ideological problems.

The LR test solves many of these problems simultaneously. The LR test uses the BCR in the maximum likelihood direction and a critical value that takes into account the distance from the alternatives on the manifold to the null, penalising alternatives that are too close and too far from the null to contribute reasonable power. It takes only one slice from each BCR boundary, namely the intersection with the inverse image of the MLE that gave rise to the maximum likelihood direction on which the

BCR was based. This determines a curved boundary that trades off the local curvature against the average global curvature at every alternative. The LR strikes a convenient compromise in terms of power against alternatives that are too close or too distant from the null, and alternatives that are a moderate distance away, against which reasonable power is desirable and can be attained.

The overall conclusion based on this presentation must be that the Wald test should be avoided, not only because of its invariance properties, but also because of the deeper questions relating to the geodesic version; the LM and PO tests can be used if the model is not too curved, preferring a PO if the model is curved locally near the null hypothesis; and, finally, the LR test can be used in any case, but when the model is seriously curved then it appears clearly favourite since it implicitly (and automatically) takes the curvature of the model into account.

References

Amari, S. (1982), 'Differential Geometry of Curved Exponential Familes – Curvatures and Information Loss', *Annals of Statistics*, 10: 357–385.

—— (1983), 'Comparisons of Asymptotically Efficient Tests in Terms of Geometry of Statistical Structures', *Bulletin of the International Statistical Institute*, Proceedings 44 Session, Book, 2, 1.190–1.206.

—— (1985), *Differential-Geometrical Methods in Statistics*, Lecture Notes in Statistics No. 28, Heidelberg: Springer.

Barndorff-Nielsen, O.E. (1978), *Information and Exponential Families in Statistical Theory*, New York: John Wiley.

Barndorff-Nielsen, O.E., D.R. Cox and N. Reid (1986), 'The Role of Differential Geometry in Statistical Theory', *International Statistical Review*, 54: 83–96.

Berenblutt, I.I. and G.I. Webb (1973), 'A New Test for Autocorrelated Errors in the Linear Regression Model', *Journal of the Royal Statistical Society*, Series B, 35: 33–50.

Borges, R. and J. Pfanzagl (1963), 'A Characterization of the One Parameter Exponential Family of Distributions by Monotonicity of Likelihood Ratios', *Zeitschrift der Wahrscheinlichkeitstheorie*, 2: 111–117.

Breusch, T.S. and A.R. Pagan (1980), 'The Lagrange Multiplier Test and Its Applications to Model Specification in Econometrics', *Review of Economic Studies*, 47: 239–253.

Breusch, T.S. and P. Schmidt (1988), 'Alternative Forms of the Wald Test: How Long Is a Piece of String', *Communications in Statistics*, 17: 2789–2795.

Brooks, R. (1993), 'Alternative Point Optimal Tests for Regression Coefficient Stability', *Journal of Econometrics*, 57: 365–376.

Buse, A. (1982), 'The Likelihood Ratio, Wald, and Lagrange Multiplier Tests – An Expository Note', *American Statistician*, 36: 153–157.

Chentsov, N.N. (1982), *Statistical Decision Rules and Optimal Inference*, Translation of Mathematical Monographs vol. 53, Providence, Rhode Island: American Mathematical Society: first published in Russian, 1972.

Cox, D.R. and D.V. Hinkley (1974), *Theoretical Statistics*, London: Chapman & Hall.

Critchley, F., P. Marriott and M. Salmon (1996), 'On the Differential Geometry of the Wald Test with Nonlinear Restrictions', *Econometrica*, 64: 1213–1222.

Davidson, R. (1992), 'The Geometry of the Wald Test', mimeo, Queen's University.

Davies, R.B. (1969), 'Beta-optimal Tests and an Application to the Summary Evaluation of Experiments', *Journal of the Royal Statistical Society*, Series B, 31: 524–538.

(1980), 'Algorithm AS155: The Distribution of a Linear Combination of χ^2 Random Variables', *Applied Statistics*, 29: 323–333.

Efron, B. (1975), 'Defining the Curvature of Statistical Problem (with Applications to Second Order Efficiency) (with Discussion)', *Annals of Statistics*, 3: 1189–1242.

(1978), 'The Geometry of Exponential Families', *Annals of Statistics*, 6: 362–376.

Engle, R.F. (1984), 'Wald, Likelihood Ratio and Lagrange Multiplier Tests in Econometrics', in Z. Griliches and M.D. Intriligator (eds.), *Handbook of Econometrics*, vol. II, Amsterdam: North-Holland, Ch. 13.

Evans, M.A. and M.L. King (1985), 'A Point Optimal Test for Heteroskedastic Disturbances, *Journal of Econometrics*, 27: 163–178.

Garderen, K.J. van (1995), 'Variance Inflation in Curved Exponential Models', Discussion Paper in Economics and Econometrics 9521, University of Southampton.

(1997a), 'Curved Exponential Models in Econometrics', *Econometric Theory*, 13: 771–790.

(1997b), 'Exact Geometry of Explosive Autoregressive Models', CORE Discussion Paper 9768.

Godfrey, L.G. (1988), *Misspecification Tests in Econometrics*, Cambridge: Cambridge University Press.

Gregory, A. and M. Veall (1985), 'On Formulating Wald Tests of Nonlinear Restrictions', *Econometrica*, 53: 1465–1468.

Hillier, G.H. (1990), 'On the Variability of Best Critical Regions and the Curvature of Exponential Models', Working Paper, Department of Econometrics, Monash University, Melbourne.

(1995), 'The Union of Best Critical Regions: Complete Classes, p-Values, and Model Curvature', Discussion Paper in Economics and Econometrics, University of Southampton.

Imhof, P.J. (1961), 'Computing the Distribution of Quadratic Forms in Normal Variables', *Biometrika*, 48: 419–426.

Jeffreys, H. (1939), *Theory of Probability*, Oxford: Clarendon Press.

Kadiyala, K.R. (1970), 'Testing for the Independence of Regression Disturbances', *Econometrica*, 38: 97–117.

King, M.L. (1987), 'Towards a Theory of Point Optimal Testing', *Econometric Reviews*, 6: 169–218.

King, M.L. and P.X. Wu (1994), 'One-sided Hypothesis Testing in Econometrics: A Survey', Working Paper, Department of Econometrics, Monash University, Melbourne.

Kumon, M. and S. Amari (1983), 'Geometrical Theory of Higher-Order Asymptotics of Test, Interval Estimator and Conditional Inference', *Proceedings of the Royal Society of London*, Series A, 387: 429–458.

Lafontaine, F. and K.J. White (1986), 'Obtaining Any Wald Statistic You Want', *Economics Letters*, 21: 35–40.

Lehmann, E.L. (1986), *Testing Statistical Hypotheses*, 2nd edn, New York: Wiley.

Moolgavkar, S.H. and D.J. Venzon (1987), 'Confidence Regions in Curved Exponential Families: Application to Matched Case-control and Survival Studies with General Relative Risk Function', *Annals of Statistics*, 15: 346–359.

Nelson, F.D. and E. Savin (1990), 'On the Dangers of Extrapolating Asymptotic Local Power', *Econometrica*, 58: 977–981.

Okamoto, I., S.-I. Amari and K. Takeuchi (1991), 'Asymptotic Theory of Sequential Estimation: Differential Geometrical Approach', *Annals of Statistics*, 19: 961–981.

Pfanzagl, J. (1968), 'A Characterization of the One Parameter Exponential Family by the Existence of Uniformly Most Powerful Tests', *Sankhyā*, Series A, 30: 147–156.

Phillips, P.C.B. and J.Y. Park (1988), 'On the Formulation of Wald Tests of Nonlinear Restrictions', *Econometrica*, 56: 1065–1083.

Rao, C.R. (1945), 'Information and Accuracy Attainable in the Estimation of Statistical Parameters', *Bulletin of the Calcutta Mathematical Society*, 37: 81–91.

(1949), 'On the Distance between Two Populations', *Sankhyā*, 9: 246–248.

(1987), 'Differential Metrics in Probability Spaces', in S.I. Amari, O.E. Barndorff-Nielsen, R.E. Kass, S.L. Lauritzen and C.R. Rao (eds.), *Differential Geometry in Statistical Inference*, Hayward, Calif.: Institute of Mathematical Statistics, pp. 217–240.

Saikkonen, P. and R. Luukkonen (1993), 'Point Optimal Tests for Testing the Order of Differencing in ARIMA Models', *Econometric Theory*, 9: 343–362.

Silvapulle, P. and M.L. King (1993), 'Non-nested Testing for Autocorrelation in the Linear Regression Model', *Journal of Econometrics*, 58: 295–314.

Væth, M. (1985), 'On the Use of Wald's Tests in Exponential Families', *International Statistical Review*, 53: 199–214.

9 Testing for unit roots in AR and MA models

Thomas J. Rothenberg

In parametric statistical models for weakly dependent data, maximum likelihood estimates are typically root-n consistent and, when standardised, have limiting normal distributions. Likelihood ratio, Wald, and score statistics for testing equality constraints on the parameters have the same limiting distribution under the null hypothesis and lead to tests with the same asymptotic power function for local alternatives. Employing higher-order asymptotic expansions of the distribution functions, one can explain the small-sample departures from the asymptotic results in terms of the statistical curvature of the likelihood function. There exist, however, statistical problems of practical importance where this standard asymptotic theory does not apply. In this chapter, we look at three examples arising in non-stationary time-series analysis: testing for a unit root in a first-order autoregressive model and in two variants of a first-order moving-average model. These three examples have very different likelihood functions, yet have many features in common. In all three cases, power functions resulting from first-order asymptotic analysis are remarkably close to those obtained from second-order asymptotic analysis in the standard case.

The examples analysed here involve one-sided, one-parameter tests in models where there are no nuisance parameters. That is, we assume that the distribution of the data depends on a single unknown parameter θ and consider tests of the null hypothesis $\theta = \bar{\theta}$ against the composite alternative $\theta < \bar{\theta}$. Since there are no nuisance parameters, the null distribution of any test statistic is known; exact critical values can always be computed by simulation. When there are nuisance parameters not specified under the null hypothesis, finding exact (or even approximate) critical values is non-trivial. This added complication is ignored here in order to concentrate on the key issues concerning power.

1   The 'standard' case

Suppose we have n observations generated according to a probability law that depends on an unknown scalar parameter θ. To test the null hypothesis that $\theta = \bar{\theta}$ against the alternative that $\theta < \bar{\theta}$, rejection regions of the form $T_n < t$ are commonly employed, where T_n is a test statistic depending on the data and $\bar{\theta}$; t is a constant critical value such that, under the null hypothesis, $\Pr[T_n < t]$ is equal to the predetermined size of the test. Tests of the same size can be compared by their power: the probability that $T_n < t$ when the null hypothesis is false. We will denote the power of the test based on T_n when the true parameter is θ by $\Pi_T(\theta)$; the size of the test is $\alpha = \Pi_T(\bar{\theta})$.

For arbitrary point $s < \bar{\theta}$ in the parameter space, let $L_n(s)$ denote the log-likelihood of the sample. By the Neyman–Pearson lemma, the best test of the null hypothesis $\theta = \bar{\theta}$ against the point alternative $\theta = s$ rejects when the log-likelihood ratio $L_n(\bar{\theta}) - L(s)$ is small. The power of this size-α NP(s) test when the true parameter is in fact θ will be denoted by $\Pi_{NP}(\theta, s)$. The function $\Pi^*(\theta) \equiv \Pi_{NP}(\theta, \theta)$ is called the power envelope since the power function of the size-α NP(s) test is tangent to Π^* at the point s. The Neyman–Pearson lemma asserts that $\Pi^*(\theta)$ is an upper bound to $\Pi_T(\theta)$ for all tests of size α.

In certain exponential models, it turns out that the power function for the NP(s) test is independent of s; there exists a uniformly most powerful test with power function identically equal to the bound. In most testing problems, even in the one-sided, one-parameter case treated here, the Neyman–Pearson bound is not attainable in finite samples. But it is often attainable asymptotically.

Since only alternatives near the true parameter value are of interest in large samples, it is convenient to reparameterise by writing the true parameter value as $\bar{\theta} - n^{-1/2}\gamma$ and a typical point in the parameter space as $\bar{\theta} - n^{-1/2}c$. We will view γ as the parameter of interest and, when developing local asymptotic approximations, hold γ and c fixed as n tends to infinity. Assuming L_n is three times differentiable, we define the standardised score $S_n(s) \equiv n^{-1/2}\partial L_n(s)/\partial s$, the average Hessian $H_n(s) \equiv n^{-1}\partial^2 L_n(s)/\partial s^2$, and the average third derivative $R_n(s) \equiv n^{-1}\partial^3 L_n(s)/\partial s^3$. By Taylor series we have

$$\frac{L_n(\bar{\theta}) - L_n(\bar{\theta} - n^{1/2}c)}{c} = S_n(\bar{\theta}) - \tfrac{1}{2}H_n(\bar{\theta})c + n^{-1/2}R_n(s^*)c^2, \qquad (1)$$

where s^* lies between $\bar{\theta}$ and $\bar{\theta} - n^{-1/2}c$. In standard cases, $S_n(\bar{\theta})$ converges in distribution to a normal random variable; $H_n(\bar{\theta})$ and $R_n(s^*)$ converge in probability to constants. Thus we find that, to a first order of approximation, the log-likelihood ratio behaves like a linear function of the asymptotically normal sufficient statistic $S_n(\bar{\theta})$. For any $c > 0$, the rejection region based on the likelihood ratio is asymptotically equivalent to rejecting for small values of the score. As n tends to infinity, the power functions tend to $\Phi(t + \sigma\gamma)$, where Φ is the standard normal distribution function, t_α is its α-quantile, and $\sigma^2 = \text{Var}[S_n(\bar{\theta})]$ is the expected information for θ (evaluated at $\bar{\theta}$). The local asymptotic power functions are independent of c and are identical to the asymptotic power envelope.

To a second order of approximation, the log-likelihood ratio is a linear combination of $S_n(\bar{\theta})$ and $H_n(\bar{\theta})$. The loss in power from using only the score depends on the amount of additional information contained in the Hessian. Efron (1975) suggested as a measure of this information the curvature

$$C = n \frac{\text{Var}[H_n] - \dfrac{\text{Cov}^2[H_n, S_n]}{\text{Var}[S_n]}}{\text{Var}^2[S_n]}, \tag{2}$$

where the score and Hessian are evaluating at the true $\bar{\theta}$. Typically, H_n and S_n are asymptotically bivariate normal, so the numerator of C is approximately the conditional variance of H_n given S_n.

Using Edgeworth expansions of their distribution functions, Pfanzagl and Wefelmeyer (1978) develop asymptotic expansions for the local power functions of various likelihood-based test statistics. The exposition here follows that of Cavanagh (1983) and Pfanzagl (1980). Under regularity conditions, the power envelope for tests of size α has the asymptotic expansion

$$\Pi^*(\bar{\theta} - n^{-1/2}\gamma) = \Phi[t_\alpha + \gamma\sigma + n^{-1/2}P(\gamma) + n^{-1}Q(\gamma)] + o(n^{-1}),$$

where P and Q are low-order polynomials depending on the particular likelihood function. The local power function for a typical admissible test has the asymptotic expansion

$$\Pi_T(\bar{\theta} - n^{-1/2}\gamma) = \Phi\left[t_\alpha + \gamma\sigma + n^{-1/2}P(\gamma) + n^{-1}Q(\gamma) \right.$$
$$\left. - \frac{C}{8n}(2\gamma_T t_\alpha + \gamma\sigma)^2\right] + o(n^{-1}), \tag{3}$$

where γ_T is a constant depending on the particular test. For example, the score test has $\gamma_T = 0$; its power curve is tangent to the power envelope at the origin where power is equal to the size α. The Wald test based on the MLE has $\gamma_T = 1$; its power curve is tangent to the power envelope at the point where power is approximately $1 - \alpha$. The maximised likelihood ratio test has $\gamma_T = \frac{1}{2}$; its power curve is tangent to the power envelope at the point where power is approximately one-half.

These power formulae have a simple interpretation in terms of power plots on normal paper. That is, suppose we graph Φ^{-1}(power) against γ. In very large samples one should get a straight line with slope σ. In small samples one will get some curvature from the polynomial terms. The curvature due to P and Q is inherent in the problem and is independent of the particular test statistic. It is captured in the power envelope. The additional curvature due to the particular test statistic is very simple. It is a pure quadratic, tangent to the power envelope, with coefficient equal to Efron's curvature measure.

Although quite elegant, this second-order asymptotic analysis need not be terribly accurate in small samples. Luckily, it can be dispensed with. In our one-parameter problem, the critical value t_α and the power functions $\Pi_T(\theta)$ can always be computed to any degree of accuracy by simulation. Indeed, that is the approach we will use in the non-standard unit-root cases where asymptotic analysis does not lead to analytically convenient approximations to the power functions.

2   The AR(1) model

Inference in autoregressive models with a near-unit root has been studied extensively, following the seminal paper by Dickey and Fuller (1979). Stock (1995) and Banerjee et al. (1993) survey some of the literature. The approach employed here is developed in greater detail in Elliott, Rothenberg and Stock (1996) and Rothenberg and Stock (1997).

Suppose an observed time-series $y_1, \ldots, y_n$ is generated by the first-order autoregression

$$y_t = \theta y_{t-1} + \varepsilon_t \qquad t = 1, \ldots, n, \tag{4}$$

where $y_0 = 0$, θ is an unknown parameter, and the ε's are unobserved i.i.d. normal errors with mean zero and unit variance. We are interested in testing the null hypothesis that $\theta = 1$ against the alternative that $\theta < 1$. Except for an additive constant, the log-likelihood function evaluated at the point s is given by

$$
\begin{aligned}
L_n(s) = &-\frac{1}{2}\sum_{t=1}^{n}(y_t - \theta y_{t-1})^2 = -\frac{1}{2}\sum_{t-1}^{n}[\Delta y_t + (1-s)y_{t-1}]^2 \\
= &-\frac{1}{2}\left[\sum_{t-1}^{n}(\Delta y_t)^2 + 2(1-s)\sum_{t=1}^{n}y_{t-1}\Delta y_t \right. \\
&\left. + (1-s)^2\sum_{t=1}^{n}(y_{t-1})^2\right].
\end{aligned}
\tag{5}
$$

Note that $L_n(s)$ is quadratic in s and that $(\sum y_{t-1} \triangle y_t, \sum (y_{t-1})^2)$ is a pair of sufficient statistics. Again it will be convenient to rewrite the model in terms of a local parameterisation around the null hypothesis value $\bar{\theta} = 1$. Writing the true parameter as $\theta = 1 - n^{-1} \gamma$ and a typical point in the parameter space as $s = 1 - n^{-1} c$, we find

$$\frac{1}{c} [L_n(1) - L_n(1 - n^{-1} c)] = A_n + \frac{1}{2} c B_n \qquad (6)$$

where

$$A_n \equiv \frac{1}{n} \sum_{t=1}^{n} y_{t-1} \triangle y_t, \qquad B_n = \frac{1}{n^2} \sum_{t=1}^{n} (y_{t-1})^2.$$

The log-likelihood ratio (6) looks very much like (1) with the remainder term set to zero. But there are three major differences:

1. To obtain finite stochastic limits, the score term A_n must be scaled by n^{-1} and the Hessian term B_n must be scaled by n^{-2}; hence the reparameterisation in terms of c involves a scaling by n instead of $n^{1/2}$.

2. Even after rescaling by n^2, B_n does not converge to a constant under the null hypothesis; the limiting likelihood ratio depends on the pair of sufficient statistics A_n and B_n.

3. The joint limiting distribution of A_n and B_n is not normal. The actual distribution function does not have a simple analytic representation, but the statistics themselves can be expressed as stochastic integrals of normal processes.

Despite these differences, the Neyman–Pearson theory discussed in section 1 is still applicable. Each member of the family of test statistics defined by (6) is admissible, with power functions tangent to the power envelope. It is only the asymptotic approximations that have to be modified. To describe the limiting behaviour of A_n and B_n, we note that, when $\gamma = n(1 - \theta)$ is fixed and n is large, the discrete time-series $n^{-1/2} y_t$ can be well approximated by a continuous-time process. Let $W(r)$ represent standard Brownian motion defined on $[0,1]$ and let

$$J_\gamma(s) = \int_0^s e^{-\gamma(s-r)} dW(r) \qquad (7)$$

be the Ornstein–Uhlenbeck process that satisfies the stochastic differential equation $dJ_\gamma(s) = -\gamma J_\gamma(s) ds + dW(s)$ with initial condition $J_\gamma(0) = 0$. For s in the unit interval, let $[sn]$ be the largest integer less than sn. Then, for parameter values local to unity such that $\gamma = n(1 - \theta)$ remains constant as n tends to infinity, $n^{-1/2} y_{[sn]} \Rightarrow J_\gamma(s)$ and

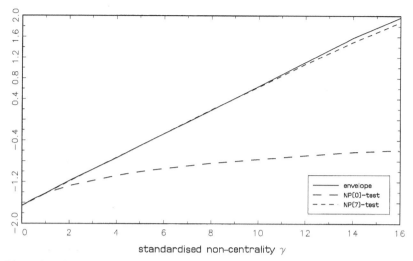

Figure 9.1 Asymptotic power functions for unit AR root (5% level; normal quantile scale)

$$(A_n, B_n) \Rightarrow \left(\tfrac{1}{2}[J_\gamma^2(1) - 1], \int_0^1 J_\gamma^2(s)\, ds \right)$$

where $\Rightarrow$ represent weak convergence (see Chan and Wei (1987) and Stock (1995)). Thus, the power functions for our family of NP tests have the form

$$\Pi_{NP}(\bar\theta - n^{-1}\gamma, \bar\theta - n^{-1}c) = \Pr\left[J_\gamma^2(1) + c \int_0^1 J_\gamma^2(s)\, ds < t(c) \right] + o(1),$$

where $t(c)$ is the appropriate critical value.

Unfortunately, there is no simple analytic expression for the joint distribution function of the pair $(J_\gamma(1), \int J_\gamma^2)$. In practice, it is simplest to compute the power function by simulating the joint distribution of (A_n, B_n) by Monte Carlo draws from the distribution of the ε's. Power functions for the NP(c) test statistics (6) were obtained from 10,000 replications of samples of size 100. The results are plotted in figure 9.1 for $c = 0$ (the score test) and for $c = 7$. In addition, the upper-bound power envelope is also drawn. To simplify comparisons, a normal quantile scale is used; that is, $\Phi^{-1}(\text{power})$ is plotted against γ. Three facts emerge from these calculations (and others not reported here):

1. With normal quantile scale, the power envelope is essentially a straight line with slope 0.24. (Note: the square root of expected information is 0.7.)

2. The Dickey–Fuller t-test (which is the signed maximum likelihood ratio test) behaves almost exactly like the NP(7) test. Their power functions are very close to the power envelope and seem to be tangent to the envelope where power is about one-half.
3. In the family of Neyman–Pearson test statistics (6), the power curves are very similar as long as $2 < c < 30$. The relative weight given to the score and the Hessian does not matter much as long as each gets some weight. The members with very small c have particularly poor power characteristics.

3   The stationary MA(1) model

Suppose the observed time-series $y_1, \ldots, y_n$ was generated by

$$y_t = \varepsilon_t - \theta\varepsilon_{t-1} \qquad t = 1, \ldots, n \tag{8}$$

where the ε's are i.i.d. standard normal variates. To avoid identifiability issues, we shall assume $|\theta| \leq 1$. The problem of testing the null hypothesis $\theta - \bar\theta$ against the alternative that $\theta < \bar\theta$ is standard as long as $|\theta|$ is much less than one. Indeed, the results of section 1 apply whenever $|\bar\theta| < 1$, although the accuracy of the asymptotic approximations will diminish rapidly as $|\bar\theta|$ tends to one. The problem of testing $\theta = 1$, however, is non-standard. Our analysis builds on the work reported by Tanaka (1990), Saikkonen and Luukkonen (1993), and Davis, Chen and Dunsmuir (1995).

Let y be the n-dimensional column vector of the observations. Then, apart from an additive constant, the log-likelihood at parameter value s is

$$L_n(s) = -\tfrac{1}{2}\log|\Omega(s)| - \tfrac{1}{2}y'\Omega(s)^{-1}y, \tag{9}$$

where $\Omega(s) = (1 + s^2)I - sD$ and $D = [d_{ij}]$ is a matrix with $d_{ij} = 1$ when $|i - j| = 1$ and zero otherwise. The characteristic roots of D are $2\cos[\pi j/(n + 1)]$, $j = 1, \ldots, n$. Hence the matrix Ω can be written as $Q'\Lambda Q$ where Q is an orthogonal matrix not depending on s and L is diagonal with typical element $\lambda_j(s) = 1 + s^2 - 2s\cos[\pi j/(n + 1)]$. It follows that $y'\Omega(s)^{-1}y$ can be written as $x'\Lambda(s)^{-1}x$, where the (observable) transformed variable $x = Qy$ has variance matrix $\Lambda(\theta)$. Thus, we can write

$$-2L_n(s) = \sum_{j=1}^{n}\left[\log\lambda_j(s) + \frac{x_j^2}{\lambda_j(s)}\right] = \sum_{j=1}^{n}\left[\log\lambda_j(s) + \frac{\lambda_j(\theta)}{\lambda_j(s)}\eta_j^2\right], \tag{10}$$

where the (unobserved) elements of $\eta = \Lambda(\theta)^{-1/2}Qy$ are i.i.d. standard normal.

When $|\bar{\theta}| < 1$, $L(\bar{\theta}) - L(s)$ can be expanded as in (1) where the remainder term is asymptotically negligible. This does not happen when $\bar{\theta} = 1$. We write the true parameter as $\theta = 1 - n^{-1}\gamma$ and the point alternative as $s = 1 - n^{-1}c$. Then, noting that

$$\lambda_j\left(1 - \frac{\gamma}{n}\right) = 2 - 2\frac{\gamma}{n} + \left(\frac{\gamma}{n}\right)^2 - 2\left(1 - \frac{\gamma}{n}\right)\cos\left(\frac{\pi j}{n+1}\right),$$

we find after considerable algebra that, as n tends to infinity,

$$-2c^{-2}[L_n(1 - n^{-1}c) - L_n(1)]$$

$$\Rightarrow \sum_{j=1}^{\infty}\left[\frac{\pi^2 j^2 + \gamma^2}{\pi^2 j^2 (\pi^2 j^2 + c^2)}\eta_j^2 + \ln\frac{\pi^2 j^2}{\pi^2 j^2 + c^2}\right]. \tag{11}$$

This implies that, asymptotically, the score evaluated at $\theta = 1$ is zero. Hence, the locally best test is based on the Hessian. It is also apparent that the higher-order derivatives of L are not asymptotically negligible. Unlike the standard case discussed in section 1 and the AR unit-root case discussed in section 2, the log-likelihood ratio is not approximately quadratic in the local parameter c. The limiting likelihood ratio depends not on just one or two sufficient statistics but on a continuum of sufficient statistics.

There are no convenient analytic expressions for the distribution functions of the limiting NP(c) statistics defined by (11). Nevertheless, it is easy to simulate the distributions. (The infinite series was truncated after 200 terms.) Figure 9.2 presents the power envelope and the power functions for a few values of c. Again, a normal quantile scale is used. We can draw the following conclusions.

1. With a normal quantile scale, the power envelope has noticeable curvature for small values of g but is approximately linear for large values of g.
2. The power curve for the NP(7) test is very close to the envelope. It is tangent to the power envelope at a point where power is about one-half.
3. In the family of Neyman–Pearson tests of the form (11), the power curves are fairly similar as long as $2 < c < 30$. The members with very small c have somewhat poorer power characteristics.

4   A non-stationary MA model

Suppose the observed time-series $y_1, \ldots, y_n$ was generated by

$$y_t = \varepsilon_t - \theta\varepsilon_{t-1}, \tag{12}$$

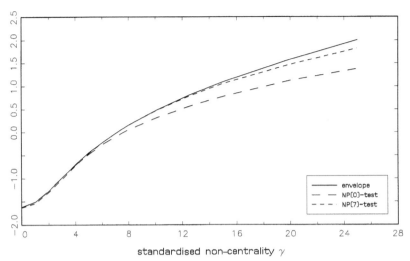

standardised non-centrality γ

Figure 9.2 Asymptotic power functions for unit MA root (stationary model; 5% level; normal quantile scale)

where $\varepsilon_1, \ldots, \varepsilon_n$ are i.i.d. standard normal variates and $\varepsilon_0 = 0$. This model is identical to the one considered in section 3 except for the first observation. When the hypothesised value $\bar{\theta}$ is less than one in absolute value, the modification has no effect to a first order of approximation and has only a trivial effect to second order. When $\bar{\theta} = 1$, the effect is non-negligible even asymptotically.

Note that the joint density for $\varepsilon_1, \ldots, \varepsilon_n$ is proportional to $\exp\{-\frac{1}{2}\sum \varepsilon_t^2\}$. But (12) defines a one-to-one mapping of the ε's to the y's with Jacobian equal to one. Recursively solving for the ε's in terms of the y's, we find that, apart from an additive constant, the log-likelihood function evaluated at parameter value s is

$$L_n(s) = -\frac{1}{2}\sum_{t=1}^{n}\left[\sum_{i=0}^{t-1}s^i y_{t-i}\right]^2. \tag{13}$$

Again we transform into local coordinates, writing the true parameter value as $\theta = 1 - n^{-1}\gamma$ and an arbitrary point is the parameter space as $s = 1 - n^{-1}c$. It is convenient to define the artificial (unobserved) variable

$$x_t^c \equiv \sum_{i=0}^{t-1}(1 - n^{-1}c)^i \varepsilon_{t-i}.$$

Then we find that

$$\sum_{i=0}^{t-1}(1 - n^{-1}c)^{i}y_{t-i} = \sum_{i=0}^{t-1}(1 - n^{-1}c)^{i}(\Delta\varepsilon_{t-i} + \gamma n^{-1}\varepsilon_{t-i})$$

$$= \varepsilon_{t} + n^{-1}(\gamma - c)x_{t}^{c}.$$

Thus we find the log-likelihood ratio for testing $\theta = 1$ against the alternative $\theta = 1 - n^{-1}c$ is given by

$$L_{n}(1) - L_{n}(1 - n^{-1}c) = \frac{1}{2}\sum_{t=1}^{n}\left[\sum_{i=1}^{t-1}s^{i}y_{t-i}\right]^{2} - \frac{1}{2}\sum_{t=1}^{n}\left[\sum_{i=1}^{t-1}y_{t-i}\right]^{2}$$

$$= \frac{1}{2}\sum_{t=1}^{n}[\varepsilon_{t} + n^{-1}(\gamma - c)x_{t-1}^{c}]^{2}$$

$$- \frac{1}{2}\sum_{t=1}^{n}[\varepsilon_{t} + n^{-1}\gamma x_{t-1}^{0}]^{2}. \tag{14}$$

Noting that the process $n^{-1/2}x_{[sn]}^{c}$ converges to the continuous time process $J_{c}(s)$ defined in (6), we find that the likelihood ratio converges to the stochastic integral

$$\tfrac{1}{2}(\gamma^{2} - c^{2})\int_{0}^{1}J_{c}^{2}(s)\,ds - \tfrac{1}{2}\gamma^{2}\int_{0}^{1}J_{0}^{2}(s)\,ds + (\gamma - c)$$

$$\times \int_{0}^{1}J_{c}(s)\,dW(s) - \gamma\int_{0}^{1}J_{0}(s)dW(s). \tag{15}$$

Again, there is a continuum of sufficient statistics asymptotically. Differentiating and evaluating at $c = 0$, we find that the score test statistic has the simple asymptotic representation

$$\lim_{c\to 0}c^{-1}[L_{n}(1) - L_{n}(1 - n^{-1}c)] = \frac{1}{2}\sum_{t=1}^{n}\left[\sum_{i=0}^{t-1}y_{t-1}\right]\left[\sum_{i=0}^{t-1}iy_{t-1}\right]$$

$$\Rightarrow \frac{1}{2} - \frac{1}{2}\left[W(1) + \gamma\int_{0}^{1}W(s)\,ds\right]^{2}. \tag{16}$$

Except for the score statistic, which asymptotically is a linear transform of a chi square, there are no convenient analytic expressions for the distribution functions of the limiting NP(c) statistics defined by (15). Nevertheless, it is easy to simulate the distributions using the representation (13). The sample size n was set at 200 and 10,000 Monte Carlo replications were used. Using a normal quantile scale, figure 9.3 presents

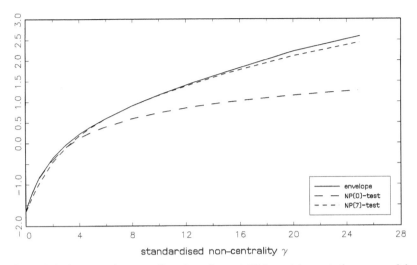

Figure 9.3 Asymptotic power functions for unit MA root (non-stationary model; 5% level; normal quantile scale)

the power envelope and the power functions for a few values of c. We can draw the following conclusions.

1. With a normal quantile scale, the power envelope has strong curvature for small values of γ but is approximately linear for large values of γ.
2. The power curve for the NP(7) test is very close to the envelope. It is tangent to the envelope at a point where power is slightly greater than one-half.
3. In the family of Neyman–Pearson tests of the form (11), the power curves are fairly similar as long as $2 < c < 30$. The members with very small c have much poorer power characteristics.

5   Conclusions

The large-sample power curves and power envelopes for the three 'non-standard' examples presented here look very much like the small-sample power curves and envelopes predicted by second-order theory for 'standard problems'. Although the test statistics themselves are not even close to being normally distributed, the power curves are not very far from looking like normal power curves. Curiously, the NP(7) test seems to behave similarly in all three examples.

For the AR(1) model, van Garderen (1997) shows that Efron curvature, viewed as a function of θ, increases very sharply when θ is near one.

Thus, standard second-order theory seems to explain why the score test of the unit-root hypothesis performs rather badly. The result that the power curve for the maximum likelihood ratio test is tangent to the power envelope at the point where power equals one-half is also consistent with standard second-order theory, although the standard proof is not applicable.

For the MA unit-root problem, it is not so clear that standard asymptotic theory provides any explanation for our empirical findings. In particular, Efron curvature is not a very useful measure in these models. When $\theta = 1$, all the derivatives of the log-likelihood are the same order of magnitude, so it does not seem useful to concentrate only on the first two. The results presented here cannot be viewed as a solution to the problem of explaining the behaviour of tests in non-standard situations. Rather they are really just a description of some of the facts that have to be explained.

References

Banerjee, A., J.J. Dolado, J.W. Galbraith and D. Hendry (1993), *Cointegration, Error Correction, and Econometric Analysis of Nonstationary Data*, Oxford: University Press.

Cavanagh, C.L. (1983), 'Hypothesis Testing in Models with Discrete Dependent Variables', Ph.D. thesis, University of California.

Chan, N.H. and C.Z. Wei (1987), 'Asymptotic Inference for Nearly Nonstationary AR(1) Processes', *Annals of Statistics*, 15: 1050–1063.

Davis, R., M. Chen and W. Dunsmuir (1995), 'Inference for MA(1) Process with a Root on or near the Unit Circle', *Probability and Mathematical Statistics*, 15: 227–242.

Dickey, D. and W. Fuller (1979), 'Distribution of the Estimators for Autoregressive Time Series with a Unit Root', *Journal of the American Statistical Association*, 74: 427–431.

Efron, B. (1975), 'Defining the Curvature of a Statistical Problem', *Annals of Statistics*, 3: 1189–1242

Elliott, G., T. Rothenberg and J. Stock (1996), 'Efficient Tests for an Autoregressive Unit Root', *Econometrica*, 64: 813–836.

Garderen, K. van (1997), 'Exact Geometry of Explosive Autoregressive Models', unpublished working paper.

Pfanzagl, J. (1980), 'Asymptotic Expansions in Parametric Statistical Theory', in P. R. Krishnaiah (ed.), *Developments in Statistics*, vol. 3, New York: Academic Press.

Pfanzagl, J. and W. Wefelmeyer (1978), 'An Asymptotically Complete Class of Tests', *Zeitschrift für Wahrscheinlichkeitstheorie*, 45: 49–72.

Rothenberg, T.J. and J. Stock (1997), 'Inference in a Nearly Integrated Autoregressive Model with Nonnormal Innovations', *Journal of Econometrics*, 80: 269–286.

Saikkonen P. and R. Luukkonen (1993), 'Point Optimal Tests for Testing the Order of Differencing in ARIMA Models', *Econometric Theory*, 9: 343–362.

Stock, J. (1995), 'Unit Roots, Structural Breaks, and Trends', in R. Engle and D. McFadden (eds.), *The Handbook of Econometrics*, vol. 4, Amsterdam: North-Holland.

Tanaka, T. (1990), 'Testing for a Moving Average Unit Root', *Econometric Theory*, 6: 433–444.

10 An elementary account of Amari's expected geometry

Frank Critchley, Paul Marriott and Mark Salmon

Differential geometry has found fruitful application in statistical inference. In particular, Amari's (1990) expected geometry is used in higher-order asymptotic analysis and in the study of sufficiency and ancillarity. However, we can see three drawbacks to the use of a differential geometric approach in econometrics and statistics more generally. First, the mathematics is unfamiliar and the terms involved can be difficult for the econometrician to appreciate fully. Secondly, their statistical meaning can be less than completely clear. Finally, the fact that, at its core, geometry is a visual subject can be obscured by the mathematical formalism required for a rigorous analysis, thereby hindering intuition. All three drawbacks apply particularly to the differential geometric concept of a non-metric affine connection.

The primary objective of this chapter is to attempt to mitigate these drawbacks in the case of Amari's expected geometric structure on a full exponential family. We aim to do this by providing an elementary account of this structure that is clearly based statistically, accessible geometrically and visually presented.

Statistically, we use three natural tools: the score function and its first two moments with respect to the true distribution. Geometrically, we are largely able to restrict attention to tensors; in particular, we are able to avoid the need formally to define an affine connection. To emphasise the visual foundation of geometric analysis we parallel the mathematical development with graphical illustrations using important examples of full exponential families. Although the analysis is not restricted to this case, we emphasise one-dimensional examples so that simple pictures can

This work has been partially supported by ESRC grant 'Geodesic Inference, Encompassing and Preferred Point Geometry in Econometrics' (Grant Number R000232270).

be used to illustrate the underlying geometrical ideas and aid intuition. It turns out that this account also sheds some new light on the choice of parameterisation as discussed by Amari (1990), extending earlier work by Bates and Watts (1980, 1981), Hougaard (1982) and Kass (1984). There are also a number of points of contact between our presentation and Firth (1993).

A key feature of our account is that all expectations and induced distributions are taken with respect to one fixed distribution, namely, that assumed to give rise to the data. This is the so-called preferred point geometrical approach developed in Critchley, Marriott and Salmon (1993, 1994), on whose results we draw where appropriate.

Our hope is that the following development will serve to broaden interest in an important and developing area. For a more formal but still readable treatment of differential geometry, see Dodson and Poston (1977). For broader accounts of the application of differential geometry to statistics, see the review chapters or monographs by Barndorff-Nielsen, Cox and Reid (1986), Kass (1987, 1989), Amari (1990) and Murray and Rice (1993).

The chapter is organised as follows. The elementary prerequisites are established in section 1. The key elements of Amari's expected geometry of general families of distributions are briefly and intuitively reviewed in section 2. In particular, his α-connections are discussed in terms of the characteristic statistical properties of their associated affine parameterisations. Section 3 contains our account of this geometry in the full exponential family case, as outlined above, and section 4 considers the effect of changing the sample size.

1   Preliminaries

1.1   The general framework

Let

$$M = \{p(x, \theta) : \theta \in \Theta\}$$

be a p-dimensional parametric family of probability (density) functions. The available data $\mathbf{x} = (x_1, \ldots, x_n)^T$ is modelled as a random sample from some unknown true distribution $p(x, \phi) \in M$. Let the parameter space Θ be an open connected subset of $\mathbf{R}^p$. The family M is regarded as a manifold, with the parameter θ playing the role of a coordinate system on it. Formally, certain regularity conditions are entailed. These are detailed in Amari (1990, p. 16).

1.2   The score function

The score function

$$s(\theta, \mathbf{x}) = \left(\frac{\partial}{\partial \theta^1} \ln p(\mathbf{x}, \theta), \ldots, \frac{\partial}{\partial \theta^p} \ln p(\mathbf{x}, \theta) \right)^T$$

is very natural to work with statistically as it contains precisely all the relevant information in the likelihood function. Integrating over Θ recovers the log-likelihood function, l, up to an additive constant which is independent of θ. This is equivalent to the likelihood up to a multiplicative positive factor which may depend on $\mathbf{x}$ but not on θ. As discussed by Cox and Hinkley (1974, p. 12), two different choices of the constant do not affect the essential likelihood information, which we refer to as the shape of the likelihood. Visually, the graph of the score function displays the shape of the likelihood in a natural and direct way. We use this to advantage later.

The score function is also a very natural tool to work with geometrically. An important concept of differential geometry is that of the tangent space. We can avoid the general abstract definition here as we have a concrete representation of this space in terms of the score function. Regarding $\mathbf{x}$ now as a random vector and following Amari (1990), we identify the tangent space TM_θ at each fixed $p(\mathbf{x}, \theta) \in M$ with the vector space of random variables spanned by

$$\{s_i(\theta, \mathbf{x}) = \frac{\partial}{\partial \theta^i} \ln p(\mathbf{x}, \theta) : i = 1, \ldots, p\}.$$

Under the regularity conditions referenced in section 2.3 of chapter 1, this vector space has dimension p, the dimension of M.

1.3   Distribution of the score vector

Naturally associated with each fixed tangent space TM_θ is the joint distribution ρ_θ^ϕ of the components of the score vector $s(\theta, \mathbf{x})$. This may be known analytically but can always, by the central limit theorem, be approximated asymptotically by the multivariate normal distribution $N_p(\mu^\phi(\theta), g^\phi(\theta))$, where

$$\mu^\phi(\theta) = \mathbf{E}_{p(x,\phi)}[s(\theta, \mathbf{x})] = n\mathbf{E}_{p(x,\phi)}[s(\theta, x)]$$

and

$$g^\phi(\theta) = \mathrm{Cov}_{p(x,\phi)}[s(\theta, \mathbf{x})] = n\mathrm{Cov}_{p(x,\phi)}[s(\theta, x)].$$

These last two quantities are statistically natural tools that we shall employ in our account of Amari's geometry. The matrix $g^\phi(\theta)$ is assumed to be always positive definite.

Note that, for all ϕ,

$$\mu^\phi(\phi) = 0 \quad \text{and} \quad g^\phi(\phi) = I(\phi) = ni(\phi),$$

where I and i denote the Fisher information for the sample and for a single observation, respectively.

For later use we define the random vector $\epsilon^\phi(\theta, \mathbf{x})$ by the decomposition

$$s(\theta, \mathbf{x}) = \mu^\phi(\theta) + \epsilon^\phi(\theta, \mathbf{x})$$

so that $\mathbf{E}_{p(x,\phi)}[\epsilon^\phi(\theta, \mathbf{x})]$ vanishes identically in θ and ϕ.

In the one-dimensional case there is a particularly useful graphical representation of the three tools on which our account is based. For a particular realisation of the data $\mathbf{x}$, the plot of the graph of $s(\theta, \mathbf{x})$ against θ can give great insight into the shape of the observed likelihood function. We call this graph the observed plot. Together with this we use the expected plot. This is a graph of the true mean score together with an indication of variability. We make extensive use of this graphical method for several important examples below.

1.4   Reparameterisation

So far, we have worked in a single parameterisation θ. It is important to consider what happens under a reparameterisation.

We consider reparameterisations $\theta \to \xi(\theta)$ that are smooth and invertible. Define

$$B_i^\alpha(\theta) = \frac{\partial \xi^\alpha}{\partial \theta^i} \quad \text{and} \quad \bar{B}_\alpha^i(\xi) = \frac{\partial \theta^i}{\partial \xi^\alpha},$$

for $1 \le i, \alpha \le p$. By the chain rule, the components of the score vector transform as 1-tensors. That is:

$$s_\alpha(\xi(\theta), \mathbf{x}) := \frac{\partial l}{\partial \xi^\alpha} = \sum_{i=1}^{p} \bar{B}_\alpha^i(\xi(\theta))\frac{\partial l}{\partial \theta^i} := \sum_{i=1}^{p} \bar{B}_\alpha^i(\theta)s_i(\theta, \mathbf{x}) \tag{1}$$

for each fixed θ. This amounts to a change of basis for the vector space TM_θ. By linearity of expectation, the components of $\mu^\phi(\theta)$ are also 1-tensors. That is:

$$\mu_\alpha^{\xi(\phi)}(\xi(\theta)) = \sum_{i=1}^{p} \bar{B}_\alpha^i(\theta)\mu_i^\phi(\theta). \tag{2}$$

As covariance is a bilinear form, we see that $g^\phi(\theta)$ is a 2-tensor. That is, its components transform according to:

$$g_{\alpha\beta}^{\xi(\phi)}(\xi(\theta)) = \sum_{i=1}^{p}\sum_{j=1}^{p} \bar{B}_\alpha^i(\theta)\bar{B}_\beta^j(\theta)g_{ij}^\phi(\theta). \tag{3}$$

By symmetry, the assumption of positive definiteness, and since $g^\phi(\theta)$ varies smoothly with θ, $g^\phi(\theta)$ fulfils the requirements of a metric tensor (see Amari (1990), p. 25). It follows at once, putting $\theta = \phi$, that the Fisher information also enjoys this property.

In parallel with this tensor analysis, plotting the observed and expected plots for different parameterisations of the model can be extremely useful in conveying the effects of reparameterisation on the shape of the likelihood and the statistical properties of important statistics such as the maximum likelihood estimate (MLE). The question of parameterisation is therefore an important choice that has to be taken in statistical analysis.

2   Some elements of Amari's expected geometry

2.1   Connections

Formally, Amari's expected geometry is a triple (M, I, ∇^{+1}) in which M is a family of probability (density) functions and I the Fisher information metric tensor, as described above. The major difficulty in understanding revolves around the third component, ∇^{+1}, which is a particular non-metric affine connection. In section 3 we obtain a simple, statistical interpretation of it in the full exponential family case. Here we note certain facts concerning connections and Amari's geometry, offering intuitive explanations and descriptions where possible. For a formal treatment, see Amari (1990). We emphasise that such a treatment is not required here, as our later argument proceeds in terms of the elementary material already presented.

A connection allows us to (covariantly) differentiate tangent vectors and, more generally, tensors (see Dodson and Poston (1977), chapter 7). A connection therefore determines which curves in a manifold shall be called 'geodesic' or 'straight'. Generalising familiar Euclidean ideas, these are defined to be those curves along which the tangent vector does not change.

A metric tensor induces in a natural way an associated connection called the Levi–Civita or metric connection. In Amari's structure the Fisher information I induces the affine connection denoted by ∇^0. The Levi–Civita connection has the property that its geodesics are curves of

minimum length joining their endpoints. No concept of length is associated with the geodesics corresponding to non-metric connections.

Amari shows that the two connections ∇^0 and ∇^{+1} can be combined to
produce an entire one-parameter family $\{\nabla^\alpha : \alpha \in \mathbf{R}\}$ of connections,
called the α-connections. The most important connections statistically
correspond to $\alpha = 0, \pm\frac{1}{3}, \pm 1$, as we now explain.

2.2   Choice of parameterisation

For each of Amari's connections it can happen that a parameterisation θ
of M exists such that the geodesic joining the points labelled θ_1 and θ_2
simply consists of the points labelled $\{(1 - \lambda)\theta_1 + \lambda\theta_2 : 0 \leq \lambda \leq 1\}$. For
example, Cartesian coordinates define such a parameterisation in the
Euclidean case. When this happens, M is said to be flat, such a parameterisation is called affine, and the parameters are unique up to affine
equivalence. That is, any two affine parameterisations are related by a
non-singular affine transformation. In the important special case of a
metric connection, M is flat if and only if there exists a parameterisation
θ in which the metric tensor is independent of θ.

For a connection to admit an affine parameterisation is a rather
special circumstance. When it does, we may expect the affine parameterisation to have correspondingly special properties. This is indeed
the case with Amari's expected geometry. When an α-connection has
this property, the manifold is called α-flat and the associated parameterisations are called α-affine. Amari (1990, Theorem 5.12, p. 152),
established the following characteristic features of certain α-affine parameterisations:

1. $\alpha = 1$ corresponds to the natural parameter, θ.
2. $\alpha = \frac{1}{3}$ corresponds to the normal likelihood parameter.
3. $\alpha = 0$ gives a constant asymptotic covariance of the MLE.
4. $\alpha = -\frac{1}{3}$ gives zero asymptotic skewness of the MLE.
5. $\alpha = -1$ gives zero asymptotic bias of the MLE.

These correspond to the $\delta = 0, \frac{1}{3}, \frac{1}{2}, \frac{2}{3}, 1$ parameterisations, respectively, of
Hougaard (1982), who studied the one-dimensional curved exponential
family case. In any one-dimensional family an α-affine parameter exists
for every α. A full exponential family, of any dimension, is always $+1$-
flat and -1-flat, with the natural and mean value parameters, respectively, being affine. Amari (1990) also established the duality result that
M is α-flat if and only if it is $-\alpha$-flat. This duality between ∇^α and $\nabla^{-\alpha}$
has nice mathematical properties but has not been well understood
statistically.

3   The expected geometry of the full exponential family

3.1   Introduction

We restrict attention now to the full exponential family. In the natural parameterisation, θ, we have

$$p(x, \theta) = \exp\left\{\sum_{i=1}^{p} t_i(x)\theta^i - \psi(\theta)\right\}.$$

The mean value parameterisation is given by $\eta = (\eta^1, \ldots, \eta^p)$, where

$$\eta^i(\theta) = \mathbb{E}_{p(x,\theta)}[t_i(x)] = \frac{\partial \psi}{\partial \theta^i}(\theta).$$

These two parameterisations are therefore affinely equivalent if and only if ψ is a quadratic function of θ, as with the case of normal distributions with constant covariance. As we shall see, this is a very special circumstance.

In natural parameters, the score function is

$$s_i(\theta, \mathbf{x}) = n\left\{\bar{t}_i(\mathbf{x}) - \frac{\partial \psi}{\partial \theta^i}(\theta)\right\} = n\{\bar{t}_i(\mathbf{x}) - \eta^i(\theta)\}, \tag{4}$$

where $n\bar{t}_i(\mathbf{x}) = \sum_{r=1}^{n} t_i(x_r)$. From (4) we have the useful fact that the maximum likelihood estimator $\hat{\eta}^i := \eta^i(\hat{\theta}) = \bar{t}_i$. Further, the first two moments of the score function under $p(x, \phi)$ are given by

$$\mu^{\phi}{}_i(\theta) = n\left\{\frac{\partial \psi}{\partial \theta^i}(\phi) - \frac{\partial \psi}{\partial \theta^i}(\theta)\right\} = n\{\eta^i(\phi) - \eta^i(\theta)\} \tag{5}$$

$$g^{\phi}{}_{ij}(\theta) = n\frac{\partial^2 \psi}{\partial \theta^i \partial \theta^j}(\phi) = I_{ij}(\phi). \tag{6}$$

3.2   Examples

The following one-dimensional examples are used for illustrative purposes: Poisson, normal with constant (unit) variance, exponential and Bernoulli.

Although, of course, the sample size affects the ϕ-distribution of $\bar{t}$, it enters the above equations for the score and its first two moments only as a multiplicative constant. Therefore our analysis, which is based solely on these quantities, is essentially invariant under independent repeated samples. Our third and fourth examples implicitly cover the gamma and binomial families and together, then, these examples embrace most

Table 10.1. *One-dimensional examples: Poisson, normal, exponential and Bernoulli*

	Poisson (θ) (Figure 10.1)	Normal $(\theta, 1)$ (Figure 10.2)	Exponential (θ) (Figure 10.3)	Bernoulli (θ) (Figure 10.4)
$t(x)$	x	x	$-x$	x
$\psi(\theta)$	e^{θ}	$\frac{1}{2}\theta^2$	$-\ln\theta$	$\ln(1+e^{\theta})$
$s(\theta, \mathbf{x})$	$n(\bar{x}-e^{\theta})$	$n(\bar{x}-\theta)$	$n(-\bar{x}+\theta^{-1})$	$n[\bar{x}-e^{\theta}(1+e^{\theta})^{-1}]$
$\mu^{\phi}(\theta)$	$n(e^{\phi}-e^{\theta})$	$n(\phi-\theta)$	$n(-\phi^{-1}+\theta^{-1})$	$n\dfrac{e^{\phi}}{1+e^{\phi}}-n\dfrac{e^{\theta}}{1+e^{\theta}}$
$g^{\phi}(\theta)$	ne^{ϕ}	n	$n\phi^{-2}$	$ne^{\phi}(1+e^{\phi})^{-2}$
$\xi(\theta)$	$\eta(\theta)=e^{\theta}$	$\theta^{1/3}$	$\eta(\theta)=-\theta^{-1}$	$\eta(\theta)=e^{\theta}(1+e^{\theta})^{-1}$
$\bar{B}(\theta)$	ξ^{-1}	$3\xi^2$	ξ^{-2}	$[\xi(1-\xi)]^{-1}$
$s(\xi, \mathbf{x})$	$n(\bar{x}-\xi)\xi^{-1}$	$3n(\bar{x}-\xi^3)\xi^2$	$-n(\bar{x}+\xi)\xi^{-2}$	$n(\bar{x}-\xi)[\xi(1-\xi)]^{-1}$
$\mu^{\xi(\phi)}(\xi)$	$n[\xi(\phi)-\xi]\xi^{-1}$	$3n[\xi^3(\phi)-\xi^3]\xi^2$	$n[\xi(\phi)-\xi]\xi^{-2}$	$n\dfrac{[\xi(\phi)-\xi]}{[\xi(1-\xi)]}$
$g^{\xi(\phi)}(\xi)$	$n\xi(\phi)\xi^{-2}$	$9n\xi^4$	$n\xi(\phi)^2\xi^{-4}$	$n\dfrac{\xi(\phi)[1-\xi(\phi)]}{[\xi(1-\xi)]^2}$
ϕ	0	0	1	0
n	10	10	10	10

of the distributions widely used in generalised linear models (McCullagh and Nelder, 1989).

The examples are summarised algebraically in table 10.1, and are displayed visually in figures 10.1 to 10.4, respectively. For each example, for a chosen ϕ and n shown in table 10.1, we give observed and expected plots, both in the natural parameterisation θ and in a non-affinely equivalent parameterisation $\xi(\theta)$.

We take $\xi(\theta)$ to be the mean value parameter $\eta(\theta)$ except in the normal case, where we take $\xi(\theta)=\theta^{\frac{1}{3}}$. We use this last parameterisation for illustration only, even though it is not invertible at $\theta=0$. In each case, ξ is an increasing function of θ. In the expected plots, we illustrate the first two moments of the score function under the true distribution (that is, under $p(x, \phi)$) by plotting the mean ± 2 standard deviations. In the observed plots, to give some idea of sampling variability, we plot five observed score functions corresponding to the 5%, 25%, 50%, 75% and 95% points of the true distribution of $\bar{t}$ for the continuous families and the closest observable points to these in the discrete cases. Recall that these

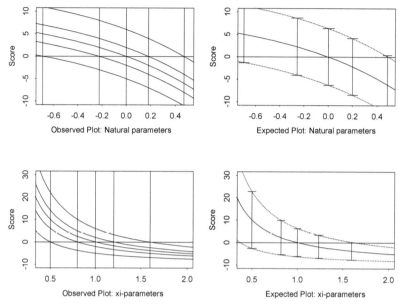

Figure 10.1 One-dimensional Poisson example

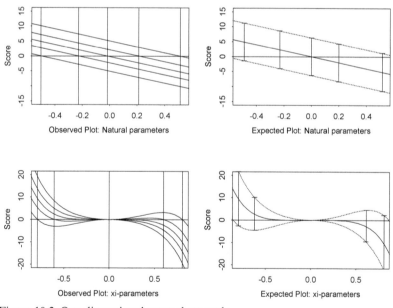

Figure 10.2 One-dimensional normal example

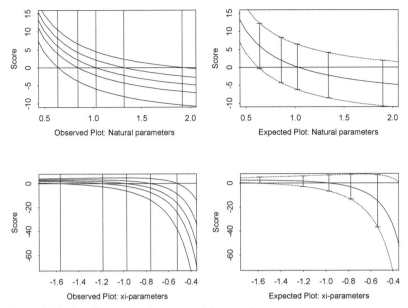

Figure 10.3 One-dimensional exponential example

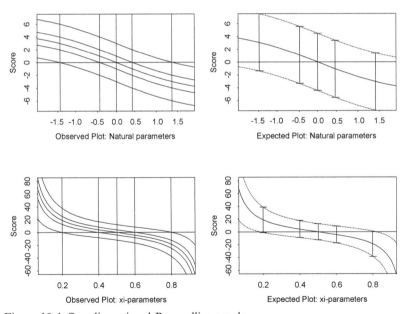

Figure 10.4 One-dimensional Bernoulli example

plots precisely contain the shape of the observed and expected likelihood functions and thus are a direct and visual representation of important statistical information.

The observed score graphs do not cross since, for each fixed parameter value, the observed score function is a non-decreasing affine function of $\bar{t}$. This holds in all parameterisations, using (1). From (1), (2), (4) and (5) it is clear that, in any parameterisation, the graph of the true mean score function coincides with that of the observed score for data where $\bar{t}(\mathbf{x})$ equals its true mean $\eta(\phi)$. In the examples, the true distribution of $n\bar{t}$ is given by Poisson($\phi + \ln n$), normal($n\phi, n$), gamma(ϕ, n) and binomial(n, ϕ), respectively.

The most striking feature of the plots is the constancy of the variance of the score across the natural parameterisation, and the fact that this property is lost in the alternative parameterisation. Also remarkable is the linearity of the normal plots in the natural parameterisation. A close inspection reveals that for each example, in the natural parameterisation, each of the observed plots differs by only a vertical translation. Again this property will not hold in a general parameterisation. We use these and other features of the plots to better understand Amari's expected geometry.

Certain information is evident from the plots straight away. Under standard regularity conditions, the unique maximum likelihood estimate of a parameter for given data occurs when the graph of the corresponding observed score function crosses the horizontal axis from above. Thus, as $\bar{t} = \hat{\eta}$ in our examples (even in the degenerate Bernoulli case), these five crossing points are the 5%, 25%, 50%, 75% and 95% points of the true distribution of the maximum likelihood estimate. The position of these five crossing points gives visual information about this distribution, in particular about its location, variance and skewness.

Of more direct relevance to our present concern is the fact that, in these one-dimensional cases, there is a straightforward visual representation of the tangent space at each point. TM_θ can be identified with the vertical line through θ, and ρ_θ^ϕ with the distribution of the intersection of this line with the graph of the observed score function. Identical remarks apply in any parameterisation. These tangent spaces are shown in both parameterisations, at the above five percentage points of the maximum likelihood estimator, as lines in the observed plots and as vertical bars in the expected plots.

In the observed plot, the five intersection points with any given tangent space TM_θ are the five corresponding percentage points of ρ_θ^ϕ. The same is true in any increasing reparameterisation ξ. Thus, comparing the position of these five intersection points at corresponding parameter values in the two observed plots gives direct visual information on the difference between ρ_θ^ϕ and $\rho_{\xi(\theta)}^{\xi(\phi)}$; in particular, on changes in skewness. The observed plots also show very clearly that, as the natural parameter varies, the true distribution of the score changes only in its location, whereas this is not so in a general parameterisation.

This brings to light a certain natural duality between the maximum likelihood estimator and the score function. Consider the observed plots in the natural and mean value parameterisations. For any given point consider its corresponding tangent space TM_θ and $TM_{\eta(\theta)}$ in the two plots. In each plot we have five horizontal and five vertical crossing points, as above, giving information about the distribution of the maximum likelihood estimator and the score function respectively in the same parameterisation. Now, these two plots are far from independent. As $\hat{\eta}(\mathbf{x}) = \eta(\theta) + n^{-1}s(\theta, \mathbf{x})$, the horizontal crossing points in the mean parameter plot are just an affine transformation of the vertical crossing points in the natural parameter plot. The converse is true asymptotically. As we discuss below, this simple and natural duality between the maximum likelihood estimator and the score function corresponds with the duality present in Amari's expected geometry.

3.3   Amari's + 1-geometry

The above one-dimensional plots have already indicated two senses in which the natural parameterisation is very special. We note here that this is so generally. Our analysis then provides a simple statistical interpretation of Amari's + 1-connection.

From (4) we see that in the natural parameterisation the score function has the form of a stochastic part, independent of θ, plus a deterministic part, independent of the data. Recalling (1) and (4) we see that this property is lost in a non-affine reparameterisation ξ, since $\bar{B}(\theta)$ $(:= \bar{B}_1^1(\theta))$ is independent of θ if and only if ξ is an affine transformation of θ. An equivalent way to describe this property is that the 'error term' $\epsilon^\phi(\theta, \mathbf{x})$ in the mean value decomposition of $s(\theta, \mathbf{x})$ defined at the end of section 1.3 is independent of θ. Or again, as $\mu^\phi(\phi)$ vanishes, that this decomposition has the form

$$s(\theta, \mathbf{x}) = \mu^\phi(\theta) + s(\phi, \mathbf{x}). \tag{7}$$

Note that ρ_θ^ϕ differs from $\rho_{\theta'}^\phi$ only by the translation $\mu^\phi(\theta) - \mu^\phi(\theta')$. In this parameterisation, from one sample to the next, the whole graph of the observed score function just shifts vertically about its ϕ-expectation by the same amount $s(\phi, \mathbf{x})$.

As a consequence of (7), the ϕ-covariance of the score function is independent of θ (and therefore coincides with $g^\phi(\phi) = I(\phi)$). But $g^\phi(\theta)$ is a metric tensor (section 1.4) and, in this parameterisation, the metric is constant across all tangent spaces. Recalling section 2.2, we note that if a metric is constant in a parameterisation then the parameterisation is affine for the metric connection. All tangent spaces thus have the same geometric structure and differ only by their choice of origin. For more details on this geometric idea of flatness, see Dodson and Poston (1977).

The metric connection is the natural geometric tool for measuring the variation of a metric tensor in any parameterisation. But Critchley, Marriott and Salmon (1994) prove that, in the full exponential family, the metric connection induced by $g^\phi(\theta)$ coincides with Amari's $+1$-connection. Thus we have the simple statistical interpretation that ∇^{+1} is the natural geometric measure of the non-constancy of the covariance of the score function in an arbitrary parameterisation. In the one-dimensional case, the $+1$-connection measures the variability of variance of the observed score across different points of M. Looking again at figures 10.1 to 10.4 we see a visual representation of this fact in that the ± 2 standard deviation bars on the expected plot are of a constant length for the θ-parameterisation, and this does not hold in the non-affine ξ-parameterisation.

3.4   Amari's 0-geometry

The fact that in the natural parameterisation all the observed score functions have the same shape invites interpretation. From (7) we see that the common information conveyed in all of them is that conveyed by their ϕ-mean. What is it?

The answer is precisely the Fisher information for the family. This is clear since μ^ϕ determines I via

$$I_{ij}(\theta) = -\frac{\partial \mu_j^\phi}{\partial \theta^i}(\theta),$$

while the converse is true by integration, noting that $\mu^\phi(\phi) = 0$. Thus, in natural parameters, knowing the Fisher information at all points is equivalent to knowing the true mean of the score function (and hence all the observed score functions up to their stochastic shift term). In particular, in the one-dimensional case, the Fisher information is conveyed visually by minus the slope of the graph of $\mu^\phi(\theta)$ as, for example, in the natural parameter expected plots of figures 10.1 to 10.4.

Amari uses the Fisher information as his metric tensor. It is important to note that, when endowed with the corresponding metric connection, an exponential family is not in general flat. That is, there does not, in general, exist any parameterisation in which the Fisher information is constant. The multivariate normal distributions with constant covariance matrix and any one-dimensional family are notable exceptions. In the former case, the natural parameters are affine. In the latter case, using (3), the affine parameters are obtained as solutions to the equation

$$\left(\frac{\partial\theta}{\partial\xi}(\theta)\right)^2 \psi''(\theta) = \text{constant}.$$

For example, in the Poisson family where $\psi(\theta) = \exp(\theta)$ one finds $\xi(\theta) = \exp(\theta/2)$, as in Hougaard (1982).

Thus far we have seen that, in the case of the full exponential family, the fundamental components of Amari's geometry (M, I, ∇^{+1}) can be simply and naturally understood in terms of the first two moments of the score function under the distribution assumed to give rise to the data. I is defined by the true mean, and ∇^{+1} by I and the true covariance. Further, they can be understood visually in terms of the expected plots in our one-dimensional examples. We now go on to comment on duality and choice of parameterisation.

3.5   Amari's -1-geometry and duality

The one-dimensional plots above have already indicated a natural duality between the score vector and the maximum likelihood estimator, and that there is a natural statistical curvature, even in the one-dimensional case, unless the manifold is *totally flat*; that is, unless the graph of the true mean score function is linear in the natural parameterisation. We develop these remarks here.

Amari (1990) shows that the mean value parameters

$$\eta(\theta) = \mathbf{E}_{p(x,\theta)}[t(x)] = \psi'(\theta)$$

are -1-affine and therefore, by his general theory, duality related to the natural $+1$-affine parameters θ. We offer the following simple and direct statistical interpretation of this duality. We have,

$$\hat{\eta} = \eta(\theta) + n^{-1}s(\theta, \mathbf{x}).$$

Expanding $\theta(\hat{\eta})$ to first order about η gives an asymptotic converse

$$\hat{\theta} \doteq \theta + n^{-1}\bar{B}(\theta)s(\theta, \mathbf{x}) = \theta + n^{-1}s(\eta, \mathbf{x}),$$

the right-hand equality following from (1) and where we use $\doteq$ to denote first-order asymptotic equivalence. Note that $\bar{B}(\theta) = i^{-1}(\theta)$. Thus the duality between the $+1$ and -1 connections can be seen as the above strong and natural asymptotic correspondence between the maximum likelihood estimator in one parameterisation and the score function in another. In fact this simple statistical interpretation of Amari's duality is not restricted to the full exponential family (see Critchley, Marriott and Salmon (1994)). It is established formally in a more general case than $+1$ duality here in section 3.7.

3.6   Total flatness and choice of parameterisation

The above approximation to $\hat{\theta}$ is exact when θ and η are affinely equivalent. In this case, $\hat{\theta}$ and $\hat{\eta}$ are in the same affine relationship and so their distributions have the same shape. In particular, as normality is preserved under affine transformations, these distributions are as close to normality as each other whatever the definition of closeness that is used. In the case where M is a constant covariance normal family, $\hat{\theta}$ and $\hat{\eta}$ are both exactly normally distributed.

Affine equivalence of θ and η is a very strong property. When it holds, much more is true. It is the equivalent in the full exponential family case of the general geometric notion of total flatness defined and studied in Critchley, Marriott and Salmon (1993). Recall that the natural parameterisation θ has already been characterised by the fact that the true covariance of the score function is constant in it. Total flatness entails this same parameterisation simultaneously has other nice properties. It is easy to show the following equivalences:

θ and η are affinely equivalent

$\Longleftrightarrow$ ψ is a quadratic function of θ

$\Longleftrightarrow$ $I(\theta)$ is constant in the natural parameters

$\Longleftrightarrow$ $\mu^\phi(\theta)$ is an affine function of θ

$\Longleftrightarrow$ $\exists \alpha \neq \beta$ with $\nabla^\alpha = \nabla^\beta$

$\Longleftrightarrow$ $\forall \alpha, \forall \beta, \quad \nabla^\alpha = \nabla^\beta$

$\Longleftrightarrow$ the θ parameterisation is α-affine for all α

(see Critchley, Marriott and Salmon (1993)). In particular, the maximum likelihood estimators of any α-affine parameters are all equally close (in any sense) to normality.

It is exceptional for a family M to be totally flat. Constant covariance multivariate normal families are a rare example. In totally flat manifolds the graph of $\mu^\phi(\theta)$ is linear in the natural parameterisation, as remarked upon in the one-dimensional normal example of figure 10.2. More usually, even in the one-dimensional case, a family M of probability (density) functions will exhibit a form of curvature evidenced by the non-linearity of the graph of $\mu^\phi(\theta)$.

Recall that the graph of $\mu^\phi(\theta)$ enables us to connect the distribution of $\hat{\theta}$ and $\hat{\eta}$. In the natural parameterisation θ, each observed graph is a vertical shift of the expected graph. This shift is an affine function of $\bar{t} = \hat{\eta}$. The intersection of the observed plot with the θ axis determines $\hat{\theta}$. When the expected plot is linear (the totally flat case), then $\hat{\theta}$ and $\hat{\eta}$ are affinely related and so their distributions have the same shape. When it is non-linear they will not be affinely related. This opens up the possibility that, in a particular sense of 'closeness', one of them will be closer to normality.

In all cases, the 0-geometry plays a pivotal role between the ± 1-geo-metries. That is, the graph of $\mu^\phi(\theta)$ determines the relationship between the distributions of the maximum likelihood estimators $\hat{\theta}$ and $\hat{\eta}$ of the ± 1-affine parameters. We illustrate this for our examples in figure 10.5. Both distributions are of course exactly normal when the parent distribution is. In the Poisson case, the concavity of $\mu^\phi(\theta)$ means that the positive skew-ness of $\hat{\eta}$ is reduced. Indeed, $\hat{\theta}$ has negative skew, as figure 10.5a illus-trates. The opposite relationship holds in the exponential case, where $\mu^\phi(\theta)$ is convex (figure 10.5c). In our Bernoulli example, the form of $\mu^\phi(\theta)$ preserves symmetry while increasing kurtosis so that, in this sense, the distribution of $\hat{\theta}$ is closer to normality than that of $\hat{\eta}$ (figure 10.5d).

3.7 Amari's $\pm\frac{1}{3}$-geometry and duality

Amari's $\frac{1}{3}$-connection can be simply interpreted in terms of linearity of the graph of the true mean score function, at least in the one-dimensional situation where the $\frac{1}{3}$-affine parameters are known to exist. If M is totally flat, this graph is linear in the natural parameterisation, as in the normal constant covariance family. It is therefore natural to pose the question: Can a parameterisation be found for a general M in which this graph is linear?

This question can be viewed in two ways. First, for some given $p(x, \phi)$, is such a parameterisation possible? However, in this case, any parame-terisation found could be a function of the true distribution. In general, there will not be a single parameterisation that works for all ϕ. The

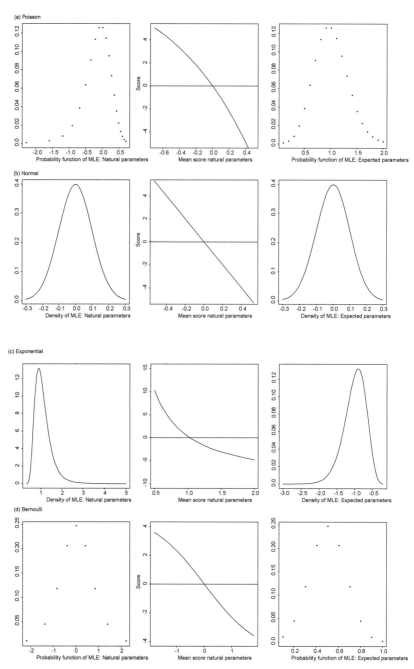

Figure 10.5 The distributions of the natural and expected parameter estimates

second way is to look locally to ϕ. This is the more fruitful approach statistically. The question then becomes: Can a single parameterisation $\theta \to \xi$ be found such that, for all ϕ, the graph of the true mean score is linear locally to $\xi = \xi(\phi)$? In the one-dimensional case, we seek ξ such that

$$\forall \phi, \quad \frac{\partial^2 \mu^{\xi(\phi)}(\xi)}{\partial \xi^2}\bigg|_{\xi = \xi(\phi)} = 0.$$

Such a local approach is sufficient asymptotically when the observed score function will be close to its expected value and the maximum likelihood estimate will be close to the true parameter. Thus in such a parameterisation, whatever the true value, the observed log-likelihood will asymptotically be close to quadratic near the MLE. Hence the name, normal likelihood parameter. Amari (1990) shows that such parameters always exist for a one-dimensional full exponential family, and that they are the $\frac{1}{3}$-affine parameters.

The vanishing of the second derivative of the true expected score function in one parameterisation ξ finds a dual echo in the vanishing of the asymptotic skewness of the true distribution of the maximum likelihood estimator in another parameterisation λ. This is called the $-\frac{1}{3}$-affine parameterisation, because it is induced by Amari's $-\frac{1}{3}$-connection. Note again that the duality is between the score function and the maximum likelihood estimator, as in section 3.5. This can be formalised as follows.

Consider any one-dimensional full exponential family,

$$p(x, \theta) = \exp\{t(x)\theta - \psi(\theta)\}.$$

Let ξ and λ be any two reparameterisations. Extending the approach in section 3.5, it is easy to show the following equivalences:

$$\hat{\xi} \doteq \xi + n^{-1}s(\lambda, \mathbf{x}) \iff \hat{\lambda} \doteq \lambda + n^{-1}s(\xi, \mathbf{x}) \iff \frac{\partial \lambda}{\partial \theta}\frac{\partial \xi}{\partial \theta} = \psi''(\theta).$$

In this case, we say that ξ and λ are ψ-dual. Clearly, the natural (+1-affine) and mean value (−1-affine) parameters are ψ-dual. A parameter ξ is called self ψ-dual if it is ψ-dual to itself. In this case we find again the differential equation for the 0-affine parameters given in section 3.4. More generally, it can be shown that for any $\alpha \in \mathbf{R}$

$$\xi \text{ and } \lambda \text{ are } \psi\text{-dual} \Rightarrow [\xi \text{ is } \alpha\text{-affine} \iff \lambda \text{ is } -\alpha\text{-affine}].$$

For a proof see the appendix to this chapter. Thus the duality between the score function and the maximum likelihood estimator coincides quite generally with the duality in Amari's expected geometry.

Note that the simple notion of ψ-duality gives an easy way to find $-\alpha$-affine parameters once $+\alpha$-affine parameters are known. For example,

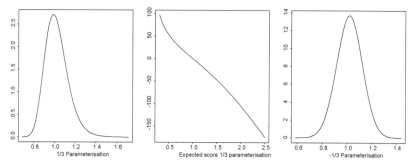

Figure 10.6 The distributions of the 1/3 affine parameter estimates: the exponential case

given that $\xi = \theta^{\frac{1}{3}}$ is $\frac{1}{3}$-affine in the exponential family (Hougaard, 1982) where $\psi(\theta) = -\ln(\theta)$, one immediately has

$$\frac{\partial \lambda}{\partial \theta} = 3\theta^{-4/3},$$

whence $\theta^{-1/3}$ is $-\frac{1}{3}$-affine. Again, in the Poisson family, $\xi = \exp(\theta/3)$ is $\frac{1}{3}$-affine gives at once that $\exp(2\theta/3)$ is $-\frac{1}{3}$-affine.

The local linearity of the true score in $+\frac{1}{3}$-parameters suggests that asymptotically the distributions of the maximum likelihood estimator of the $\pm\frac{1}{3}$-affine parameters will be relatively close compared, for example, with those of the ± 1-affine parameters. In particular, it suggests that both will show little skewness. Figure 10.6, which may be compared with figure 10.5(c), conveys this information for our exponential family example.

4   Sample size effects

In this section we look at the effect of different sample sizes on our plots of the graph of the score vector. For brevity we concentrate on the exponential model. In figure 10.7 we plot the observed scores, taken as before at the 5%, 25%, 50%, 75% and 95% points of the distribution of the score vector. We do this in the natural θ-parameters and the -1-affine mean value η-parameters, for sample sizes 5, 10, 20 and 50.

In the natural parameters we can see that the distribution of $\hat{\theta}$ approaches its asymptotic normal limit. Its positive skewness visibly decreases as the sample size increases. More strikingly, the non-linearity in each of the graphs of the observed scores reduces quickly as n increases. For the sample size 50 case, we see that each graph is, to a close degree of approximation, linear. This implies that at this sample size

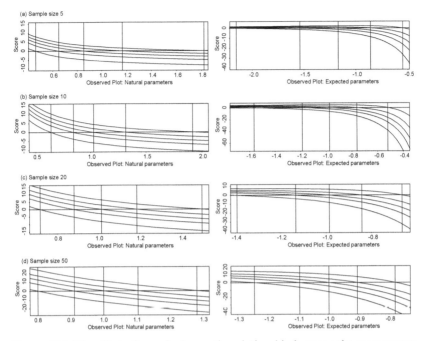

Figure 10.7 The effect of sample size on the relationship between the score vector and the MLE: the exponential case

there will be almost an affine relationship between the score in θ coordinates and the maximum likelihood estimator $\hat{\theta}$, thus demonstrating their well-known asymptotic affine equivalence. It also throws light on the familiar asymptotic equivalence of the score test, the Wald test and (given the asymptotic normality of the maximum likelihood estimate) the likelihood ratio test.

For any model in any smooth invertible reparameterisation of the natural parameters asymptotically the graphs of the observed score will tend to the natural parameterisation plot of the normal distribution shown in figure 10.2. In this limit the graphs become straight and parallel. We can see both these processes in the η-parameterisation of figure 10.7. In this example, a higher sample size than for the natural parameter case is needed to reach the same degree of asymptotic approximation. The highly non-linear and non-parallel graphs of sample size 5 and 10 have been reduced to a much more moderate degree of non-linearity for sample size 50. However, this sample size is not quite sufficient to produce the parallel, linear graphs of the θ-parameterisation, thus there will still not quite be an affine relationship between the score and the maximum likelihood estimator.

Appendix

We give the proof of the equivalence claimed in section 3.7. We assume here familiarity with the use of Christoffel symbols (see Amari (1990), p. 42).

Theorem *Let M be a one-dimensional full exponential family, and assume the parameterisations ξ and λ are ψ-dual. Then ξ is $+\alpha$-affine if and only if λ is $-\alpha$-affine.*

Proof From Amari (1990) we have in the natural θ-parameterisation

$$\Gamma^{\alpha}(\theta) = \left(\frac{1-\alpha}{2}\right)\psi'''(\theta).$$

Thus in ξ-parameters, by the usual transformation rule, the Christoffel symbols are

$$\Gamma^{\alpha}(\xi) = \left(\frac{\partial\theta}{\partial\xi}\right)^{3}\Gamma^{\alpha}(\theta) + i(\theta)\frac{\partial\theta}{\partial\xi}\frac{\partial^{2}\theta}{\partial\xi^{2}}$$

$$= \left(\frac{1-\alpha}{2}\right)\psi'''(\theta)\left(\frac{\partial\theta}{\partial\xi}\right)^{3} + \psi''(\theta)\frac{\partial\theta}{\partial\xi}\frac{\partial^{2}\theta}{\partial\xi^{2}}.$$

Thus ξ is α-flat if and only if

$$\left(\frac{1-\alpha}{2}\right)\psi'''(\theta) + \psi''(\theta)\left(\frac{\partial^{2}\theta}{\partial\xi^{2}}\right)\left(\frac{\partial\xi}{\partial\theta}\right)^{2} = 0. \tag{A.1}$$

Similarly in λ parameters we have λ is $-\alpha$-flat if and only if

$$\left(\frac{1+\alpha}{2}\right)\psi'''(\theta) + \psi''(\theta)\left(\frac{\partial^{2}\theta}{\partial\lambda^{2}}\right)\left(\frac{\partial\lambda}{\partial\theta}\right)^{2} = 0. \tag{A.2}$$

Since ξ and λ are ψ-dual we have

$$\frac{\partial\theta}{\partial\lambda}\frac{\partial\theta}{\partial\xi} = (\psi'')^{-1}(\theta).$$

Differentiating both sides with respect to θ using the chain rule gives

$$\frac{\partial^{2}\theta}{\partial\lambda^{2}}\frac{\partial\lambda}{\partial\theta}\frac{\partial\theta}{\partial\xi} + \frac{\partial^{2}\theta}{\partial\xi^{2}}\frac{\partial\xi}{\partial\theta}\frac{\partial\theta}{\partial\lambda} = -\left(\frac{1}{\psi''}(\theta)\right)^{2}\psi'''(\theta),$$

and multiplying through by $(\psi'')^{2}$ and using the ψ-duality gives

$$\frac{\partial^2\theta}{\partial\lambda^2}\left(\frac{\partial\lambda}{\partial\theta}\right)^2\psi''(\theta) + \frac{\partial^2\theta}{\partial\xi^2}\left(\frac{\partial\xi}{\partial\theta}\right)^2\psi''(\theta) = -\psi'''(\theta). \tag{A.3}$$

Substituting (A.3) into (A.2) gives (A.1), and (A.3) into (A.1) gives (A.2) as required.

References

Amari, S. (1990), *Differential-Geometrical Methods in Statistics*, 2nd edn, Lecture Notes in Statistics No. 28, Berlin: Springer-Verlag.

Barndorff-Nielsen, O.E., D.R. Cox and N. Reid (1986), 'The Role of Differential Geometry in Statistical Theory', *International Statistical Review*, 54: 83–86.

Bates, D.M. and D.G. Watts (1980), 'Relative Curvature Measures of Non-linearity', *Journal of the Royal Statistical Society*, Series B, 40: 1–25.

(1981), 'Parametric Transforms for Improving Approximate Confidence Regions in Non-linear Least Squares', *Annals of Statistics*, 9: 1152–1167.

Cox, D.R. and D.V. Hinkley (1974), *Theoretical Statistics*, London: Chapman & Hall.

Critchley, F., P.K. Marriott and M. Salmon (1993), 'Preferred Point Geometry and Statistical Manifolds', *Annals of Statistics*, 21: 1197–1224.

(1994), 'On the Local Differential Geometry of the Kullback–Leibler Divergence', *Annals of Statistics*, 22: 1587–1602.

Dodson, C.T.J. and T. Poston (1977), *Tensor Geometry*, London: Pitman.

Firth, D. (1993), 'Bias Reduction of Maximum Likelihood Estimates', *Biometrika*, 80: 27–38.

Hougaard, P. (1982), 'Parametrisations of Nonlinear Models', *Journal of the Royal Statistical Society*, Series B, 44: 244–252.

Kass, R.E. (1984), 'Canonical Parametrisation and Zero Parameter Effects Curvature', *Journal of the Royal Statistical Society*, Series B, 46: 86–92.

(1987), 'Introduction', in S.I. Amari, O.E. Barndorff-Nielsen, R.E. Kass, S.L. Lauritzen and C.R. Rao (eds.), *Differential Geometry in Statistical Inference*, Hayward, Calif.: Institute of Mathematical Statistics.

(1989), 'The Geometry of Asymptotic Inference', *Statistical Sciences*, 4: 188–234.

McCullagh, P. and J.A. Nelder (1989), *Generalised Linear Models*, 2nd edn, London: Chapman & Hall.

Murray, M.K. and J.W. Rice (1993), *Differential Geometry and Statistics*, London: Chapman & Hall.

Index

For EU product safety concerns, contact us at Calle de José Abascal, 56–1°,
28003 Madrid, Spain or eugpsr@cambridge.org.

www.ingramcontent.com/pod-product-compliance
Ingram Content Group UK Ltd.
Pitfield, Milton Keynes, MK11 3LW, UK
UKHW042211180425
457623UK00011B/158